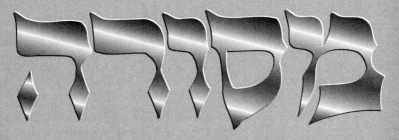

ArtScroll Series®

Rabbi Nosson Scherman / Rabbi Meir Zlotowitz

General Editors

Rabbi Zelig Pliskin

MARR

Published by

Mesorah Publications, ltd

IAGE

*A wise and sensitive guide to
making any marriage even better*

FIRST EDITION
First Impression ... November 1998
Second Impression ... February 1999
Third Impression ... June 2001
Fourth Impression ... August 2002
Fifth Impression ... December 2003
Sixth Impression ... July 2007
Seventh Impression ... July 2009

Published and Distributed by
MESORAH PUBLICATIONS, LTD.
4401 Second Avenue / Brooklyn, N.Y 11232

Distributed in Europe by
LEHMANNS
Unit E, Viking Business Park
Rolling Mill Road
Jarow, Tyne & Wear, NE32 3DP
England

Distributed in Australia and New Zealand
by **GOLDS WORLDS OF JUDAICA**
William Street 3-13
Balaclava, Melbourne 3183
Victoria, Australia

Distributed in Israel by
SIFRIATI / A. GITLER — BOOKS
Hayarkon Street 6
Bnei Brak 51127

Distributed in South Africa by
KOLLEL BOOKSHOP
Ivy Common
William Road 105
Norwood 2192, Johannesburg, South Africa

ARTSCROLL SERIES®
MARRIAGE
© Copyright 1998, by MESORAH PUBLICATIONS, Ltd.
4401 Second Avenue / Brooklyn, N.Y. 11232 / (718) 921-9000

ISBN 10: 1-57819-273-0 / ISBN 13: 978-1-57819-273-1 (hard cover)

Typography by CompuScribe at ArtScroll Studios, Ltd.

Printed in the United States of America by Noble Book Press Corp.
Bound by Sefercraft, Quality Bookbinders, Ltd., Brooklyn N.Y. 11232

LETTER FROM RABBI NOACH ORLOWECK, *shlita*

(Mashgiach Ruchni, Trainer of educators, Consultant, and author of "My Disciple, My Child," and "My Child, My Disciple")

Jerusalem, 24 Tishrei 5759

Differences between husband and wife are often the focal point for problems in marital harmony. But the reality is that every home is a blend of differences. The letter *beis,* when spelled out, reads ב-י-ת, which means home. The letter *beis* consists of parallel lines that are connected by a third line. Parallel lines are lines that will never intersect, even if they were extended to Pluto. It is the third line, the connector, that causes the home to be complete. As Rav Shlomo Wolbe, *shlita,* says, peace is the connecting of opposites (*Alei Shur,* vol. 1, p. 257). This was the essence of Jerusalem, the city of Peace, where the various Tribes met three times a year; their very differences caused them to love each other more.

How husband and wife can be so different, and how much needs to be invested in understanding each other's nature and background, can be put into focus by the following situation, which was related to me by the husband himself.

A couple, several months married, was doing well, with the wife always being home to greet her husband. One day the husband arrived home and his wife wasn't home. She had left no message on the answering machine, and after half an hour the husband started to become concerned. After an hour and a half, the wife entered the home, and the husband blew up at her. "Where were you!? Couldn't you let me know where you were and why you were going to be late!?" The husband then stalked out of the room. A little while later, he came back and was ready to apologize to his wife for his blowup. He found her crying — tears of joy. She had grown up in a home where she felt that no one really cared or noticed if she was around. As a young girl, she had even run away, only to return the next day to find that no one had missed her! Now that she saw how her husband actually cared about where she was and why she wasn't home, she knew that he truly loved her and that they would share a wonderful, happy life together.

What for another woman would have been a traumatic blowup, was for this woman, because of her upbringing, an affirmation of love.

For over two decades it has been my honor to call myself a friend and colleague of Rav Zelig Pliskin, *shlita*. Often we have worked together on the issues that people have presented to us, and time and again I have seen his wisdom, insight, practicality, caring and *yiras shamayim* at work. He never fails to shed light, both intellectual and intuitive, on a problem at hand.

Whenever Rav Zelig comes out with a new book, I always have the same thought. It has been said that many authors write books that are greater than they, that is, they themselves do not embody the ideas and insights about which they write. Rav Zelig, however, is a living repository of these ideas in each of his varied and enormously important works that have enriched *Klal Yisrael*. So too with his newest book, *Marriage*. Rare is the person who can compete with Rav Zelig in caring about others and showing how differences between people can be cause for love and mutual enrichment rather than strife and estrangement.

There is no doubt in my mind that those who read this book, which comes not just from the writer's mind but from his heart and his essence, will be affected and transformed. Our Sages tell us (*Berachos* 6b) that whoever has *yiras shamayim*, his words are heard, and, as is more popularly quoted, words that emanate from the heart penetrate the heart.

May Hashem give Rav Zelig many years of health and *siyata dishmaya* so that he can continue to enrich *Klal Yisrael*, both by his personal counseling and through his worthy writings.

B'Yedidus U'B'Ahavah,
Noach Orloweck

Table of Contents

INTRODUCTION

arriage is for growth. By its very nature your marriage will continuously give you opportunities to develop your character. The more challenging one's marriage, the greater the growth possibilities.

The *mitzvah* to develop our character is the *mitzvah* to walk in the ways of our Creator. Viewing events and situations in this light will elevate the mundane, for in the ultimate view of life nothing is mundane. Every moment presents its unique, once in a lifetime opportunity. By acting and reacting in ways that are kind, compassionate, understanding, and sensitive, you emulate the Creator and bring the *Shechinah* (Divine presence) into your home. No accomplishment could be greater.

Many people tend to speak of marriage as if it were the same for everyone, rather than the unique experience it is for anyone who is married. Since every individual is different from any other individual who ever was or ever will be, every marriage partnership is inevitably one of a kind. Marriages range from being a source of great joy to being the source of much pain.

he young couple was married for a month. As they both thought about their present situation, this is what went through their minds: "I can't believe how fortunate I am. I appreciated him/her when I was engaged, but he/she is even better than I had ever imagined. I am forever grateful to my Creator for creating such a wonderful person just for me. Our differences enhance our lives. I only pray that I will continue to be worthy of such a fantastic blessing. He/she brings out the best in me and I feel so wonderful about myself when I am in his/her presence. This is just the beginning of our marriage, and I can already see us having a marvelous family. I am committed to do my part to maintain the quality of our marriage."

Now let us compare this with what went through the minds of another young couple at the end of the first month of their marriage.

"I can't believe how disappointed and sad I am. I looked forward to getting married but never imagined there would be so many arguments over petty issues. I feel totally frustrated. Nothing goes smoothly. Not only am I in pain about the behavior of the person I married, but I am disgusted with myself. I speak in ways that I never thought I would. We act towards each other like kindergarten children. I think I made a serious mistake in deciding to marry this person. We are different even in areas that I thought we were similar. This is just the beginning of our marriage; what will be when we have children? The future looks bleak and dark. And it's all my spouse's fault for not acting towards me the way I wish."

Now let us take a look at two other couples, both married for close to forty years.

"As I look back over the past forty years, I see how fortunate I have been. I have a treasury of wonderful memories. My spouse has been so kind, sensitive, and understanding. I am a better person myself because of the person I married many years ago. We have experienced many hardships together, but they have brought us closer. The trait that I have developed the most has been patience. The Creator has sent me thousands of opportunities to increase my level of patience and tolerance. I keep focusing on the positive qualities and actions of my spouse and the list keeps growing. Our marriage was truly made in Heaven."

Compare this with the thoughts of another couple married equally long.

"The past forty years have been a tragedy. We have argued and fought countless times. What could have been days of joy were ruined by anger and insults. With almost everyone else I act like a decent human being, but with my spouse I am selfish and insensitive and that is all because of the way I am treated. If only my spouse would have acted better towards me, I would have acted better towards my spouse. Why couldn't my spouse change? I was impatient at the beginning of our marriage, and I have become even more quick-tempered. My memory bank is full of painful memories. Our marriage might have been made in Heaven, but it was destroyed on earth."

Torah principles give us the wisdom and concepts that are needed to have a harmonious marriage. But just knowing these ideas will not automatically guarantee a happy marriage. Torah ideas need to be internalized and practiced. You have your strengths and weaknesses, positive qualities and faults, and so does the person you married. You have a unique life history; you came from a specific family and so did your spouse. You have a unique genetic makeup, with a unique combination of intellect and emotions, and so does every other human being on our planet. Your temperament, personality, communication style, and myriads of other factors need to interact with the temperament, personality, and communication style of your spouse. This will inevitably create many challenges. Your response to these challenges will either create problems, pain, and quarrels, or will be the source of elevating you spiritually and emotionally. You will have daily opportunities to keep developing your character.

Being prepared for the challenges that arise will make them easier to handle. In *Marriage* you will find insights and stories that will help you gain a better understanding of what is happening and what you can say and do to bring out the best in yourself and the best in your spouse.

The wise person learns from everyone (*Pirkei Avos* 4:1). The concepts and stories in this book come from hundreds of interviews which took place over many years. They will enable you to learn from the experiences of others. You will see what it is wise to increase and what to decrease or eliminate. The stories are all written from the perspective of either the husband or the wife. You will be "hearing" the inner thoughts of other people as they faced the challenges with which they were tested. You will get more in touch with your own feelings and the feelings of your spouse. Hopefully, this will enable you to enhance your ability to enter the thought patterns of your spouse. By understanding your spouse, you will find it easier to say and do what is helpful and elevating and to avoid what is counterproductive and detrimental.

Every time you reread this book, you will find ideas and insights that you will see in a new light. As time passes, different issues and challenges will arise in your life. An idea that seemed too obvious or even irrelevant to you the first time you read about it might now be exactly what you need.

Be patient in your efforts to integrate and internalize these ideas, tools, and patterns. It is normal to experience ups and downs. Don't let difficulties discourage you. Growth and change are lifetime processes. Feel joy with every degree of improvement.

At all Torah weddings the newly married couple is blessed that they should experience the joy of the Garden of Eden. May this book serve as a vehicle to help you experience more of that joy.

ACKNOWLEDGMENTS

I wish to express my profound gratitude to *Hashem Yisbarach* for all that He has given me.

I thank Rabbi Meir Zlotowitz of Artscroll for suggesting that I write a book on marriage, and I very much appreciate his encouragement.

It is a pleasure to work with Reb Shmuel Blitz of Artscroll. His expertise, practical insight, and efficiency are greatly appreciated.

My great thanks to Mrs. Roberta Chester for her skillful editing and helpful feedback. Her indispensable work is strongly appreciated.

I thank Mrs. Dvora Rhein for her fine editing and input in this book.

I am very grateful to Rabbi Noach Weinberg, *Rosh Yeshivah* of Aish HaTorah in Jerusalem. Aish HaTorah's Executive Learning Center (The ELC) has been a forum for many of the ideas contained in this book.

My father, of blessed memory, was a wise and brilliant Torah scholar. I value all that he taught me, more and more as the years go by.

My mother's love and devotion has had a major influence on me throughout my life. Her compassion has been a great teacher.

May Hashem grant long life and good health to my wonderful in-laws, Rabbi and Mrs. Simchah Weissman. May they have much *nachas* from their children, grandchildren, and great-grandchildren.

I would like to take this opportunity to express my deep gratitude to my wife, who has made this and my other books possible. She is the personification of an *aishes chayil.* May Hashem grant us much *nachas* from our children and grandchildren.

AN IMPORTANT NOTE TO THE READER

Some of the stories might give the impression that people just need to hear an idea or concept once and then they will immediately change. Change is a process that usually takes effort and time. The stories are frequently a condensed version of a sequence of events. It is unrealistic to expect that someone will read or hear about a new pattern and will consistently apply it from then on. Be patient with your spouse, and hopefully your spouse will be patient with you.

Men and women have different natures and there are a number of books written for men or women only. This book addresses general principles that are applicable to both. It is crucial for men to attend classes or read books directed especially for them, and the same goes for women. Furthermore, this book is limited in scope and there are major areas of marriage that need to be studied with a personal teacher.

There is a problem intrinsic to books on marriage. Reading about the ideal might cause a reader to become angry at his or her spouse. The true ideal of this book is that each of us needs to grow and develop in the reality in which we find ourselves. We can't always change someone else, but if we are respectful and loving we have a much better chance of succeeding. Regardless of the outcome, we can grow in the process.

MARRIAGE

Chapter One

Growth Through Marriage

∞ *Echoes of Gan Eden: the blessing of joy*

∞ *Bringing out the best in each other*

∞ *Basic Torah principles*

∞ *You and your spouse are unique;
   therefore your marriage is unique*

∞ *Problem solving: focus on solutions*

∞ *Growth from challenges*

∞ *Growing with joy*

ECHOES OF GAN EDEN:
THE BLESSING OF JOY

ashem, our loving Father and King, Who created the world for our benefit, created the first couple, Adam and Chavah. The Creator placed Adam and Chavah, our great-grandparents of many generations ago, in *Gan Eden* and brought them much joy. He was the original matchmaker, and He is ultimately your matchmaker also. At all weddings you are blessed that He should give both of you the same joy that He gave the first human couple on the planet in the Garden of Eden. No blessing could be greater.

You and your spouse are partners in creation. You create yourself and you create each other. Your bond creates a unique partnership unlike any other that exists, has existed, or will exist. When you merit it, the Almighty's presence, the *Shechinah*, is with you (*Sotah* 17a).

The Talmud (*Shabbos* 119a) states that someone who prays on Friday evening and recites the verses of *Vayechulu* is a partner with the Creator. Recognizing that Hashem is the Creator of the universe makes you a partner with Him. Your awareness that both you and your spouse are created in His image and are His children, and that your marriage was planned and orchestrated by Him, adds to this partnership.

You and your spouse are faced with constant choices about

how you will speak and act with each other. Some choices will make you partners in fulfilling the blessings that you received under the *chuppah* and at the *sheva berachos.* Other choices will take a couple far away from those blessings. Hopefully, you and your spouse will make the wise choices that will make your life an echo of *Gan Eden.*

Rabbi Chaim Shmulevitz, *zt"l, Rosh Yeshivah* of Mir in Jerusalem, said that when Adam, the first man, was alone in the Garden of Eden, G–d, the Creator, called this, "*Lo tov*" ("It is not good"). As is stated in the Torah (*Bereishis* 2:18): "Hashem said, 'It is not good that man be alone; I will make him a helper corresponding to him.'" *Gan Eden* was the most perfect place possible. The food was the best that could be. The climate was perfect. The location was a scenic paradise. Yet all this was "not good." What was missing? A life partner. Adam without Chavah was missing the one thing that he needed the most, his companion. And because of this void in his life, in spite of all that he had, he was missing the key ingredient that would have made his the best situation any human has ever experienced. Adam needed a life partner to be a complete person.

Nevertheless, the Mirrer *Rosh Yeshivah* would constantly point out, the Torah contains an entire section about divorce. Not every marriage turns out to be the *Gan Eden* that everyone aspires to. What is wrong? It comes from making the wrong choices in word and deed. These are the choices that are the source of much pain, the choices that lead to dashed hopes, bitter arguments, and hurtful words. Each partner needs to focus on what he or she can do to create the atmosphere in the home that will make life together a source of the joy with which they were blessed when they first started out together.

*A*fter being married a number of years, I attended the wedding of a friend's son. I didn't know most of the people at the wedding and during the chuppah I had time to reflect on my own marriage. My friend was a few years older than me, and it would still be a *number of years before my oldest child would be ready to get married. I thought about how this young couple was certainly looking forward to a joyous life together.*

Everyone else seemed very happy, but deep inside I was sad. I remembered my own wedding and my own expectations. I never expected to argue and quarrel with my wife the way I frequently did. I didn't think I would lose my temper so often. I wished my wife spoke to me with more respect and understanding. I was certain that she wished that I spoke to her like that, as well.

Then I heard a prominent Rabbi recite the blessing that Hashem give this couple the same joy that He gave to the very first couple in Gan Eden. This heightened my pain. My own marriage wasn't anywhere close to this. I felt like leaving right after the chupah, but I decided to stay for the meal as I had originally planned.

During the dancing, I saw the joy radiating from the face of the chasan as his closest friends rejoiced with him. Then an elderly Rosh Yeshivah danced the chasan back and forth amidst the exuberant singing of all those present.

"Look how this Torah scholar is dancing with the chasan to help him rejoice," I said to myself. "It is difficult for him to walk, yet to give joy to the chasan he is forcing himself to make the effort."

Then it hit me. When all was going well, I acted all right and so did my wife. But when we were under stress and not at our best, we vented our irritation on each other. This caused suffering for both of us. I made a commitment right then and there to give my wife as much joy as possible, whether I felt like it or not.

A few years later my own daughter got married. From the time of my friend's son's wedding onward, I had kept the commitment I had made and my own marriage had improved greatly. I faced strong challenges and experienced ups and downs, but the trend was constant improvement. I learned to control my anger and how I spoke even when I was frustrated. My marriage was transformed from a source of pain to a source of much joy and nachas.

Now, standing under the chuppah at my daughter's wedding a few years later, I remembered how I had felt at my friend's son's wedding. Since then my marriage was transformed. When I heard the blessing of the joy of Gan Eden, I was very happy that I could hear that same blessing with joy rather than with sadness and regret. I realized that I had come a long way. I was now able to experience deep gratitude to Hashem for giving me the understanding to improve my own patterns of speech and bring joy into my home. I blessed the new young couple that they should feel the same joy in the future when they would marry off their first child.

BRINGING OUT THE BEST IN EACH OTHER

When we are on our best behavior we act quite differently than when we are at our worst. We even seem to be two different people. This is not a rare case of multiple personality disorder, rather it is the result of failure to think clearly at a time when we are stressed or angry.

We all have met people who bring out the best in us. Around them we feel better about ourselves. We think more clearly. We act in a kindly and more elevated fashion. However, there are other people with whom our interaction is not as successful. This will be true for you and true for the person to whom you are married. Your task is to bring out the best in yourself and the best in your spouse. Before you complain that this seems unfair, remember that your spouse has the same task.

If you were to ask someone before getting married, "When you get married, would you like to bring out the best in your spouse?" you wouldn't expect him to respond, "No. My hope is that we will bring out the worst in each other so we can really mess up our lives." Yet, in many situations, otherwise bright and reasonable people fall into counterproductive patterns. They become upset and angry and say and do things that will bring about an undesirable result.

Sometimes a couple will not say and do things to bring out the worst in each other, but they will still fail to make an effort to bring out the best. When two people first get married, they realize that they are the most important people in each other's lives. They appreciate one another. They are enthusiastic and happy to be married, and this newness enables them both to speak and act in ways that bring out the best in each other. But after time has passed, children, jobs, studying, projects, and a host of other activities become their priorities. The ideal of bringing out the best in each other can decrease in importance and can even be forgotten.

Knowing that someone is trying to help you bring out the best in yourself will usually give you good feelings about that person. The reason I say "usually" instead of "always" is because it is important that a person who tries to bring out the best in another person does it in a way that is helpful. There are some people who feel that by criticizing someone, telling him or her off, giving him or her an intense *mussar* lecture, and getting across how awful he or she is, they will motivate that person to do his or her best. Maybe this will work for some people. But for the vast majority of people, a heavy-handed approach becomes a source of distress and quarrels, not growth.

Directly confronting weaknesses and deficits can have its appropriate time and place. In a marriage, however, this approach often is counterproductive. It is preferable to help your spouse elicit strengths and virtues and thereby overcome whatever needs correcting and improving.

Having the skill to bring out the best in another person is one of the greatest challenges we can master. Parents who bring out the best in their children will have much *nachas*. So will a teacher who brings out the best in his or her students. Employers and managers who bring out the best in their employees will be successful, and not just financially. And a husband and wife who know how to bring out the best in each other will live blessed lives. They will cherish each other and create a wonderful environment in which to raise their children.

I have been married for more than two years and am now a totally different person than I was before I got married. I have a dreamy nature, and am easily distracted. I enjoy reflecting on the thoughts and images that come into my mind. I love to read and this gives me much material to think about.

When I was a teenager both my father and mother would often become irritated by my nature. My father was always busy and in a rush and he accomplished much with his dynamic personality. Often when he asked me to do something, I wouldn't hear him the first time. When he repeated his request a second time, I would only be partially conscious and not get all the details. By the third repetition, he would become impatient and often say, "Don't be so dreamy. When you get married, your husband will become angry at you if he has to repeat everything he says." This prediction didn't heal my dreaminess, but it did make me apprehensive about getting married.

My mother felt I took too long to accomplish tasks that she and most people would easily do in a shorter time. She often lost patience with me. Her favorite response to me was, "Wake up and get moving." She was right, but every time she repeated this, I felt worse about my personality.

Consequently, I had mixed feelings when I was engaged. I was joyous about my chasan, but I dreaded how he would react to my dreaminess. I told him that I was on the dreamy side, but he replied, "That's okay with me. I'm certain that you'll learn to manage just like everyone else. You seem to be very knowledgeable and capable." I didn't want to put myself down excessively so I didn't keep voicing my fears about his losing his temper at me for being dreamy.

When we were first married, my husband needed to repeat requests to me frequently. I would apologize, but he would say, "As many times as I need to repeat myself, that is my task in this world."

I would forget to do things that my husband asked me to do, and I was nervous about how he would react when I told him that I forgot. But he always put me at ease. "Any time you forget something that I ask you to do, it is an expression of my accepting Hashem's will to take it calmly. Whatever happens is what was meant to be."

My husband always spoke to me gently and patiently. This relaxed me, and I felt totally calm taking care of our house. I was grateful to my husband for being so accepting of my personality. I made an effort to become more efficient. When I shared this with my husband, he responded, "I thank you profusely for all your efforts on my behalf. But don't feel any pressure to be any different than you are."

His gentle way of reminding me to take care of things enabled me to become proficient at tasks I was never good at before. Slowly my skills increased. I became attuned to my husband's pleasant voice, and as soon as he began speaking to me, I immediately paid attention to what he was saying.

At the end of my first year of marriage, both my father and mother told me independently that they had been worried about how I would run a house on my own. Both were pleasantly surprised at how well I manage. I owe it all to my wonderful husband. He has brought out the best in me and I am grateful.

The greater your mastery at bringing out the best in people, the fewer people there will be with whom you will have difficulty. In a marriage, the one person who counts is the specific person to whom you are married. Ask yourself, "What do I need to say and do that will bring out the best in my spouse?"

How do you bring out the best in another person? First of all, believe in the other person. See your spouse as if he or she is at his or her best. View him or her as a competent, well-intentioned, intelligent, kind, and good person who basically wants to do the right thing. This is how the average person acts at his or her best. When you decided to marry this person, most likely you saw him or her in this way. Or at least you felt that he or she had enough positive qualities for you to decide to get married. If that is not the way you presently see your partner, it can take real effort to see him or her in a positive light. But by making that effort you have a much better chance of bringing out the best in him or her.

This is what Aharon, Moshe's brother, did. When he knew that someone did something wrong, he went out of his way to greet that person in a respectful and friendly manner. Then the person would say to himself, "If Aharon treats me like this, I must live up to his expectations." This is what Hillel advised us to do. "Be a disciple of Aharon. Love peace and pursue peace" (*Avos D'Reb Noson* 12:3). By bringing out the best in another person you will create more peace within that person. When that person is the one you are married to, you have much to gain, for your own inner peace will be increased as well.

Speak with sincere heartfelt compassion and understanding and you will often see an immediate transformation in the person with whom you are interacting. Someone who was just angry, upset, or resentful will quickly become a much softer, open person. Add sincere, unconditional, selfless love, and inevitably you will see this transformation even in people whom others call difficult or challenging, or even impossible. Will this be true 100 percent of the time? Probably not, but that is only because of our own difficulty in accessing a state where we radiate sincere, unconditional, selfless love. We are not talking about a superficial smile. We are not talking about just saying, "I love you." We are referring to a true inner feeling. This can take time and patience to develop.

Remember times in the past when you have brought out the best in your partner. How did you talk then? What did you do? Learning from what has already worked well for you, you will be more likely to replicate similar patterns in the present and the future.

Each move you make affects the next move of your spouse. In games like chess and checkers this is obvious. But the same applies in any relationship, especially in marriage. Negative moves, that is, words and actions, usually elicit negative reactions, while positive moves tend to elicit positive reactions. There is always a chain reaction. Whenever a husband and wife get into a quarrel and either one tries to relate his or her side of the story to another person, many moves that have added to the problem are omitted. That is why it is so usual for a husband or wife who speaks to someone else, without one or the other being there, to return with a report, "I was told that I am right." However, if you keep your main focus on making positive moves that create positive outcomes, you will both gain.

What can you do if you have no idea how to bring out the best in someone? Watch how those who do bring out the best in this person talk and act with him or her. Perhaps you can think of someone who has done so in the past. Also, observe people who generally bring out the best in others. Listen to the way they talk and see how they act. Maybe you can model yourself after them.

Ultimately, the best person to ask is the person himself. But how you speak will make a difference. Let's look at a way that is guaranteed not to be effective: "You are totally inconsistent. You act awful most of the time. Tell me what I should say to someone who acts as badly as you do to make you act right for a change." If you want to prove that nothing will work, the way to do it is to keep asking in ways that resemble this approach.

The exact wording of what to say to bring out the best in your spouse will depend on the nature of your relationship until now. But whatever you say, your spouse must sense your respect and caring. Perhaps something like: "There are many times when I deeply appreciate the way you are. What can I do that would make it easier for you to be that way more often?"

If a couple feels a need to consult someone about how to improve their relationship, a good way to present the situation to the person they consult would be, "We are interested in learning the skill of bringing out the best in each other, and we are looking for specific ways to do this." In many instances this positive approach is a better way to start than by just giving over a list of complaints.

Please note that when two people bring out the best in each other, they will have pleasant interactions even when they disagree over an issue. This attitude will free them from anger, resentment, and quarrels and often they won't even realize how much they have accomplished in a difficult situation.

Taking the good for granted occurs frequently with couples who are used to having nasty quarrels over many issues. When such couples improve the way they speak to each other, they realize the difference and appreciate the positive changes that each has made. Others, however, say, "We didn't fight this week because we didn't provoke each other, so it doesn't count." If they were in different cities and didn't see or speak to each other, I agree that it wouldn't count. They didn't have any interaction that would cause each other pain. But if they were in the same house and did interact, and things went smoothly when they hadn't before, that is progress. Remember this if you are trying to improve a situation. Once a situation is improved it might seem so natural and obvious that you might not appreciate your progress and that of your spouse. But this is growth.

I once saw this advertisement: "Make sure you're part of a winning team." The way to be part of a winning team in marriage is to bring out the best in your spouse. Remember to keep your focus on your spouse's strengths and not on his or her weaknesses. Remember to believe in the potential of your spouse. Believe that your spouse has untapped wisdom and goodness that both of you can reach. Remember to notice positive changes and to express your appreciation. Express appreciation and gratitude for positive words and actions, even if they are not totally what you would have wanted. By giving positive reinforcement to a movement in the right direction, you encourage your spouse to keep moving along the best path for both of you.

If your spouse portrays a picture of him/herself more positively than you feel is accurate, accept it. Build upon it. It is frequently a mistake to try to demolish this picture. By building upon it, you create a more positive future reality. People tend to act in ways that are consistent with their view of themselves. For example, your spouse might say, "I consider myself to be very considerate." Let's say you disagree and feel that your spouse has a long way to go to fit this picture. You would like your spouse to be more considerate, wouldn't you? Therefore, it is best to express gratitude for the consideration already displayed. By doing so you have a better chance of having a more considerate spouse. If you argue, there is a good chance you will end up in a no-win quarrel. Even if your spouse ends up agreeing with you, it is not likely that your approach will improve his or her character.

Don't limit yourself to the present reality. What potential strengths and resources do you see in your spouse that have not yet been accessed? Keep asking yourself, "What can I say and do to encourage my spouse to activate these resources?"

What if you try to bring out the best in your spouse, but you feel that your spouse is not trying to bring out the best in you? Then you have the task of bringing out the best in yourself. Since this one-sided effort makes the job more difficult, the growth that you personally experience is greater than if you were both doing this. Ideally, it is preferable for both to try and bring out the best in each other. Nevertheless, if you need to do it alone, understand that your spouse has been your partner in helping you become even greater than you would have otherwise. Even though this might not be the choice that you would have wanted, your gain is eternal.

My wife brings out both the best and worst in me. We are very different from each other and communicating often leads to misunderstandings. With the vast majority of people, I am calm and pleasant, but my wife often provokes my anger. When I lose my temper, I tend to speak in ways that I later regret.

But my wife also brings out the best in me. The way she talks to me when she is irritated with me, which is quite often, arouses my resistance, defensiveness, and resentment. I often need to overcome these negative tendencies. I am reminded of the man the Rambam praises for stating that the happiest day in his life was when he transcended his natural tendency and remained totally serene even though he was being insulted. It's easy to be pleasant to someone who treats you with love and respect; it's a great challenge to be kind to someone who often speaks to you with contempt.

When I am able to stay centered and think clearly even if my wife speaks to me condescendingly, I speak respectfully and kindly in return. This has a positive effect on my wife and her moments of irritation quickly pass. If, however, I respond with frustration or anger, the situation gets worse. My wife's patterns are a constant test of my ability to bring out the best in myself. Whenever I am successful, we both gain and there is a peaceful atmosphere in our home.

BASIC TORAH PRINCIPLES

There are a number of basic Torah principles that will build a foundation for your marriage. Those that are listed here will be further elaborated upon throughout this book.

[1] When a husband and wife get along harmoniously, they bring the *Shechinah* (Divine Presence) into their home (*Sotah* 17a).

I witnessed a Torah scholar leave a Kiddush on Shabbos in what seemed to be a big hurry. He started walking very quickly towards his home. A colleague of his casually asked him, "Why are you rushing on Shabbos? On Shabbos we need to walk at a more leisurely pace."

"I'm rushing for the sake of the Shechinah," he replied. "My wife will be waiting for me. My not making her wait any longer than necessary helps bring the Shechinah into our home."

I loved my late father-in-law, who was a second father to me. I was extremely grateful to him for his generosity. He didn't have much money, but what he had he shared with us with an open heart. My wife was an only child, and on his yahrtzeit I was the one designated to say Kaddish for him.

The night of his fourth yahrtzeit I was delayed in a traffic jam and missed Maariv in shul. I ended up going to sleep very late that night and therefore was very tired the next morning after only three hours of sleep. I nevertheless woke up on time for davening, but my mind was in an altered state and I forgot to say Kaddish in shul that morning.

As soon as I came home from davening and entered our kitchen, I noticed the yahrtzeit candle my wife had lit the evening before. I felt awful that I hadn't said Kaddish. I thought that my wife would be angry at me and, to my mind, rightfully so.

But when I told my wife that I hadn't said Kaddish, she

commented, *"We say Kaddish on a yahrtzeit to sanctify Hashem's name. When a husband and wife have harmony and peace, that brings the Shechinah into their home. May my forgiveness be a sanctification of our Creator and a merit for my father."*

"Your father was such a wonderful person, no wonder he had such a fantastic daughter," I said to my wife with tears in my eyes.

I grew up in a home where my father would constantly say, "Things can't be better," whenever he was asked about how things were going.

After I was married, whenever my wife asked me how my day went, I would reply, "Things couldn't have been better." To me, this seemed like the ABC's of emunah. If Hashem would want things to be better, they would be.

My wife kept complaining that I wasn't sharing my day with her and she felt lonely. I told her that I felt it would be wrong for me not to answer in the exact same way that my father did.

My wife insisted that I consult a posek. I did and asked him if it was appropriate for me to answer the way I did.

"How does your wife feel about the matter?" the posek asked me, intuitively feeling that I had left some details out.

"She tells me that she feels depressed that all I give is a platitude for an answer and that I don't share with her the details of my day."

"You will connect more with the Shechinah by making your wife happy than by using this type of expression. While the attitude projected by the expression is praiseworthy, it is even more praiseworthy to speak to your wife in a way that makes her feel valued and more connected with you," the posek told me.

[2] The Rambam describes how a husband and wife are required by the Torah to relate to each other:

"The Sages commanded that a husband honor his wife more than himself and love her as himself. He should increase his spending for her welfare in proportion to his wealth. He should speak pleasantly to her. He should be neither sad nor quick to anger.

"The Sages commanded that a wife honor her husband exceedingly. She should revere him, and all of her actions should be in accordance with his will. He should be in her eyes as a prince or king. She should do as he desires and refrain from doing whatever he dislikes" (*Yad HaChazakah, Hilchos Ishus* 15:19, 20).

Rabbi Chaim Shmulevitz, the late *Rosh Yeshivah* of Mir, would often repeat this most important principle when he spoke about the Torah requirements for marriage: "If a husband will do all he can to fulfill his obligations and the wife will do all she can to fulfill her obligations, they will live a happy and harmonious life together. Troubles begin, however, when each is only concerned with the other's obligations."

While the Mirrer *Rosh Yeshivah* was describing the ideal, if a husband or wife feels that the other one is not treating him or her with proper respect, it would be appropriate to ask for improvement. But there is a major prerequisite. If you wish to ask for more respect, the manner in which you ask will either improve the situation or make it worse. First of all, be resolved to do your share and meet your obligations. Secondly, don't speak in a tone of voice that communicates condemnation. Rather, express your concerns and goals in a way that invites a fair hearing. It is often wise to add that you personally feel a need to improve in this area also. For example, you might say, "I feel that we both would benefit by speaking to each other with greater respect. I personally would like to improve in this area. By working on this together we will both gain."

It should be noted that the Rambam is essentially telling us a *halachah*, a Torah law: "You have an obligation to honor each other whether you feel like it or not." This is a *halachah* like any other Torah law. We need to keep kosher whether we feel like it or not. We need to observe Shabbos whether we feel like it or not. Similarly, we need to be respectful to our spouse whether we feel like it or not.

I was in Miami, and I met a man in shul who told me about the first time he met his wife's grandfather. When he became engaged, he was introduced to his kallah's family. Her grandfather had been a professional strongman. As a child in Europe in the early part of the century, he was beaten up for being Jewish. He decided then and there to become physically strong to protect himself and others.

When he came to the United States, he earned a living by demonstrating his amazing physical strength. He picked up heavy weights that even the super-strong were unable to lift. His nickname was "The Mighty Atom," and newspapers carried his picture pulling a car with a chain attached to his body.

The kallah's grandfather spoke to the chasan in a very friendly manner. Then he took a thick metal horseshoe and twisted it as easily as if it had been made out of putty. Handing the younger man the twisted horseshoe as a souvenir, the grandfather said, "I'm certain that you will always treat my granddaughter with respect."

Needless to say, this made a lasting impression on the young man. I heard this from him many years later when he himself was a grandfather.

I told this story to a few married fellows. One of them came back to me a few days later and said, "That amusing anecdote you told me had a powerful impact. The next time I touched the mezuzah when I entered my house, the following thought hit me. The mighty Creator and Sustainer of the universe is telling me to treat His child, the bas melech I am married to, with respect."

❖ ❖ ❖

*B*efore I was married I thought that the person I married would act towards me exactly the way I had always dreamed. My vision was one of a totally harmonious marriage which exemplified all the beautiful thoughts that I had heard at weddings and sheva berachos about a marriage based on Torah. I expected to be treated royally and was open to reciprocate. My disappointment came fast and heavy. The person I married was much moodier than I expected, and I wasn't spoken to with the respect that I felt people deserved regardless of who they were.

I am embarrassed to admit that I treated my spouse the way I was treated. I returned anger with anger, insult with insult, and in a passive-aggressive way, I didn't take care of everything I was asked to do. We were in a downward spiral and the speed of our descent was as rapid as if we were free-falling from a plane.

I told my spouse that we both needed to improve, and I expected agreement. But the response I received was, "It's all your fault. If you act better towards me, I will act better towards you."

I saw that I had a choice. I could wait until we both would simultaneously treat each other better and until then refuse to make things better; or, I could unilaterally do everything possible to improve things. I have always felt a strong need for things to be fair. My sense of fairness at first prevented me from upgrading my behavior towards my spouse without a reciprocal agreement. But after thinking it over, I felt it would be stupid of me to ruin my life when I could take action to enhance it.

I gathered every bit of strength I had and treated my spouse exactly the way the Rambam advised. I viewed the words of the Rambam as his personal advice to me.

I was committed to maintaining this resolve regardless of how I would be treated in return.

At first, my improvements were met with skepticism. I was the butt of sarcastic remarks: "Oh, did you attend a lecture or read a book on improving your marriage? I bet it won't last." I realized that this was the worst thing for my spouse to say. I would have appreciated a positive comment such as, "I like the way you are acting. I hope you keep it up." But I knew that I would just have to strengthen my determination to do all I could to keep up my half of the obligation.

Every day I would think, "Will I be treated better today? Can I keep this up if I am not?" We both had a lot of resentment towards each other, so I knew I had to be patient to prove that my change of behavior would last. It took over a month for me to see results. I have to admit that I was ready to give up a number of times. I had to control an inner sense of outrage many times. I felt a total commitment to do all I could. I believed that eventually my hard work would pay off. And it did.

I was greatly rewarded when one day my spouse finally told me, "I have to apologize. You have been treating me so wonderfully and I haven't been very nice to you. It hit me that you deserve better treatment. I am now resolved to change how I speak and act towards you. If you are ever dissatisfied with what I say or do, please tell me. I want to treat you like you are treating me. Thank you for not allowing my stubbornness to prevent you from continuing your heroic efforts."

When my spouse said this to me, I felt as if I had won the Nobel Peace Prize. It was like being married anew, even though I recognized that we still had a lot of hard work ahead of us in order to learn to treat each other properly. We are very different from one another and our spontaneous reactions are not always what the other would want. But being in a partnership when, despite dif-

ferences, you each treat the other with love and respect is an awesome experience after having suffered so much.

Two years later, I look back at that time as the turning point in my life. I wish I had had the wisdom to treat my spouse properly from the start. But I guess that I appreciate the wonderful relationship we now have more than if all had gone smoothly from the beginning.

I had more stress than I could bear. We had a number of small children and I was feeling worn out with a flu that just wouldn't go away. A number of other stressful factors were adding up and I found it hard to cope. What I really wished for was a two-week vacation in which I would be totally free of all obligations and responsibilities. But this didn't seem likely with all the practical things I needed to take care of.

A major cause of my stress was that I wished my husband were different. I compared him to my father who worked hard every day. He woke up very early each morning to learn Torah and daven and then utilized his time to the maximum to provide for his family. I was one of the top students in my class both in high school and in seminary. I envisioned myself marrying someone who was brilliant, who would be a super masmid, who would have strong opinions about the proper Torah outlook on major life issues, and who would be able to take charge of raising the children.

My husband was very different from the picture I had imagined. He hadn't been that successful in yeshivah. He wasted much time and didn't have strong opinions on most issues. He didn't have a clue as to how to raise children. In addition to all this, he was sloppy, unlike my father and brothers who were always neat and clean. My general state of frustration caused me to be short-tempered with my husband and also with the children.

My husband would do anything I asked him to do, but he didn't take the initiative to do things on his own. Why did I have to remind him of everything? Why couldn't he figure out what needed to be done by himself and just take care of it? This wore me out.

I finally spoke to someone about my situation and asked him for advice on how to cope. The person I turned to asked me a lot of questions to get a comprehensive picture of what my husband was like, what my background was, what was important to me, and what steps I already had taken to try to improve the situation.

He then told me that I was making a fundamental error. I was living with the disappointment that my husband was not the way I had hoped he would be. Instead I should realize that my task in life was to handle my actual situation in the best way possible. My husband was very kind and tried to do what I suggested. I needed to learn to be patient and calm with him. Instead of speaking with exasperation, I needed to calmly point out step by step what had to be taken care of. Although I had wanted a "take charge" husband, I had to take the initiative to see what was needed and to set the pace. If I wasn't prepared to do this with a joyous attitude towards carrying out my life's task, I would eat myself up with frustration, endangering my health. Continually getting irritated and angry at my husband would be problematic for the entire family. The person I spoke to was sympathetic about my difficulty with giving up the vision of how I would have wanted things. But that is the essence of accepting the Almighty's will. I had the option of choosing to carry it out with joy.

"But how can I respect him when he is sloppy and doesn't take the initiative?" I asked.

"If you would automatically respect your husband, you wouldn't need the Rambam to tell you to do so," I was

told. "The very fact that the Rambam needs to tell a wife to respect her husband means that it doesn't necessarily come naturally or automatically. You have a lot to respect. He is especially kind and he has high values. Be patient and don't expect the messages you suggest to have an immediate effect. By repeating them in a way that your husband finds pleasant, you will have a positive influence on him. You will be accomplishing more with your husband than you would with someone who was perfect on his own."

I left the meeting dedicated to developing a calm attitude in giving suggestions and treating my husband with respect. This would be no different from my approach to making berachos and doing all the other mitzvos.

[3] Whenever a husband or wife do anything to help each other, they are doing an act of kindness and should take pleasure in it (Rabbi Noson Tzvi Finkel; *Tenuas HaMussar,* vol. 3, pp. 250-1). Couples who master this Torah principle live happy lives. They each enjoy doing things for each other.

I once attended a sheva berachos in the Toldos Aharon community in Meah Shearim. If you want to meet a group that is dedicated to following traditions and customs in their entirety, it is this group.

As is the custom at sheva berachos, there were a few speakers. The main speaker was a Rabbi from their community who is a keynote speaker at events such as these. I was curious to see what points he would emphasize.

This is what he said to the chasan and the men who were there: "A great Chassidic Rebbe said that one of the biggest segulos for a harmonious marriage is a broom. Yes, dear chasan, take the broom in your house and do your part in keeping the house clean. This is one of the best ways to have a happy marriage."

[4] I heard from Rabbi Shlomo Wolbe, author of *Alei Shur* and a great *mussar* authority, that he considers the five attributes which Rabbi Yochanan ben Zakkai's students chose as fundamental to life, to be the five basic qualities necessary for a successful marriage. The Mishnah (*Pirkei Avos* 2:9) states that Rabbi Yochanan ben Zakkai had five special students and each one had a unique greatness. He told them to go out into the world and investigate the one quality that would make a major difference in a person's life. Each one came back with one attribute. These five are guidelines for us to integrate into our marriage.

They are: having a good eye; being a good friend; being a good neighbor; seeing the outcome; and having a good heart.

When you have a good eye, you are able to see the good in your spouse. This enables you to focus on what is right, and allows you to consistently judge him or her favorably. A good eye allows you to experience pleasure for every good thing and success in your spouse's life. When you are a good friend, you are totally accepting of the other. You will do all you can to help your friend in every way, spiritually, financially, physically, and emotionally. You can be encouraging and supportive. When you are a good neighbor, you are available when your neighbor needs you. You also allow your neighbor privacy and give your neighbor space when it is needed. When you see the outcome, you are careful not to say or do anything that will cause your spouse distress or suffering. You think first and ask yourself, "What will be the outcome of what I am about to say or do?" When you have a good heart, you will have selfless love, compassion, and you will experience much joy.

These attributes require much effort to master, and that is why they enable us to grow throughout our marriage.

[5] The Torah (*Bereishis* 2:24) states that a husband and wife are considered as "one." As the Ramban states in his commentary,

"Through the sanctification of marriage, a husband and wife become the closest of relatives."

A couple that views themselves as "one" will be sensitive to the needs and wishes of one another. They will do all they can for the other's welfare, and will avoid saying and doing anything that will cause distress.

[6] Working on our character traits is a fulfillment of the Torah commandment of walking in the ways of the Almighty (*Devarim* 28:9; Rambam, *Hilchos Dei'os,* ch. 1). Interacting with your spouse gives you unlimited opportunities to develop your *middos* in unprecedented ways. Not only will you enjoy the process, but you will experience constant growth.

[7] The mitzvah of "Love your neighbor as yourself" (*Vayikra* 19:18) applies to the person you are married to just as it applies to everyone else. Your actions should give your spouse pleasure rather than pain. When you view your spouse as "yourself," your spouse's needs, wants, and feelings will be just as important to you as your own.

[8] Be especially careful not to violate the Torah commandment which prohibits *ona'as devarim* (words that cause pain). When a couple is careful not to cause pain with their words, they help to avoid a major pitfall that can cause much distress and damage.

[9] "According to the difficulty is the reward" (*Pirkei Avos* 5:22). If you find that you and your spouse's personalities, styles, approaches, and patterns tend to clash, and it is difficult for you to act in the ideal Torah manner, this difficulty can serve to make you a better person. You are working with a handicap. In a race, those without handicaps might objectively run faster, climb the mountain first, or swim further. But those who participate with handicaps have mastered a greater obstacle and achieved a greatness unmatched by those without the handicap. You may

feel handicapped because of the difficulties in your marriage, but it is this very situation that can cause you to be a greater success in your *avodas Hashem* (service of G-d) and *tikkun hamiddos* (character development).

[10] "Let all of your actions be for the sake of Heaven" (*Pirkei Avos* 2:12; see *Shulchan Aruch, Orach Chaim* 231:1). This elevates the mundane to the holy. Everything you do — such as eating, resting, and exercising — can be a spiritual experience.

If a husband gets angry about the taste of a meal, he needs to ask himself why he is eating. The ideal is to eat to get energy to serve Hashem. You serve Hashem with your positive *middos,* as you are sensitive not to hurt your wife's feelings. Even if you feel a practical need to point out that something might be spoiled, do so with tact.

[11] Use the power of prayer to enhance your marriage. Pray to our Creator, the One Who united you, to give you both joyous lives. If problems arise, pray to your Father, your King, Creator and Sustainer of the universe, to give you the wisdom to solve the problem in ways that will be good for both of you.

I am a grandmother with much life experience. I knew a great tzaddik who was very successful in making peace between couples who previously didn't get along. His approach was the following: He would speak to the husband and wife separately, listening to each spouse complain and criticize the other.

When the wife finished relating her complaints, he would say to her, "Every day for a month stand by a mezuzah in your house and bless your husband for ten full minutes. This might be difficult for you to do for such a long time. Nevertheless, this is what you must do. Think of every possible blessing for success and happiness. Bless him to have good health. Bless him to be successful in financial matters. Bless him to be successful in

Torah study and mitzvos. Bless him to enjoy himself and experience much joy."

When the husband finished relating his complaints, he would say to him, "Every day for a month when you finish the regular prayers in shul, pray for your wife's welfare for ten whole minutes. This might be difficult for you to do for such a long time. Nevertheless, this is what you must do. Think of every possible blessing for success and happiness. Bless her to have joy and nachas. Bless her to have healthy children and that she should have an easy time raising them. Bless her to have wonderful experiences during the entire day. Keep on blessing your wife for ten full minutes."

While the complaints might have been different, the suggested solutions for both were identical, with slight variations. Using this approach, this tzaddik helped many people for whom standard marriage counseling was of no help. When you regularly bless one another for ten minutes a day, you are bound to make positive changes in your interactions.

YOU AND YOUR SPOUSE ARE UNIQUE; THEREFORE YOUR MARRIAGE IS UNIQUE

Each human being is unique. You are one of a kind. There is no one else exactly like you. You are the only one with your specific blend of character traits, temperament, personality, patterns of thought, and behavior. We can hear this many times, but as often as we hear it we need to hear it again. The person you are married to is also one of a kind. No one else is exactly like him or her. This means that the relationship between the two of you will be unique. Only you can fulfill your life's mission in this world, and only you have the exact marriage that you have. This can give you a sense of your specialness as well as of the significance of your life's task. Only you can serve your Creator in your unique manner.

In your marriage you will be tested and challenged, just as everything that occurs in our lives is meant to be a test and challenge (see *Mesillas Yesharim*, ch. 1). The Divine plan for your tests will be distinctly your own. Your marriage is a major part of your life's mission. Your union is the only time in world history that this exact test will exist for anyone. Let this thought empower you to fulfill the will of Hashem with a profound sense of meaning throughout your life. Having a sense of meaning gives a person strength in times of adversity. The ultimate meaning in life is devoting your entire being to serving Hashem. You will be able to do this throughout your marriage as you emulate Him by being kind, compassionate, and giving. It is your Divine mission to create a loving and respectful relationship with this special and unique union.

This uniqueness also means that when you hear advice about marriage, you will need to think seriously about each idea, concept, approach, and technique. See what is appropriate for you in your situation, given the unique mixture of personalities and temperaments. Your reactions to what each of you says and does will be unique. Some ideas and techniques can be perfect for one couple but inappropriate for another. How can you know? Observe the reactions of your spouse to what you say and do. Get feedback, both verbally and nonverbally, to see what you are doing right and what needs to be changed or modified.

PROBLEM SOLVING:
FOCUS ON SOLUTIONS

Since we live in the post-*Gan Eden* era, everyone's life will contain problems that need solutions. At times, this can be a desperate need. How you approach the problem will either make it worse or improve the situation. Even before you have a solution to a problem, if you are able to think clearly, you are more likely to come up with a solution that will be acceptable to both you and your spouse. When you think clearly about a problem, your emotional state will be much more centered and balanced, and this, too, facilitates better solutions.

What makes something a problem? If you think something is a problem, then it is a problem. If you don't think it is a problem, but your spouse thinks it is, then it is a problem. If someone tells his or her spouse, "I don't have any problems at all. It's all your problem," the very fact that the spouse is suffering and the other party doesn't consider this his or her concern, is an issue that needs rectifying. If you both don't think there is a problem, but people who are close to you tell you that you have a problem, that in itself is a problem that needs a solution. If you both don't think there is a problem and no other person tells you there is a problem, but the Creator would consider your situation a problem, then you have a problem. Denial of a problem can be the greatest problem.

What is the most important rule for dealing with problems? To me it is: When you think about a problem, keep your main focus on finding solutions. This one piece of advice makes a major difference in every life situation, and especially in marriage. We will deal with this at length in the chapter on outcome thinking. Let me say that it is worth reading this book if the only benefit you gain is that now you will focus on finding solutions instead of rehashing over and over again what you don't like.

When the major focus is on the problem, a couple can get into the totally counterproductive argument of, "Whose fault was it?" or, "Even if we are both to blame, who started, or who is more to blame?" This leads to angry arguments and quarrels. The way a husband and wife discuss a problem can be a bigger problem than the original problem itself. It is much wiser to focus on, "What can we do now to find a solution?" Then it's not very important to figure out who started or who is more to blame. Rather, you will be thinking constructively about things you can say or do to rectify the situation. For example, when one person nags, the other is likely to withdraw. The more that person withdraws, the more the other one is likely to nag. When you think in terms of solutions, it makes no difference if the nagging caused the withdrawing or the withdrawing caused the nagging.

At times the person who is less to blame can be the initiator of the positive changes that will influence his or her partner to also make changes that will enhance both of their lives.

The verbal exchanges of married couples have been compared to the steps of a dance. These patterns are repeated, usually without the conscious awareness of either the husband or the wife. But once a pattern is recognized and acknowledged, it can be changed. Even if a couple maintains the old pattern, it will no longer have the same intensity. Each partner will observe his statements and recognize what he or she is doing. This is a major step forward towards making improvements.

Every problem can be looked at in many ways. Your perspective will either make a solution easier to find or make it more difficult. "The question of a wise person is half a response" (*Migdal Oz, Hilchos Teshuvah,* ch. 5). That is, the very way that the wise person formulates the question points us in the direction of a solution. Whenever you are in a dilemma or in the middle of a problem, think about the best way to word your question. This applies not only when you ask your question to someone else, but even when you pose a question to yourself.

At times it is necessary to figure out the exact root of a problem to find the solution; at other times it isn't. Causes can be highly complex. Speaking about the past can be exactly what some couples need to do to work things out and to improve their relationship. For other couples, however, this would just be the source of more resentment, hard feelings, and quarrels.

It is possible to make a problem worse by overreacting to something that bothers you. By mistakenly defining some abstract concept as the root, you might be trying to overcome something that is so vague and abstract that you will never know whether or not you have succeeded. By looking objectively at what each person is saying and doing, and how that causes distress, you can make changes in the way you both speak and act. This will automatically change the way you both feel. Then you can see if the problem still exists.

For example, someone might say, "The fact that you forgot to buy what I asked for shows me you don't care about me at all." In truth, it doesn't. It only shows that the person didn't remember. If the situation is viewed as one of not caring, it is much more difficult to solve. If the problem is viewed as, "What would help my spouse remember things next time?" it is easier to find a solution. One can write a list and keep looking at it. One can buy an electronic organizer and set it to ring as a reminder. One can wear a string tied around the finger.

Let's say that the forgetful one now remembers to take care of things. If that alleviates the problem, then the solution was successful. If the person who felt neglected still feels that way, then another solution is needed. But first it would be necessary to define and describe what needs to happen for this person to feel cared for. It is very possible that the spouse does many considerate acts that get ignored and only the forgetful episodes are noticed. It is also possible that the person who feels uncared for has a definition of caring that is almost impossible to meet. Then a more realistic definition is required.

Suppose you feel that your spouse does not care about you. Then the problem can be stated: "My husband/wife doesn't care about me. What can I do in order for him/her to care about me?" Stated this way, you focus on what you personally can do in order to create the caring that you want. Thinking about a solution, you would make an effort to do things that would make your spouse feel so positive about you that it would be likely for him or her to respond by being more considerate. This is the exact opposite of what someone would do if he or she just blames and berates the other spouse for not caring. Angry attacks are not known for their effectiveness. Kindness, love, respect, and consideration have a much better chance of succeeding. Of course, this is difficult when someone doesn't feel cared for. But at least it gives you a chance to get what you want. The complaining, blaming, and berating approach is almost guaranteed to worsen the situation.

Another example: Suppose one spouse asks the other questions about something just said or done. The wording or tone of voice of the questions may be distressing to the one being asked. Someone might say, "The fact that you are asking me questions shows me that you don't trust me." Then the issue is a lack of trust which can be very emotionally charged. If every question is a sign of a lack of trust, then the couple will have many landmines that can easily explode. But asking questions could just mean that he or she wants more comprehension. It could be a sign of interest in what the other person is doing. And, yes, it could also be an opportunity to make positive suggestions about better ways to do things. The awareness that the wording of the questions or the tone of voice can cause distress, makes it easier to find a solution that will eliminate the problem. The problem will be resolved by editing the wording of the questions, or by choosing to ask questions in a more pleasant tone of voice.

People who have resented questions in the past might find them totally acceptable if they are asked in a way that doesn't make them feel attacked or confronted. If the questions are now asked in an acceptable manner, but the person on the receiving end of these questions still feels that they show a lack of trust, then clarify what needs to change in order for this person to feel trusted.

Trust is an important concept but also an abstract one. It means different things to different people. The goal is to view the issue as one in which both the husband and wife want a win-win solution. They can then have a more peaceful discussion over the issue, rather than a heated battle. This is definitely more conducive to building trust.

Some problems may have been with you for a long time. But whether a problem is simple or difficult to solve depends on the nature of the solutions available rather than the length of time you have experienced the problem. Take, for example, a person who is wearing a shoe that is one size too small. She's been wearing this shoe for many years, resulting in her feet constantly hurting. Let's even imagine that she has gone to doctors about the problem but x-rays have shown nothing wrong and the doctors can't find a way to rid her of the pain. As soon as she realizes that she needs to wear a larger size shoe, the problem will be solved. Similarly, if a man wears a shirt that is one size too small, and he always wears a tie and keeps the top button buttoned, he will experience much distress. This could have been going on for a long time, but as soon as he gets a larger size, the problem is solved.

Not all problems are solved this easily. But there are many long-standing problems that have fairly simple solutions if the problem is viewed properly. One of my favorite case histories involves a problem that was solved by an internationally famous psychiatrist. An elderly woman was deeply depressed. She lived by herself and didn't have any special talents, skills, or intellectual pursuits. Most methods for overcoming depression might not have worked for her since she was socially isolated and didn't have any stimulation in her life.

The psychiatrist, Dr. Milton Erickson, found that this woman did have one special interest — she loved African violet plants. He suggested that she buy 200 flower pots and cultivate them. Making sure they had sunlight and water would take a lot of work. Then she should give them as gifts one by one to anyone she knew celebrating a special occasion. She followed this suggestion. She became known as "The African Violet Queen" of her city and was constantly invited out to special events where she was always greeted warmly. She was constantly busy with an activity that she found enjoyable, and she regularly met people who were happy to see her. Her depression disappeared after just one session.

There are, of course, people who are clinically depressed who might need medication. Other people might need more than one session. Many people would not find it pleasurable to cultivate plants and therefore this would not be an appropriate solution for them. But at times even a problem that is chronic and serious can have a creative solution that might be resolved in a fairly short amount of time.

Many marriage situations are similar. If both husband and wife are totally committed to speaking to each other consistently with respect, years of problematic interchanges can be a thing of the past. This will eliminate the aftermath of ona'as devarim, the entire gamut of words that cause pain. Often the big obstacle is getting both parties motivated to improve the way they speak and act towards each other. You have a great deal of control over one of the parties in your marriage: yourself. You have a more limited influence on your partner. But by mastering the way you speak and act, you are likely to have a positive influence on both parties of the marriage.

When problems arise, think about exceptions. When is there no problem? Look for circumstances that might make the difference between times when the problem exists and times when the problem does not exist. This might help you find ways to eliminate the problem. For example, the problems between a couple might arise only when they are both tired and under special stress. Or the problems might arise when preparing for Shabbos only when they expect a lot of company. Or the problems might not exist when there is someone to help clean the home. Just looking for times when the problem doesn't exist is helpful since you will be looking for what is working well, rather than what isn't.

There are problems and dilemmas in life that are so painful and so serious that regardless of how clearly we are thinking, there are no easy answers and solutions. Your spouse might have patterns that you find difficult to deal with. For example, he or she is someone who gets angry very easily, someone who is highly irrational, someone who is highly critical. You might speak to different authorities and experts and still not know what to do. You might hear contradictory advice from various people. You might find some of the suggestions and recommendations too difficult to handle and cope with right now. In such situations clear thinking will prevent you from making impulsive choices that prove to be unwise.

Keep in mind that there have indeed been situations in which it seemed impossible for a particular condition to get better, but that it did, in fact, improve. At times, someone might suggest a brilliant move that can suddenly turn an entire situation around. Even very difficult circumstances become stabilized. Just not getting worse can be an important accomplishment too, and with time, things might improve little by little.

When a problem persists, the questions we can ask are: (1) What is maintaining the problem? (2) What words or actions will solve or remove the problem? For example, when one spouse is under stress, he or she can be transformed from a kind, reasonable, and composed individual into someone who is totally irrational. Viewing the stress as the root of the problem, you might find something to say or do that will decrease your spouse's level of stress.

The best preparation for difficult situations is to practice thinking objectively when smaller problems arise. If past preparations have not been sufficient, we need to make two goals for ourselves. One is to have greater mastery over our emotional states. The second is to find a solution to the issue at hand.

When a problem seems insurmountable, handle it one step at a time. Take one aspect of the problem and deal with that first. This alleviates that awesome feeling that the problem is too big to solve.

One basic perspective on problems and dilemmas, whether large or small, is that it is our life task to handle the tests that we are given. And this brings us to the next section.

GROWTH FROM CHALLENGES

Life after the wedding is very different from the way it is between the time that two people first meet until they get married. There is unique drama in the dating process. It contains a certain suspense with both parties trying to present themselves at their best. After the engagement, both the *chasan* and *kallah* are involved in preparations for the wedding. The focus is on the hall, band, and photographer. The *chasan* and *kallah* have a special relationship. Both while dating and while being engaged, problems, disagreements, and unpleasant surprises can arise. But during this time there is a special excitement filled with the joy and anticipation of finding one's life partner and entering a new stage in life. The wedding is often the most thrilling day in a person's life. But after the *sheva berachos,* things settle down and the respective personalities and character traits of the new husband and wife will either create harmonious ways of interacting or they will clash.

Prospective marriage partners need to face the fact that they will be married to a human being who is imperfect. For some this is a painful awareness. Others accept this as part of the Creator's creation. Our task is to grow from reality.

Difficulties will occur in everyone's life. We are much more aware of our own difficulties than of those of others. This can easily breed unwarranted envy. But knowing that everyone has challenges in life can make your own easier to cope with. Marriage is a constantly changing, fluid, evolving process. Hashem will always be sending you new challenges. Each stage of marriage has its unique *middos*-development opportunities. Hashem will set you up in situations that will challenge you and enable you to access hidden strengths that you might not have previously realized you possessed.

"Every challenge in your life is meant as a *nisayon,* a life challenge, from which you can grow" (*Mesillas Yesharim,* ch. 1). Believe that the Almighty has given you the strength and potential to not only cope with what happens to you in your life and marriage, but to grow from the experience. Marriage will add depth to your character. It will test you in a way that you've never been tested before. Being together with your parents and siblings, roommates and friends, is a totally different relationship from the experience of being married. You can plan consciously all you want. G-d will frequently send the unexpected into your life. Utilize whatever happens in your life and marriage for growth.

When someone thinks of getting married, he or she doesn't seek difficult challenges. People just want to be happy. When someone speaks to a *shadchan,* he or she doesn't ask for a person who will be a challenge. We look for the type of person with whom we will feel compatible. We want someone with good character traits. We want someone with similar values. We want to marry a person whose looks please us. We want someone who will be supportive emotionally and, often, financially.

A *shadchan* will make suggestions emphasizing the positive qualities of the prospective husband or wife. It is unlikely that a *shadchan* will say, "I would like to suggest someone you will find difficult to live with. He/she will test your character in many ways. You will have numerous opportunities to learn to control your anger. The tone of voice and the contents of what this person says will make you utilize every ounce of strength that you have. You might have a totally miserable marriage, but if you are successful in growing in this marriage, you will come out in the end on a high spiritual level." But this is exactly what our Heavenly *shadchan* has in mind for many people. Before you decided to get married you wanted reassurance that you would have someone you find easy to get along with, someone who would consistently make you happy. But looking back from the vantage point of eternity, the person you would want to choose is the one who would be most beneficial for your soul.

When you are faced with a challenge, you have many choices as to how to view it. Some ways of viewing challenges in life and marriage cause more pain than necessary even when, objectively speaking, anyone would agree that the situation is distressful. Your spouse might push your buttons more than anyone else. But, you can look at each challenge as a vote of confidence from our Creator. You can say to yourself, "Hashem believes in me. He believes that I can face this challenge and grow from it. If He believes that I can handle it, I, too, will believe that He gave me the intelligence and emotional strength to deal with it." Be the best person you can be. The more difficult the situation, the better person you become by acting in an elevated way. Our purpose in this world is to keep growing and developing our character. Without challenges our growth is limited.

Some people love to create drama in their lives, and some want to live a life of peace and quiet. We usually want both, but each at a time when we are ready for it. Our Creator, though, might test us and give us drama when we would prefer quiet, and quiet when we would like more excitement in our lives. We are forced to always be on our toes, ready for anything. Our task is to utilize each state in the best way.

Think right now of a challenge that you handled well. What did you think, say, and do that enabled you to handle it well? There were certainly many challenges that you handled so smoothly that it might not have registered in your mind that you were handling a challenge at all. As you remember them, you will feel more confident in your future ability to handle challenges. Every time in the future that you deal well with a potentially difficult situation, consciously add it to your mental data base. This data will serve as a valuable resource for the future.

Take, for example, the challenge of learning how to talk when you were a young child. You began without the ability to understand any language at all. You didn't even know one word. Little by little, over years, you learned how to understand what was said to you. At the same time you learned how to speak. You even learned how to read and write. While now you take these skills for granted, they were awesome accomplishments. By investing a similar effort to learn ways of talking and acting with your spouse, you will develop and master the skill of bringing out the best in each other.

When you first met your spouse, you might have felt the excitement of being with the person you always wanted to marry. Or, you might have begun to like the person more and more over time. Or, you were indecisive, but thought it was a good idea. Or, you felt pressured into your marriage. In a book on choosing and deciding whom to marry, this is an important issue. For a book on marriage, in one way it's irrelevant. Regardless of how you met, how you felt during dating, what you liked and disliked then, or why and how you came to the decision to marry this person, you are married. Now your life task is to grow from your marriage.

Even though, practically speaking, you are now married to your spouse, how you felt emotionally about him or her when you first met, when you continued going out, and how you reached your decision to marry him or her, will play a role in your present feelings. At times, this role can be a major one. For example, someone who felt pressured into marrying a person he or she really didn't want to marry, might still feel that without that pressure there would not have been a marriage. That person will then fail to try to make the marriage everything it could be. When problems arise in marriage, some standard reactions are:

(1) Anger: feelings of bitterness and resentment.

(2) Sadness: pain, disappointed, depression.

(3) Fatalistic acceptance: "Life is rough, and unfortunately my life is rougher than most."

(4) Divorce: "I can't stand this any longer, so I am cutting my losses and getting out of this marriage."

(5) Joyous acceptance together with a resolution to improve the situation: "If this is what Hashem wants for me, I accept His will with joy. I will read books on marriage, listen to tapes, and even speak to a Rabbi, Rebbetzin, or marriage counselor to do my share to improve what I can."

One does not need to define a marriage as happy or unhappy, successful or unsuccessful, or even functional or dysfunctional. Rather, each interaction is another opportunity to grow or not to grow. Each interaction is another opportunity to fulfill a mitzvah by doing *chesed*. Each interaction can elevate you and make you a better person.

When a marriage begins with resentment, the challenge is greater. Some people feel resentful that they weren't told certain truths about the other person. It could be the person's age. It could be that the person has a health issue about which you weren't aware. It could be that there are problems with a parent of the spouse and you weren't informed about them. It could be that you were promised a certain amount of financial assistance and it didn't materialize. It could be that you made certain assumptions that didn't have an actual basis, but you feel resentful that those assumptions weren't actualized. Let go of the resentment. As we will discuss in a later chapter, make it a high priority to live in the present. Be resolved to grow from the present challenges.

Utilize all that happens as an opportunity for growth. When your spouse makes a mistake, you have a chance to be compassionate and sensitive. You have a chance to judge favorably. You have a chance to fulfill the *mitzvah* of loving another person as yourself and to treat your spouse the way you would wish to be treated when you make a mistake. You have a chance to communicate love and concern. You have a chance to elevate your power of speech by helping to alleviate any distressful feelings over the mistake, instead of adding to them.

Grow from the challenges that Hashem gives us. That is what brings us closer to Him and prepares us for our soul's eternal destiny.

I wasn't satisfied with my marriage. I kept thinking that if only I had married someone else, my entire life would have been much smoother. This thought came to me fairly often and was a constant source of distress.

A sentence I heard from someone helped me discard this thought. I was told by an elderly Rabbi whom I respected greatly, "If you were married to someone else, you would also have problems."

The saintly Torah scholar then elaborated on this theme. "Many people think that if they had only married a different person, they would be free from all of their present problems. But that's not the way Hashem runs the world. As Mesillas Yesharim states in Chapter One, 'This world is a world of suffering.' If you wouldn't have the problems you presently have, you would have an equal number of different problems. Someone might marry a person who seems perfect for them, but illness, poverty, and other life tests can come their way. Whatever number of problems was destined for you will come your way in one form or another. Your task in life is to grow from each challenge."

What had been a long-standing obsession was erased with this insight.

I love to have the windows closed and my spouse demands to have them open. My spouse has a strong need for fresh air. I have a strong need to keep dust and noise out. We've argued over this many times.

Our choice of food is also different. I like my food rather bland. My spouse likes sharp, spicy food.

When music is playing, I like it to be soft and peaceful. My spouse likes music to be loud and blaring.

"Why did Hashem, our ultimate matchmaker, decide to put us together? Couldn't He have found someone more similar for both of us?" I asked my Rabbi.

"That's exactly the point," my Rabbi told me, with an understanding, hearty laugh. "You are perfect for each other. This way you both have to work on your middos. As you work out practical solutions in a way that is acceptable to both of you, you each build your character."

Many years ago before I got married, a Torah scholar advised me to consult a certain hidden tzaddik. This man appeared to most people as quite ordinary. But this well-known Torah scholar assured me that he was very special. He told me to ask him for advice on having a good marriage. When I spoke to that

righteous person, he told me that I should constantly remember that marriage, like everything else in life, is meant as a test. Knowing this will make the tests easier. Some people fail their tests because they expect them to be easy and therefore don't prepare for them as well as they should. They get caught off balance when the tests turn out to be very difficult. Besides studying hard for a test, there are tips and techniques that can help you deal with tests in the optimal way. The tzaddik shared with me these ten ideas and said, "Those who follow this list of ten will find it easier to pass the tests in marriage that Hashem sends them."

1. *The best preparation for Yom Kippur is to say to Hashem, "I forgive my wife for everything and anything she ever said or did wrong to me." And the best time to say this is this very moment or any time you think about her having said or done anything wrong. Once you forgive her, keep in mind that you have already let it go.*
2. *If you want a happy marriage, decide that you will consistently be happy with all that Hashem sends your way.*
3. *Tell your wife, "You are perfect the way you are." Even if she is not perfect for herself, she is perfect for you.*
4. *Right after saying "Modeh Ani" in the morning, expressing your gratitude for being alive, say, "And thank You for giving me my wife. I realize that she is exactly what I need for fulfilling my purpose in this world."*
5. *Before going to sleep at night, think about any mistakes you made when interacting with your wife. Mentally see yourself handling those situations better in the future. Feel joy that you are in the process of improving.*

6. As you stand before Hashem at the end of the Shemoneh Esrei, when saying the blessing, "Hamevarech es amo Yisrael bashalom — He who blesses His nation, Israel, with peace," think to yourself, "And bless me and my wife with peace."

7. Ideally we should do chesed out of sincere love for other people. But if you don't have these feelings, you are still obligated to do chesed. The same holds true in a marriage. Ideally you should have love and respect for your wife. If not, you are still obligated to treat her the way you would if you did have these feelings. Keeping this up will eventually increase your positive feelings.

8. If you ever feel that things are not as they should be between you and your spouse, pray that Hashem should bring harmony to all couples who need it. Praying for others helps your own prayers to be answered.

9. Increase your level of bitachon and you won't have to worry about anything. This will improve your marriage. When your wife sees how confident you are that things will work out well, she, too, will be calmer.

10. Each day say the first fifteen verses of Chapter 34 in Tehillim at least three times. This is one of the greatest segulos for shalom bayis.

GROWING WITH JOY

Everyone wants a happy marriage. The best way to ensure a happy marriage is to master the ability to experience joy in your life with each moment of growth. And each moment is an opportunity to grow.

There are many forms of growth in marriage. Growth can mean you are happy with your marriage and constantly feel grateful to Hashem. Growth can mean that you have a Torah partnership that is eternal for both of you. Growth can mean that you are increasing your appreciation for *chesed.* Growth can mean that you are improving in your character traits. Growth can mean that you act in an elevated manner even though things are difficult. Growth can mean that you develop resources to turn around a difficult situation. Growth can mean that you transcend your natural tendencies in order to be compassionate and forgiving. Growth can mean that you make sacrifices for the benefit of your spouse and children. Growth can mean that you sustain a loving and respecting way of being even though this is not reciprocated. Growth can even mean that you have the courage to end an abusive situation. Growth always means that you act according to Hashem's will. Growth always means that the Torah is your guide as to which patterns of speech and action to increase and which to eliminate from your repertoire.

"The wise person lives a life of pleasure" (*Chochmah U'Mussar,* vol. 1, p. 75). Why is this so? Because a wise person consistently keeps growing and therefore experiences joy each day. As the Chazon Ish wrote: "There is no greater joy for a wise person than the joy of improving character traits" (*Emunah U'Bitachon* 4:15).

Some people might think that they can only feel joy if they see that they have made a major transformation in their character. So keep in mind these words of the late *mashgiach* of Slobodka, Rabbi Avraham Grodzinsky, *zt"l*: "Our attitude towards even the smallest degree of spiritual elevation should be similar to the happiness and excitement of someone who has found a hidden treasure" (*Toras Avraham,* p. 22).

Note the words, "smallest degree." While we should aim high, in truth, in this world we will usually grow in small increments. There are definitely special moments of inspiration which serve as a light when we find ourselves making great strides forward and upward. But day in and day out it is more realistic to expect small degrees of growth. A positive change in behavior can have a snowball effect. The initial change might be slight, but it can serve as the beginning of major change and transformation. Take daily actions to improve, even by taking small steps. Each day ask yourself, "What can I do today to improve?"

Growth cannot be measured by human beings. The more difficult something is for us to do, the greater the reward. There are difficulties that stand out as difficulties. These challenges are clearly noted in our minds as challenges and they can bring out our strengths. But overcoming inertia, boredom, sad feelings, and mild resentments is difficult too. That is exactly why growing at these moments is an act of greatness. So when you find yourself still acting with love and respect in a moment when this is difficult, visualize yourself finding a major treasure. You have found an eternal fortune. Allow yourself to rejoice.

"Feel joy with every moment of awareness of the Almighty that you attain" (Rabbeinu Avraham ben HaRambam; *HaMaspik L'Ovdei Hashem*, p. 66; Chofetz Chaim in *Chomas HaDas*, ch. 17, footnote). If you had an entire stadium of people applauding and cheering for you because you accomplished something difficult, the difficulty would be much easier. You know that the efforts you put into your accomplishment have been noted and acknowledged. Awareness of Hashem's recognition of your efforts when you are faced with a challenge makes the entire process of growth that much easier. It can still be difficult, but the inner feelings you will experience will illuminate your life.

What if you seek awareness of Hashem but are not yet totally there? Rabbi Leibush of Apelia commented on the verse, "May the heart of those who seek Hashem rejoice" (*Divrei HaYamim* 1:16:10): "When one seeks a certain object, he feels no joy until after he finds what he is looking for. But when we seek the Almighty, the very act of seeking Him can give us joy" (*Siach Sarfei Kodesh*, vol. 5, p. 48). When a married couple live in harmony, the Almighty is there. Therefore, preparing for marriage by developing plans to treat your spouse with love and respect, or working on enhancing an already good marriage, or exerting the effort to improve a stormy relationship, are ultimately ways of seeking Hashem. Feel joy in the entire process. This joy will make it easier for both of you to increase the level of joy in your home as you bring the *Shechinah* into your lives.

Whenever we have repeated a pattern many times, it can be difficult to change. But all patterns ultimately can be changed. It is a question of having a clear goal as to what pattern you want to modify, and then being motivated to take action. It is easier to change patterns when both parties are willing to work together. If you are the only one, it takes more strength, more courage, and more resilience. The Almighty leads a person on the path on which he wants to go. May He gave you the wisdom to make the right decisions and choices, and the strength and courage to follow through.

Grow from both the good and the bad. Grow from the pleasant and the unpleasant. Grow from moments of joy and from moments of sadness and grief. Grow when things go the way you wish, and when they don't. Grow from your best moments and from your worst. Each and every moment of life provides a potential for inner growth.

Chapter Two

Building the Foundation

- Chesed — giving consciousness:

  the heart of marriage

- Appreciation and gratitude

- Respect

- Love

- Common goals:

  partners in fulfilling your life's mission

- Your spouse is your closest relative; you are one

- Your marriage partner is your Creator's choice

  for you

- The first year of marriage:

  a time to gain understanding

- Hashem will send you messages; learn from them

CHESED —
GIVING CONSCIOUSNESS:
THE HEART OF MARRIAGE

hesed is one of the three pillars supporting the world (*Pirkei Avos* 1:2). It is also a major pillar for your marriage. *Chesed* means caring sincerely about the needs, wants, and wishes of your spouse. Although we all need to both give and take, a person with a giving consciousness places a higher priority on giving than on taking.

"Develop a love for doing acts of kindness." When you have this love for *chesed,* you will be very happy every time you have the opportunity to do something for another person (Chofetz Chaim; *Ahavas Chesed,* part 2, ch. 2). In marriage you have many opportunities to be giving for your husband or wife. Each action you take that will benefit or help the other in some way is an opportunity to do *chesed* and can be transformed into a source of joy. This will guarantee you much joy in your married life.

Rabbi Eliyahu Eliezer Dessler used to tell newlyweds that the key to a successful marriage is for each partner to always try to make the other happy. But when one constantly makes demands of the other, happiness will not be theirs (*Michtav MeEliyahu,* vol. 1, p. 39).

In the words of one of the great *mussar* personalities, *chesed* is not merely giving material goods to others. A friendly smile and a kind word are also forms of *chesed*. We must learn to understand others in order to fulfill our obligation of doing *chesed*. Try to sense the problems of another person, and feel their suffering. Help others without being asked. This is a very difficult task since others might be lacking something that you yourself do not deem necessary. When a person is able to recognize that others are in need of help, an enormous number of opportunities for *chesed* present themselves (*Alei Shur*, vol. 1, p. 22).

"Any favor or kindness that you do for someone is a fulfillment of the commandment of loving other people as yourself" (*Yesod V'Shoresh HaAvodah* 1:7,8). With every act of *chesed* that you do for your husband or wife, you are making the foundation of your marriage stronger and stronger. Doing any act of *chesed* even for a stranger is the fulfillment of a *mitzvah*, all the more so when you do a *chesed* for your spouse. With each kind act, you are strengthening the foundation of your marriage.

The Chofetz Chaim wrote that even if someone can afford to buy clothes himself, you nonetheless fulfill a *mitzvah* by helping him choose clothes. Any effort to help someone acquire clothing is included in the *mitzvah* of emulating the Creator (*Ahavas Chesed*, part 3, ch. 7, footnote; *Sotah* 14a). Helping your spouse choose an item of clothing might seem like a mundane act, but it is a spiritually elevating act of *chesed*.

Every time you hand something to your spouse, you are doing an act of *chesed*. Every time you tell your spouse good news, it's *chesed* (*Shnei Luchos HaBris*, vol. 1, *Shaar HaOsiyos*). Every time you give your spouse change for a larger coin, it's *chesed* (*Machaneh Yisrael* 2:2). Every time you greet your spouse in a friendly manner, it's *chesed* (*HaKesav V'HaKabbalah, Vayikra* 19:18). Every time you pray for your spouse's welfare, it's *chesed* (*Eved HaMelech, Bereishis*, p. 74b). Every time you forgive your spouse for something, it's *chesed* (*Mei'am Loez, Bereishis*, vol. 1, p. 404). Every time you warn your spouse about a potential harm or damage, it's *chesed* (*Yesod V'Shoresh HaAvodah* 1:8). Every time you cheer your spouse when he or she needs an emotional boost, it is an act of *chesed* (*Ahavas Chesed* 3:5). Every time you pick up an item from the floor to prevent it from getting damaged, it's *chesed* (*Yesod V'Shoresh HaAvodah* 1:8). Of course, a husband or wife should not needlessly cause the other extra work, that too is *chesed*. And this is just a start. The amount of *chesed* the two of you can do for each other is unlimited. As you feel the joy of doing *chesed*, your married life will consequently be filled with joy.

There are many stories of great people who focused only on giving and not on taking. While these stories are inspiring, they must be understood within the context of the personality of the people involved. These Torah giants and righteous people had great pleasure from the Torah that they mastered, and they experienced intense pleasure from praying and doing *mitzvos*. Therefore their personal needs in other areas were much less than those of most people. The vast majority of even great people have wants, needs, and wishes. When most of us fail to receive some of these wants, needs, and wishes, we build up resentment. We might even keep score. "I've done this much. What have I received in return?" Therefore, we need a balance in the area of giving and taking. It is definitely appropriate for even a very giving person to make reasonable requests of his or her spouse. Those who are more idealistic and *chesed*-oriented need to allow themselves the right to be normal human beings to whom the Creator gave wants, needs, and wishes.

On the other side of the giving/taking spectrum, some people always have strings attached when they do acts of kindness for another person. They will demand gratitude and claim that since they did things for you, you now owe them. In the extreme, you can never do enough in return. They will use guilt tactics to intimidate others to continually do things for them because of what they have done. The demands they make will be way out of proportion to what they have done. They need to learn that *chesed* should be done with no strings attached. Rabbi Chaim

Shmulevitz used to say that the fact that the Torah forbids taking interest on a financial loan teaches us that when you perform a *chesed*, do so only for the sake of helping another person. Don't demand or even ask for anything in return. While these restrictions do not apply to other forms of kindness that you do for someone, they teach us the general principle that our acts of kindness for others must benefit the other person. Ultimately, as a result of these acts, the attribute of kindness becomes an integral part of us.

However, some people complain, "I'm tired of giving and giving and not getting anything in return. I do a lot for my spouse and my spouse does not do an equal amount for me."

There are two basic solutions to this situation: The first approach involves finding ways to motivate and influence your spouse to be more giving towards you. Ask yourself, "What would my spouse need in order to feel so good about me that he/she would be happy to do things for me in return?" The other approach requires developing such an intense love for doing acts of kindness for your spouse that even if your spouse doesn't reciprocate, you will be in a constant state of joy for the *chesed* that you consistently do. It makes sense to apply a combination of both solutions.

A student of Rabbi Noson Tzvi Finkel related that his Rebbe once asked him, "Do you help your wife in the house before Shabbos?" He replied that he did, and added that he well appreciated the importance of honoring Shabbos. The Talmud (Shabbos 119a) relates that even the most prominent Sages performed menial tasks to prepare for Shabbos.

Instead of praising him, however, Rabbi Finkel admonished the student for his attitude. "It is a Torah commandment to help someone who needs assistance," he said. "This applies even to a total stranger; all the more so does it apply to one's wife. On Friday afternoon, women are usually tired and it is a very great chesed to assist them" (Tenuas HaMussar, vol. 3, p. 250).

I used to help out a lot around the house. But to tell the truth, I sometimes resented it. Even when I realized that it was my obligation, I often did it reluctantly. But I knew that it's an act of chesed to help out. Moreover, when my wife does things around the house, she is doing them for me and our children and the least I can do is my comparatively small part.

I remember hearing in the name of Rabbi Chaim Friedlander, zt"l, of the Ponovezh Yeshivah, "If you are going to do it anyway, you might as well do it with joy." This piece of advice is precious in all areas of our lives, and especially when it comes to marriage.

To help me improve my attitude and emotional state, I developed the habit of saying, "I'll be happy to do it," whenever I was asked to do something. When I first began saying this, I didn't feel very happy doing things, but with time I've internalized this message. This one expression created a much happier atmosphere in our home.

❖ ❖ ❖

I am very moody, and have many emotional ups and downs. When I feel up, I am one of the kindest people in the world. When I am down, however, my personality changes and I don't feel like doing anything for anyone. Besides my frequent emotional cycles, the way my husband talks to me is a key element in how I feel towards him. When he is sensitive and considerate, I love him and will do anything for him. If he talks to me gruffly or abruptly, however, I don't feel like doing anything for him. At times I will refuse his requests with a sharp, "No. Do it yourself." At other *times, I will passive-aggressively find excuses why I can't do things for him: "I am too busy now." Or, "I don't feel so well."*

I attended a lecture on chesed which dealt with the idea of doing acts of kindness for others even if we don't feel like it. The speaker cited the Gemara which states that if two people need our help, with one person needing help to load his animal and the other needing help to unload his animal, normally we have to first help the person who wishes to unload his animal. This is because both the person and the animal need our help. By unloading, we are making the animal's load lighter. Therefore this takes precedence. But there is an important exception to this rule.

Imagine that you see two people having a difficult time, one with loading and the other with unloading their animals. A close friend of yours is the one who needs to unload his animal. But nearby is someone whom you dislike and that person is having a difficult time loading his animal. Here you need to help the person you dislike first. The Talmud states the reason: "Lachof es yitzro — to exercise your spiritual muscles and force yourself to do what you don't feel like doing."

Hearing this, I realized that when I don't feel like doing chesed for my husband, that is exactly when I have a greater obligation to do chesed for him. Even if someone else needs my help also, my negative feelings towards my husband are exactly the reason I need to help him right away.

When I put this into practice, my husband acted so kindly towards me in return that my feelings were transformed into positive ones towards him.

"**Y**ou are so selfish. Whey don't you do more chesed for me?" Who said this the most times: my spouse or me? I couldn't tell. But the concept of chesed was used by both of us as a tool that resembled a weapon.

Perhaps if I instill enough guilt, my spouse will be motivated to meet more of my needs. This was the practical rationale when both of us expressed the need for more chesed in our home.

Chesed is one of the pillars of the world. Chesed is the beginning and end of the Torah. But in our house chesed is just a leverage tool for manipulation. Instead of being an expression of selflessness, we use it to attack the self-esteem of the other.

I remember the day we hit our lowest ebb. I started it. "You feel that chesed is important, don't you?" I asked my spouse.

"Of course. It's one of the most important attributes one can have," my spouse replied.

"Then how come you lack it to such a large degree?" I challenged.

"Who are you to say that I don't have chesed?" my spouse responded. "You and chesed are an oxymoron."

"Well if one of us is an ox and a moron, it's definitely you," I said.

"Idiot!" my spouse said. "You are so stupid that you didn't even understand what I was saying."

"I do understand that you are a self-centered egoist, and you don't have a sense of humor," I said.

My spouse left the room in a rage, and we were both angry with each other until the next day. After I had time to calm down, I thought about the situation objectively. The reality is that both my spouse and I want to do chesed for others and even for each other. But we dislike feeling manipulated or pressured into doing things.

"I'm sorry that I started the argument this time," I said.

"Let's both pledge not to misuse the Torah ideal of chesed."

"I agree," said my spouse. "Let's use the ideal of chesed to motivate ourselves and not as a means of attacking each other."

APPRECIATION AND GRATITUDE

"A person who has mastered the attribute of appreciating what he has is in the same state and emotionally as high as the person who is inebriated during the height of the pleasure of a party" (Vilna Gaon; *Mishlei* 15:15).

The way to live a joyous life is to appreciate all the gifts that the Almighty has given you. As long as you are alive you will have many things to appreciate. Don't take anything for granted. Each and every day, from the moment you say *Modeh Ani* in the morning to express your gratitude for once again being alive to experience another day, throughout each breath you take, until you go to sleep at night, focus on what you have rather than on what you are missing.

Every husband and wife have many reasons to be grateful to each other. Just being married gives you benefits that enable you to exercise the attribute of gratitude. The more grateful you are to your spouse, the stronger the foundation of your marriage.

Expressing gratitude gives pleasure to your spouse. And it serves as positive reinforcement for motivating your spouse to continue doing those things for which you sincerely express your gratitude.

Why isn't everyone grateful? Because the nature of each person is to want more. "He who has 100 wants 200. He who has 200 wants 400." It is so much easier to focus on what we don't have rather than to keep focusing on what we do have. Some people feel that they can only be grateful if the person they are married to meets all their wants, wishes, and needs; only if the person is totally perfect can they be grateful. But the Torah attitude is that we should be grateful for anything anyone has done for us. The Talmudic Sage, Rabbi Chiya, was married to someone who consistently did things to cause him pain. Nevertheless, out of gratitude for the positive things she did for him, such as bearing him a child, he would always be on the lookout for gifts he could bring to her (*Yevamos* 63a).

We should even be grateful for those things we received from our spouse unintentionally. We see in the Torah (*Shemos* 7:19): "And Hashem said to Moshe, say to Aharon, 'Take your rod and stretch out your hand over the waters of Egypt, over their streams, their rivers, and their pools. And over every gathering of their water, that they may become blood, throughout all the land of Egypt, both in vessels of wood and in vessels of stone.' "

Rashi cites the *Midrash* (*Shemos Rabbah* 9:10) which explains that Aharon rather than Moshe was chosen to initiate the plagues of blood and frogs because the water had protected Moshe when he was cast into it as an infant. It would therefore not be proper for Moshe to smite the water.

Rabbi Chaim Shmulevitz repeated frequently that water is an inanimate object which does not have free will. When something floats in water and does not sink, it would not occur to us to give thanks to the water for its buoyancy. Nevertheless, we learn from this verse that if a person derives pleasure from an object, he should show his gratitude by being careful not to cause harm or damage to the object, even though it would not suffer pain. As the Talmud (*Bava Kamma* 92a) states: "If you drink water from a well, do not throw stones in it." Although this advice is basically meant as a metaphor for people who have given you something, the literal meaning should not be ignored either (see *Shitah Mekubetzes, Bava Kamma,* ibid.). Since our obligation to be grateful for benefits gained applies to inanimate objects, all the more so must we show gratitude towards people.

One way to increase your level of gratitude towards your spouse is to keep a gratitude journal and write down a list of things for which you can be grateful. Don't forget the things you might take for granted. Make a note of the spiritual benefits you gain from being married, any amount of money your spouse brings home, the food your spouse cooks, kind words, any shopping that your spouse does, clean dishes or your clean laundry, and your house being neat and clean. Above all be grateful for the kindnesses you can do for your spouse.

If someone does and says everything exactly as you would wish, it's easy to have gratitude. The challenge is to feel and express gratitude for what someone does for you even though they are imperfect and even though they don't always do exactly as you would wish.

We can feel more grateful for what we have when we appreciate that we are spared the suffering of those who are missing what we might take for granted.

*A*n older single woman had this to say about being single: "To me being single is like living in a holocaust. I know that this sounds extreme, but this is my inner reality. I don't have family. I don't have what to look forward to. I am lonely. I don't have children. When I think of the future, I think of being all by myself in an old-age home. People who are married don't know how fortunate they are. I suffer each day in the present, and the future looks bleak. I know that not everyone who is single suffers as much as I do, and I wish I could make myself happier than I am. My one and only wish is to find someone appropriate to marry."

If you are grateful for not suffering this kind of loneliness, catch your spouse doing positive rather than negative things. We easily take for granted the positive qualities that we are used to. Don't take even the smallest positive virtue or attribute for granted. People with this attitude live happy lives, and those who think with gratitude and appreciation about their husband or wife have happy marriages.

I feel that gratitude is a highly important attribute, and I consider it my responsibility to be grateful to those who do things for me. But I find it difficult to be grateful to someone who demands it from me.

My spouse constantly tells me, "I do a lot for you. You must express your gratitude in word and deed. Right now I want you to ..."

How can this possibly make me feel? Even if I'm about to do what I'm being asked to do, when the demand for gratitude is being shoved down my throat I feel like I'm choking.

How would you feel if on a regular basis you were told: "Remember what I did for you when we were engaged. Now you owe me." "That's pretty ungrateful of you — to refuse to do what I ask." "The Sages say, 'Whoever shows ingratitude to a human being will end up without gratitude to Hashem. You'd better watch out.' " "I'm not going to go out of my way to do anything for you unless you express more gratitude."

Here is my challenge. I do have many things for which to be grateful. But the way I'm constantly reminded of it makes me not want to express it. I know it's the right thing to express my gratitude anyway. I'm reframing the counterproductive pattern of my spouse as an opportunity to develop the quality of gratitude even more than if it were easier. I now have to overcome the resistance I feel because of the way my spouse uses the request for gratitude. My sense of gratitude needs to be so strong that it lifts me above my initial feelings. Whenever I succeed, my gratitude to our Creator also increases.

RESPECT

"Who is honorable?" the Mishnah (*Pirkei Avos* 4:1) asks. "Someone who honors other human beings!" the Mishnah answers. Why? Because honoring other humans, who were created in His image, ultimately honors our Creator. This applies to every person you meet. The person you are married to is a descendant of the first couple created by our Creator. You have a common ancestry and are both children of G-d. Besides our regular obligation to honor everyone, the Rambam cites the special obligation of a husband to honor his wife more than himself, and the obligation of a wife to honor her husband like a member of royalty.

When husband and wife feel that the other respects them, the foundation of the marriage is strong. If the foundation of a major structure is weak, anyone in that building is at risk. One can never know when it will collapse, injuring everyone inside. The highest priority in such instances is to fortify the foundation to ensure that it will remain strong and sturdy. The same applies to respect in marriage. Build up an inner respect and express it with your words and actions.

Rabbi Yitzchak Blauser wrote about his teacher Rabbi Yisrael Salanter that even though the sage personally kept a distance from all forms of honor, he was nevertheless very careful to show proper respect and honor to other people.

It is natural for a person who works on himself and nullifies the concept of honor to eventually find that honor is not important in his eyes. Consequently, it might be hard for him to worry about the honor due to others. Even though you refrain from seeking honor yourself, however, be very careful to show respect to others (Rabbi Yechezkel Levenstein; *Ohr Yechezkel, Middos,* pp. 21-22).

Rabbi Yitzchak Blauser used to say that a man should treat his wife as respectfully as he would treat a stranger. Just as a person is careful to be polite to strangers, so should a husband be polite to his wife (*Kochvei Ohr,* vol. 2, p. 16).

The *Menoras HaMaor* cites a *Midrash* which relates that a wise woman told her daughter: "Serve your husband as if he were a king. For, if you will act towards him like his maid, he will act as if he were your servant, and will honor you like a queen. If, however, you try to dominate him, he will be your master, and you will be in his eyes like a maidservant" (*Menoras HaMaor, Ner*, 3 part 4, ch. 2).

*W*hen I was engaged, I spoke to a number of people for advice on what I could do to have a good marriage. An elderly woman, a friend of my grandmother, who was one of the most joyous people I've ever met, was on top of my list of people to whom to speak. She and her husband have been married for over fifty years and when you see them together you see two youthful people. They seem to have the same vibrancy as two newlyweds a few weeks after their wedding.

"What is the secret of your happy marriage?" I asked my grandmother's friend.

"My dear, I'm sorry to disappoint you," she told me, "but I don't have any secrets."

"But there must be some principles or formulas that you follow," I said. "From all the stories you've told me, you didn't seem to have it too easy financially."

"That's right. My husband was a teacher before he retired," she told me. "We never did have a lot of money, but we've always had exactly what we needed. I don't have an original formula or any secret. But there are two basic Torah ideas that have been my guiding light. I'm certain you know them."

"What are they?" I asked impatiently.

"I hope you're not disappointed with what I'm about to tell you. I'm positive that you already know them."

"I see that they work for you. I also see that not everyone has the type of marriage that you do and very few people are so consistently happy."

"I guess that both ideas I'm about to tell you fit together as sort of a package. You probably learned in the first grade the statement in Pirkei Avos that the wealthy person is the one who has joy with what he has. I've always had things to be joyous about, so I'm always joyous. Of course there have been many sad and difficult times in my life. But much more often I am grateful to Hashem for the good He has given me. Even in the most difficult of times there is something for which to be grateful. I'm not even an optimist. I don't know how anything will work out. But I've found over and over again that as long as we are alive, we will be able to find things for which to be grateful. All the children growing up today have much more than I did when I was young. Even then there were some people who went around praising Hashem for His kindness and others who would always find something to complain about. I chose to live a life of gratitude. I am grateful right now that I have an opportunity to add something to your life, if you find what I say useful.

"About marriage, when I was engaged, my grand-mother blessed me with her grandmotherly blessings. Then she said to me, 'My beloved granddaughter. You have a very nice chasan. But you still have a choice of acting in ways that will make your marriage happy or unhappy. Treat your husband like a king and you will be married to royalty. Whatever you do for him, feel like you are doing it for a king. He might not always act as royally as he should. Still, treat him like a king. Feel it an honor to do as much as you can for him. I guarantee you that he will treat you equally well.'

"Those words of my grandmother are no secret. They are a basic Torah principle. I've found that it worked for me. I've lived long enough to see that those women who apply it are much better off than those who feel that this isn't for them. I hope that fifty years from now this is the advice you will be giving your grandchildren when they ask you why your marriage is so wonderful."

When I was engaged, I wanted to make certain that after marriage I would treat my husband with respect. I asked a few teachers with much life experience, "What suggestions do you have for me on how to treat my husband properly?" One piece of advice stuck with me for over thirty years.

"Go to at least five fancy restaurants," I was told. "Observe the waiters and waitresses carefully. Observe their excellence in the chesed of serving guests. Notice how they greet the guests who come to their restaurant. See how they speak and how they serve. Listen to how they ask if all is satisfactory. See how they offer more food."

"That sounds like a good idea," I said to myself.

"Do you know why they give excellent service?" my teacher asked me.

"They want to keep their jobs, and they want larger tips," I replied.

"Exactly," said the teacher. "Money motivates them. Always remember that a happy marriage is worth even more than money can buy."

Since then I have given this advice to many kallahs, both before and after they were married. My favorite reaction was the bride who paid a professional waitress to give her private lessons. Five months later the bride came back to me and said that it was the single most meaningful advice she ever heard in her life.

We need to respect every human being because they are created in our Creator's image. When you realize that your spouse is a child of our Father, our King, Creator and Sustainer of the universe, you will give respect. If you don't yet actually feel this way, act as if you do, and little by little it will become internalized.

*J*okingly, my wife and I decided to address each other as King and Queen of the world. We agreed to try this for an entire week and see what would happen. We only did this when no one else was present because we didn't want anyone else to think that we were weird. "And how is the Queen of the universe feeling today?" I would ask. "I thank the King of the world for asking me. Fine, baruch Hashem," my wife would respond with a big smile. "The King's supper is ready now," my wife would tell me. "I thank Her Majesty, the Queen, for preparing and offering me the meal. It was kind of Her Royal Highness," I would respond. I can just say that this had a more powerful effect on us than we had expected. We each used to complain that we weren't being treated respectfully enough. At the end of a week we laughed about how far we had come in such a short time.

How Can I Respect Someone Who Is Imperfect?

All humans have faults and limitations. Unless you can respect someone who is imperfect, you will never respect anyone. Even if a person has faults, he or she is still created in G–d's image; he or she is still a child of G-d. Respect is what is due all human beings and ideally should be unconditional.

The Dubner Maggid (*Parashas Emor*) offers the following parable in reference to another topic, but it applies to our subject as well. A father became angry at his son and kicked him out of the house. The son decided to travel to another city, but first he wanted to beg people for money so he could afford to travel. He went door to door to raise the money. Since people recognized him they gave him more than they would have given a mere stranger. He decided to knock on the home of his parents to beg money from them. When his father opened the door and saw him, he was furious. "I kicked you out of the house. Why are you asking me for money?" The son replied, "I realize that you don't want to support me like a father would do for his child. But I was hoping that you would give me charity just like you would give to a total stranger."

This parable can apply to marriage. Even if you aren't entirely happy with the person to whom you are married, at least treat him or her with the respect and kindness that you would a stranger.

The reality is that each person will have some quality that you can respect. Keep your focus on what you can respect about the person you married:

- He/she might be lazy. But you can focus on his/her kindness.
- He/she might be of average intelligence. But you can focus on his/her honesty and diligence.
- He/she might be disorganized. But you can focus on his/her creativity.
- He/she might be awkward. But you can focus on his/her sense of humor.
- He/she might be emotionally underdeveloped. But you can focus on his/her willingness to do many things for you even when it is difficult.

*M*y father always woke up early in the morning for Shacharis. I was so disappointed that my husband would get up relatively late for davening. "How can I respect him if he consistently gets up late," I asked myself.

I spoke to an understanding teacher who knew my husband's family and she said to me, "Your husband has so many positive qualities on which to focus. He is serious about studying Torah. He is kindhearted. He is easygoing and noncritical. True, he is missing a certain drive that your father has, but he has a wealth of positive qualities that you can focus on. He gets many things accomplished in his own way. Focus on what he does right, not on what is missing."

This talk with my teacher changed my focus. What she said enabled me to be happy with my marriage. We are married a number of years now, and I see the wisdom of what she told me.

❖ ❖ ❖

My mother is a very organized person. She is neat and orderly, and even with a large family and busy schedule, she always kept our house running efficiently and effectively. My wife is the extreme opposite. She is always late. Nothing is ever done on time. She constantly procrastinates and postpones things. I feel that our house is always in a state of chaos.

I spoke to my Rabbi and asked him how I can possibly respect someone who is so not together. He told me that I am making a fundamental error. My Torah obligation is to love and respect my wife. The Rambam does not state, "You are free from this obligation if your wife is disorganized and procrastinates."

"Your wife was given to you to improve your middos and to help you raise a Torah family," the Rabbi continued. "She is a total success at both. She is idealistic and the Torah attitudes she lives with are on a high level. Her lack of organization gives you opportunities to do many acts of kindness to help her out. You have constant challenges that can help you develop humility and patience. Your entire marriage is an opportunity to accept our Creator's will. Your wife deserves your love and respect just as every other child of our Creator."

After that talk I viewed my wife's lack of organization as exactly what I needed for my personal growth. As a fringe benefit she has become more organized. Previously, she hated my constant nagging and griping. Now that I have increased my inner feelings of respect and let go of trying to control her, she feels greater motivation to become more organized. I was pleasantly surprised when she told me that she signed up for a course on efficient home-management. But regardless of how she ends up in this area, I am totally committed to respecting her.

Focus on Your Spouse's Potential

What if your spouse has many serious faults and negative qualities that outweigh the positive aspects? The answer is that in such instances you can still focus on the potential positive qualities.

My favorite example of this is how Rabbi Yochanan viewed Reish Lakish the first time they met (*Bava Metzia* 84a). I feel that the message of this *Gemara* is so powerful that we need to review it frequently.

Rabbi Yochanan was one of the great Sages of the Talmud. Reish Lakish was the leader of a gang of robbers. Reish Lakish observed Rabbi Yochanan swimming in the Jordan River, dived into the water and energetically swam to him.

Immediately, Rabbi Yochanan said to Reish Lakish, "Your strength should be used to study Torah."

Rabbi Yochanan didn't focus on the fact that Reish Lakish was the head of a gang of robbers and was very far from living a total Torah way of life. Instead, he focused on the fact that Reish Lakish had intense energy and potential to become a great Torah scholar.

The only problem is, "How do you motivate this person to give up his present profession as a leader of robbers and devote that energy to becoming a Torah scholar?" Motivating someone requires understanding what is important to him. Listen carefully and people will tell you what is most important to them.

Reish Lakish retorted to Rabbi Yochanan, "Your beauty is fitting for a woman."

Now Rabbi Yochanan saw the way to influence Reish Lakish.

"Immerse yourself in Torah study," said Rabbi Yochanan, "and you can marry my sister who is even more beautiful."

Reish Lakish agreed and became a great scholar who is frequently quoted in the Talmud, especially in reference to his debates with his brother-in-law, Rabbi Yochanan.

When an artist sees an empty canvas, he immediately imagines the beautiful picture that he can paint. This can be our model regarding human beings with faults. See people for their potential when they utilize their strengths in positive ways. Each person needs to be motivated in a way that addresses specific interests, wants, and desires. Don't give up before you even start. People who believe in other people can do amazing, even miraculous, things.

One of the major challenges in marriage is to develop the strength of character to act with respect towards your spouse: even when your feelings have been deeply hurt; even when you are angry; even when you feel that your spouse has been unfair; and even when acting with respect is the last thing you feel like doing.

When you act with kindness and respect towards someone, you increase that person's tendency to treat others with more kindness and respect. In your marriage, you will be the one to gain when your spouse reciprocates.

It isn't advisable to say to your spouse, "If you treat me with respect then I will treat you with respect." Your spouse might respond, "So you acknowledge that you aren't treating me with respect. When you treat me with respect, I will do the same for you."

It's much more effective to say, "I will treat you with respect. I hope that you will do the same towards me." Or, you might say, "I want to treat you with great respect. It will make it a lot easier for me to treat you right, if you treat me right."

LOVE

What Is Love?

In my book, *Gateway to Happiness*, I have only one footnote. And that is: "Words cannot really define happiness. Happiness is an emotional state and this needs to be experienced to be understood. Just as colors need to be seen to know what they are and music needs to be heard, emotions need to be felt."

Most simply, love may be defined as having positive feelings for another person. Some define love as affection based on admiration, benevolence, or common interests. Others define love as warm attachment, enthusiasm, or devotion. Yet others define it as unselfish loyal and benevolent concern for the good of another.

Many people cite the Torah description of Yitzchak's feelings for Rivkah, where we read that first Yitzchak married Rivkah and then he loved her (*Bereishis* 24:67). But we also find in the Torah that Yaakov loved Rachel right from the first moment he saw her (*Bereishis* 29:18), and this motivated him to agree to work for seven years for her father so he would consent to their marriage. The *Ohr HaChaim* comments that the source of Yaakov's love for Rachel was that he felt she was his life partner. Thus, in the Torah we find various possibilities for the experience of love.

In the Talmudic based blessings recited under the *chuppah,* we say, "*Same'ach tesamach, rei'im ha'ahuvim* — Cause to rejoice the friends who love each other." Rashi on *Kesubos* 8a explains that this refers to the groom and the bride who are friends and who love each other. They are designated as partners to fulfill their life's mission.

However we define it, love is giving. This is a valuable concept that works both ways. We want to give to the person we love. It is also true that when we constantly give to someone, we increase our positive feelings for that person. Even if we don't spontaneously love someone, giving consistently is the way to create or increase those feelings.

Regardless of how anyone else defines love, what will count for you is your understanding and experience of this emotion. A marriage in which both the husband and wife feel a strong sense of love for each other has a better chance of going smoothly if those feelings last. When love is strong, a person will overlook the faults and mistakes of another (*Mishlei* 10:12). The wording in Mishlei is, "*Al kol pesha'im techaseh ahavah* — Love covers over all iniquities." That is, regardless of the faults that someone has, if you love that person, you will focus not on what you don't like but on what you do like.

This verse in *Mishlei* can be understood by thinking of a beautiful expensive carpet covering over a floor that has many scratches and spots. Even if you always remember the scratches and spots, when you look at the floor you will see the beautiful designs and colors that are on the carpet. So too, with strong feelings of love. You might still know that a person has faults, but you will see the qualities that you like and respect and not the faults.

This can be dangerous when someone needs to make a choice about whom to marry. One might ignore serious faults that he or she will have a difficult time coping with, in the event that those strong feelings subside, which is the norm rather than the exception. But once you are married, it is in the best interests of everyone that you keep your main focus on what you do like and not on what you don't.

When a husband and wife feel positive about each other, even such issues as where they live becomes secondary.

I appreciated being married to my husband so much when we first got married that I kept saying, "I don't care where I live as long as it's with him." But Hashem tested me. The first apartment we rented had three rooms, but then for financial considerations we moved to an apartment that had only one room. My husband and I lived in that one-room apartment for three years, and I am happy to say that if we lived in a magnificent mansion, we couldn't have been happier.

Yes, every time I needed to put a load of clothes in the washing machine, we had to move the machine out of the tiny corner it was squeezed into. When we had guests, we had to turn the table to a different angle to make enough room. But we enjoyed each other's com-

pany. We studied together and we had many enjoyable discussions.

We both viewed our tiny apartment as a wonderful introduction to married life. We felt that when we would eventually move into a larger apartment we would enjoy it so much more than if we had started out in a large flat.

I am bulimic and so embarrassed about it that I did everything I could to hide my eating disorder from my closest friends. My weight was about standard for my height so no one noticed that anything was wrong.

I lived with dread during the first four years of my bulimia. I wondered how a prospective husband would react to my condition.

I asked a posek and was told that I should reveal the information only after we met a few times, and if I thought there was a good chance we would get married. That is what I did.

My future husband reacted calmly. "I've kind of heard about bulimia," he said. "But I really don't know very much about it. You look healthy to me and I feel that whatever it takes to deal with it, I will help you."

I had dreaded this moment for over four years. To my great relief, my husband-to-be handled it remarkably well. He told me that his love for me was because of my Torah ideals and positive character qualities. He looked at my challenge to conquer the bulimia as a partnership and he was glad to do anything for me that would be helpful.

After we were married, he handled it even better. "You might have negative associations with bulimia, but I don't," he reassured me. "We will find an expert on eating disorders and will do whatever needs to be done. I am behind you and want you to be healthy physically and emotionally. I love you just the same whether or not you ever overcome this or anything else."

My husband's wonderful attitude gave me the strength to consult a professional. My husband didn't push or pressure me but gave me only gentle encouragement. This and his unconditional love enabled me to make progress much more quickly than I had thought possible. My husband sincerely reiterated that I shouldn't feel any pressure at all from his side. I didn't, and this was the greatest help he could give me.

Even if two people love each other, they will still have misunderstandings. They still will not be able to read each other's minds. Each of them will still need time to be by themselves. There still will be differences in their personalities, needs, and wishes. But feelings of love make it easier for them to handle the difficulties that inevitably occur. Someone can act positively out of feelings of obligation. But when obligation is combined with love, it makes all that they do much more pleasurable. Even when there is emotional storminess in one's marriage, the positive feelings that are at the foundation of the marriage will enable the couple to weather the storm.

Applying the Wisdom of *Mishlei*

Maintaining love and respect when our spouse doesn't talk to us the way we would wish is difficult. Maintaining love and respect when we feel unloved or disrespected is exceedingly hard, but it is the wisest course of action. We all want to be loved and respected. This is a basic and universal need. Responding to a lack of love and respect with anger, resentment, animosity, and hatred is likely to increase these qualities in the other person. We will then increase the probability that we will be on the receiving end of more of what we don't want. If, however, we can transcend ourselves and reflect sincere love and respect to someone who lacks these feelings towards us, we increase the chances of receiving what we do want.

This wisdom is found in *Mishlei* 27:19: "As water reflects a face back to a face, so one's heart is reflected back to him by another." What would you like to see reflected back to you when you look in a pond? A smile or a frown? It's your choice. Whatever you wish to see, that is the model of what you need to project. This too is the secret of how to influence someone to feel more positive towards you.

Why should we choose the path of love and respect? We have one of two reasons. First, we can do so because we want to live our life the way our Creator wants us to live it. In that case, we will choose love and respect. However, it is not easy to radiate love and respect to someone who doesn't send these feelings back to you; but life wasn't meant to be easy, it was meant to test us. The more difficult it is for us, the greater we become by passing that test.

Secondly, we ought to choose love and respect because it is the choice of enlightened self-interest. True self-interest says: Act in ways that are most likely to get you what you want. Causing pain to your spouse through words or deeds creates a negative loop. Like an echo and a boomerang, what you send out will come back to you. Consistently talking and acting with love and respect will usually bring you these feelings in return.

"But what if they don't?" you might ask. First of all, you have lost nothing by trying.

"What do you mean I lose nothing; don't I make myself vulnerable?" is a common question. Although this question is common, there is no objective basis for it in reality. Whether or not you perceive yourself as vulnerable is your subjective choice. When you act in an elevated manner, you raise your spiritual level. Even if you didn't presently get what you wished for in return, your spiritual gains are eternal! When you increase resentment and bitterness, you are making yourself vulnerable to all forms of psychosomatic and spiritual ills. You will act and react badly to your spouse, and will be creating a problematic loop. But by increasing love and respect, you are strengthening yourself. You are increasing your own emotional independence. Even if the other person doesn't change for the better, you have won a tremendous victory.

You are deluding yourself if you are only acting and talking in ways that on the surface might seem to be positive, but inwardly you keep talking to yourself in patterns that increase your feelings of bitterness and resentment. You are also deluding yourself if you build up your expectations that after a short duration of positive behavior on your part, your spouse will magically become the way you wish. This can lead to great disappointment. Moreover, some personalities might even treat you worse than before if you act in ways that you consider sweet and loving, but they find irritating and annoying. This is the exception rather than the rule. The vast majority of people will reciprocate your positive feelings.

Increasing Feelings of Love and Respect

How do we create love and respect for another person if these feelings don't come spontaneously? Since the Torah commands us to love other people, it is clear that there must be something we can do to create and increase these feelings. It is a common error to think that either we will spontaneously love someone or else the positive feelings just won't be there. What can we do? When you focus on the positive qualities and virtues of another person, your positive feelings towards that person are increased.

I heard a beautiful lecture from Rabbi Noach Weinberg, Rosh Yeshivah of Aish HaTorah, based on the theme, "Love is the pleasure of seeing the virtues of another person." I was single at the time and felt that this was going to be very easy for me. I tend to see the good in people and was certain that when I got married I would automatically see the good qualities and traits of my spouse.

When I met the person I chose to marry, I saw so many positive qualities that I was even more certain that I would always keep my focus on those virtues and that my positive feelings would keep growing.

About four years after our wedding, when cleaning for Pesach, I found the notes that I had taken during classes, and I came across the sentence, "Love is the pleasure of seeing the virtues of another person." To me right at that moment, this wasn't at all the same sentence I had written at the time of the class. At that time I felt a great sense of anticipation for the future. I was dedicated to putting this concept into practice. But now I found that I was largely focusing on the mistakes and faults of my spouse. I kept thinking about what I didn't like and what was annoying. Now this sentence hit me like a slap in the face.

The idea had made total sense to me when I first heard it. Now it made even more sense. But with experience I knew that it wasn't going to be as easy and automatic as I had thought. I kept repeating the words "positive qualities" whenever I saw or thought about my spouse. The traits of "honesty, dedication, hard work, integrity, responsibility, and dutifulness," would immediately pop into my head.

What did my spouse do for me? Literally, thousands of things. Whenever I needlessly thought about what wasn't done, I quickly asked the question, "What am I grateful for?" And I acknowledge that I have a lot to be grateful for.

What did this do for my marriage? A lot. I now tell this to other young couples. I tell them to write this idea on a piece of paper and to put it into their Yom Kippur machzor. This way they will remember it at a time when they are more open to committing themselves to following their resolutions.

*M*y spouse and I get along quite well. I didn't think that either of us had to do anything special to improve our relationship. As the saying goes, "If it's not broken, don't fix it." But reading about how major companies constantly try to improve their products and services, I realized that even though we don't have any specific problems, we probably could enhance our lives together. I made a list of the five qualities I most admire and respect in my spouse and repeated them at least ten times a day. I was surprised at how much this increased my positive feelings.

Some people find it easier to focus on their complaints about other people in general, and their spouse in particular. They keep building up their data base of resentment. They repeat to themselves over and over again what they dislike about their spouse and the distressful things he or she has said or done. The list keeps growing. Moreover, as they themselves build up resentment, they talk and act in ways that further elicit even more negative words and behaviors, and then the negative list grows even faster.

One way to build up a positive data base about your spouse is to write an appreciation list. Write a list of your spouse's positive qualities. Every time your spouse says or does something you appreciate, write it down. Keep rereading your list. As you focus on the positive actions and words of your spouse, you will notice things that you previously had taken for granted and overlooked. Moreover, your positive feelings will create an atmosphere in which your spouse will say and do more positive things.

Remember the positive things that were told to you about the person you married around the time you first met. In the future, whenever you hear someone else say positive things, add these to your list.

A grateful neighbor once sent this thank-you note to my wife. I have saved it and enjoy reading it over and over again.

Dear Mrs. _____ ,

How lucky we are to have such wonderful neighbors! Every time we need something, you are always there to help us. To borrow things, to ask advice, or just to share ideas — you always greet us with a warm and welcoming smile.

Thank you for everything,
Malky

I once heard a father bless his son who was about to get married, "I bless you that you and your wife should always see each other with the eyes of a shadchan. A shadchan always sees the good in every potential chasan and kallah. Whether the motive is the pleasure of making a shiduch or getting professional fees, a shadchan is an artist at seeing virtues. No virtue is too small to magnify. And no fault is too big to minimize. In order that you should have a joyous and harmonious marriage, may you both do the same."

This reminds me of the story of the professional shadchan who approached a young man and told him, "I have a wonderful suggestion of a young lady who would make a fantastic wife for you."

"That sounds good," said the young man. "Who is she?"

As soon as the shadchan mentioned her name, the young man exclaimed, "You're just making fun of me."

"Of course not," the shadchan said defensively. "What objections do you have?"

"She's blind," said the fellow.

"That's a virtue, not a fault," said the shadchan. *"She won't see what you are doing and how you look, so she won't have complaints about you. If you fix or paint something and it's not a perfect job she won't notice it."*

"But she's mute," said the young man.

"That's another virtue," argued the shadchan. *"She won't say anything to you and you won't have to listen to her talking nonsense. She certainly can't yell and scream at you."*

"But she has an awful limp," said the young man.

"That's also a virtue," the shadchan explained. *"If you want to leave the house, she won't be able to run after you."*

"She's hunchbacked," complained the young man.

"You're not perfect either," said the shadchan. *"You would be married by now if you were. You should really be able to tolerate one little fault which is trivial compared to all of her virtues."*

COMMON GOALS: PARTNERS IN FULFILLING YOUR LIFE'S MISSION

When two people know that they have common goals and are partners in reaching those goals, they feel like a team. The success of one is the success of the other. Both members of the team encourage each other. There are many ways that you and your spouse are partners. You are partners in fulfilling your life's mission. Each one might have a different role to play, but together you help each other fulfill that mission. You are partners in bringing the *Shechinah* into your home. You are partners in *avodas Hashem,* in service to our Creator, in Torah, in fulfilling *mitzvos* and doing *chesed.* You are partners in raising a family. You are partners in *middos* development. You are partners in creating a meaningful and emotionally fulfilling life.

Business partners can have many disagreements. But there is a big difference between two partners in a business arguing with each other and arguing with a competitor and adversary. When two partners in a business argue, they both want the business to prosper. They might have diverse opinions as to the wisest and best course of action, but they both want the other to be successful, because the success of the other is their own success. A competitor, on the other hand, is viewed as an opponent, at times even an enemy. The success of one results in the failure of the other.

It is a very painful sight to observe a husband and wife acting towards each other as opponents, when they could view themselves as mutual partners in a great venture and project. You build your marriage when you see your spouse as a partner whose interests you care about just as you care about your own.

In a debate or a boxing match you have an advantage when you get your opponent off balance. When people are off balance, they make mistakes. But in marriage, you and your partner are on the same team. So if you get your spouse off balance, it is up to you to correct that balance.

When both parties have as their highest ideal to do the will of our Creator, they will both have peace and harmony as a high priority.

What are your best skills and talents? What are your spouse's? Used together, you are a team that has more skills than either one has alone.

I spoke to a couple who felt that they are so different from one another that they don't have any common goals. I first asked one, then the other, "Would you like to live a happy life?" Both the husband and wife replied, "Yes, very much so." "Great," I commented, "this is your common goal. Let's see how you both can treat each other in a way that will give each of you a happy life."

They both said that they hadn't looked at it that way, and yes, it made sense that they had this in common.

"You both have a lot more in common than you think," I told them. "You both want to live a Torah way of life. You both need to breathe and eat. You both want to raise a family. Compared to

what you have in common, your differences are in the minority."
I suggested that they spend an entire week trying to find more
things that they had in common and should keep a written list
of their findings. When they spoke to me a week later they said
that they were amazed at their similarities. When they prepared
for Shabbos, they both viewed it as a joint venture to observe the
Almighty's day of rest. They realized that they were both children
of the Creator. They had a common ancestry dating back from
Adam and Chavah, Noach, Avraham and Sarah, Yitzchak and
Rivkah and their son, Yaakov. They felt similarly about health
issues and both wanted world peace. They couldn't wait to find
even more factors that they had in common.

*I was eaten up with envy. My spouse was okay, but not
everything that I had wished for. Every time I heard
about the positive qualities of someone else who just
became engaged, I felt more than a tinge of jealousy. I
was consumed by it.*

*I went to an elderly Rabbi who was known to be an
elevated spiritual scholar. He listened to my story non-
judgmentally and with total acceptance and compassion.*

*Then he said to me, "Each individual has a unique
tikkun or mission in this world. Only you have your
unique task to fulfill. People are not envious of the eye-
glasses of someone else. Each person needs glasses that
are appropriate for his eyes. So too, each person has a
marriage partner who is exactly what he or she needs for
his or her life's mission. Your own accomplishments are
independent of what anyone else has or does.*

*"Carry out your mission in this world with joy. This joy
is an aspect of ahavas Hashem, love and respect for your
Creator, Who in His infinite wisdom has given you what
is for your ultimate, eternal best interests."*

*I left inspired by this thought. I can't say I was able to
integrate it immediately. But little by little this concept*

became integrated into my everyday thinking and has made a tremendous difference in my life.

*A*ll through High School and Seminary I was more introverted than most of the other girls I knew. I was told by my parents, teachers, and friends, "You must become more outgoing before you get married."

Deep down I said to myself, "I know that Hashem will find a chasan for me who will appreciate my love for silence." I once heard that an introvert is someone with such a rich inner life that he or she doesn't have such a strong need for others. I planned to marry a super masmid. We would both share a love for his Torah study and I would do everything I could to prevent disturbances while he was learning.

I mentioned this to a couple of people and they said I was a dreamer. It's almost impossible to find anyone as I pictured.

I called up a Rabbi who I thought might be sympathetic and I asked him if my plans were realistic. He validated my position by telling me, "Most fellows would not be suitable for you as you are now. But you only need one person in order to get married. The Chofetz Chaim's son wrote that his father would praise his wife as being the source of his success in Torah. She took care of all the material needs of the home without involving him. His merit in Torah was a partnership and she was an equal partner."

The person I called told me that he once attended an entire day of lectures given by nine different Rabbis. It was for chasanim and newly married kollel men. Over 200 young men attended. The Rabbis were from different backgrounds: Chassidic, Sephardic, Litvish, Israeli, and from English-speaking countries. One speaker said *that it's very important for a couple to talk together each day for at least fifteen minutes. Another speaker said, "That is not our way. When you are totally immersed in Torah studies and have internalized bitachon, your wife will respect you and you will have shalom bayis."*

I knew what type of bachur I was looking for and passed up many potential shiduchim which sounded good, but would not be for me. Finally someone suggested the man who would eventually be my husband. He was the biggest masmid in his yeshivah. He was friendly and had a healthy personality, but he didn't waste time. He told the shadchan that he wanted a quiet girl who wouldn't merely tolerate his constant devotion to Torah study, but had the same ideals as he did.

Even on our first meeting, he told me Torah thoughts. He told me how his ideal was Rabbi Akiva Eiger's discussing words of yiras Shamayim with his wife. That is exactly what I was waiting to hear.

We are now married a number of years and I greatly appreciate my husband's total devotion to Torah study. He appreciates my enabling him to learn without unnecessary disturbances. He shares divrei Torah with me and we study from sefarim together on a regular basis. Because we are both totally satisfied with each other, we are free from conflicts and quarrels. We feel as joyous together as other couples who spend much more time speaking to each other.

YOUR SPOUSE IS YOUR CLOSEST RELATIVE; YOU ARE ONE

The Torah (*Bereishis* 2:24) states that a husband and wife are considered as one. As the Ramban states in his commentary, "Through the sanctification of marriage, a husband and wife become the closest of relatives" (ibid.). This oneness is even stronger than being partners. In a regular partnership, you care about the welfare of your partner, but the partner is still separate from you. When you see yourselves as one, however, there is a total sense of unity.

When a husband and wife view themselves as being one, the pain and pleasure of both are important to each other. You see yourself as a single entity. Having this consciousness will automatically make you both closer. You will both consider the total welfare of each other to have the same high priority as taking care of yourself. This will make you more understanding and accepting of your spouse.

Imagine sitting down to drink a cup of coffee. You are a bit tired and you are expecting the coffee to give you a lift to begin the day or to revive you in the middle of the day. Or you might not be a coffee drinker for health reasons, but on a special day, in order to celebrate, you indulge in a cup of coffee. As you take the first sip you barely contain yourself from spitting it out. Instead of containing sugar, this cup contained salt. The big question is: Will you get angry at the person who made the mistake?

Regardless of your temper, the one instance when you wouldn't lose it is when you yourself are the one who put in salt instead of sugar, even if all you had to do was read the word "SALT" printed in large letters on the container. You might even find a positive aspect to it: Isn't it great that I usually do it right? Or, you might think to yourself that sugar in coffee tastes so much better than salt that I am grateful to the Creator for creating this difference.

When you view yourself and your spouse as one, just as you would not criticize yourself for this error, so too, you shouldn't say anything derogatory to your spouse. And if you do feel a strong need to say something, how about, "I am grateful to you for usually putting in sugar."

What if your spouse doesn't consider both of you as "one"? Can you still view yourselves as one? Yes, you can. Your perspective is dependent on how you personally view things. There is no question that if both the husband and wife see themselves as being one it is a lot easier than if only you decide to do so. There is a chance that if you take the initiative, your spouse might follow your example. Even if it takes time until your spouse does so, you still gain immensely by integrating this perspective. This is our Creator's view in the Torah. It makes sense to adopt the Creator's view rather than the view of a mortal.

W*e were married a number of years with many ups and downs. My wife and I had questions about our compatibility. While we knew that we would stay married, we both viewed ourselves as two totally separate people who were destined to spend their lives together. If that was our life challenge and our tikkun in this world, so be it. We accepted the Almighty's will for us. We tried going to counseling a few times but any changes we made were just temporary. Someone advised us to speak to a Torah scholar who would check the compatibility of our names. I was reluctant because I didn't grow up with this idea, and it felt a bit awkward to me. But we figured that it couldn't hurt. The worst that would happen is that we would be advised to change our names. Then we would ask our posek for advice. My wife and I were told that according to our names we were a match. We both smiled, "That's nice," I said to myself. "But we still have the same issues as before."*

Then we spoke to someone who asked us what held us back from viewing ourselves as being a single unit, as one.

"We are so different from each other," I said.

"Of course you are. Every couple is. The only question is to what degree. But you are still one unit. Isn't your right hand different from your right ear?" he asked.

"Certainly," I said.

"But aren't they both part of the one and only you?"

"Yes," I replied, "but that's different."

"No, it's not," he insisted. "Your heart and your brain

are different. Your nose and your toes are different. Your eyes and your lungs are different. And they are all part of the one you. I realize that some couples have a much easier time viewing themselves as one unit. Others find this much more difficult. But the Torah view is that as soon as you get married you are one unit.

"Try this as an experiment. For an entire week both of you view each other as if you are a single entity. See yourselves as one. Make a mental note of how this improves your interactions. If one of you suffers, your entire unit suffers. If one of you needs something, the entire system needs it. Most couples who try this find that they are automatically much more careful about not doing and saying things that cause pain. Both husband and wife become much more open to doing things to help each other. Even when they disagree, they view it as if they themselves have mixed feelings about the matter."

When we returned after a week, we were able to report that it was one of the best weeks we'd had in a long time. The Rabbi then told us both, "Every time you enter the house, you pass the mezuzah. It is a reminder that Hashem is One, and He made you as one. Let the mezuzah remind you of this."

We aren't always able to maintain this awareness, but when we get off track one of us will usually remind the other, "We are one. And I want my other half to be happy. What can I do for you?"

Before I was married, someone told me, "Since a husband and wife are supposed to be like one, ('Ishto kegufo') you shouldn't say, 'Thank you,' to your wife. Just as you don't thank yourself, you don't thank your wife. Of course, you should give compliments, but don't say *thanks. I wanted to do the right thing, so I carefully refrained from saying those forbidden words."*

After I was married for some time, I accidentally said, "Thank you," when my wife cooked something special. She thanked me profusely. "I really appreciate your finally saying thank you."

"You do?" I asked. "I was told that you wouldn't like it because then it means a lack of feeling that we are one."

"That's ridiculous," my wife laughed. "You are such a nice person I was puzzled why you never thanked me for anything."

From then on, I was careful to say "thank you" as often as I could. A few days before my younger brother's wedding, I made certain to tell this to him so he wouldn't make the same mistake that I did. Interestingly enough, someone had given him the same advice that I'd gotten. I'm glad that I was able to spare his wife the distress that my wife experienced.

YOUR MARRIAGE PARTNER IS YOUR CREATOR'S CHOICE FOR YOU

A basic Torah principle is that your marriage partner is your Creator's choice for you. The Talmud (*Moed Katan* 18b) cites verses where this fundamental concept is stated. The first is in the portion of *Chayei Sarah* (24:50). Besuel, Rivkah's father, and Lavan, her brother, both told Eliezer, Avraham's servant, together, "The match of Rivkah to Yitzchak comes from G-d (*MeiHashem yatza hadavar*)." Although Besuel and Lavan were not the epitome of righteousness, they recognized this reality. This concept is also stated in *Shoftim* 14:4 and *Mishlei* 19:14.

The individual Hashem has chosen for you is for your ultimate good. Internalizing this awareness is the foundation for answering the question: "How can I love and respect someone who is not exactly the way I wish him or her to be?"

Since your Creator has selected this person for you, and He wishes you to speak and act with love and respect, do so out of love and respect for Him. If in your particular circumstances you find this difficult, realize how this elevates you. Let the thought reverberate in your mind, "I am talking and acting with love and respect to carry out the will of my loving Father, the Creator and Sustainer of the universe." Imagine the profound spiritual experience this will be as you consistently repeat this message.

Some couples flow harmoniously together. Others don't. In each instance the parties have opportunities to grow. Accept the situation that the Creator gave you as your mission in this world. One issue that many new couples have is, "Did I make the right choice?" Once you are married, view your choice as the Divinely ordained choice for you. This will enable you to put your heart and soul into making your marriage work well. Some people claim "temporary insanity" as the reason why they chose to marry the person they did. But in most instances there are psychological factors that motivated you to choose the person you did. The ultimate reason for your choice, however, is that through *hashgachah pratis* — Divine intervention — it was meant to be. This doesn't guarantee that a marriage will last, only that your marriage is a Divinely prepared plan to help you grow. Being married to a person with faults, or with whom you initially find it difficult to get along, can bring out your strengths in a way that being married to someone else might not.

Some people spend years not being committed to the marriage. "I think I made a mistake," they say to themselves, and sometimes to others. They never really settle into the marriage. No marriage is a mistake. Each marriage was a choice we made and there is *hashgachah pratis.* Your marriage partner might be very different from what you were hoping for. But whatever the person is like, there is a Divine purpose in your being married to this particular person. The person you are married to is exactly the person with whom, at present, it is in your best spiritual interests to interact.

The Dubner Maggid has a parable about a person who had a buried treasure hidden away on his property. But the person didn't know about it and never in his entire life was he able to benefit from it. There is a similar well-known story about someone who had a dream that he would find a buried treasure in another city. As he was digging there, a spectator asked what he was doing. This spectator told him that he doesn't believe in dreams. But if he did, he would be digging for treasure in such and such a place — for he just had a dream that a great treasure could be found there. That was exactly in the backyard of the person who was digging for the treasure. He rushed home and found the buried treasure in his own backyard. Likewise, in marriage, your spiritual treasure is to be found in your own home. If you are having a challenging time with your spouse, realize that this is exactly why your Creator chose to put the two of you together. This is your area of growth. Others might experience growth in different ways. Your life mission at any given moment is exactly where you are.

When I first met my spouse, I had doubts as to whether or not we should get married. I wanted to be able to have flowing conversations with the person I married, but we found it difficult to talk to each other. I wanted to be understood, but I felt that this person didn't really understand me. I wanted someone who would be very accepting, but instead this person was highly critical.

I expressed my doubts to someone I respected. I was told, "Don't worry. Everything will turn out all right. After you get married these issues will all be resolved and you will have a happy marriage. I've seen a lot of young people with doubts, but after marriage they are glad they married."

I listened but I wasn't totally convinced.

I spoke to two more people and asked them for their advice. I was told by one, "Everyone is nervous beforehand. I was also. I have a good marriage, and so will you."

The other person told me, "You're being too picky. You're not perfect either. You need to get married. The person you are considering marrying sounds like a wonderful person. The practical, daily issues of raising a family will keep you so busy that you won't have time to worry about the things you are concerned about now."

I listened to the advice I heard from these people, although I had my misgivings. I had been told that I should be patient and that after time, we would be just as happy as all the happy couples I see everywhere.

Guess what? This might have been someone else's reality, but not mine. I kept waiting for things to change, but they never did.

I felt resentful towards all the good-intentioned people who told me, "It will work out just fine." This resentment blocked me from seeing my spouse's good points. I kept focusing on what I didn't like, and I was consistently miserable.

I toyed with divorce a number of times. But I kept hearing how difficult it would be. "You can't just start all over again. Now you have heavy baggage." I was told, "It's better to make it work than to give up."

I'm not going to relate all the anguish I suffered. But it was painful.

Taking an objective look at my situation, I realize that maintaining the resentment was a form of self-torture. I have to accept that it was my own choice to listen to the advice that I heard. No one forced me to do so. Giving up resentment is difficult. But it was either that or ruining my life. I realized that those who advised me to get married were telling me what they felt was best for me. They did know people who had doubts, got married, and were forever grateful that they did. Maybe some people weren't so happy, but they kept it to themselves. Also, people who are advised to marry someone don't always come back to the person who advised them to get mar-

ried and tell them that it didn't work out according to the way it was supposed to. The feedback is usually more positive than the reality.

I have finally accepted the Almighty's will for me. I have accepted the idea that although things are not the way I would have wished, being married is much better than being single. I have a lot to be grateful for in my spouse. For an entire month, I kept a written "Gratitude List." I wrote down at least five things a day that I am grateful for that my spouse has done for me. On some days I have over fifteen items on my list. This has changed my focus from, "What don't I like?" to "What do I appreciate?"

The key concept that helped me was the realization that accepting the will of Hashem with love is the most elevating attribute one can have. By making this my number one goal, I have gained spiritually and emotionally.

The Bas Kol (Heavenly Voice)

Some people feel that the person they married is perfect for them. They are fortunate. But others who find that the differences between them cause much stress and lead to quarrels have doubts about the wisdom of their choice. If you find yourself in this category, think about the following. Imagine that a prophet told you it was G-d's will for you to marry exactly the person you did. Wouldn't that be reassuring? Wouldn't it be wonderful if you heard a Heavenly voice telling you, "The person you married is exactly the one I have chosen for you"?

Right at the first moment you came into being, a Heavenly voice decreed, *"Bas Plony l'Plony"* ("This person's daughter will marry so-and-so"). If you ever feel doubtful, in your mind's ear, hear the Heavenly voice calling out into the cosmos, "You are married to exactly the right person for you!" See how this affects your feelings and the actions that result from those feelings.

I have a strong inner voice. At times this inner voice gives me encouragement. It tells me positive messages such as, "You can do it." "Keep going and you will succeed." "Start again and you will make it."

But at other times the inner voice is excessively critical or gives me negative messages.

One day when I was in a down mood and irritable, my spouse said something to me that I didn't like. All of a sudden, my inner voice popped up with the sentence, "You might have made a mistake. Another person might have been better for you." I knew that if I would allow this voice to become louder it would cause me a lot of grief. I decided to drown out the voice of the yetzer hara with the powerful voice of the Divine Bas Kol: "The person you are married to was destined to be your partner for your ultimate benefit."

I mentally replayed this voice over and over again. I added the music of an orchestra and visualized tremendous light. This drowned out the problematic voice, and I felt myself becoming much more comfortable about my decision to marry the person I did.

Rabbi Chaim Zaichyk, a great *mussar* personality, wrote, "The one Torah concept that will make the most practical difference to the emotional quality of your life is the awareness that everything the Almighty does is for your benefit. This realization is a great wisdom that will help you in both this world and the next. There is no greater wealth than mastering this attitude. When you reach this level, you will not be broken or become sad, regardless of how the Almighty sets up your life. You will accept whatever happens with love" (*Maayanei HaChaim*, vol. 3, p. 176).

This is a fundamental Torah principle that will serve as a light throughout your life. This concept is especially important when it comes to viewing your marriage with a Torah outlook. When a husband and wife both see daily life events from this perspective, they are guaranteed a wonderful life together.

THE FIRST YEAR OF MARRIAGE:
A TIME TO GAIN UNDERSTANDING

A man is exempt from certain obligations during the first year of his marriage. This is the time when the new couple build the foundation of their future family life. They need time to build the bond and to gain an understanding of each other. It is quite common to discover many surprises after the marriage. The person you thought you were marrying will be different from the person you actually married. The whole question is to what degree. In the courtship and engagement stages there is often an illusory buildup of what the other person is really like. In the first year of marriage both parties deal with the reality of the interaction of their personalities: their unique characters, ideals and attitudes, positive and negative traits, virtues and faults, strengths and weaknesses.

There is a common expression, "The first year of marriage is the hardest." Like many other cliches, this is frequently the reality. It takes time for two people to really understand each other. Every person has a unique personality and communication pattern. Each person needs to understand the other's way of saying things. Each needs to understand the other's emotions and feelings. Each needs to understand the other's wants and needs. Each needs to learn how to negotiate and discuss difficulties. While this is a lifetime process, it often takes a couple an entire year to build a proper foundation.

But like most cliches, "The first year of marriage is the hardest," is not always true. There are other possibilities: The first year can be wonderful and remain wonderful. This is possible when the two partners are highly compatible. It is also possible for two people who both work on their character and are dedicated to be givers rather than takers. And this is also possible for two people who are both flexible and easy to please.

*M*any years ago I asked a student who was married approximately half a year, "Is marriage similar or different from what you thought it would be?"

I loved his answer and repeat it frequently. "Marriage is exactly what I thought it would be," he said. "I thought that I would have to work hard. I would need to work on my character. I would need to think before I speak and be sensitive to my wife's needs. I thought that it was a learning process that needed to be studied just as any other difficult topic."

"No wonder that for you marriage is exactly what you thought it would be," I patted him on the back with respect. "If others had the same attitude, much suffering and misery could be avoided."

Unfortunately, there are some marriages in which the first year is very difficult, but instead of things getting easier they just get more and more difficult as time goes on. Resentment keeps building up. The husband and wife keep arguing about more things as well as remembering past grievances.

On the other hand, while for a good percentage of couples the first year is the hardest, it gets easier as time goes on. Knowing this can help a newly married couple cope better with the fact that being married is more difficult for them than they had expected. Awareness that the difficulties are temporary makes them much easier to handle. This is the power of the saying, "This too shall pass."

For my wife and me our marriage gets better and better all the time. But I recall how difficult that first year was. We loved each other, but my wife felt sick and weak almost the entire year. Her emotional state was not the same as it was when we were dating. I am an easygoing person and get along well with others, but I found that understanding my wife's reactions was more difficult than understanding other people. I remember saying to myself, "It's so rough now. Is this how it will always be?" But after our first baby was a few months old, we both saw that we understood each other better.

As time went on, our sense of being connected kept getting stronger. A highlight for me was that after five years of marriage, my wife once said to me, "I was thinking about your positive qualities. I have trouble deciding whether your best quality is your emunah peshutah, your total awareness that all that happens is from G-d, or your lev tov, your good-heartedness." Personally, I didn't care which one wins, I just felt so happy that my wife sees me in a positive light and that her only problem was deciding which trait was stronger.

I had heard from my mother-in-law a number of times, "The first year of marriage was the most difficult for us." I figured that her daughter might have been programmed with this attitude, and I braced myself for the first year's difficulties. But to my surprise the first year wasn't difficult at all. Yes, it took a bit of adjusting, but we had moved to Eretz Yisrael and life was exciting. For us, however, as the family grew larger we had a more difficult time. We had a number of children and didn't get as much sleep as we needed. We disagreed about how to handle the children and there was always so much to do. I'm not complaining, since no one said that life is supposed to be easy, but if I would have realized that things could get harder later on, I would have been better prepared.

The attitude that "life is a constant problem" is not conducive to joy in marriage or in life. A person with a globally negative view of life must be totally committed to finding more joy in the positive aspects of his or her life. For someone who views everything as difficult, learning the skill of joy is just as difficult as other skills, if not harder. But the cost of not developing a more joyous attitude is much greater than the investment of reading about how to acquire joy, speaking to other people about it, and keeping joy and self-mastery lists. Once you develop attitudes of appreciation and gratitude for the gifts the Creator has given you, and accept your mission in life with joy for the opportunity to do the Almighty's will, everything becomes easier.

HASHEM WILL SEND YOU MESSAGES; LEARN FROM THEM

A basic Torah principle is that there are no accidents in this world. Whatever happens, happens for a reason. Throughout your life, Hashem will send you messages. The wise person learns from everyone (*Pirkei Avos* 4:1). Be wise and learn from all the messages that have been sent your way in the past and those that will be sent your way in the future.

Every time you see a couple interact it can be educational. Even listening to the way a newly married couple or an elderly couple speak together in a line at the supermarket can teach you something. At times you will hear a positive way of talking that you can emulate. At other times you will hear a negative way of talking that you will find similar to your own. This can be a wake-up call to make a change. And then there are situations that will enable you to feel fortunate for your own situation. You will now have greater appreciation and gratitude for what previously you might have taken for granted.

Hashem's messages can come in many forms. When you are open to see and hear them, you will find you have constant reminders to upgrade your way of being.

A chance remark by an elderly stranger greatly enhanced my marriage. My husband and I and our two little children were returning to Eretz Yisrael from the United States. At the airport while we were waiting to board the plane, I was sitting next to a little old lady who was all by herself, knitting. I asked her if she was traveling with anyone.

"I'm almost eighty years old, but thank G-d, I'm healthy," she told me. "My sister's grandson is getting married in Jerusalem and I'm going to the wedding. I was never married and the only family I have is my sister and her children."

We made small talk for a few minutes and then they announced that passengers with young children could board the plane first. "You are incredibly fortunate," this woman said to me before we parted. "Your husband looks like a wonderful young man and you have two beautiful children. I know the pain of loneliness. Always cherish your husband."

To tell the truth, I hadn't always cherished my husband. I was painfully aware of his shortcomings. But looking at him through the eyes of this kindhearted, lonely lady, I began to feel that she was right. I am incredibly fortunate. I don't know who that woman was or anything else about her, but those four words, "You are incredibly fortunate," were the most valuable I've ever heard.

I was highly irritated. My wife and I needed to find a certain office in a neighborhood that was far from where we lived. She told me she had been there before and knew where it was. When we got there, we found a sign saying they had moved to the other side of the city.

We took a taxi to the new address. When we got there, it was dark, and we had a difficult time finding the address we needed. The taxi left us off at the wrong place. I was carrying a heavy package and my arms had begun to hurt. I blamed my wife for giving me the wrong address.

"It's your own fault for not calling them up to see if they moved," my wife replied angrily. "I was just being helpful by giving you the address."

"Why should I have thought they would have moved?" I replied in an even angrier voice.

"So how come you are blaming me for the same thing that you feel you couldn't have guessed?" she responded.

Just then an elderly blind man walked by and called out for help. "What can I do for you?" I asked him.

"Can you please help me cross the street and walk me to the bus stop?" he asked.

I was happy for this opportunity to do an act of chesed for this blind man. By the time we reached the bus stop both my wife and myself felt much better. My arms still hurt, but after helping that man, my package felt much lighter.

The next time my wife and I began the game of blame and counterblame, we said almost simultaneously, "Let's be grateful that we can see."

A couple of years ago my spouse and I got into a major argument during dinner. Each of us brought up past grievances. Needless to say, we both lost our appetite and didn't finish our meal. Nothing was resolved, but I had to go someplace and therefore called a truce so I could recite Birkas HaMazon.

I wasn't able to concentrate on most of the words I was saying. The bitter argument had left its fallout. Gratitude to G-d for the food He has given you and intense fury at your life's partner are incongruent.

But when I reached the latter part of Birkas HaMazon, I reflected on the words, "He who makes peace in the Heavens, make peace among us, and among all of Israel." What does it mean "among us"? It means among those who are sitting together at our table right now.

"That's amazing," I said to myself. "Every time my spouse and I have eaten together from the first day we were married, we have both asked Hashem to give us peace. Wouldn't it be wonderful if we both enabled Hashem to allow us to have this peace?"

As I meditated on thoughts of what this peace would be like, I became calmer. My spouse saw that my mood had changed and said to me, "You look calmer. What thoughts were you thinking?"

I explained that I had just started looking at the words of Birkas HaMazon in a new light. That recital of the prayer of gratitude that I had repeated so many times since I was a young child is now viewed by both of us as the turning point of our marriage.

During the height of the Intifada in Israel, my spouse and I were traveling on a dangerous road. We were in yet another one of our heated quarrels about some trivial matter. Now, neither of us can recall the topic that at the time brought out mutually intense feelings of anger.

All of a sudden, our car was hit by a barrage of stones. Instantly our quarrel was forgotten and we fervently prayed that we would be saved. Thank G-d, the only damage was a broken back window, and we came out of the incident unscathed.

My spouse and I were shaken up by this threat to our lives. It was timely that we were attacked by real stones just as we were hurling verbal stones at each other. Enemies of our people are trying to destroy us. We shouldn't do anything to destroy ourselves. From then on we were much more careful to be respectful towards each other when we had differences of opinion.

❖ ❖ ❖

I was talking to my wife on a public telephone. We were discussing different events that occurred since the last time we had spoken that morning. It was an enjoyable conversation and we both felt good.

But then I saw a sight that increased our positive feelings. A pair of doves were walking together and stopping every few minutes to peck for food. One would walk a little faster than the other, and then the slower one would jump faster than usual to keep up with the pace of its mate.

As I saw this, I interrupted our discussion to describe the scene, play by play. "And now they are going at the same speed. And now the one on the right is going faster. And now the one on the left just caught up, and they are again matching each other's pace." My wife cooed with delight at hearing this description.

It's amazing how Hashem keeps sending these wonderful opportunities to teach us lessons. We can't always go at the same pace, but we can make an effort to catch up and once again be in harmony.

The Almighty will send you many messengers to help you improve your marriage. Be open to them. They will come in many forms. Passing up an opportunity to learn from someone who could help you is a loss greater than the loss of a large amount of money.

I went to the Western Wall to pray for a relative who was ill. On the way back, I walked through the Jewish Quarter in the Old City. I passed by a young couple who were in the midst of a heated quarrel. They were clearly tourists and instead of enjoying themselves in Jerusalem, they were fighting. The husband shouted at the wife, and the wife shouted back. The wife then stormed off and left her husband stewing.

Should I go over to him and try to say something that might be helpful, or shouldn't I? I asked myself. He was a stranger and might not appreciate someone intruding. On the other hand, what if he would be open to listen to beneficial advice and suggestions? Could I just walk by when perhaps this encounter could change his life?

I built up my inner courage and walked over to him. "Perhaps you would like to talk?" I offered.

"No, thank you," he said. "I prefer to be alone right now."

I walked back to the Kosel to pray for the welfare of this couple. They needed Hashem's blessings to heal their marriage as much as the physically ill person for whom I originally went to pray.

*M*y husband and I were in an elevator in a large office building. I thought that he had pressed the button for the floor we needed and he assumed that I had. Because neither of us pressed the button, when we reached the floor right below our destination, the elevator started going down.

We had an important meeting and we would now be a few minutes late. The person we were going to meet ran a major business and had a tight schedule. We both felt he would be angry with us.

I started to blame my husband for not pressing the button. "It's your own fault," he said. "You should have pushed the button."

"Don't blame me," I replied. "You should have pressed it yourself."

"You always blame me for your own mistakes."

The tone of our voices was escalating and then I noticed that everyone in the elevator was staring at us.

An elderly fellow who looked like he had suffered through many adversities, commented to us, "Life is like an elevator. It has many ups and downs. It's crazy that a couple who got married to help each other go up, should cause each other to go down."

As he got off at his stop, my husband and I were left to reflect on what he had told us. From then on, if either my husband or I started saying something that seemed to be leading into a needless quarrel, the other would say, "Let's take the 'up' elevator," and we would both smile.

Chapter 3

The Ultimate Five-Word Formula:
Don't Cause Pain, Give Pleasure

Introduction

I. Don't Cause Pain
- *If you're not getting what you want, ask for it, negotiate, motivate, and influence, without causing pain*
- *Ona'as devarim: insults and put-downs*
- *Watch the content of what you say: choose your words*
- *Tone of voice: What is the music of your voice?*
- *Your facial expression and the look in your eyes can speak louder than words*
- *Ask yourself, "What should I stop saying or doing that is causing my spouse distress?"*
- *Habits: make it a habit to eliminate habits that cause distress*
- *Getting even lowers you*
- *Asking for forgiveness and forgiving*

II. Give Pleasure
- *Express your realization that your spouse is important*
- *Smiles*
- *Marriage gives you unlimited opportunities for chesed*
- *Express your appreciation and gratitude*
- *Be generous with your sincere praise*
- *Listening is a powerful act of respect, kindness, and validation*
- *Communication connects*
- *Look for positive activities that you can do together*

Introduction

Marriage can be either the source of life's greatest joys and *nachas* or the root of much misery, even tragedy. There is a formula that can be stated in five words that is the key to a joyous marriage. "Don't cause pain, give pleasure." In the original Hebrew verse (*Tehillim* 34:15), this is a four-word formula, *"Sur mei'ra, va'asei tov."* That is, "Keep away from evil, and do good." Both with words and deeds be careful not to cause your spouse needless pain. And do as much as you can to give your spouse pleasure from your potentially unlimited capacity for *chesed.*

It can be challenging to avoid causing pain. Only a rare person is sadistic and really enjoys causing pain. But in marriage it's easy to feel frustrated or angry when wishes and needs clash. These clashes can breed arguments and quarrels with hurt feelings on both sides. Marriage gives you constant opportunities to develop the attribute of doing *chesed,* and the self-mastery and sensitivity not to cause your spouse pain.

Those who believe in other people believe that everyone has the resources they need to effect change. In many areas of life we need new information and knowledge, and marriage is no exception. But the basics of how to cause pleasure rather than pain can be taught in less than ten minutes to the vast majority of normally intelligent adults.

Here's the lesson on how not to cause pain: Sit quietly for thirty seconds without saying one word. Have a fairly pleasant expression on your face as you do so. If you can do this at will, you will eliminate most of the pain caused in marriage. Someone might get angry at you for just sitting in one place and not doing something or speaking to them. But most of the pain is caused by saying the wrong things, having a negative look on your face, and doing things that are annoying and irritating. If you were quiet for those thirty seconds, you know how to avoid all the negative things. You just need the willpower when it is difficult. It is not easy, but we were not put in this world to have it easy.

Regarding the subject of giving your husband or wife pleasure, what have you done in the past that gave him or her pleasure? For that matter, what have you said or done for anyone else on the planet that was helpful, useful, kind, or pleasurable to them? Answering these two questions gives you some basic ideas on how to give pleasure. If you still have no idea, try asking your spouse, "What can I do for you that you would like, appreciate, or want?" But what if your spouse tells you, "You should know on your own"? Or, "Now you ask me, after all this time." Or, "If I have to tell you, it doesn't mean anything to me." If this is how your spouse responds, then you will need to put more effort into your research project. Think of a few people you can ask.

The author of the classic work, *Orchos Tzaddikim*, writes that when it comes to perfecting our character traits there are two potential problems. One is not knowing what to do. The second is knowing what to do but not having the motivation to follow through. He offers a metaphor: You might look for a certain person named Reuven, but you won't find him because you don't know what he looks like. Then there is another possibility. You know what he looks like, but you aren't motivated enough to look for him. Either way you won't find him. The same applies to the ultimate formula. The first step is to know what to do and say, and what to avoid doing and saying. The second step is to be motivated to put this into action. A book can give you ideas about how to give your spouse pleasure rather than pain, but it is up to you to implement these ideas and bring harmony and peace into your home.

People pay a lot of money to paint their homes, believing that the right colors will lift their emotional state, while the wrong colors will cause distressful feelings every time they walk into the room. People pay a lot of money to have nice furniture in their homes, convinced that elegant furniture creates a special atmosphere. But having a harmonious marriage is more valuable than the most beautiful colors and the most expensive furniture. Harmony in one's home makes it beautiful regardless of the shade of the paint and the quality of the furniture, while a lack of peace and harmony results in negative energy in the home regardless of the fancy and expensive decor and furnishings.

It is advisable to make a long list of your spouse's likes and dislikes. Increase the number of times you do what your spouse likes and decrease or eliminate what your spouse dislikes. The sections that follow will give you some ideas. If you can, ask your spouse to help you compose the lists.

I. DON'T CAUSE PAIN

IF YOU'RE NOT GETTING WHAT YOU WANT, ASK FOR IT, NEGOTIATE, MOTIVATE, AND INFLUENCE, WITHOUT CAUSING PAIN

Most of the pain husbands and wives cause each other is not because either of them is mean or vicious. Rather, they want something from their spouse and feel frustrated or upset by not getting it. Husbands and wives need to accept the fact that no one in this world gets everything he or she wishes for. At the same time, both you and your spouse benefit by your becoming proficient at asking for what you want in a way that will result in your spouse feeling good about meeting your needs.

Therefore be willing to ask for what you want in a way that your spouse will find pleasant. Some husbands and wives resent the idea of having to ask for what they want. "I shouldn't have to ask for what I want," they say. "He/she should know on his/her own." Where is the source of this life principle? Since we humans don't have telepathy, of course we have to ask for what we want. And if you find yourself in a situation in which you feel that it is quite obvious that you shouldn't have to ask, actually having to ask is the Divine test of your character traits. It is a test that will enable you to further develop your level of patience and sensitivity.

Avoid giving orders when you ask your spouse to do something for you. It is much more preferable to say something like, "Could you please ..."; "I am sorry to trouble you, but could I please ask you to ..."; "Would you mind if ..."; "Please say no if it's too difficult for you. Would you be able to ..."; or "I have a problem. Perhaps you could help me ..."

When you need undivided attention, ask for it. Don't just be upset that you aren't getting it. Some people might feel hesitant about asking, as if this is demanding too much. Others might feel bad that they need to ask, but it is important to speak up when something bothers you. Failure to do so might build up negative feelings of resentment and frustration and lead to a blow-up that could have been avoided. Express yourself clearly and directly without blaming. For example, if your spouse speaks to you in a way that increases the pressure you experience, you might say, "I work better when I'm not under pressure." In general, make your requests in a simple and straightforward manner. If you have a complaint, be specific and offer a solution.

Most people don't associate negotiations with marriage, but rather with two countries dealing with each other about important issues. Actually, negotiation is a tool we use in many areas of our lives. For example, we are willing to work many hours, doing things that may not interest us, in exchange for the money we earn. The art of making win-win negotiations is highly important in marriage. Couples that don't know how to negotiate well are likely to argue and quarrel in a way that causes both parties pain. If either the husband or wife has a stronger personality and gets his or her way without taking the other's feelings into consideration, resentment will keep building, causing depression or anger, as well as strife and suffering.

Similarly, when you want your spouse to do something for you that your spouse isn't that interested in doing, think, "What can I do for my spouse so that in return my spouse will be willing to do this for me?" If you make a request and your spouse initially responds with "No," you don't necessarily have to take this as a final position. In many instances a "no" is really a "not yet." If you calmly explain why this is important to you, the other person might change his or her mind. Ask yourself, "How can I negotiate to get a 'yes'?" At the same time, be prepared to accept a "no." In the long run, your acceptance of a "no" can lead to an ultimate "yes." The person who thinks, "I'm going to get what I want whether my spouse likes it or not," will be creating a lot of trouble for both of them.

When you try to motivate or influence your spouse to do something for you personally or even something that you feel would be for his or her benefit, and he or she won't do it without your asking, how you ask will make a world of difference. There are ways to make that person happy to comply with your requests, and there are ways to motivate and influence that are highly painful. Take, for example, the practice of yelling at someone until he or she takes action. What are you really doing? You are making noise in a way that is highly distressful. The person being yelled at might then choose to do what you asked rather than suffer from your yelling. Does this work? You may get immediate results, but in the long term the pain you cause creates negative energy in your home, and can lead to the disintegration of a marriage. Even if the marriage lasts, it will be missing love and respect. This will be a short-term tactical victory at the cost of a long-term strategic loss.

For example, fixing things can be a source of contention when the party who is the designated fixer procrastinates or is so busy that things that need to be taken care of don't get done without repeated requests. (The first and most important rule is to ask in a way that makes the person want to take action and consequently feel good about it. Follow this rule the first time you ask for something. Follow it the second time and every other time as well.) If you need to repeat yourself more times than you appreciate, you might want to say, "I realize that what I'm asking of you might be difficult to fit into your schedule or that you find the task unpleasant. I would greatly appreciate it being taken care of. What would make it easier for you to do it?"

Sometimes, no matter how often you ask for something, negotiate, and try to motivate and influence, you won't get your spouse to agree. Anger and yelling may be effective, but if you end up getting what you want by causing pain, you lose out more than you would by not getting what you originally wanted. Part of not causing pain is the acceptance that even if you don't get your way entirely, you might still get part of what you wanted. If you do, appreciate the agreement you did get, and work on yourself to gain greater mastery over your own emotional states.

*B*efore my wedding, I asked a number of people for the three ideas that they felt were most helpful for a harmonious marriage.

The one idea that helped me the most was from a man who was now happily married after two divorces.

"I'll tell you a question to ask yourself that cost me a great deal to learn. Before I asked this question, I ruined two marriages. I suffered a lot and caused suffering to others. Now that I consistently ask myself this question, I am happily married. I am certain that if I would have asked myself this question, my first marriages would have been successful.

"Before asking your spouse for anything, the question to ask yourself is, 'How can I make my spouse feel good about complying with my request?'

"The first two times I was married, I gave orders in a commanding voice. If my request wasn't met, I spoke in anger. I instilled guilt and fear. At times I got what I asked

for but, like the old saying, 'The operation was successful, but the patient died.' If you want a healthy, vital marriage, speak and act in ways that will make your spouse happy to do the things you need and want."

I hated the way my mother treated my father. She would frequently scold and nag him. I felt my father was henpecked and pledged that when I got married, I would never treat my husband that way. When I got engaged, I was so thrilled with my chasan that I was certain I would find it easy to keep my earlier pledge. When I made it, it was theoretical. Now that I was going to be married to such a wonderful person, I was absolutely positive that I would never speak to him disrespectfully.

I was in for a big shock when a few days after the wedding, I heard myself nag my beloved chasan the same way my mother did my father. I could hardly believe how I used the same words and tone of voice that my mother did, as if I had a tape recorder in my brain that played itself automatically.

I remembered hearing that if you want to change a pattern, you need to clarify the exact pattern you do want. I repeatedly practiced more respectful approaches. I even looked in a mirror when I rehearsed the pleasant ways of speaking that I wanted to integrate.

I felt this was so important that I was willing to repeat this technique thousands of times. My practice sessions paid off. Even when I am dissatisfied, I speak in ways that are acceptable to my husband and I feel good about myself for doing so.

I liked my spouse very much but there were a number of things that my spouse said and did that I felt would be looked at negatively by others. I kept telling my spouse that there was a need for change in these areas, but to no avail. It wasn't easy for my spouse to change these patterns. I guess the fact that they didn't really bother me personally added to the lack of motivation to put in the effort necessary to make changes. My constant harping on these patterns was a frequent source of contention.

I attended a class that discussed approval-seeking as one of the three qualities that Pirkei Avos lists as destroyers of life. "Envy, desires, and honor-seeking takes us out of the world." This applies to both this world and the next, the speaker said.

When I heard an elaboration on this theme, I realized that my real problem was not with my spouse. It was with my own strong desire for honor and approval. I began to realize that I shouldn't disturb my shalom bayis over issues that are not against the Torah, just because I'm concerned with the way others view them. I told my spouse that I am committed not to nag about these patterns. While I would appreciate changes, I will work on myself alone. I kept my word. My spouse did modify some of these patterns and I have utilized what remained as reminders to become less emotionally dependent on the approval and disapproval of others.

M y parents were divorced when I was a child. I grew up with my mother and saw my father only rarely. My memories of their marriage were painful. My father had a bad temper and would frequently yell at my mother.

I have always said, "I didn't have a healthy role model of how a husband should speak to his wife."

My wife didn't like the way I often spoke to her and we went to a Rabbi for advice. I told him how I lacked a role model. He, however, disagreed with me saying, "You have had many positive role models, and even some great role models. You just didn't realize it.

"Were you ever a guest at anyone's home for Shabbos?" he asked me.

"Plenty of times," I replied.

"Did you ever hear husbands speak in positive ways to their wives?" he asked.

"Of course, many times," was my response.

"Then you have had many role models. Each of those scenes is engraved in your mental library. Just think of the different married men you observed. And keep selecting the best scenes to emulate."

"But each time lasted only a short duration," I argued.

"Even if you only hear someone speak for a few minutes, he can serve as a role model," he said to me.

"I never saw it that way before," I said. "But of course what you are saying makes sense."

"Let me also point out something else to you," said the Rabbi. "You have been speaking very pleasantly and courteously to me throughout our entire conversation. Use this as a role model for the way to speak to your wife."

Realizing that I did have positive role models gave me guidelines that have greatly improved the way I now speak to my wife.

I was waiting on a long line in a post office in a rough inner city neighborhood. A tougher than average guy was smoking a cigarette. The look on his face gave the

message, "I'm going to smoke in here whether anyone else likes it or not."

Someone who didn't like it raised his voice and said to him, "Hey, you can't smoke in here."

"You gonna try and stop me?" he said. "You'll be sorry if you do."

"Stop smoking. It's illegal to smoke here," a tall and husky fellow called out to him.

"Okay, big guy. You tryin' to uphold the law," the smoker snarled. "You got a badge or something? If you try to take away my cigarette, your hands won't be able to do much else for a while."

Then a meek-looking little fellow who had witnessed this scene, politely said to the smoker, "I'm sorry to inconvenience you, but I'll greatly appreciate it if you would be so kind as to wait until you go outside to smoke. I don't mean to tell anybody what to do, but my father died of cancer and my doctor told me to avoid cigarette smoke."

To my amazement, the smoker complied with the request. "No problem. This cigarette's almost gone. I'll wait for my next one until I get into the fresh air."

After this, I began to apply the power of, "I'm sorry to inconvenience you," and "I'd greatly appreciate it if you would be so kind," with my spouse. I have to admit that the side-effects of this approach are a lot better than, "Stop that! You're bothering me," and, "I've already told you a bunch of times not to do that."

ONA'AS DEVARIM: INSULTS AND PUT-DOWNS

The Torah (*Vayikra* 25:17) prohibits all forms of causing pain with words. The Mishnah and Talmud (*Bava Metzia* 58b) elaborate on the prohibition against *ona'as devarim,* and more details are cited in the *Shulchan Aruch, Choshen Mishpat* 228. The

Talmud (ibid. 59a) states that a man must be especially careful not to cause his wife pain with words, since women tend to be more sensitive than men. Nevertheless, the *ona'as devarim* of either the husband or the wife can cause much anger, resentment, and quarrels. Because husbands and wives know each other so well, one can easily find the other's weak points.

In my book, *The Power of Words*, I have elaborated on this Torah prohibition. To summarize: It is forbidden to say anything that will needlessly cause pain to another person. The speaker mustn't say, "You shouldn't be so sensitive." If the listener will experience pain, the speaker is forbidden to say it.

Some people who cause pain with their words tell their victim, "It's not what I said that caused you pain; it's your perception. Just change your perception, and you will be free from pain." It is true that one's perception is a key element, but the Torah prohibition is clear. When you speak to someone who will feel hurt by what you said, you are responsible for the pain your words caused. It's like throwing a rock at someone's head and then saying, "If you would have ducked, the rock wouldn't have hit you." The person didn't duck, the rock did hurt him, and you are guilty of causing pain. So too, with your words. The fact that this person might have worked on mastering the ability to be impervious to all insults doesn't allow you to throw verbal rocks that hurt.

It is forbidden for a husband or wife to speak in a way that would be considered: mocking, belittling, scoffing, derisive, insulting, or a put-down. Sarcasm is often pure *ona'as devarim*. Jokes at your spouse's expense that cause distress are a cruel way to get pleasure. Reminding a husband or wife of past wrongs is considered *ona'as devarim*.

If your spouse failed to listen to something that you suggested and then ended up suffering, it will cause distress if you say, "I told you so." This is just ego satisfaction at the expense of your spouse's pain. It's much more preferable to say, "I'm sorry that you suffered."

Rushing your spouse by saying, "Come on already. What's taking you so long?" in a loud tone of voice so everyone can hear is highly likely to cause pain. When we are late and are being delayed further, we feel anxiety. The challenge is how to access a more relaxed state and remind your spouse to hurry in a way that will not be distressing. You might find it more helpful to say, "You're worth waiting for. Nevertheless, I would appreciate it if you could hurry."

If your spouse claims that your words caused him or her pain, don't argue that you think they really didn't. Apologize.

Think about any patterns of speech of yours that cause distress to your husband or wife. Be resolved to eliminate these patterns in the future.

I attended a lecture on the prohibition against ona'as devarim. I am usually pretty careful not to hurt anyone's feelings with words. So when I heard the lecture, I thought about how I sometimes find my husband's way of talking to me distressful. He's not cruel or mean, and although his manner of speaking might have been acceptable in the family in which he grew up, it causes me pain. I have a more sensitive nature than the members of his family.

The woman who gave the class related that if her husband ever inadvertently said something that could constitute ona'as devarim, he appreciated it greatly if his wife pointed it out to him. And he gave her permission to mention this when she teaches.

I started a new custom in our house. "That's ona'as devarim," I would tell my husband. "And so is that and that." I don't think a conversation lasting over five minutes went by without me pointing out that something was ona'as devarim.

After a couple of weeks of my commenting on every subtle nuance of ona'as devarim, my husband finally blew up at me. "I can't take it anymore!" he shouted. "I don't want to cause you any pain or suffering. But I refuse to be told every few minutes that what I'm saying is ona'as devarim when I talk in a way that most people would consider normal. To me you are the one in this house is who is the most guilty of ona'as devarim."

After that I decided to point out only major violations of ona'as devarim. And there weren't too many of these. Even then I minimized my use of the term "ona'as devarim." The situation still isn't perfect, but it's much improved for both of us. I appreciate my husband's greater sensitivity with his words and he appreciates my restraint in correcting him.

❖ ❖ ❖

Whenever my wife failed to notice anything that I felt she should have seen, I told her, "You are as blind as a bat."

Whenever she didn't understand something, I commented, "How come you don't understand? I didn't think you were that stupid."

If she dropped something, I would say, "You're really klutzy."

If she forgot to take care of something, I would say, "You're quite young to have Alzheimer's."

A younger brother of mine was our guest for Shabbos. He came early on Friday and left long after Shabbos was over. During his visit, I spoke to my wife as usual. On Tuesday he called me up.

"Ever since I visited you," he told me, "I have been disturbed by the way you speak to your wife. It could be that you do this so often that you both don't realize how awful it sounds. You have no right to speak to your wife the way you do. I was your guest on Shabbos and I did not feel like mixing into your life if I wasn't asked. But I kept thinking how upset we both would be if our sister's *husband talked to her the way you do to your wife. Please take this as advice from a younger brother who cares for you."*

My initial reaction was to tell my brother to mind his own business. But I realized it had been difficult for him to say what he did. I told my wife that I was sorry for any pain I caused her. Since then I have almost totally eliminated these derisive remarks, which I now realize were mean and hurtful.

A couple who loved each other but got into frequent quarrels made a resolution to speak to each other with mutual respect. They needed to work out patterns of communication that were mutually acceptable. They had someone listen to the way they spoke to each other and give suggestions of better ways to get their points across.

The husband was asked, "What is the motivating factor behind your wishing to change the way you speak?"

He replied, "I've decided I don't want to be in pain and I don't want to cause pain. When I speak to my wife in a way that distresses her, she gets angry and, knowing my vulnerable spots, she responds with painful verbal barbs."

From then on, the person who helped them communicate would ask other couples, "Can I ask you two questions?"

"Of course," he is always told.

"Do you want to be in pain?" he asks.

"No," is the answer that everyone always gives.

Then he asks, "Do you really want to create pain for your spouse?" Again, the answer is, "No." Both husband and wife usually respond this way.

"So any pain that is caused by either of you is inadvertent. Since you both don't want to cause pain, let's see what patterns cause the pain and let's learn different patterns that will prevent it."

In some instances one party will say, "I think he/she wants to cause me pain." In response, a straight denial by the other partner is usually not accepted as being true.

Therefore both parties would be asked, "If you were convinced your spouse doesn't want to cause you pain, would you be resolved not to cause pain in return?" The answer is almost always, "Yes." And the couple is instructed, "Let's see how you can speak to each other in ways that will prove your goodwill."

Then both of the partners can be asked, "If your husband/wife truly had goodwill and really didn't want to cause you pain, what is the least amount of proof that you would need to show you that there is goodwill?" This often points to the direction of the improvement.

WATCH THE CONTENT OF WHAT YOU SAY: CHOOSE YOUR WORDS

"Death and life are in the power of the tongue" (*Mishlei* 18:21). This definitely applies to the life of your marriage. An article for a newspaper or magazine or a letter to someone you consider very important requires choosing your words carefully. You might even ask others for suggestions on how to edit what you wrote. It is equally crucial to watch what you say when you speak to your husband or wife.

Your words to your spouse can create feelings of joy, love, closeness, gratitude, and maybe even radiant bliss. Your words to your spouse can console, comfort, inspire, motivate, elevate. But other words can create feelings of pain, distress, and anger.

When you choose the right words, you can say things that would create a quarrel had you said them differently. Take, for example, situations when you need to say "no" to a request. Some people say "no" in a way that causes resentment or ill will. For example, "You don't meet my requests when you don't feel like it, so I'm not going to do what you asked." But you can also say "no" in a different way. "I would love to meet your request at a different time. But I'm afraid that I can't say 'yes' right now." As someone once said, "If you can't oblige, at least speak obligingly."

I once saw a sign on someone's refrigerator, "Be careful of the words you say. Keep them soft and sweet. You'll never know from day to day, which ones you'll have to eat." The thought went through my mind that one's refrigerator is the perfect place to keep this reminder. Just as we need to be careful about what we eat, regarding both *kashrus* and health, so too, we need to be careful about how we speak, regarding both *kashrus* and the health of one's marriage.

Every statement you make can be phrased in many ways. Choose positive ways to word things. Marriage is a great opportunity to learn tact. Tact is when you say your position in a way that is sensitive to the feelings of the person to whom you are talking. Speaking without tact can be a violation of the Torah prohibition against *ona'as devarim*. Some examples:

- "That's ridiculous." Compare this with: "I see some difficulties with that."
- "That's totally stupid." Compare this with: "Let's look at this in another way."
- "How could anyone in their right mind think that?" Compare this with: "I think that another position has its merits."
- "You are totally wrong." Compare this with: "This seems to me to be the right way."
- "Only an idiot would say that." Compare this with: "I think that if we both took a closer look at this we might agree that ..."
- "You are dumb for not knowing that." Compare this with refraining from commenting when your spouse doesn't know something. If you yourself know something your spouse doesn't know, feel joy for the opportunity to do *chesed* by sharing your knowledge and information.

If your spouse didn't understand you, it would be tactful to say, "I must not have expressed myself clearly. Let me explain what I mean."

Do everything you can not to embarrass your spouse or put him or her on the spot. There is no need to point out every single error and mistake. If a mistake is likely to be repeated or needs to be corrected, it is important to point it out, but even then do it with finesse. In many situations, the mistake is a one-time error and there is absolutely no need to point it out. If there is a healthy relationship between husband and wife and both have high self-esteem, this is not an issue. But there are many marriages in which pointing out mistakes is the primary focus of communication, and this causes much distress.

Here are some don'ts when it comes to communication with your spouse:

- Don't criticize small and irrelevant mistakes unless you know that your husband or wife will appreciate it. Some partners constantly correct the other's grammar, choice of words, and patterns of speech. If you find someone's grammar or pattern annoying, correct it in a way that enables the other person to feel good. Don't do it in a way that sounds like an attack on the intelligence and competency of your husband or wife.
- Don't mumble comments under your breath that you know you shouldn't say.
- Don't say what you are not saying. "I'm not going to tell you what I think of your intelligence, competence, insight, etc."
- Don't say, "I'm not your father/mother." Of course, you aren't. Nobody ever thought that you were.

Some people claim, "I can't control what I say and how I say it," but the control depends on their motivation. Many people actually believe this about themselves. But the very same people can usually control what they say and how they say it if someone they respect knocks on the door. And most people can do this even if the person at the door is a total stranger whom they will never see again.

I interviewed a retired American Rabbi who settled in Jerusalem, not far from most of his married children and grandchildren. I asked him about the first thought that comes to mind when he thinks about an important principle for marriage.

"Don't say everything that comes to your mind," he said.

In contrast, someone who got divorced responded to my question about personal qualities or patterns that led to divorce, saying, "I believe strongly in the importance of saying everything I feel. If I don't like something, I consider it dishonest not to express my thoughts frankly and bluntly. We would have had a good marriage except for the fact that my wife was so weak. She couldn't take hearing the truth. She kept telling me to keep my critical remarks to myself. But she's wrong. I was hoping that she would become stronger, but she quit the marriage instead. She's a coward and afraid to face herself."

This anti-Torah attitude towards speech is many people's downfall. Most people are not as extreme as this fellow. But unless one is careful with what one says and how he/she says it, his or her marriage won't be harmonious.

*M*y husband tends to quote the statements of others to attack me and put me down. I recall the first time he did it. We were guests in someone's home, and I inadvertently said something inappropriate. My husband felt embarrassed and as soon as we left the hosts' house, he said to me, "Your mother told me that you are socially inept. And she sure is right."

This was rechilus at its worst. Why did my mother do this to me? She probably meant well, but my husband used it against me.

When I was fired from my job, my husband said, "Your therapist told me that you have trouble keeping jobs."

I kept hearing, "Remember the taxi driver who said he wouldn't want you as a passenger again." "My Rabbi told me he had questions about whether you were right for me."

Sometimes my husband would say this in a positive style. "My teacher would be proud of us the way we are talking so pleasantly to each other." I didn't want anyone else's shadow in our house. I insisted that these quotes should be eliminated. Our Rabbi backed up my position. "It's obvious that negative quotes are wrong," he told us. "But if your wife finds the positive quotes distressful, you should avoid them as well. And please don't quote me in your home if it will cause distress."

My spouse and I frequently became embroiled in fiery quarrels. We would both say things to each other that we would be embarrassed to repeat to any of our friends or relatives. Our verbal battles were replete with lethal weapons of speech.

We decided that we needed to consult a third party to learn how to speak to each other without such intense verbal battles.

The person we spoke to tried a number of approaches to influence us to change the way we tried to resolve our differences. At the sessions we spoke respectfully to each other. But once we got home, we again insulted and attacked each other with our verbal weapons.

The counselor suggested a homework assignment that proved to be highly effective. He told us, "I thought of an idea that will help you change your patterns. I want both of you to transcribe word for word what the other person says when you quarrel. We will then discuss the contents of what you have written at our next meeting."

We carried out the homework according to the instructions we were given. After doing this for an entire week, we only needed one more session with the counselor.

Whoever was transcribing word for word what the other one said had to keep requesting that the speaker speak slower. Seeing your spouse writing down each word you say makes you think a little bit more objectively about your communication. Also, speaking slower prevents you from spewing forth angry words.

When we met with the counselor to read what we had written, he suggested ways we could "edit" what we had said. He told us to keep asking for what we wanted and to express our opinions in a way that is both self-respecting and respectful of each other.

Seeing your words transcribed is a great reminder of the Mishnah in Pirkei Avos which says that all of our deeds and words are written in an eternal book. Politicians and diplomats are much more careful with what they say when reporters are present. My spouse and I became each other's reporters. We agreed to have weekly meetings together to discuss the written highlights of the week. The caustic barbs ended. Our meetings were transformed into conversations between a young couple who care deeply for each other. My most thrilling "report" was when I quoted my spouse as saying, "I think that you are a super wonderful person. And I feel fortunate to be married to you."

My husband was leaning back on one of our dining room chairs so that all his weight was only on the two back legs of the chair. I heard a slight cracking noise and was afraid that the chair would break and he would hurt his back.

"Please sit on the chair upright," I said to him. "I'm afraid the chair might break."

"You only care about the chair and not about me getting hurt," my husband said in a pained voice.

"I don't care a drop about the chair compared to your getting hurt," I told my husband, and he saw how sincere I was.

This interchange with my husband taught me that I need to be explicit about my concern for his welfare.

❖ ❖ ❖

"I see that you hate me," the husband said to his wife.

"No, I don't. I just don't like the way you acted towards me," the wife replied.

"What didn't you like?" he asked.

"The way you spoke to me," she said.

"But the only reason that would bother you is because you hate me," he responded.

"Just because I want you to speak differently doesn't mean that I hate you," the wife said. "I'm not your enemy."

This couple had a different definition for the word "hate." To the wife, "hate" means you consider that person a mortal enemy. To the husband, however, "hate" was a negative word, but not to the same extent as it was to his wife. He came from a home where people said, "I hate you," when most other people would say, "I'm angry at you."

"Hate" is a powerful word. It's so much better to say, "I don't like what you said (or did). And I wish you would refrain from saying (doing) that again."

TONE OF VOICE:
WHAT IS THE MUSIC OF YOUR VOICE?

"The Torah ideal is to speak to others in a manner that makes it a pleasurable experience. Your tone of voice should be calm and pleasant when you speak to anyone. Do not speak in anger or raise your voice" (Rabbi Eliyahu Lopian; *Lev Eliyahu,* vol. 1, p. 66).

The tone of voice you use to express something will have an effect on the reaction of the listener. There are tones of voice that are enjoyable to listen to, just like beautiful music. And there are tones of voice that remind one of scraping chalk on a blackboard. Each tone of voice gives off a different energy and conveys a specific message. An angry tone of voice or one that is soft and gentle give very different messages. Everyone sounds totally different in their best tones than when they say things in their worst tones. Your tone of voice reflects your feelings and emotions. Every change in mood will be reflected in your tone of voice. Even if someone is speaking a language you don't understand, you can often comprehend what is being conveyed by listening to the tone of voice with which the words are spoken.

Frustration, irritation, anger, and disappointment can all be detected in the tone of voice. Some people are more sensitive to this and some less sensitive, but almost everyone will be affected. The same message that would be difficult for the listener to listen to if said in the wrong tone of voice, might be acceptable if the wording and tone of voice reflect compassion and respect.

Learn to apologize without sounding too self-effacing; disagree without sounding as if you are condemning, attacking, or blaming; be reasonable without sounding boring or robot-like.

When calling your spouse from a different room, be careful not to sound disrespectful when you raise your tone of voice. If you ever yell, or speak angrily to your spouse to stop him or her from saying or doing something, ask yourself why you do it. It's like the question: Why did the chicken cross the road? To get to the other side. It's obvious, you want him or her to stop, so how about speaking in a gentle, loving tone of voice? How about humor that would be appreciated?

Some husbands and wives begin their requests for help in an angry tone of voice. For example, a husband might say, "What's the matter with you! You didn't sew my shirt that I left on the sewing machine." Or a wife may say in an angry tone of voice, "Can't you take the plates off the table to help out around here!"

Three almost simultaneous reactions occur in this type of situation. First, both notice that their spouse didn't do something to help them. Then they say to themselves, "He/she should have known on his/her own to do this. It's not right of him/her to have failed to help me." Then both express their angry feelings via their tone of voice and in the kinds of words they select. This entire process happens with lightning speed.

Awareness of this pattern will enable you to make your requests for help in a friendly, cheerful tone of voice, or at least in a relatively calm one. When your tone of voice conveys cheerfulness, respect, love, or sensitivity, the message you give is more likely to be received with a similar feeling.

If someone has a business and wants to keep his customers, speaking pleasantly is a necessity. Failure to do so will cause him to lose customers. When customers enjoy the way someone who is running a store or business speaks to them, they are likely to increase the monetary profits of that person. This is even more important in a marriage. With a business, if a customer doesn't like the way you speak to them, you will just lose out financially. In a marriage, however, the loss caused by speaking in ways that cause distress is much worse.

Be aware of the effects of your tone of voice on your spouse. In counseling couples I frequently point out how their tone of voice keep changing. I have them find a range of tones that their spouse finds comfortable. The listener is always more sensitive and aware of the tone of voice of the speaker than the speaker is. The more aware you are of your own tone of voice and the effect it has on the listener, the easier it will be for you to recognize when there is a change in your tone. One way to become more aware of your tone of voice is to ask your spouse for feedback, by saying, "If my tone of voice ever distresses you, please point it out to me. And when you especially like a certain tone of voice, please tell me."

I hate to be spoken to in a tone of voice that sounds controlling or demanding. If my spouse ever asked me to do something in a tone of voice I didn't like, I used to respond with, "I'll only do what you asked if you ask again in a pleasant tone of voice." The frequent response was, "What are you, a baby? If it's the right thing to do, you should do it anyway regardless of the tone of voice I use."

"But tone of voice means a great deal to me," I explained, not in my best tone of voice. "If I give in to your requests when you speak in an unpleasant tone of voice, then I am training you to continue speaking to me like that. I hate it when I hear your demanding tone of voice."

This brought out the worst in my spouse. My spouse would never repeat the request in a more pleasant tone. Instead I got a speech about how immature, insecure, and childish I was.

I tried to ignore the harsh or shrill tone of voice if a reasonable request was made, but I couldn't. Try ignoring the sound of chalk on a blackboard if that sends chills down your spine.

I finally thought of a sentence that was very effective. When I didn't like the tone of voice with which a request was made, I would say, "I'll do what you asked regardless of how you say it. But I would prefer if you could speak pleasantly."

That was it. I didn't add another word to my request for an improvement in the way my spouse spoke to me. I immediately took care of what I was asked to do. Interestingly, even though there was no acknowledgment that there was anything wrong with the way that the original request was made, the next requests were expressed in a much more pleasant tone of voice.

Someone advised me to wait at least two days before I criticized my husband. I was told that by waiting two days I would be calmer when I spoke.

I found, however, that during those two days my inner critic was busy at work. I kept thinking of how much the thing I was critical of bothered me and how important it was for me that my spouse make a change. I would say to myself that perhaps my husband wouldn't listen to me and we would get into an argument. The more I thought about it, the more the resentment kept building up.

After forty-eight hours, I felt so resentful that I would blast my husband. I came to the realization that speaking up immediately enabled me to speak more tactfully. Furthermore, my husband has a strong personality and doesn't mind it at all if I make suggestions about how he can improve. He doesn't always follow through right away, but he doesn't mind me repeating my request a few days later. He can't stand it, though, if I criticize in an angry tone of voice. So for me, the challenge is to control my tone of voice. Since I see that he is open to my criticisms, it is easier for me to remain calm when I point out things.

My husband and I get along very well, and our biggest nachas in life is our children and grandchildren. My husband tends to blame me for any mistake that happens, but I've become used to that over the years and it no longer bothers me too much. For example, if I don't understand something he says, he tells me, "What's the matter with you? Why don't you understand?" But if he doesn't understand something that I say, he tells me, "You didn't explain yourself clearly." It seems to me that any objective outsider could see that one could say the exact opposite. But this is really a minor issue in our lives.

The factor that is an issue for us is the tone of voice we use to speak to each other. We usually speak in ways that the other is comfortable with. But we can both easily speak in a tone of voice that the other will find irritating. We developed a practice that has worked well for us. We bought chimes. Whenever either of us doesn't like the other's tone of voice, the one on the receiving end of the message tickles the chimes and lightly says, "Tone." This has proven itself to be an effective reminder for the speaker to change to a more pleasant tone of voice.

❖ ❖ ❖

*O*nce when our family was having our Shabbos meal together, I was irritated about something my husband said. While I didn't shout or yell, my tone of voice was critical and the words I chose were not the most tactful.

My teenage daughter looked at me with a cute smile, and went out of her way to say in a playful, childlike tone of voice, "Please be nice to him, he's my daddy." I couldn't help but smile. I was so proud of my daughter for her sensitivity.

The way she almost sang those words caused them to reverberate in my mind and definitely serve as a motivating factor for my speaking with greater sensitivity in the future.

YOUR FACIAL EXPRESSION AND THE LOOK IN YOUR EYES CAN SPEAK LOUDER THAN WORDS

We communicate in many ways. We communicate with our words, with our body language, with the expression on our face, and the look in our eyes. There are expressions that give the message: "I like you very much." "I care about you." "I respect you." And there are facial expressions that give a message, "I have contempt for you." "You are highly displeasing to me." "I wish you would get out of my presence."

My late *Rosh Yeshivah*, Rabbi Chaim Mordechai Katz, used to say that we can even kill another person, so to speak, with the way we wrinkle our nose at the mention of his name. On the other hand, you can make a facial expression that puts someone at ease and lifts up his or her spirits.

Be aware of the message you are giving with your face. Create inner positive feelings that will be reflected in the look on your face and in your eyes.

When my husband didn't like something I did, he would show his displeasure by staring. I found this distressing, but got so used to it that I didn't say anything.

One Shabbos when we had guests for the meal, the topic discussed was anger. One of the guests asked my husband if he gets angry frequently. I was certain that my husband would reply that he doesn't, but I know he really does.

To my surprise, my husband was totally open. "Unfortunately, I naturally have a bad temper that I consistently need to keep under control. As a child I used to shout a lot at my younger brothers and sisters. As I got older, I learned to control my temper, but inside I frequently felt frustrated and critical. I realized that before I got married, I would need greater mastery over my emotions. I worked on developing attitudes that would decrease my inner feelings of anger. I keep on practicing all kinds of techniques that increase my patience and tolerance. I feel guilty that I become impatient, but I am improving. I know that I still have a long way to go."

This was an eye-opener to me. I didn't realize that my husband was working on his temper. I only observed the look in his eyes which I interpreted as his impatience with me. Now I realize that the fact that he only expresses his displeasure with his eyes is the result of his program of improvement.

The next time I saw that look in his eyes, I said to myself, "I appreciate his efforts at controlling what he says." After a few more times, I expressed my appreciation for his efforts. He was thankful that I gave him credit for trying and has stepped up his efforts.

ASK YOURSELF, "WHAT SHOULD I STOP SAYING OR DOING THAT IS CAUSING MY SPOUSE DISTRESS?"

There is a general question that you should ask yourself regularly: "What should I stop saying or doing that is causing my spouse distress?" Each person will need to decide on his or her own how often to ask this question. But as you are reading this now, try to think of a few things. If you can't think of anything yourself, you can ask the person to whom you are married. This can also serve as a treasured gift to your spouse. You can write a gift certificate stating, "The bearer of this certificate can ask me to stop saying or doing one item." Some couples might enjoy bartering, "I will stop saying or doing an item that bothers you, in exchange for a similar action from you."

Whenever I would comment that something bothers me, my spouse would respond, "I don't see why this should bother you. It doesn't bother me."

I kept arguing that every human being is different. "Our Torah obligation is to be sensitive to the individual likes and dislikes of the other person, even though our own portfolio of likes and dislikes might be totally different," I said.

"But if it doesn't bother me, most likely it doesn't bother the vast majority of normal people. If you have a reaction that is abnormal, that's not my problem," my spouse would insist.

I would try and try to get my spouse to see that individual sensitivities and irritations need to be respected, but to no avail.

"When I was growing up," said my spouse, "if any of my siblings would be bothered by something that didn't bother anyone else, we were told, "You need to learn to live with this. Everyone's life has potential irritants. The more you learn to accept them, the better off you'll be in life."

Finally one day my spouse heard something that was convincing. "In a lecture that I attended," he said, "I heard that the laws of ona'as devarim are subjective. Even if you wouldn't mind if someone said a certain thing to you, it's forbidden to say it to someone else who wouldn't want it to be said. This illustrates that in all areas of interpersonal relationships, an individual's reactions are the key factor in whether they are acceptable or not."

Since then, my spouse has stopped saying, "If it doesn't bother me, it shouldn't bother you." Rather, if it bothers me, my spouse tries to stop saying or doing it.

HABITS: MAKE IT A HABIT TO ELIMINATE HABITS THAT CAUSE DISTRESS

Since each person is different, we all have habits that the person we are married to finds annoying or upsetting. There are habits that might bother one person but not another. It is very possible that the people you grew up with in your home were not bothered by a habit you have, but your husband or wife finds it extremely irritating. It is almost impossible for a person to suddenly eliminate lifelong habits, but if a habit of yours causes distress, make it a priority to overcome it.

Here it is important to mention that if you want your spouse to stop a habit, mention it politely and tactfully. You will probably have to repeat your request a number of times. Many people are unconscious of their habits. View your efforts to motivate your spouse to stop these habits as your personal effort to build up your level of patience. Gentle reminders that are repeated often will eventually change the habit. Anger and aggressive approaches can create more harm than the habit you are trying to eliminate.

One habit that usually causes distress is that of making someone wait for you. In every marriage one party will need to wait for the other many times. Nevertheless, we should put in the effort to minimize this when we can.

*O*ne summer night in a Tel Aviv hotel before the evening prayer, Rabbi Noson Tzvi Finkel gave a long lecture on ethics to a number of his former students. Before he had finished, his wife interrupted him with a whisper, "They have wives." In the midst of a most enlightening talk, he stopped and said, "We must start Maariv already."

One of those present said, "But our wives won't mind."

"First of all," replied Rabbi Finkel, "I'm not certain that is so, and you have no right to make your wives wait for you. Secondly, my wife is surely hungry and I don't have permission to make her wait."

He refused to finish the lecture. Moreover, after the evening prayers, he made certain that everyone went home as soon as possible (Tenuas HaMussar, vol. 3, p. 250).

*"I*t's not fair!" As a child I would frequently say this to my parents, to my teachers, and to my friends.

Fairness was a high value for me. I always tried to be fair. And I demanded that others treat me fairly also.

When we were making our wedding plans, I would repeat, "It's not fair!" quite often. I had a vision of how I wanted things to be and felt it was unfair that I should be deprived of all that I had pictured in my mind for a long time now.

In my first year of marriage, I would constantly be upset about things not being fair. Even if a matter seemed trivial to my husband, to me it was highly important to get my way if I felt that it would be unfair for my wishes not to be met.

On our first anniversary, my husband gave me a beautiful gift. He told me that he appreciated me greatly. He added, however, that he had one request.

"Please stop using the expression, 'It's not fair!' It's not fair to me that I have to hear it all the time. It's not even fair to you. Thinking that things aren't fair increases your irritation and anger. So many times an objective observer would see that the question of fairness and unfairness has no relevancy to the matter at hand."

I said I would try to decrease my use of this expression. After a month of not saying, "It's not fair," I see that many things don't bother me as much as they used to.

I had a habit of asking, "Can I raise a point?" before I commented on what my husband said. In my home, my parents always told me to ask permission before I commented on what they said. I did this so many times growing up that I didn't think anything of it. The importance of not interrupting someone when they were speaking was instilled in all my brothers and sisters. Our conversations at home weren't as spontaneous as in some other homes, but they were always respectful.

One day my husband said to me, "Please don't ask

permission before you say something to me. Of course, you can always make any comments you wish on anything I say. When you ask me for permission, I feel as if you think that I might prevent you from sharing what's on your mind. And this I never want to do."

❖ ❖ ❖

My husband likes to make comparisons. When he was single, he constantly did this and he has continued to do so with everything I do.

"This cholent is great. But a cholent I had at my cousin's aufruf Shabbos two years ago was even better."

"You look wonderful, almost as good as you did in that other outfit."

"I had an enjoyable time during this morning's conversation. The last time that it was more enjoyable was three months ago."

"Our son brought home a good report card. But it wasn't as good as his younger brother's."

No matter what I do, I feel I am being rated and judged. My husband has a fantastic memory. Professionally, his ability to remember facts and to make comparisons in trends has made him financially successful. But only those who are very confident and secure can cope with him. His constant measuring and judging make a lot of people uneasy. He isn't mean or cruel, but his awesome memory and automatic comparisons can be devastating.

I have tried to point this out to him on numerous occasions. But he argues, "I don't do this on purpose. My mind automatically compares anything I see or do with anything similar. I do this to myself all the time, and I enjoy it and gain from it, too. After I daven, I compare today's Shemoneh Esrei with previous ones. I compare my learning and creative ideas with previous experi-

ences. I compare the amount of time something takes me with the time these things took previously. I find that this enables me to keep improving myself in all areas of life."

"But I find it highly distressful," I said to him.

"Do you find it equally distressful all the time, or is it getting better or worse?" he asked.

"I really don't care," I responded. "Just stop it."

"But I can't stop it," he replied. "My brain just happens to work this way."

"At least keep your comparisons to yourself when it comes to me and anything I do," I requested.

"That will be difficult," he responded.

"Then you can compare each time whether it's more difficult or less difficult than other times," I suggested. "Each time you control yourself, you are fulfilling the mitzvah of not causing pain to others. Count how often you do this. Compare the number of times you do this each day of the week. Eventually you can make yearly comparisons."

While I said this half as a joke, I knew that it would appeal to my husband. He agreed and since then he has turned his comparison game into a one-man game of solitaire.

GETTING EVEN LOWERS YOU

There is a strong human tendency to want to get even when someone wrongs us. If someone refuses to lend us money or any other article, we tend to want to refuse that person in return. If someone causes us pain, we are likely to want that person to suffer in some way. But the Torah (*Vayikra* 19:18) explicitly prohibits us from taking revenge and bearing a grudge.

What is the pattern of "getting even"? "You spoke to me in a way that I didn't like, so I'll speak to you in a way that you don't like." "You didn't do what I asked you to do, so I won't do what you ask me to do." "You caused me distress, so I'll do things that distress you."

While the wording that is used when taking revenge is "getting even," we really become lowered by letting our hurt feelings lead us to act in an anti-Torah manner. You become elevated when you transcend personal slights and hurts and act with kindness and compassion towards someone who did not act that way towards you. This applies even to strangers; all the more so it applies to the person to whom we are married. When someone tries to get even, he or she is creating a negative loop that will boomerang and cause more suffering.

The ultimate concept that will enable us to refrain from getting even is the idea expressed by the *Sefer HaChinuch* (241): "Realize that everything that occurs to us is Hashem's will. If someone causes you pain or anguish, it is Hashem's decree. Awareness of this fact will prevent you from taking revenge."

I'm not the type of person who will try to take revenge by actively doing things to cause my spouse to suffer. But if my spouse insults me, I tend to act passive-aggressively for some time to come. I will act as if I did not hear requests that were made. I will find things to do outside the house instead of taking care of something my spouse wants me to take care of. I feel bad about my acting this way. But when I am hurt, I have a strong need to cause distress in return. This outweighs all of my ideals and natural desire to do acts of kindness.

One day I was speaking to a close friend who was able to maintain a joyous attitude in spite of difficulties. This friend was having an especially hard time with a relative who thought very differently from my friend on almost every issue that they had to deal with together. My friend said to me, "Years ago these types of incidents used to get me very angry, and I would become embroiled in a heated quarrel with my relative. But now I am much more aware that all that happens to me is not really from this relative, but from Hashem who is testing me. I realize that all that Hashem causes to happen to me in my life is for my ultimate good. This has totally removed negative feelings towards that relative. Now I am able to interact peacefully regardless of any obstacles this relative causes."

This is exactly the message that I needed to hear about dealing with my spouse. While I don't find it easy, I realize that my spouse is Hashem's agent to test me for my benefit. Since then, whenever I felt like acting passive-aggressively with my spouse, I would repeat to myself, "This isn't my spouse causing this to me; it is my loving Creator who does this for my benefit. I will treat my spouse with as much kindness as possible." When I am able to actually do this, the feelings of spiritual accomplishment are greater than the dubious pleasure of getting back at my spouse.

We should also realize that all matters concerning this world are so trivial and inconsequential that it is simply not worthwhile to take revenge for them (Rambam; *Hilchos Dei'os* 7:9).

Keep in mind the metaphor of *Talmud Yerushalmi* (*Nedarim* 9:4 and *Korban Eidah*): "If you cut your left hand while slicing meat, would your left hand take revenge on your right hand for cutting it? For this reason we should not take revenge on others, since we are all one." All the more so, this applies to your spouse, with whom you have an even greater oneness. Let the pleasure of acting in an elevated manner override the potential pleasure of getting even.

I am embarrassed to admit that whenever my spouse said or did anything that was distressful to me, I felt pleasure if there was a measure for measure retribution during the next few days.

I felt an inner glee and joy when my irritation and distress was avenged with cuts, disappointments, slights, or insults from various sources. As a matter of fact, it became difficult for me to let go of my inner feelings of resentment until my spouse suffered in one way or another.

Whenever I came across the verse in Pirkei Avos that states we shouldn't rejoice at the downfall of our enemies (Mishlei 24:17; Pirkei Avos 4:19), I felt a tinge of guilt. But I quickly rationalized that this was referring only to an enemy. My spouse isn't my enemy but my friend.

Then one day I received an intense wake-up call. There is someone I know well and care about whose life is full of difficult challenges and suffering. I wasn't compassionate enough towards this person who has suffered a lot from others minimizing his pain and anguish. "I wish you would experience what I was experiencing," I was told, "so you would be more understanding and compassionate towards my plight."

It was a painful lesson, but I got the message loud and clear. I saw that when I made a mistake and didn't treat someone exactly right, I didn't want that person to wish me suffering. I saw that my interpretation of that Mishnah was an inaccurate rationalization. I no longer feel a need for my spouse to have a measure for measure experience before I let go. I now use every ounce of spiritual strength to try to let go of resentment as fast as I possibly can.

I once met a very wealthy person who traveled far to learn about joy. He owned numerous factories and had thousands of employees. His present wealth was enough to last him several lifetimes even if he would buy every luxury he could ever wish for. But it hadn't bought him happiness.

"Okay, teach me the formula for happiness," he demanded.

"I'll tell you some Torah principles that, if you apply them, will enable you to find much happiness in your life," I told him. *"But first can you give me a picture of your present emotional situation? What gives you joy right now, what has given you real joy in the past, and what detracts from it?"*

"I love to make great business deals, and I hate to lose out in a negotiation," he replied.

"Will the amount you win or lose make a practical difference in your life?" I asked him.

"Of course not," he said with a smile. *"I have enough money to buy whatever I need even if I don't make another penny. I can also afford to lose large amounts and maintain my present lifestyle."*

"What are the most pressing issues that prevent you from enjoying your life?" I asked.

"My wife," he replied. *"I want a divorce and she is trying to take too large a percentage of my money. My main goal in life is to make her miserable. I'll fight her in court as long as it takes to give her less than she demands."*

"Do you actually enjoy this?" I asked.

"Not really," he said. *"But it's my number one priority to make certain that she loses more than I do."*

"That's crazy," I retorted. *"You say you want happiness. But your main focus is on being spiteful and you are harming yourself as much as you are harming her."*

His powerful determination enabled him to amass a fortune. But his obsessive resentment and desire for revenge prevented him from enjoying his wealth. What a pity!

Not everyone has this man's wealth. But everyone reading this has something that is more precious than wealth. And that is life. Every moment of life is precious. With every moment of life you have the ability to amass a spiritual fortune. Every moment of life can be lived to the fullest with joy (when that is appropriate), or at least with a sense of meaning and accomplishment. Even if at present you have not mastered the ability to access joy at will, you can work towards developing your mind in a way that will give you more happiness and joy. Resentment towards one's spouse is incompatible with joy. Make it a high priority to increase your level of joy.

ASKING FOR FORGIVENESS AND FORGIVING

Just as we have an obligation to ask forgiveness of any person we have hurt, damaged, or caused emotional pain to, so too, we have an obligation to ask our spouse for forgiveness if we have caused him or her any suffering.

"When a person you wronged sees that you sincerely regret having hurt him and that you will not repeat your error, he will forgive you. When your regret is sincere, you will find the proper words to say to him. Some people, however, seem to ask forgiveness but are not sincere and their words are deceitful. Such a way of asking for forgiveness will not be successful" (Vilna Gaon; *Mishlei* 10:32).

If you ask forgiveness in a tone of voice and manner that does not sound sincere, it's as if you are saying explicitly, "I'm not sorry that I caused you pain." The person being asked for forgiveness might still forgive you, and it would be appropriate to do so in a marriage in order to facilitate *shalom bayis,* but if the pain and suffering you caused were severe, it is understandable that your spouse will not be open to forgive you unless it is clear that you sincerely regret what you have said or done.

When we are sincerely approached by someone and are asked to forgive him or her, we are required to do so. At times this can be routine. For example, before Yom Kippur, husbands and wives will ask each other for forgiveness and both are happy to forgive the other for any minor irritants. But at times, forgiving can be extremely difficult. One party might have hurt the other so deeply or so frequently that the feelings of resentment are too strong in the present to forgive. It can be a heroic act on the part of the forgiver to forgive. Since the Almighty works measure for measure when it comes to forgiveness, let the knowledge that you will be forgiven for the wrongs that you did serve as a motivating factor to make it easier for you to forgive.

I am basically a kind person, and I love to do acts of kindness for others. If my friends need anything, I will run to help them get it. I am even kind to total strangers. When I give charity to someone begging in the street, I always add words of compassion and encouragement.

But if someone wrongs me in any way, I feel a knee-jerk reaction of getting back at them. I reacted this way with my parents. If I ever felt they treated me inappropriately, I would act passive-aggressively towards them in return. Someone warned me that I should be careful not to repeat this pattern when I get married. I didn't think this would be a problem because I would only marry someone who was consistently gentle, kind, and sensitive.

My husband is kind, but not always as kind to me as I would wish. If he ever speaks to me roughly, I tend to overreact and say things I know I shouldn't say. He then wants me to apologize. But I feel that I'm not going to crawl to him and apologize because I only overreacted after I was provoked.

But then I heard a talk on the greatness of asking for forgiveness. Even though I felt he should ask me for my forgiveness first, I realize that if he doesn't, I still have an obligation to ask forgiveness for what I did wrong. This isn't crawling, I was told, it's climbing. This new metaphor has motivated me to take the initiative to ask for forgiveness. Then my husband would also apologize and we both felt much better.

❖ ❖ ❖

I was much too frazzled to deal with it. I felt that I was at the bottom of a bottomless pit. This impossibility reflected my sense of being totally at a loss as to what to do. We were about to lose our house even though I had told my husband that taking out a mortgage for his risky business venture was not very wise. Now I wasn't speaking so politely.

"How could you have been so stupid? We are going to be homeless and out in the street."

I imagined myself as a bag lady. I was in a total panic, and my husband was the target of my rage and chaotic feelings. I was sure he was going to defend himself, telling me why he wasn't to blame. I planned to verbally blast him into admitting that he had made a serious mistake.

But my husband stopped me by saying, "I don't blame you one bit for being angry. You are right. This was one of the most stupid things I've ever done. It's all my own fault. I beg your forgiveness, and I understand if you don't feel ready to forgive me yet."

I couldn't keep up my anger at my husband when faced with his sincere acknowledgment of error. But I was still in a panic.

"Where are we going to live?" I said with tears flowing.

"I take full responsibility for what happened, and I will come up with enough money to rent a place for us to live. We won't be out in the street. I assure you of this 100 percent. I will do everything that is humanly possible to take care of you."

Although I was still worried, my panic subsided. I was grateful to my husband for the way he was handling this crisis.

*M*y wife would frequently apologize to me for anything she said or did that distressed me. She would also say, "I'm sorry" if she ever unintentionally forgot to say or do something.

But I grew up in a family where no one ever said, "I'm sorry." My wife told me a number of times that saying "I'm sorry" would mean a lot to her. But I always responded, "I can't say 'I'm sorry.' I'll gladly take action to rectify anything I've done. But what's the difference if I do or don't say 'I'm sorry'?"

I spoke to my Rabbi and asked him what I should do. He smiled and said, "First of all, when you told me you can't say 'I'm sorry,' you already said those words. So I know with 100 percent clarity that you are able to say them.

"Now," he said, "let's practice. Tell me, 'I'm sorry I don't say I'm sorry.'" I hesitated, but he gently encouraged me saying, "I know you can do it."

With great effort, I forced myself to say, "I'm sorry."

"Now let's repeat it together at least twenty times."

With repetition it got easier. When I got home, I practiced repeating, "I'm sorry," and looked in a mirror as I did so in order to engrave the image on my brain.

The next time it was appropriate, I said "I'm sorry" to my wife. Her positive reaction made it much easier for me to repeat this afterwards.

I refuse to apologize to someone who might misconstrue my apology. I told my Rabbi, "If someone wrongs me and I say I'm sorry for what I did, that person might think that he can get away with speaking to me in a way that causes me distress."

"I hear your concerns," my Rabbi responded. "But did you say anything to your wife that caused her pain?"

"Well, yes," I admitted. "Nevertheless, if I say that I am sorry, she'll think she didn't do anything wrong."

"Maybe yes, and maybe no," he said. "But regardless, if you cause pain you have to ask forgiveness. My experience has been that most people will admit their own culpability when their adversary admits his. But if you were on the proper level it would be more important for you to ask forgiveness for your own wrongs than to worry whether or not someone else admits their mistakes."

I thought it over and realized that my failure to ask forgiveness resulted from gaivah (arrogance) and not because of a concern for my wife's spirituality. It was difficult for me, but I intensified my resolve and asked my wife to forgive me for what I had said to her. My Rabbi was right. She immediately responded, "Yes, of course I forgive you. And I hope that you forgive me for what I said to you."

II. GIVE PLEASURE
EXPRESS YOUR REALIZATION THAT YOUR SPOUSE IS IMPORTANT

Human beings have a great emotional need to feel important. We truly are important because we are created in our Creator's image. Someone who expresses respect and honor for everyone is considered an honorable person because he or she recognizes this reality. When people are treated with respect, they feel better about themselves. This understanding is especially crucial for a husband and wife.

Asking your husband or wife, "How do you feel about this?" indicates that his or her feelings are important.

Saying, "I won't do this if it bothers you," in a tone of voice that affirms your sincerity, tells your spouse that he or she is important to you.

Not doing something that you would like to do because you

would rather take care of something that your spouse needs, shows you consider him or her important.

Doing something that you would prefer not to do but doing it because your spouse would appreciate it, conveys your message that he or she is important.

Not making a decision until you check it out with your spouse is a form of showing respect. However, the types of decisions requiring joint approval will depend on your particular relationship.

*W*hile I have talents and skills, I still have deep feelings of insecurity. Whenever I fall into that bottomless well, my husband reaches out and gives me reassurance. No matter how many times I express my insecurity, he just continues to reassure me. Gradually, over a period of years, this has given me a sense of trust not only in him, but also in myself. Still I am always afraid that he will get tired and impatient, but about this, too, he reassures me.

"You are the most important person in my life, and it gives me pleasure to help you out in any way possible," he has told me numerous times.

I consider his willingness to reassure me an infinite number of times as the way he emulates Hashem.

SMILES

When you smile sincerely to your husband or wife, you send positive energy. Your smile gives a valuable message to your spouse. There is a saying, "A smile is a small curve that sets many things straight." Master the art of the genuine smile. For a smile to be genuine, it must come from the heart. A smile is actually what you feel inside and your face is just an external expression of that inner smile. Being on the receiving end of an artificial smile or a real smile that comes from within are totally different experiences.

A young man once came to Rabbi Noson Tzvi Finkel to announce his engagement. Noticing that he had a very solemn facial expression, Rav Noson Tzvi lectured him on the importance of having a cheerful countenance. Rabbi Finkel stressed that while this is a great obligation at all times, it is especially necessary in the presence of his fiancee (*HaMeoros HaGedolim,* p. 234).

❖ ❖ ❖

*M*y wife is good natured, but she tends to be serious and doesn't smile as often as I would like her to. When guests come to our house, they would probably feel more comfortable if greeted with a smile.

I asked my wife if she would be willing to smile more, but she said, "I don't feel comfortable wearing a false smile. If it's not real, it's not considered a smile at all."

I asked a person who smiles a lot how he does it. He told me that we all have memories of when we laughed or smiled in the past. Vividly remembering one of those memories in the present makes us smile, and this smile is just as real as any other.

He also suggested that we can emulate Rabbi Avraham Grodzinsky, author of Toras Avraham. He spent much time perfecting his smile since smiling to someone is a great act of chesed. He would practice smiling while looking in a mirror, never forgetting that he was really practicing the performance of chesed. The person I consulted would also practice waving and smiling to the image he saw in the mirror. This idea may sound funny but it works well.

I shared these two ideas with my wife and she was open to them. While she still doesn't have the smile of someone to whom it comes more naturally, I appreciate her efforts and feel that her smile is an even greater accomplishment.

I asked a friend who travels a lot and stays at hotels in various cities around the world what important lessons he's learned.

"I feel good whenever the staff members of the hotel smile to me when I return after a hard day's work," he replied. "I know that most of them don't mean anything personal and their smiles are part of their job description. Nevertheless, the smiles of the man at the front door and behind the desk give me a lift. Now I, too, smile to others since I see how much it means."

This has taught me to appreciate the smiles of my wife whether or not they are spontaneous. And I have made it a rule to smile to my spouse and children whenever I walk in or out of the house, regardless of how I feel.

MARRIAGE GIVES YOU UNLIMITED OPPORTUNITIES FOR CHESED

Both husband and wife have many opportunities to do or say something kind. Every friendly greeting, everything you hand one another, every piece of information you share, is *chesed*. Every effort you make, every smile is *chesed*. Some understand this in the verse (*Mishlei* 18:22): "He who finds a wife finds something that is good." The good is the multitude of acts of kindness that a husband can do for his wife. And the same applies to the many acts of kindness that a wife can do for her husband.

"Great is *chesed*, for the Torah begins with *chesed* and ends with *chesed*" (*Sotah* 14a). In the beginning of the Torah (*Bereishis* 3:21) we read that the Creator gave the first couple clothing; at the end of the Torah we read that Hashem buried Moshe. When you want to know about a book, read the beginning and read the end. Everything in between deals with this same topic. The essence of the Torah is the Almighty's kindness. A life filled with *chesed* is a life in which one emulates our Creator. A marriage filled with *chesed* will be a joyous relationship. The more joy you experience for each opportunity to do *chesed* with word and deed, the more joy you will experience yourself and will create for your spouse.

*R*abbi Naftali Amsterdam, one of Rabbi Yisrael Salanter's closest disciples, moved to Jerusalem in his old age and married an elderly woman. Soon after their marriage, she became ill and he, a weak man of eighty, had to take care of her. He washed the dishes, cleaned the house, and did other household chores. Another man in his place might have felt sorry for himself, but Rav Naftali cheerfully accepted his situation, for it was an opportunity to do chesed (MiGedolei Yerushalayim, p. 180).

When you focus on the fact that you are fulfilling the Torah commandment of doing acts of kindness, what could have been mundane and even frustrating becomes transformed into an elevated act. Every action on behalf of your spouse is spiritually uplifting as you increase your awareness of every action's eternal value.

Refraining from bothering someone is also a form of *chesed* (see *Noam Elimelech*, cited in *Chamishim Shaarei Chassidus*, p. 55). Husbands and wives both need each other, but at times the amount of effort required for something that is not that important to you will be very bothersome. By telling your spouse not to bother, you are doing an act of kindness.

*O*nce while the Chazon Ish was walking with a disciple, a sad woman approached him and insisted that he take money from her to pray for *her welfare. She handed the Chazon Ish ten shillings which he readily accepted. He blessed her wholeheartedly and cheered her with pleasant words. When she left them, she was in good spirits. Knowing that the Chazon Ish never accepted presents or donations from others, the disciple was puzzled as to why he agreed to take this woman's money.*

Noticing the puzzled look on his student's face, the Chazon Ish told him, "Everyone is required to do chesed in every possible way. In this instance, the biggest chesed I could do for this lady was to accept her money"(Pe'er HaDor, vol. 4, p. 22).

This principle will have many manifestations in marriage. For example, your spouse might give you a present which doesn't appeal to you and which you might even want to refuse. By accepting the gift you are doing an act of kindness.

The Two Questions to Keep Asking

There are two important questions that will greatly increase the level of *chesed* in your marriage. One question is for you to ask your spouse; the other question is one you should keep asking yourself.

The question to keep asking your spouse is, "What can I do for you?" The question to keep asking yourself is, "What can I say or do to give my spouse pleasure?"

EXPRESS YOUR APPRECIATION AND GRATITUDE

When we know that our efforts are appreciated and we hear expressions of gratitude, it usually makes all those efforts worthwhile. Even someone who does not pursue honor and glory wants to know that he or she made a difference. It is so easy for a husband and wife to feel that the other one takes their hard work for granted. This breeds stress and resentment. The amount of effort that it takes to express gratitude is slight, but the benefit is enormous.

Some people express gratitude because of selfish reasons. They know that if they want to motivate someone to continue working at the same standard as before, they'd better tell the person they are grateful. But the ideal is to express gratitude because you are truly grateful and know that it will make your husband or wife feel happy. Every expression of gratitude that will be appreciated by your spouse is the fulfillment of the Torah commandment to love other people as you love yourself. Feel the joy of the mitzvah and this will increase the positive energy in your tone of voice. And remember that appreciation to a human being is like sunlight to a plant.

M*y marriage was a rough one. If I have to think of a single pattern that was a constant source of suffering for me, it was this: Whenever I said or did something my spouse "appreciated," I was challenged with, "How come you didn't do this before?" or, "Finally, you woke up."*

At times, if I really went out of my way to do something extra special, I heard an angry outburst: "You have deprived me of this for a long time. If you are able to do it now, you should have done this many times before."

As you can imagine, this is not a very effective way to motivate someone to do positive things. I pointed this out a number of times, but whenever I did, I was told, "It's important for you to know that you can't get away with all the things you didn't do before. It would be a travesty of justice for me not to point out your deficiencies."

I hungered for expressions of gratitude, or at least a positive acknowledgment of my efforts. The only consolation I had, if you want to call it that, was that my spouse had never really been happy. His distorted thinking prevented him from enjoying life. The good just reminded him of what was missing.

BE GENEROUS WITH YOUR SINCERE PRAISE

People can give all kinds of reasons why they are hesitant to praise others. Sometimes praise might be counterproductive, but in the vast majority of instances when you sincerely praise someone, you are doing that person a great service. I heard many times from Rabbi Chaim Shmulevitz, *Rosh Yeshivah* of Mir, in the name of Rabbi Yisrael Salanter, that praising others is a spiritual act, as opposed to flattery which is a compliment someone gives in order to get something from him in return. Sincere praise, however, expresses your recognition of someone's good qualities or of a positive action. This is the way to build up someone. Growing up without praise will compromise a child's emotional well-being. A marriage without praise will be missing a vital source of positive energy. Many people are ready to find fault. We should find it much easier to acknowledge the good in others, and be a hundred times more careful before we blame and complain.

A general rule to keep in mind: Only praise if it is appreciated. Praise perceived as insincere, exaggerated, or condescending, will not be appreciated. Watch the non-verbal reaction of your spouse to see if there is a positive response. Some people tend to belittle praise, even though they really enjoy hearing it. They might offer some slight resistance to the praise out of modesty, but the look on their face shows that they love it.

Keeping words of praise on the tip of your tongue will make it easier for you to spontaneously express them. If words don't come easily to you, plan them out carefully ahead of time. Of course there are many, many ways to express feelings of appreciation, but the following list might be a good starting point. Use words of praise such as: excellent, exquisite, delightful, extraordinary, fascinating, fantastic, etc. It is, of course, far better to have developed your own list, coming straight from your own heart, but one must always start somewhere.

Even more important is the ability to communicate statements that express positive feedback. Again, optimally, these statements should come from deep within your heart, but the following samples can get you started on the right path:

- I admire what you did.
- I am touched by what you said.
- I appreciate that I can always depend on you.
- I benefited greatly from what you told me.
- I enjoyed it immensely.
- I feel safe in your presence.
- I feel secure when you are handling things.
- I find you calming.
- I was impressed with the way you spoke.
- That was an insightful comment.
- That was courageous.
- That was highly thoughtful of you.
- That was one of the nicest things anyone ever said to me.
- You have my admiration and respect.
- You made my day.
- Your caring has meant a lot to me.
- Your feedback is tremendously helpful.
- Your understanding has meant everything to me.

We were married a week after Shavuos, but it took until Purim, nine months later, until our relationship was the kind I always wished for. My husband was kind, but quiet. He had difficulty expressing his feelings. I knew he cared about me, but this was shown by the actions he did for me, rather than by anything he explicitly said.

The first Purim after we were married, we went to my parents' house for the seudah. I was the last child in our family to get married, and the house was filled with my married siblings and their children.

My husband didn't seem the type to get drunk, but he announced at the meal, "I've never been drunk on Purim before. In honor of my first year of marriage, I will drink until I won't know the difference between praising Mordechai and cursing Haman."

My husband mixed his drinks, not the wisest thing to do. He drank wine, beer, and whiskey and became drunk surprisingly fast.

He then stood up and pounded on the table to get everyone quiet. In a booming loud voice, he said, "I've never really done this properly. But I want to tell everyone here how happy I am to be a member of your family. I thank my father-in-law and my mother-in-law for raising such an amazing daughter. I thank Hashem for sending me the most terrific wife in the whole world. May we have many joyous years together. L'chaim, everyone!!"

My husband's true feelings that were expressed that Purim have reverberated in my mind every time I have heard anyone say "L'chaim." Since then my husband has been much more expressive with his positive feelings and I appreciate this immensely.

I live on Panim Meiros Street in Jerusalem, which translates to "shining face." It could refer to smiling, or it could even mean having a radiant face. On a rainy day, I hailed a taxi and told the driver that I was going to Panim Meiros Street. The driver, who was about sixty years old, commented, "That's a nice name for a street."

"You are right," I agreed. "The street is named after a Torah book with that name. It is also a reminder to smile to other people."

The taxi driver, who was a total stranger, said to me, "I appreciated your saying that I am right. I am married thirty-five years and my wife never tells me that I am right."

What a shame, I thought to myself. I'm certain that she could find a lot of things to compliment regardless of any differences of opinion that they might have.

I was furious at my husband. He was in a self-pitying mood and slightly hypochondriacal. He was acting weak and wimpy, and I couldn't stand it. His complaining was getting on my nerves and it took a tremendous amount of self-discipline for me not to shout at him, "Stop it already! Be a man. Have true bitachon and stop worrying so much. Pull yourself together and gain control over yourself!"

I grew up in a house with a cheerful atmosphere. The general interaction between family members was upbeat. From a young age we were taught not to complain needlessly. If you had a real problem, you discussed it to find solutions. Anyone who didn't feel well would express his or her feelings, and would receive nurturing and sincere concern. But we didn't immerse ourselves in self-pity.

Earlier in the marriage I would complain to my husband that he overdid it when he didn't feel well. But he would angrily tell me that I was lacking chesed, and that I was being insensitive to his needs. His response forced me to keep my contemptuous feelings about his self-pity to myself. Self-pity was an art in which my husband excelled, but in me he certainly didn't have an appreciative audience for his dramatic performances.

Just as I was feeling angry at my husband and holding myself back from sharing my opinion about his complaining, a group of young girls came to our bungalow for a Torah class that I had spent a long time preparing. With all of my inner strength, I forced myself to enter a better emotional state and put my entire heart and soul into giving the best class I could.

When my students left, my husband commented, "You really did a good job. I heard you from the other room. You must have inspired them."

The anger I had felt before totally melted away. My husband probably didn't realize how much his enthusiastic praise meant to me, but I experienced a glow of appreciation for my husband's sincere words of praise.

I love to give compliments and praise, and couldn't wait until I was married to be able to compliment and praise my spouse. Bringing a smile to someone's face is one of my greatest pleasures in life. It was a disappointment to me that after I was married, my spouse consistently deflected all my compliments and praise.

"When I praise you, why do you always argue and say that it is nothing?" I asked.

"I've always reacted this way when people praise me," said my spouse.

"When someone praises you and you belittle what they say, you make them feel bad," I pointed out.

"I don't want to make you feel bad, but I feel uncomfortable when I am praised," my spouse told me.

"What thoughts go through your mind when you are praised?" I asked.

"First of all, it's a lack of humility to want praise. But more than that, I feel I don't deserve the praise. I have so many faults and there are so many positive attributes and qualities that I am missing. Also, when I'm praised I'm afraid that you will keep demanding more from me than I am able to sustain."

"Speak to our Rabbi about it," I suggested.

My spouse did. He was told that pursuing praise and honor is a fault. But if someone sincerely praises you, the appropriate response is to say, "Thank you."

"If you really appreciate praise," our Rabbi said, "be honest with your feelings to your spouse. Praise between husband and wife brings greater harmony and therefore is a mitzvah. Belittling praise often comes from a lack of positive self-esteem. Humility requires not a denial of your strengths, but a realization that they are gifts from Hashem. When you are praised in the present, don't worry about what will be in the future."

LISTENING IS A POWERFUL ACT OF RESPECT, KINDNESS, AND VALIDATION

Listening might seem passive because you just stand or sit there and let the words enter your ears. But listening can be one of the greatest acts of kindness you can do for someone. As a person speaks to you and you listen carefully to what he or she is saying, that person knows that someone cares and considers that what is being said is important. Listening is a powerful act of respect, kindness, and validation.

Someone once said that the difference between a monologue and a dialogue is that in a monologue only one person talks to himself and in a dialogue there are two people talking to themselves. This won't happen in your marriage if you listen carefully to what your spouse says when he or she speaks.

When your spouse shares his or her feelings with you, it is

not helpful to respond, "You shouldn't feel this way." Feelings don't usually disappear by one's being told that one shouldn't feel a certain way. For many people, expressing distressful feelings enables those feelings to become lighter. Give your spouse the right and the chance to talk about worries and problems that bother him or her. Some people insist on talking only about positive topics. If someone complains to them about something, they will say, "You shouldn't talk about that. Be happy. Don't worry." But if a person is not happy and does worry, it might be necessary to talk about the issues that bother him or her.

A person who often came to speak with Rabbi Dov Berish Wiedenfeld, the Rabbi of Tshebin, enjoyed telling the Rabbi his Torah thoughts. Although this person was very long-winded and what he said did not have much content, Rabbi Wiedenfeld would listen patiently. Someone once asked the Rabbi of Tshebin why he wasted so much precious time on the man. Rabbi Wiedenfeld smilingly replied, "Isn't this *chesed?*" (*Rabboseinu*, p. 237).

When you enjoy listening to your spouse talk, listening is something you are doing for yourself. However, when you find it difficult to listen, then what you are doing is an act of *chesed* and listening is a spiritual act that is nourishing for your soul.

Rabbi Avraham Baharan, zt"l, author of HaChevrah VeHashpaatah and principal of a girls high school, told me the story of a young man who wanted to marry a highly intelligent girl. He asked Rabbi Baharan if he could suggest any girls who had graduated from his school. Rabbi Baharan suggested a number of possibilities, but whenever the fellow met one of the girls, his reaction was, "She might be bright and intelligent, but she doesn't meet my standards."

Someone else suggested another graduate of the school and the fellow was highly impressed after meeting her. After the first meeting, he spoke to Rabbi Baharan and expressed how pleased he was with the intelligence of this young lady. Rabbi Baharan, however, knew that this girl was not as scholastically intelligent as the other girls this fellow had met. But the young man told him, "This is the most intelligent girl I've ever met. She is a wonderful conversationalist."

A few days later, Rabbi Baharan asked the girl, "Could you please describe to me how you respond to what he says on dates?" She replied, "I like him very much. I don't always understand everything that he is saying, but I enjoy the way he expresses himself. Throughout the conversation I keep making comments like, 'That's very interesting,' 'That's brilliant,' 'What a deep idea,' 'Ummm,' 'Wow!' 'Yes, tell me more.' We both enjoy the dates very much."

They got married and a few months later Rabbi Baharan met his former student and asked her how things were going. "Just wonderful," she replied. "He keeps talking a lot and I enjoy responding with the same kind of comments I made when we first met."

Rabbi Baharan concluded, "There's a lot to learn here. This young lady was brighter in the area of emotional intelligence than others who received higher grades in school."

Being a good listener can be interpreted as being a great conversationalist. Is your spouse satisfied with the way you listen to him or her? If not, make a concerted effort to listen and concentrate on giving feedback that shows you are listening.

I asked a fellow who was married for two weeks, "Before your wedding you heard a lot of advice about marriage from different people. What ideas helped you the most? And was anything you heard counterproductive for you?"

"Much of the advice was great," the young man said. "The only issue I have is that I need to remember to implement all that I heard."

"But what was especially valuable?" I persisted.

"I consider two pieces of advice the most helpful for me. One, don't try to find solutions when your wife sounds as if she is complaining about something. Rather, listen empathetically. My first impulse is to try to find practical solutions or to express a rational argument as to why this issue is not really a problem, but I was told to listen and try to understand before saying anything. I see that when I do this, my wife feels much better, and the issue is resolved just by her being able to talk about it. Secondly, when I come home, even if I really want to be the first one to talk, I need to have the patience to listen to what my wife has to say first. She appreciates my listening to her."

*B*efore I was married, I was told, "When your wife complains about things, don't try to find solutions. Just listen empathetically." I heard this from a few people, and I wanted to be a good husband.

Whenever my wife had a complaint about anything, I would say, "That's really rough." Or, "I'm sorry that happened." Or, "Yes. That is frustrating, isn't it?"

After a month of this, my wife blew up at me. "Why don't you give me any advice or suggestions? All I hear from you are inane statements of sympathy. Do you think I'm a baby? I want you to brainstorm solutions with me. I don't need you to make irrelevant comments. I'm a practical woman and I would appreciate your respecting that."

❖ ❖ ❖

I like to read books on self-development and personal growth. Some speak to me more than others. But I find that I gain from each book that I read, even if it's only a few points. A quality that I've read about that I feel is of extreme importance to master is: listening with one's heart.

I have studied in a few yeshivos away from home so I have been a guest at the homes of many people for Shabbos. The thing that bothers me the most is when a husband doesn't pay attention to his wife when she speaks. I feel that every husband needs a course in how to really listen so his wife will know she is heard.

Someone once pointed out to me that when I listen, I experience the distress and pain of others. He asked me if this came naturally to me. It didn't. I had to work on this for over two years until it became spontaneous.

I knew that I greatly appreciated talking to people who were good listeners. What is a good listener? Someone who listens with undivided attention, who has nothing else on his mind except what you are saying, who leans forward when he listens to what you have to say, who looks directly at you, and who makes short sounds and comments that express an understanding of the heart.

When I first began developing this quality, I didn't actually feel the distress of anyone else. But I practiced the proper body language and comments. When someone told me about a painful incident or situation I would say such things as, "I'm sorry," "Oy!" "That's difficult." And when someone would tell me good news, I would say, "That's great," "Wonderful," "You must be very happy."

For two whole years I consciously and consistently worked on this. At present, I actually feel the suffering and joys of others. This quality is valuable for interacting with anyone, and all the more so for a husband with his wife.

I have a great need to repeat my points over and over again. My husband is highly intelligent and understands what I say even before I finish the entire thought once. He used to become impatient with me and would try to stop me by saying, "I hear you."

Someone advised my husband to repeat the essence of my messages to show that I've been heard. But I know that he hears me. I still feel a need to repeat my points so I can feel satisfied that I have expressed myself adequately.

My husband spoke to an insightful Rabbi. The scholar told him, "Your wife wants to feel a close emotional connection with you. She does this by talking. It's similar to singing. People enjoy repeating the same song over and over again. You are doing your wife a chesed by being patient when she repeats herself. The more difficult it is for you, the greater the reward."

Since then my husband has been unbelievably patient with me and I appreciate it greatly. I try to save him time in many other ways to compensate for his willingness to hear me out even though my way of talking is not really concise enough for him.

❖ ❖ ❖

I tend to comment on what I see and this often arouses my husband's irritation. For example, I noticed a large water spot on my son's suede shoes. When I pointed this out to my son, my husband said to me, "You're always bothering him about these kinds of things. Leave him alone."

"It's very cold today," I said in the car.

"You are so negative," my husband responded. "You just notice what you don't like."

The Ultimate Five-Word Formula / 181

Although I am a highly qualified professional with a position of responsibility, my husband often says to me that at home I act like a child and he can't speak to me.

My husband's biggest complaint is that I don't really listen to him when he speaks. He's right. I do tend to space out when he talks and I am mentally far away. With my friends and clients I am usually a wonderful listener, but not with my husband.

I was told to increase the amount of positive comments that I made. This included: giving my husband as much praise and positive feedback as I could; also doing the same to our children; and going out of my way to make positive comments in general about scenery, about weather, and about as many things as I honestly could.

The next thing I was told was to improve my listening skills with my husband and children. I realized that this would take a lot of effort on my part, but it is worth it. The way things are now, I suffer a lot. I am highly committed to practice praising, making positive comments, and listening with total concentration. I pray that when I apply what I know it will improve my marriage and my general level of joy in life.

W hen my son was a teenager, one of his favorite expressions was, "What's the connection?"

It was especially annoying when he said this at a time the family was having meals together. If someone would bring up a topic that my son wasn't interested in, he would say, "What's the connection?"

I thought he would grow out of this habit, but off and on he kept this up for years. As he got older, I told him, "When you get married and your wife makes a comment that to you might seem irrelevant and on a different topic from the one you originally started speaking about, please don't challenge it as not having a connection. Often, people speak just to have an emotional connection. Even if you don't see the logical connection, your wife who made the comment does. If you challenge the connection, you might make her feel bad."

I was so concerned that I repeated this every couple of months. The first time my son's kallah ate a Shabbos meal at our house, I was relieved to see how open my son was to whatever she said. I have been even more relieved over time to see that in the years he has been married, he reacts with respect to all of his wife's comments and remarks.

COMMUNICATION CONNECTS

When a couple is able to have enjoyable conversation, those conversations build up a sense of connection. (Problems arise when conversations lead to quarrels and this will be dealt with in a later chapter.) Couples differ as to what their communication needs are. Some couples can have a very happy marriage with a minimal amount of conversation, and some individuals have a greater need for longer conversations. A problem that needs to be worked out is when one party has a much greater need for conversation than the other.

I tend to be quiet and introverted. My wife, on the other hand, is usually outgoing and talkative. She has told me a number of times that the reason she decided to marry me is because she always felt it would be preferable for her to marry a good listener. Another talkative person would compete for the right to talk when she wanted to do the talking.

After we were married for over a year, my wife began to complain to me that I should speak to her more than I had been doing, which I acknowledge hadn't been too much.

She still would like to do most of the talking in our home, but she would like me to share my thoughts and feelings.

I often don't have anything to say, and I appear guarded and secretive. I saw that my wife was feeling bad about my absence from the conversation. I personally didn't feel a need to speak, but my wife kept insisting that communication is the tool for creating closeness.

Since I hadn't the faintest idea of what to do, I spoke to a friend who was an expert in communication. He gave me a number of suggestions that I was able to put into practice.

First, I should ask clarification questions. For example, if my wife tells me that someone she knows got engaged, I should ask such questions as, "Who is the chasan?" "What does he do?" "How did they meet?" "Where are they planning to live?"

Second, I should tell my wife stories from books she hasn't read yet.

Third, I should listen carefully to the comments others make when they speak to someone in my presence. This would give me ideas on what I could comment on myself.

Fourth, I should observe things that happen in my presence wherever I am. Even when I walk or ride there will always be things to notice that are a bit out of the ordinary. For example, acts of chesed that I see, new products in stores, and funny occurrences all are good topics for conversation.

Fifth, I should listen to my wife's side of the conversation when she talks to family and friends and acquire the patterns she would appreciate.

My parents weren't able to communicate well with each other, and I always wished they could. I hoped to discuss my thoughts, opin-

ions, and feelings, and I was certain that I would marry someone who would feel similarly.

When I was dating, my future spouse and I spoke freely and easily. When I said, "Good communication is important to me," I was told, "It's important to me also."

Shortly after the wedding, I saw that we had very different ideas about what we considered "good communication."

The statement that bothered me the most was, "I refuse to talk about that." When I asked, "Why?" I was met with, "I just told you. I refuse to talk about that."

The list of things that my spouse didn't want to talk about grew. I couldn't even talk about subjects that we had been able to talk about in the beginning of our marriage, if they caused my spouse discomfort or stress.

"What can I do to make it easier for you to talk about more subjects?" I asked.

"I don't want to talk about it."

If I kept insisting, my spouse walked out of the room. I realized that I had a choice. I could keep nagging about improving our communication, which I saw was not getting me effective results, or I could just accept the fact that many topics were off limits. I chose the latter, since I saw that it would be the most conducive for shalom bayis. While I am aware that I will always want better communication, I make the best of the situation by keeping my focus on what I do enjoy and benefit from in our marriage.

I still hope that one day I will find a way to influence my spouse to be more open to discuss things. But until then I am dedicated to live up to my Torah obligations.

*O*ur conversations, punctuated by long, silent breaks, didn't exactly flow smoothly. I liked what my husband had to say, but he wasn't a conversationalist. He would deliberate about what he would say and speaking seemed to take more effort for him than for most people.

He would always say, "It's better to say a little that means a lot than to say a lot that means a little."

"Why don't you talk more?" I would ask him.

"I don't like to talk just for the sake of talking," he'd reply.

Fairly quickly I saw that I had a choice. I could focus on the fact that my husband doesn't speak to me as much as I wish, or I could focus on what I like about him. I admire and respect my husband greatly. He's a serious ben Torah and he loves learning.

I accepted upon myself to appreciate my husband for being the idealist that he is. I reasoned to myself, "Rabbi Akiva's wife was so willing to sacrifice for her husband's learning that he was away from home many years. My husband comes home every day and I enjoy the conversations we do have. It's just that I wish they were longer. By focusing on what I was missing I would miss out on what I did have." I had heard this piece of wisdom many times, but it is difficult to put into practice. This was my challenge and I was committed to appreciate what I had.

That was thirty years ago. Now my husband has many students who study under him. For many years already I haven't felt that I'm missing anything. My husband's accomplishments in Torah study are more valuable to me than the long conversations that we didn't have — which I wouldn't have remembered by now anyway.

Gifts

When you give a gift to your husband or wife, you are giving more than just the actual gift. You are giving a message of caring. The more thoughtful your gift, the more it will be appreciated, regardless of the cost.

If your spouse wants to give you an affordable gift, don't deprive him or her of this pleasure. If you don't really want gifts and you let him/her give them to you, it is an act of giving on your part and not of taking.

Surprise your spouse; every once in a while do something that will make him or her feel good unexpectedly.

*A*n elderly halachic authority in Bnei Brak saw a newly married chasan in shul at the morning prayers the day after his wedding. The distinguished posek approached the young man and told him, "Two blocks from here is such and such a store. Before you go home, go to that store. Ask for such and such a perfume. Tell them to wrap it with the fanciest wrapping paper they have. Then go home, and give the perfume to your wife as a gift."

The chasan was surprised that this great person came over to him and made this suggestion. He took it as an obligation to follow these directives. When he brought the gift to his kallah, she was thrilled at his thoughtfulness. A few months later she was still talking about how considerate he was.

*A*major mussar personality spoke to a group of married students. He told them that they should frequently bring home small presents. And he added, "But don't mention that you heard this from me. Your wife will appreciate it more if you do it on your own."

One fellow objected, "But it costs money, and I'm not wealthy."

"Matzah, a lulav and an esrog also cost money," he replied.

❖ ❖ ❖

*O*ur family lives on a tight budget. But I like to splurge when it comes to buying my wife presents. I saved up a relatively large amount of money and bought my wife an expensive gift. I had joy when I bought the gift for her and anticipated a big smile and warm expressions of thanks.

But to my great dismay, my wife made a stern face and announced, "You shouldn't have bought this, it's too expensive."

"Aren't you grateful for the present?" I asked, taken aback by her lack of appreciation for the gift I so lovingly bought.

"How can I be grateful when you buy things we can't afford?" she responded.

I was deeply hurt. I was certain that she would be grateful, but instead this present just made her angry. This wasn't the first time we had an exchange like this. I asked my Rabbi about how to deal with this. He was sympathetic to my disappointment, and at the same time tried to set me straight.

"You are making a fundamental mistake about gift giving," he said. "The purpose of a gift is to make the recipient happy. Even if your intentions are totally pure, it is wrong to give a gift that you know will just cause distress. Perhaps you want your wife to feel positive about you, not just that she should be happy. It is quite normal to have mixed motives, but it's important to know why you are doing things. Either way, learn from her reactions and consider them the next time you want to give a gift.

"You don't need to spend much money; it's the thought that counts. Buy her items that are symbolic of your positive feelings but don't cost much. One gift that is easy to give but doesn't cost you anything is a cookie or piece of cake from a bris or bar mitzvah. You can ask the baal simchah if it's okay to take something home, and from my experience it almost always is."

I could tell that my wife was upset with me, but I did not know why. I would ask her, "What's bothering you about me?" and she would reply, "Nothing." Then I would ask, "What would you want me to do differently than I am doing now?" and she would say, "Who says I want you to do anything differently?"

I approached an older family member for advice on what I could do to improve things. "She won't tell me what's wrong. But I'm certain that something is bothering her. What can I do?"

This relative told me, "I'm going to teach you how to write poetry. You probably won't write anything that will be included in volumes of 'The World's Greatest Poetry,' but if you do what I suggest, your wife will feel that you are the greatest poet in the world."

"But I don't know anything about writing poetry," I insisted.

"Don't worry, it's quite simple," I was told. "Here it is in a nutshell. Think of words you like. Write them down. Then find a word that rhymes with each of those words. Then make up sentences that end with both those words. Only think of two lines at a time.

"Your goal is to make your wife happy. Forget about grammar and any rules about writing you might have learned in school. Don't worry if what you write sounds corny. If you write from the heart, your wife will appreciate it. This might not be everyone's cup of tea, but I believe that you can do it. I know that your wife will appreciate it immensely."

I agreed to try it out and I found rhyming words like great and create, love and above, heart and smart, boy and joy, fine and mine. With practice I got better and better at composing short poems. This became a weekly ritual for me and I gave these poems to my wife each week on Erev Shabbos. I never found out what was bothering my wife before, but whatever it was, it is quite clear that it no longer matters.

LOOK FOR POSITIVE ACTIVITIES THAT YOU CAN DO TOGETHER

When couples are first married they naturally spend a lot of time together. The wedding and *sheva berachos* are dramatic events that they share, and setting up a new home involves many decisions that need to be discussed and dealt with. A couple's first Shabbos in their own home is a memorable experience. There is a lot to talk about and there are many adjustments to make. But after a while, it is common for couples to be so busy that they don't spend much quality time together unless they plan to do so. For many couples this is not at all a problem, but for others it is a major issue.

I have asked many people, "What have you done to enhance your relationship?" Here are some of the ideas I've heard. Depending on many factors (time, financial situation, personalities, etc.) some are appropriate for certain couples and not for others. This list is only a beginning. Couples can brainstorm together or ask others for more suggestions:

- We have begun to take daily walks together.
- We study together from a *sefer* at least five times a week.
- We have an elaborate *melaveh malkah* each *Motza'ei Shabbos* after the children have gone to sleep.
- We have "official" meetings once a week where we can each bring up any issues that otherwise would be difficult to discuss. During these meetings, we don't answer the telephone or allow any other distractions.

- Once a week we each role play an interesting character and have at least a fifteen-minute conversation as these characters.
- We regularly visit different interesting people and interview them. We spend time together beforehand writing down questions to ask them. We do this with experts on *shalom bayis,* child raising, nutrition, health, financial planning, time management, and similar subjects.
- Every *Rosh Chodesh* (or close to it) we go to a restaurant together. We concentrate on reminiscing about our favorite memories.
- We take trips together to interesting places.
- We look for enjoyable stories to tell each other.
- We go together to visit people in the hospital.
- We play scrabble once a week. Once in a while, we work on a crossword puzzle together. We work on jigsaw puzzles together.
- We teach each other skills that one has and the other doesn't.
- We have both learned to play a musical instrument, and we practice together.
- Once a month we have a brainstorming session to generate money-making ideas and projects.
- From time to time we have a picnic together in a park or garden.
- Every two weeks we designate a time to trade off doing things one of us likes to do and the other doesn't.
- We have learned a foreign language together that most people we know don't understand.
- We both regularly leave cute notes and cards for each other.
- We leave humorous messages on our answering machine for each other. We often imitate various accents and personalities.
- We go to the *Kosel* together to pray.

- We have opened a business together.
- We regularly watch the sunset together.
- From time to time, we light a candle, turn off the light in the room, and concentrate on the flame for two or three minutes as we both pray that Hashem should bring light into our lives.
- Once a month we each type up a list of statements for each of us to say to the other.
- Every day we bless each other for an entire minute.
- Every day we call each other at work at least once to ask how things are going.
- We stay out of the way to give each other space.

W*hile commuting, a colleague told me the following story about a couple he once spoke to. He received a long-distance call from a husband who complained about various problems in his marriage. The Rabbi asked a number of questions to get a clear picture.*

During the telephone interview, he found out that they had a television in their bedroom. When they were living in Eretz Yisrael, they never watched television at all. But now it had become a major distraction.

He told them, "Take your television and throw it out. Then you'll see a significant improvement in your lives." A follow-up call indicated a major improvement in their marriage after the television was removed.

The Rabbi explained this on both a spiritual and practical level. Spiritually, a television isn't conducive to having the Shechinah in one's home. The messages given on television and the Torah view of shalom bayis are antithetical.

On the practical level, they spent too much time watching television and not enough time with each other. The removal of the television and the improvement in their marriage ensured they would also do what was necessary to enhance their lives together.

❖ ❖ ❖

A Rabbi told me that one Friday night a number of years ago, when he was taking a walk with his wife, they passed a young couple. The young wife was very unhappy with the marriage and openly spoke about the option of divorce. The Rabbi was happy that the fellow agreed to take a walk with his wife, for he frequently refused to do so.

But as the two couples passed, the fellow called out to the Rabbi, "The next time our wives want to take a walk, let them walk together. Then you and I can study together."

The Rabbi said to himself, "Oh no, he messed it up. He's certainly going to lose credit for agreeing to the walk. Now his wife will get angry with him."

Sure enough, fifteen minutes later they passed each other again. The Rabbi heard the wife berating her husband and telling him how awful he was.

The Rabbi suggested to his Rebbetzin, "Perhaps you can tell his wife to ask her husband, 'What can we talk about that will increase your willingness to take these walks?' Or perhaps you might tell the wife to say to her husband, 'I realize that you are only taking these walks to please me even though it is difficult for you. I appreciate your effort to make me happy.' "

Both the young husband and his wife were making a mistake. The husband was wrong for trying to get out of the walk that was so important to his wife, especially since he knew that his wife was unhappy in the marriage. Instead he should have done everything in his power to improve things. The wife erred by making the walks unpleasant. True, her distress is understandable. But it *would be wise for her to think strategically about how to make her husband want to take walks with her.*

❖ ❖ ❖

*M*y grandparents had an interesting custom. Each week after my grandfather recited Havdalah at the conclusion of Shabbos, they would each light one candle.

One Rabbi whom I told this to commented, "They've joined together in a partnership to bring light into their home. The new week begins right after Shabbos is over. They've created new light to illuminate the entire week. I would recommend this custom to couples who want to enhance their marriage."

Chapter Four

Outcome Thinking:
The Pattern of the Wise

- ∞ *Outcome thinking*

- ∞ *Ask yourself: "What is my goal? What do I need to say and do to achieve that goal?"*

- ∞ *Your own changes are likely to elicit changes in your spouse*

- ∞ *Motivating and influencing wisely*

- ∞ *Learn to become wiser from each experience*

OUTCOME THINKING

The Sages (*Tamid* 32) define a wise person as someone who sees the outcome. When you speak to someone, you have a choice of just saying whatever you feel
like saying, or you can think for a moment about what you wish
to accomplish with what you say. Since wisdom is seeing the
outcome of what you say or do, stupidity is just speaking and
acting without concern for the outcome. Master the pattern of
the wise. This is the path to a harmonious marriage. This pattern
will give you and your spouse a more joyous life.

Imagine asking someone to give you a job you desperately
need. You are very short on money, and the salary would enable
you to keep your house and feed your family. You ask for an
interview and are given fifteen minutes to state reasons why the
employer should hire you. You are told that you can say anything
you want during your interview. You will not be asked questions,
nor will you be told you are saying the wrong things. At the end
of the fifteen minutes you will be hired if you convince the boss
that you will do a good job. You are told only one thing about
the employer's policy. He will only hire you if he feels that you
will be beneficial to the company.

Imagine that someone who is an expert communicator comes
over to you and says, "I have written two scripts. Look them over.
I am not going to tell you which one to choose. Take them both

and follow the pattern that you feel will be in your best interest. If you choose the wrong pattern, you will not be given a job. I hope you make the right choice."

Script one: "I sure hope that you will give me a job. I like your place very much and think that I would enjoy myself here. I need the money and it's very important to me to get the job. If you fail to hire me, I will consider you evil and cruel. I will keep feeling this resentment and will wish you harm. I think that you should feel guilty and ashamed of yourself for not hiring me. I'm sure that you've done a lot of wrong things already in the past and this would be just another one to add to your list. How could you be so selfish? Now give me the job."

Script two: "I have researched your company's needs and feel that I can be very helpful to you. Based on my education and work experience, I will be able to help you increase your profits. I have much experience working with personnel similar to those who are working for you, and I feel confident that I can motivate your employees into a unified team. Let me show you my plans for creating an incentive program that will increase employee loyalty and raise your profits."

It is quite obvious that any normal person would choose script number two which tells the employer how he will benefit from hiring you. No one wants to hire someone who tries to bully him by making him feel guilty, or just talks about his own needs rather than about how he can be of service to the company. The second script is based on outcome thinking. The first script isn't.

In harmonious marriages of mutual love and respect, both the husband and wife speak to each other in ways that bring out their best. Unfortunately, there are couples who don't. It's amazing how many otherwise normal and intelligent people ask for things in their marriage using scripts similar to script one because they often forget to think about the outcome they really want. They become frustrated, resentful, or angry, and then they just say whatever comes to mind, provoking their spouse to respond in kind.

Take, for example, the person who asks his or her spouse to take care of something by saying, "You don't make good use of your time anyway, so go ahead and ..." This is not a very effective way to make a request. Thinking about the potential outcome of such a statement would instantly suggest that this approach needs editing.

Another example is saying, "I know you won't do this for me, but I'll ask you anyway ..." This won't be conducive for putting your spouse in his or her best state.

Make it a high priority to become a wise communicator. Think first about what you want. This is outcome thinking. Not only should you think about the specific thing you want, but you should also think about the emotional state you want your spouse to be in. Then you should say only those things that will make it more likely for you to get the outcome you want together with the goodwill of your spouse.

Keep asking yourself, "What do I want?" Don't think in terms of what you don't want but about what you do want. Then ask for it in a way that makes your spouse feel comfortable. Be specific and word your request positively.

When you have mastered outcome thinking, you will consistently speak with a pleasant tone of voice. You will refrain from saying anything that will sound like blaming or attacking. In marriage, besides motivating your spouse to stop or start doing something, you also want to maintain goodwill. So this needs to be an integral part of your thinking when you consider the outcome you want.

If yours is a marriage of mutual love and respect, you will be able to communicate to your spouse in a way that influences and motivates him or her to increase what you wish to be increased, and decrease or eliminate what distresses you.

Whether this is easy or difficult depends on a number of factors. If you and your spouse love each other, and your needs and wishes are in harmony, and you both have cheerful temperaments, and you both are experts at knowing what to say and what not to say, it will be easy.

It will be difficult, however, if you both wish that your spouse were different, if your needs and wishes consistently clash, and if you both are irritable, easy to anger, and hard to appease. It will be difficult if you don't learn from your mistakes and haven't a clue as to what makes each other tick.

Even in instances when you find it difficult to elicit the responses you would like, you still have a choice to make things worse or better. By thinking about the outcome you want, you might reach the conclusion that at this moment you don't know what to say or do. However, you will still know with certainty that some modes of communication will be counterproductive. In this situation, being wise means that you remain silent until you think of something beneficial to say. At times remaining silent will have a negative outcome. If so, you might ask for time to think the matter over. "I want to improve the situation. So I need a little quiet time until I can think of something that will be good for both of us."

Some people object to the concept of outcome thinking. "But isn't it important to be spontaneous?" they ask. Yes, I think it's wonderful to be spontaneous. But it's even more wonderful to live in an atmosphere of love and respect, peace and harmony. If you are married to someone who is your dream partner, you probably can afford to be spontaneous as long as you are kind and sensitive. But if you are married to someone whom you find challenging, and instead of overflowing with feelings of love and respect you frequently feel frustrated, resentful, or angry, it is shortsighted to be spontaneous.

The vast majority of married couples who cause each other escalating distress and pain don't really want to do so. They usually just react impulsively and don't work on gaining mastery over their responses. What they say can be perceived as an attack and can elicit a counterattack which leads to a verbal boxing match. Each volley of words tends to escalate the situation and cause even more pain. Both the husband and the wife lose out in the present and set up a negative pattern that is likely to repeat itself in the future. Thinking is free, so use your brain as much as you can.

Speaking without considering your spouse's potential reaction is foolish. Your power of speech is like a powerful tool. It can be used in a positive way — for healing, encouraging, motivating, and elevating. On the other hand, it can also be a tool of destruction. Speech can be like a weapon that must be used very carefully. Failure to be careful with speech is similar to being careless with a loaded weapon.

In December 1992, a man accidentally shot himself to death in Newton, North Carolina. When awakened by the sound of a ringing telephone beside his bed, he reached for the phone but instead grabbed a Smith and Wesson .38 Special, which discharged when he drew it to his ear. This type of incident is rare. Shooting off one's mouth in a way that causes oneself spiritual and emotional injury is much more common.

When you think with the outcome in mind, it is often best to be concise. The general rule is: "Omit unnecessary words." Feel the power of this statement. When you and your spouse are feeling distressed, the more words you say, the more likely it is that you will say things that would have been better left unsaid. Long speeches are appropriate when you are involved in an interesting conversation and both you and the person you are talking to are in positive states. But when you find that the more you say, the further away you are from getting what you want, be concise. Just say the words that are essential to convey your message in a manner that makes your spouse feel good about meeting your request.

To summarize: Outcome thinking is when you first clarify what goal or outcome you are looking for. Then you say something or take an action that seems most likely to help you reach the outcome you want.

If what you said or did hasn't produced the outcome you wanted, then say or do something else. Regardless of how many times you need to change the pattern, always keep the desired outcome in mind. We won't always get what we want. But those who fail to think of the desired outcome will cause both themselves and their spouse much needless frustration and anguish.

A couple that is totally motivated to upgrade the way they speak can ask an objective third party to observe them and point out ways that they can improve.

*M*y wife and I frequently got into vicious verbal battles. She would say things to me that were infuriating, and I took the bait, expressing my anger with vivid metaphors of the violent feelings I felt. This went on for years. We both kept thinking, "This marriage is so painful, why stay in it?"

We tended to avoid each other since our conversations easily slid downhill, each of us feeling that the fault was with the other. The pattern that bothered me most was that after she infuriated me, my wife would deny that she said anything wrong.

"I don't know why you become so angry! I didn't say anything that would distress a rational person. You have inner problems with anger and self-image and that is why you react so badly," my wife would say.

"When you deny your responsibility for getting me angry, I hate you," I would answer. "I have to hold myself back from acting out on the anger and rage that I am now feeling."

I would elaborate on how awful I felt my wife was. I would remind her of times she did similar things in the past, and point out her inconsistencies.

She, in turn, would tell me that I am narcissistic, selfish, miserly, uncaring, inconsistent, hypocritical, foolish, and insensitive. Then she would calm down and expect me to go on acting towards her as if nothing had happened. I would be so angry I only wanted to talk about her faults.

I had heard about outcome thinking before, but to me it was some abstract idea that sounded nice, but didn't really have too much relevance for my life.

Then someone who had spoken to me about outcome thinking finally gave me an ultimatum. "You are an intelligent person," he said to me, "but you continuously communicate in a dumb way. You just blame your wife for your anger. You keep listing her faults. You don't meet her emotional and financial needs to the extent that you *could. You feel resentful a good part of the time. Even though you are capable of communicating with her wisely, you don't do it very often. Yet, with other people, you are wonderful. You know how to be charming. You know how to elicit the responses you wish. While I vote for you to stay married to your wife and consistently focus on the outcomes you want and speak accordingly, if you refuse to follow through on this, get divorced, because you are torturing each other."*

This made sense to me. I decided that regardless of how my wife speaks to me, I would stop blaming her for my anger. I would take total responsibility for my own state and would use all my energy to control myself. Then I would speak only with outcome thinking in mind. I would speak concisely and to the point. I would ask my wife to please not speak to me in ways that cause me pain. I would not expect her to remember to do this. Rather, I would point out any patterns of speech, tones of voice, and facial expressions that distress me. I wouldn't complain about them. But I would say to her, "I find it easier to understand you when you express your wish in a sentence or two." Or, "I find this unhelpful. Please speak in a more pleasant tone of voice." Or, "I love your smile. Would you please smile when you need to point out a mistake to me."

It was amazing! As soon as I stopped giving long angry speeches about how awful my wife was and how angry she was making me, she became much more pleasant and reasonable. She explained to me that she had been afraid of my anger, and therefore felt she had to deny any responsibility because she was afraid that I would become angrier if she acknowledged her part in getting me angry. Now that I express my wants in outcome wording, she is happy to comply with my requests.

From the wife's point of view, this is what occurred:

I find the change in my husband and our marriage remarkable. I didn't understand what I said or did that set him off so intensely. Many times his anger was way out of proportion to anything that I said. He kept telling me that he was a compassionate person, and I had nothing to be afraid of. But I didn't believe him. His anger was so strong that I felt I couldn't express myself. He kept telling me that I could disagree with anything he said. But when I disagreed with him, he got angry with me. When he wanted me to speak differently, he would go on for a long time about how awful I was, and I felt that nothing I could do would make a difference.

Once my husband accepted the idea that he would first clarify the desired outcome and actually take those steps that could achieve it, he became a totally new person. He was interesting and funny, and I enjoyed his company. He stopped blaming me for my mistakes and if he took exception to what I said, he just told me that what I was saying wasn't helpful.

When I said that I, too, wanted to communicate with outcome thinking in mind, he became much more open to explaining in specific terms how the process worked. He was totally open to listening to what I had to say. I now see that he doesn't need me to always agree with him. I learned to express myself clearly and without blaming him. I realize now that denying that I was causing him pain drove him up a wall. My husband is now wonderful to me and I attribute it all to the fact that we both consistently speak with the outcome in mind.

ASK YOURSELF: "WHAT IS MY GOAL? WHAT DO I NEED TO SAY AND DO TO ACHIEVE THAT GOAL?"

Imagine that you are walking down the street, and someone

comes running over to you and breathlessly asks, "How do you get there?"

"Where?" you ask.

"I don't know," the person replies.

Most likely you would look at such a person as being a bit strange. The only way to get somewhere is to know where you are going. Then you can either figure out by yourself how to get there or you can ask someone else to help you.

The same applies in asking for what you want. First you need to clarify for yourself, "What exactly do I want?" The next step is: "Word what you say in a way that is conducive to getting what you want." This might seem obvious, but many people make requests in ways that are almost guaranteed to fail.

Take, for example, statements that begin with, "You should have ..." Beginning a sentence to your spouse with these three words is usually not helpful. It is preferable to say, "I would appreciate it if next time ..." The same applies to asking rhetorical questions such as, "Why didn't you ...?" or, "Why did you ...?" If you are really looking for an answer, these can be valid questions. If you really mean to say, "You made a mistake," why don't you say, "I would appreciate it if next time ..."? (This is a good example of what the Sages mean when they say a person finds fault with what he himself does wrong.)

In order to put outcome thinking into action, keep asking yourself, "What is my goal?" Then ask yourself, "What do I need to say and do to achieve that goal?" Then say it positively, concisely, and gently.

Be specific when you ask for your goal. Suppose you want someone to give you money. You approach the person and ask him, "Could I please have some money?" He might give you a few pennies and he has given you what you requested. But if you want to borrow a thousand dollars from someone, it makes sense to ask for the specific amount that you want.

In marriage, a husband or wife will often say, "Stop treating me the way you do." What exactly does this mean? What exactly should the person stop saying or doing?

When you speak without your goal in mind, you are likely to make many mistakes. We can't always know in advance the exact outcome of what we will say or do. Only a prophet can know that, but very often if we would give our goal a few seconds of thought, we would know what isn't wise to say or do. Without thinking of our goal and the best way to reach it, we will create needless quarrels and arguments and cause pain and distress. When you keep your goal in mind, you will be able to gauge if what you are saying or doing is helping you reach your goal. Focusing on your goal will enable you to make wiser choices in every area of your life, and especially in marriage.

There is a question that is known as "The Miracle Question." "Suppose a miracle happened and your marriage would be wonderful. How would you know that things are different?" The benefit of this question is that it creates an image and vision of what the goal will be like when it is achieved. Then you can ask yourself, "What small step can I take now to begin to make this picture my reality?"

My life was proceeding at a mediocre pace. I wasn't very happy, but I wasn't very sad. The same could have been said about my marriage, "It's not extremely happy, but it's not too bad."

What they call "middle-age crisis," finally happened to me. I woke up one day to the fact that I was getting older and my life was slipping away. I needed to find something that would give my life more vitality and energy. I knew that the answer wouldn't be outside myself, but rather within. The more introspective I became, the worse I felt. I became painfully aware of my many faults, and I felt guilty that I wasn't treating my wife and children the way I should.

Then one day, I met an old friend whom I hadn't seen for many years. He seemed totally alive and energized. Externally his life wasn't that much different from mine, but, qualitatively, he had achieved meaning in his life. He seemed more joyous and motivated than our other friends. I asked him, "Is there a specific plan, approach, or tool that helps you achieve this quality of life?"

"I'll share something with you that has made a major impact on my life," he answered. "Wisdom is seeing the outcome. I keep making goals for myself. I consider this to be a three-part process. First, I write down a mission statement for myself, a general direction in which I want my life to go. Second, I regularly write down goals for myself that are consistent with this direction. Some goals, I end up dropping. But the goals I have reached have given my life a strong sense of meaning. The goals drive me and I feel motivated to reach them.

"Third, I keep asking myself the question, 'What outcome do I want now?' This helps me in Torah matters. It has enhanced my marriage. It has made interacting with my children much better than before, and has helped me emotionally and financially."

I thanked my friend profusely. I was anxious to put the idea of outcome questions into practice immediately. As soon as I came home, I applied it during the very first conversation I had with my wife. Wanting to make her feel good became the automatic indicator of what should or should not be said.

I now consider it a great mitzvah to share this lesson with others: One, write a mission statement. Two, keep writing goals for yourself. Three, ask yourself consistently, "What outcome do I want now?"

My wife would constantly complain, "You don't care." Whenever I didn't do something, she'd say, "You don't care. If you cared, you would have done it." If I ever said something she didn't like, she'd say, "You don't care about my feelings." If I spilled something on the floor, I would hear, "You don't care about the extra work you are making for me."

I would argue and say, "That's not right. I do care." Each time, however, my wife wouldn't believe me.

"But I do so many things for you," I would say.

"That's true. But if you really cared, you wouldn't do or say anything that is an expression of not caring."

Hearing, "You don't care" so many times got me angry. I finally challenged my wife, "Would you prefer that I care or would you really want me not to care?"

"What kind of question is that?" she answered. "Of course, I want you to care."

"Then it is a lot wiser to comment on everything I do that you like. You might say, 'That's wonderful. I see that you care.' This way you will make both of us feel better and help me reinforce the behaviors you want me to repeat."

"How can I say that?" she argued. "When you don't make me happy, I see that you don't care. It's obvious and I'm not going to deny reality."

"Looking objectively at my behavior, you will have to admit that I do many things that you like. I agree with you that I make mistakes. So if you only tell me that I don't care, you are making a greater error by ignoring my caring words and actions."

"You have a point there," she conceded.

"Let's experiment," I said. "For the next two weeks, just mention caring in reference to the caring messages I give through my words and actions. Feel free to point out any mistakes I make or anything I say or do that bothers you. But don't say, 'You don't care.'" Fortunately, my wife agreed to try this. It's worked fantastically well for both of us.

*A*t a business meeting in our house with a few people present, someone cited a statement from the Rambam. My husband immediately said, "In a used book store, I found a fascinating book called 'The Jewish Face,' published in 1948." He showed everyone the portrait of the Rambam that is in that book. Then my husband glanced through the book and came across a portrait of Rashi. "Let me read you the quotation from Rashi that is cited here. In a letter to a community seeking a decision in communal quarrels, Rashi wrote:

" 'I cannot fulfill your request to dissolve the ban, for I do not wish to set myself up as a superior judge; were I with you, I would join you in dissolving it, but who am I to claim authority in other localities? As for yourselves, however, set your hearts on establishing peace in your midst. Other communities around you have been hit hard and been dispersed; peace amongst yourselves will save you from a similar fate, as our Sages taught, "Great is peace which is the heritage of the righteous." And may He Whose Name and blessing is peace, give you peace.' "

My husband always complains that I tend to divert attention from the topic at hand and here he read the words of Rashi that had absolutely no connection with the meeting. I was about to say, "If I would interrupt a business meeting by reading something I found interesting, you would criticize me and tell me to stay on the topic and here you go doing the same thing yourself."

However, I was working on upgrading my level of communication, so I caught myself and what I did say privately to my husband was, "I am so glad that you read those beautiful words of Rashi. I tend to bring up subjects that come to my mind even though they don't have a direct connection with what we are speaking about. Now that you did the same, I hope you will be more accepting of me when I do it."

When you speak to someone, the meaning of what you are saying is dependent on the way the person to whom you are speaking understands it. Let's say you just invented a new language. Only you understand what you are saying. Then you meet someone and begin saying the most beautiful thoughts in your own language. What is the reality of what you just said? For you, these are beautiful thoughts. But for someone else, you said something that is totally meaningless. What is the reality? Since in communication the point is to get the listener to understand the way you mean it, you as a communicator need to use different words that have a greater possibility of being understood.

If you use certain words to express yourself and you think that those words express something positive, but the person you say them to understands them to be offensive, you have been offensive. The first time you said them you might not have realized that this person found them offensive. But after you do realize it, you as a communicator need to be careful not to use those words again.

So the formula to follow in marriage is: If what you said caused your spouse pain, then what you have said was painful even if that wasn't your intention. Some people tend to argue, "I don't understand why what I said caused you pain. It would be all right with me if someone spoke to me that way." This is not a valid argument. If your husband or wife finds a pattern distressing, speak with a different pattern.

Telling your spouse what you think he or she "really means" when it is unappreciated, is just a source of irritation. There are times when telling someone your interpretation of what he or she really means is highly appreciated. This occurs when the response to your interpretation is, "It's amazing how you know me even better than I know myself. That was so perceptive of you." If this is the usual response you get, keep it up. But if you see that your spouse is annoyed by your interpretation of what he or she said, avoid giving it.

The essence of the message that you send will depend on how you say it. When you make a request of your spouse, speaking in a friendly voice increases cooperation. Speaking in an unfriendly voice increases resentment, stubbornness, and resistance.

If you aren't certain how to say what you want to say in a way that is acceptable, ask your husband or wife, "How would you prefer that I express my message?" He or she might say, "It's obvious." Then calmly say, "It's not obvious to me, so I would appreciate it if you could tell me how you would like me to speak to you." If your regular way of expressing a message hasn't proved successful, think about a unique approach. When you keep your goal in mind, you might discover an approach you haven't used before. It might be an approach that someone used with you, one that you read about in an entirely different context, or some idea that another person shared with you about how someone got a message across to them. And you might be able to ask others for unique ways to communicate effectively without telling them exactly why you need to know.

Keep asking yourself, "What is the message that I want to give?" Then ask yourself, "What is the message that was received?"

If you thought that you were communicating respect, love, appreciation, or praise, and your spouse feels you were being condescending, critical, or offensive, accept the interpretation of your spouse. You can say, "I apologize. I didn't realize that this is the way it would sound."

When you apologize for the way you said something, be careful not to say it in a way that will be a further put-down. For example, "Hardly anyone else would take this the way you did; I didn't realize that you were so unusually sensitive." This is likely to be considered negative, not positive.

Remember this general rule: If your spouse found the way that you expressed yourself distressing, you spoke or asked the wrong way. Each individual person is the most authoritative expert on what causes him pain. If you feel that your spouse felt pain only because he or she misunderstood your intentions, then explain that you didn't mean to cause pain. But don't blame your spouse for feeling the way he or she did.

As an exercise, for the next week observe the way you speak to your spouse. Listen to your choice of words. Be aware of your tone of voice. Ask yourself, "Am I expressing respect, kindness, caring, understanding in such a way that it is appreciated? If I were totally motivated to speak to my spouse as a child of the Creator and Sustainer of the universe, how would I speak differently?"

I consider my husband to be much more sensitive than the average man. My father and brothers were never hurt by the way I spoke to them. My husband frequently is. I don't like to trouble him for things, so when I need his help for something, I usually apologize and explain why I am asking him to do what I want him to do. For his part, he doesn't like the apologies. He often takes them as attacks.

For example, he didn't take out the garbage when he said he would. I then said to him the next day, "Since you don't notice when the garbage is full and aren't concerned enough with how this affects me, I am reminding you to take it out." To me this seemed that I was explaining why I was asking him again. But my husband responded, "I'll gladly take out the garbage. But I don't like the way you attacked me."

"I didn't attack you," I said. "I don't think that a person with a healthy self-image would consider this an attack."

"There you go again," he said. "You are attacking my self-image."

"No, I'm not," I said. "I just want you to have more self-esteem."

It was pointed out to me that I need to be more concise when I make my requests. I needn't and shouldn't comment on my husband's self-image when all I want is for him to take care of some task that he readily agrees to do. I used to blame my husband for being too sensitive and this made the situation worse. Now I am aware that if what I say distresses my husband, I will just say a short, "I'm sorry," and I will make my request in a few positive words. This has helped us avoid many potential quarrels and our home is much more peaceful.

YOUR OWN CHANGES ARE LIKELY TO ELICIT CHANGES IN YOUR SPOUSE

There are many instances when a direct attempt to change your spouse will not be successful. He or she might resent the approach, or it might be that he or she thinks any problems in the marriage are totally your fault. Even if you get other people to agree that your spouse needs to make changes, your spouse will deny it.

When your spouse isn't open to making changes, outcome thinking in such situations means that you refrain from trying to tell your husband or wife to change. By changing yourself, however, you are more likely to change the way your spouse responds to you. If you used to get angry over your spouse's not being the way you wish him or her to be and now you are more accepting, your spouse will probably try to make you happier since you are more pleasant.

A social worker who was highly successful with individuals, couples, and families, had this to say, "Since relationships are made up of predictable, repetitive, action-reaction patterns that occur over time, even when only one partner is willing to work on solving the family problems, there is much you can do."

If you are dissatisfied with the way your spouse acts towards you, speak and act in the best possible way yourself. By doing so, you will be changing the previous action-reaction pattern. Your positive moves are likely to create a more positive reaction on the part of your spouse.

When you interact with your spouse, you are not just an objective observer, watching from a distance. Rather, everything about you — what you say and do, your tone of voice, the look on your face, and your body language — all have an effect on your spouse. If you would like your spouse to make positive changes, increase your self-awareness.

> I have a strong need for neatness and order. That's how I was raised and that's how I like my own house to be. My wife and I have young children and the floor is always a mess with toys and papers. I was experiencing difficult financial pressure. Unfortunately, I took this out on my wife when I came home in the evening.
>
> The moment I walked into the house, I would ask, "Why couldn't you have cleaned up the house? Why didn't the children put away their toys? Why don't you train the children to be neater and more responsible?"
>
> One day as I was about to open the front door, my wife pushed the door closed and said firmly, "I'm not going to let you into the house unless you pledge not to ask any, 'Why?' questions for three full days." I agreed. I didn't really have too much of a choice.
>
> It took a lot of self-discipline on my part to refrain from my usual litany of "Why?" questions. I was forced to channel my frustration into a more positive direction. When I came home and saw a mess, I took a broom and swept the house myself.
>
> Previously, I repeatedly scolded my wife to train the children to clean up after themselves. She argued that it took too much of her time and energy to try to get them to do things they didn't like to do, and she was just too exhausted to argue with them.
>
> For three whole days I kept my pledge and didn't ask, "Why?" even once. When I came home on the fourth day, it was amazing. The house was as neat as could be. I don't know exactly how she did it, whether she got the children to help or whether she did it herself, but my own changes must have motivated hers.

*M*y mother was a bit compulsive and she spent much time and energy making certain that our house was spotless. I grew up with the values of neatness, orderliness, and cleanliness being constantly emphasized.

When I had my own house, I followed her example, and I, too, spent more time and energy on cleaning my house than my friends did.

I would scold my husband if he made a mess, scratched the furniture, or dropped crumbs on the floor.

One day my husband blew up at me and said, "You care more about your furniture than you do about people."

I yelled back at him, "You are ungrateful for all the work I do! How can you be so insensitive?"

But deep in my heart, I knew that he was right. Order and cleanliness were higher on my list of priorities than the feelings of others. While I didn't want to admit to my husband that his criticism was valid, I made a resolution to make my husband's feelings my top priority. The ironic thing is that after I did this, he was more careful than before not to cause me any extra work.

❖ ❖ ❖

*M*y husband is very outgoing and sociable. He has many friends and is well liked. His sense of humor, however, has caused me much discomfort.

When we were first married, I kept asking him not to make stupid jokes. He, however, insisted that other people enjoyed them. I disagreed.

"Others often laugh just to be polite," I argued. His response was, "I've been told over and over again how much other people enjoy my company because of my sense of humor. I never make fun of other people, and you are the only one I've ever met who told me that my jokes are inappropriate."

I made it a point to observe the reactions of others when my husband cracked his corny jokes. I had to agree with him that most people did enjoy them. He has a harmless chutzpah that others appreciate. Many wish that they had the emotional courage to express whatever was on their minds the way he did.

I came to the conclusion that we would only get into painful arguments that would be lose-lose if I kept insisting that he stop joking the way he did. I made a decision to accept his sense of humor. I still cringe every once in a while. But for shalom bayis, I don't make an issue about the matter and now my husband's jokes bother me less.

When my husband saw that I was more accepting of his joking, he reciprocated by being more careful not to say things that I would find offensive or inappropriate. He even saved his corniest jokes for when I wasn't present.

MOTIVATING AND INFLUENCING WISELY

"There are two basic approaches to take when you see someone doing something wrong. One is to speak harshly to the person and correct him. But this approach does not help people know how they should behave and how they can correct what they did wrong.

"The approach of the wise is to show people how they can correct what they did wrong. This is a healing approach and the only words that are said are those conducive to healing" (Vilna Gaon; *Mishlei* 12:18).

Those who have mastered the art of motivating and influencing others wisely will have a positive influence on the lives of many people. Some people see that others excel at this and assume that it's a natural talent for them. But the reality is that this is a skill that can be learned.

When you have an important message for your spouse because you feel he or she has a major need for improvement in some important area, speak with calm assurance. Since you might be upset, this can take an act of will. But the more important the issue is for you, the more you want to ensure that your message will be well received. Speaking with calm assurance increases the possibility of your being heard more objectively.

Someone who just wants to vent frustration will speak in the tone of voice that comes automatically. When someone is upset, that distress will come through as anger and resentment and may relieve the speaker. But what about the receiver of the message? How will he or she react? The speaker is working against his or her own best interests by not speaking in a tone of voice that elicits either understanding or compassion on the part of the listener.

Many people say, "When he/she sees how upset I am, he/she will change." In reality this usually doesn't work that way. The person hearing the message feels attacked. When someone feels attacked, the response is either counterattack or being defensive. Change is much more likely to occur when you speak in a way that brings out positive feelings on the part of the listener.

A major part of motivating and influencing wisely is to know how *not* to try to motivate. Threats, screaming, guilt trips, giving authoritarian orders, and ultimatums might all have their place in extreme situations, but day in, day out, when you need to motivate or influence your spouse, do so in a manner that your spouse will find pleasant.

There are two ways to open a closed door. One is to break it down with force. This opens the door, but at a cost. The other way is to use a key or to press the right buttons on a coded lock. Getting another person to listen to you is similar to this.

Nagging leads to withdrawing. Nagging can also lead to a counterattack. With nagging you might even get the other person to take action, but this might cause resentment. Someone who nags will think he/she has a logical objection, "If I don't nag, how will I get results?" This question implies that when one resorts to nagging, the choices are between nagging and not getting the thing you are nagging about resolved. However, anyone familiar with negotiation and sales will tell you that there are other approaches. The basic principle behind nagging is: If I cause irritation by nagging, eventually the person being nagged would prefer to take action rather than continue being nagged.

One question someone who tends to nag can ask himself is, "When have I had results without nagging?" If a nagger responds, "Never," does he or she really mean to say that he or she *never* got a response without nagging? That is obviously inaccurate. If a wife says to her hungry husband, "Dinner is on the table," her husband surely came to eat. If a husband said to his wife, "I put the money on the table, for the thing you wanted to buy," there must have been some time when the wife went to get it. Why? Because in both these instances each spouse did not need nagging to be motivated.

When someone is angry, he or she must be especially careful of what he or she says or doesn't say. For example, when some people are angry with their spouse, they might accuse their spouse of being obnoxious, selfish, inconsiderate, or stupid. But throwing these words at one's spouse won't improve the situation. When a person hears these words he or she is not going to be motivated to act pleasantly, considerately, and intelligently towards the spouse.

If you are tempted to use sarcasm, ask yourself, "How do I think my spouse will react?" In the vast majority of situations, it might help to let off steam but at the price of provoking more anger or resentment. If you want to say something that will motivate and influence the other person to act better towards you, sarcasm is almost guaranteed not to work.

How do you motivate someone? Show him or her the benefit of doing what you are asking for. Express your appreciation and gratitude. The more someone likes you, the more readily they will do what you wish. The more pleasantly you speak, the greater chance that you will be heard.

An important rule of human nature is: "Most people are willing to help those in trouble when asked in the right way." Another important rule is: "People become resentful if they feel they are being treated without respect and are being taken for granted." So when you ask, express your need, but do it respectfully and gratefully.

Some husbands and wives are much more cheerful, friendly, kind, and considerate around other people than when they are at home. One option that many spouses use is to act like a lawyer in court. They try to point out to their spouse that he or she is being inconsistent. But this will usually just make him or her defensive and is not conducive to improving the behavior at home. A more effective approach is to gently tell your spouse that you would love it if the same behavior and way of speaking would be applied towards you. You might ask, "What can I say or do that will motivate you to treat me the way you treat your relatives, friends, customers, students, and strangers?"

Some people are afraid of using techniques and specific approaches to motivate and influence their spouse, because this might be viewed as being manipulative. Actually, anything you say or do to get someone to do something for you can be called manipulative. We have no choice in life. If you are going to live among other people, you will need to ask them to do or not do things. Asking directly in a regular tone of voice is a form of manipulation, but there's nothing wrong with it. Getting angry at someone is manipulation. Screaming and yelling is manipulation. Making a serious face, or a hurt one, or scowling are all forms of manipulation. Even a sincere smile is another form. So it's not a question of manipulating another person, but how one does it, and if it's in everyone's mutual best interests.

You can get more done with an olive branch than with a hammer. Hitting someone over the head with a hammer can be quite powerful and will motivate the person to do what you are asking, but the legal, spiritual, and emotional repercussions can be disastrous. It's not worth it. The same applies to motivating your spouse. Peaceful methods create a warmer and healthier home than unpleasant and distressful strategies and approaches. The olive branch approach is more tasteful, dignified, and elegant, and has greater long-term benefits.

Some people have a tendency to do the following: When they see that the person they are speaking to is not agreeing with them, they go on and on talking in ways that do not achieve their goal. Then they use examples, stories, metaphors, and parables to try to get the other person to agree with them. To be successful you need to select your examples, stories, metaphors, and parables as tools so the other person will gain greater understanding, more empathy, and an increased openness to your position. If, however, the other person just finds them boring or a waste of time, save them for people who find them entertaining or enlightening. Don't bring them up when you are trying to get the other person to agree with you. A filibuster when important issues are involved can be helpful in a senate or parliament, but not in a marriage. You need to be sensitive to your audience. And in marriage that audience is your spouse.

"There is nothing that can be done to change this person." This is not a true statement. No one on the planet knows everything there is to know about changing people. Each person is different and everyone has factors that would motivate him. Maybe you can't influence and motivate this person now, but someone else might know what to say or do. Therefore, even though at this moment you don't have the right answer, you might find it later. Also, we all change spontaneously in various degrees. As time passes, perhaps this person will change in ways that will make it much easier for you to have better interactions. If you believe that your spouse won't change, you won't notice small changes in the right direction. And this belief will prevent you from searching for the strategy that could work.

If you find it difficult to share your thoughts with your spouse, perhaps you can express yourself in a letter. Be careful to edit it, however, before sending it. Know your goal, then reread your letter imagining that your spouse is reading it. What effect do you think it will have on him or her and is this the effect that you really want?

Find out from your spouse, "When I feel a need to motivate you to do or stop doing something, what approaches do you find acceptable?" Even this question will be better tolerated by some people than by others.

There is one highly effective approach for motivating and influencing: First ask: "Between one and ten, where are you now?" Ten is "totally motivated," one is "not motivated." Then you can ask, "What would make it a ten?" Often the other party will tell you what he or she needs.

Learn from past successes. Ask yourself, "When has my spouse felt motivated to do similar things in the past? What exactly were the key factors that were useful?"

A story about an internationally famous lawyer made a big impression on me and has helped me avoid many quarrels with my husband. This lawyer's powerful arguments won him many cases in court, but his first wife couldn't tolerate his arguments at home and they were divorced.

He blamed his wife for the divorce and, without changing himself, married someone else. His first day back at work after the wedding, he was ready to go home. But he said to himself, "My first wife always insisted that I come home on time. She gave me a rough time when I was late, which was quite frequently. I refuse to be bossed around by my wife. I will show my present wife that I can come home any time I wish." He therefore purposely came home an hour after he said he would.

He was waiting for an argument when he entered the house. But his new wife said cheerfully, "I'm so happy to see you. I'll warm up your food. It got cold since I first put it on the table."

The next day, as he was about to go home, he said to himself, "She was probably angry at me yesterday that I came home late. She just controlled herself from saying anything. But I want to teach her a lesson that I can arrive home whenever I feel like it. So I'll purposely come home an hour late this evening again."

For the second time in a row, his wife greeted him cheerfully when he came home and expressed her joy at seeing him. She again told him that she would immediately warm up his supper.

"Aren't you angry that I'm late twice in a row?" he asked her.

"Not at all," she said sincerely. "I am happy to see you whenever you come home. You are an adult and can decide for yourself when you wish to come home." The lawyer related that after this he never again purposely came home late and he would do all he could to be home when he said he would.

This story hit home. My husband tends to come home late and I frequently berate him for doing so. I decided to change my approach. The next time he came home late, which was the day after I heard the story, I greeted him with a cheery, "Baruch Hashem, you have arrived. I am so happy to see you."

My husband was waiting for the rest of the speech and he braced himself. But that was it. I didn't say anything else. I continued to greet him cheerfully each day when he entered the house. After about ten times he told me, "I appreciate your greetings so much that I can't wait to come home." He has now made it a habit to be on time unless an emergency comes up.

❖ ❖ ❖

I was a nag and have to admit that the way I used to speak to my husband was highly distressing to him. But, it was his own fault, of course. All of us who nag know this to be 100 percent the absolute truth. If anyone tells us that we can speak differently, we react, "I tried everything already. Nothing works but nagging. It's impossible to speak pleasantly when you have to repeat yourself." I was a firm believer in this basic principle of human nature.

Someone told me that there are many approaches to motivation and influence that I never heard of, so it was impossible for me to have "tried everything." This person told me that she has seen positive results with wives who follow the principle, "Repeat whatever you need to say in a tone of voice that your husband will find pleasant. Do this regardless of how many times you need to repeat yourself."

"But that's impossible," I argued.

"Difficult, yes. Impossible, no," she responded. "You need to be totally committed to do this. The results are powerful so you will find the laws of operant conditioning working for you instead of against you."

"But I know my husband. It won't make any difference how I ask him to do things," I insisted.

"Experiment. You have nothing to lose. What you're doing now isn't working. Force yourself to repeat your requests as pleasantly the tenth time as the first time. You might even come up with some creative lines that are effective."

The next time I asked my husband to do something and he didn't jump to do it right away, I said to myself, "Experiment time."

"Could you please call the principal of our son's school?" I said in a pleasant voice.

"Sure, soon," my husband said.

Ten minutes later, he still hadn't called.

"Could you please call the principal of our son's school. It's important," I said in a pleasant tone of voice. As a matter of fact, my voice was more pleasant now than before since I had ten minutes to mentally rehearse.

After the fifth time I asked softly and sweetly, the response I heard was a faraway, "Of course, dear, soon."

I then said, "It's okay. If you don't feel comfortable making the call, I'll do it myself."

"Please don't," my husband said, rushing to the telephone. "I'll take care of it right now." Speaking softly and sweetly even when you're repeating yourself pays off.

LEARN TO BECOME WISER FROM EACH EXPERIENCE

"The essence of wisdom is to have a full grasp of the entire reality of a matter. A wise counselor is someone who has the wisdom to know the probable consequences of a particular course of action. Therefore, a person with experience is wise in the area of his experience. Since he has seen the outcome of his actions, he has personal knowledge of which actions produce positive outcomes and which produce negative outcomes. Internalizing the knowledge you have obtained from your experience will earn you the title, 'a wise person'" (Rabbi Simchah Zissel Ziv; *Chochmah U'Mussar*, vol. 1, pp. 63-64).

The way to become an expert at outcome thinking is to be aware of the actual outcome of what you say and do. Every time you interact with your husband or wife, you have the ability to learn more about his or her likes and dislikes. Observe your spouse's reactions to your various tones of voice and the contents of what you say.

If what you are doing isn't working, do something else. This basic rule seems obvious, but it is human nature to do the opposite. Most people keep doing what they are familiar with whether it works or not. Logically, it does not sound like a path that most people would choose to follow. It surely isn't wise to keep repeating a pattern that doesn't work, all the while hoping that somehow after five, ten, fifteen, twenty or more years that pattern will now start working.

If a pattern does not get you your outcome goal, change the pattern.

Whenever you make a mistake, view it as a learning experience. The person who just blames his or her spouse for reacting the way he or she does, fails to become wiser from what happened. Be an objective observer and let trial and error be your teacher. While no human being is infallible, eventually you will gain mastery over this most valuable skill.

If you don't like your situation and you don't make any changes, realize that the status quo is your own choice. There is a saying, "If you keep doing what you've always been doing, you'll keep getting what you've always been getting." What you need to say or do in a given situation cannot always be chosen in advance. Rather you need to tailor your response to the specific needs of the moment. You will need to think, and many times you will need to think quickly, but with more experience you will make the right moves more spontaneously.

My wife doesn't like to worry me. She consistently avoids telling me bad news. I kept telling her that I am a rational adult and can handle life's difficulties, but she still doesn't tell me about anything that went wrong.

One day I received a call from my wife at the office. "Our son is in the hospital for stitches," she told me. "But don't worry, it's nothing serious. He's all right."

I got into a panic. If my wife already told me before I came home that our son had been hurt, it might mean he is in critical condition. I had a few very important meet-

ings scheduled for that day, and I immediately canceled all of them.

I was too nervous to drive myself, so I called a taxi to take me to the hospital and I told him, "It's an emergency. Please drive as fast as you can. My son might be in critical condition." When I got to the hospital, they didn't have my son listed as a patient. I was in a state of shock. I feared that my son was no longer alive.

A doctor saw the look on my face and came over to help me. "I think my son has died," I stammered.

"Let me check it out," he said compassionately.

A few minutes later, he came back with a smile on his face. "Your son was here with a minor cut. He needed only three stitches, and compared to what I see here every day, it's nothing at all."

I felt the blood coming back to my face and I could breathe again. When I told my wife what had happened, she agreed that she would be more open with me from then on. At times this might be painful, but it's better than causing pain over nothing.

I was going on a trip and would stay for a few days at someone's home, so I wanted to bring my hosts a gift. The trip was a last-minute decision, and I was in a big rush. I went to a large department store and stopped at the leather-goods section. The salesperson in charge showed me a couple of items, but I wasn't certain which I should buy. First I called my mother who lives in a different state, but she wasn't home. Then I called my married sister for some ideas, and ended up buying the item she suggested.

When I came home, I told my wife what I had bought. She said, "Why did you buy that?" in a challenging tone of voice.

My first feeling was, "Don't I have good enough judgment to buy a present myself?"

Then, looking for support for my position, I said, "That's what my sister told me to buy."

"Why didn't you call me?" my wife said, feeling hurt.

I told her the truth. "I probably should have. I didn't think of it."

Thinking this over later, I realized that I'd made a number of mistakes. I should have called my wife first. If I did ask my mother or sister, I should not have mentioned it. If my wife was critical of my purchase, I should have accepted the fact that each person has his own unique taste. This incident taught me a number of valuable lessons for the future.

Fortunately, my wife's grandfather always told her to live by the rule, "Never go to sleep being angry at your husband." This rule has helped us resolve a number of sticky situations, including this one.

Chapter Five

Understanding Your Spouse

∽ *Learn to understand your spouse's unique reactions*

∽ *See things from your spouse's point of view: to do chesed, to prevent distress and pain, and to avoid quarrels*

∽ *Listen to understand*

∽ *Ask the right questions*

∽ *Personality differences make a major difference*

∽ *Role reversal*

∽ *Make it easier for your spouse to understand you*

LEARN TO UNDERSTAND YOUR SPOUSE'S
UNIQUE REACTIONS

One of the great mussar personalities of the generation preceding the Second World War, Rabbi Avraham Grodzinsky, *mashgiach* of Slobodka Yeshivah, elaborated on the theme that the only way to fulfill the mitzvah of interacting with another person with the love and care that the Torah obligates is to know this individual's unique wants, needs, and desires. Even if someone wants something that you don't have a need for, your obligation to do acts of kindness obligates you to understand this person and his unique reactions. When you first meet someone, it is impossible to know his exact needs. Only after daily interactions with someone will you gain the knowledge of how to treat this person. This applies to everyone we encounter. All the more so do we need to know the individuality of the person to whom we are married. Men and women have different natures and different needs. The Torah obligation is to understand what they are and only by this means can one love and respect one's spouse properly (*Toras Avraham,* pp. 399-401).

It is helpful to know generalities about the differences in needs, patterns, and reactions of men and women. A key benefit is that you will be more accepting towards your husband or wife when they act in ways not like you but typical for them. But always keep in mind that the only one whose needs, patterns, and reactions really count in your life are that of the individual to whom you are married.

The person you married is not your father, mother, brother, sister, or any other person you ever met in your life. This person is uniquely himself or herself. Moreover, every time you speak to this person, he or she is how they are at this very moment. They are not exactly who they were at any moment in the past, or how they will be in the future. So you will always be talking to this unique person as they are at this very moment.

Since each individual on the planet is unique and different, no book can tell you exactly how to act with a specific person. You are unique and your spouse is unique. When you hear general ideas about marriage, realize that they could be true for many people, but whether or not they are true for you will be dependent on your unique personality and that of your spouse. So how can you learn to interact at the most optimum level with the individual to whom you are married? He or she will teach you if you keep your eyes and ears open. Learn from every interaction which words and actions need to be increased and which need to be decreased or eliminated.

People differ greatly in many ways. Take, for instance, the need for space and boundaries. Some people have a strong need to share their experiences and feelings. Others have a great need for privacy. For example, asking your spouse, "Where are you going?" can be viewed as both a normal question and an expression of concern. Yet others, however, have a great need for independence and freedom and consider this a controlling question. It depends on the personalities of both people, their entire relationship, and the exact wording and tone of voice in which questions are asked.

Someone who grew up in a happy family, where both the father and mother cared deeply about each other and in which each of their children was treasured, has a different emotional history than someone who grew up in a family torn with strife, where anger, quarrels, and insults were a daily occurrence. Frustration and rage left over from childhood may affect an individual's present level of frustration and anger. On the other hand, someone who grew up in a cheerful home where everyone constantly spoke with love and respect to each other might experience greater pain with a minor quarrel than someone for whom this was a frequent occurrence.

For some individuals marriage is an escape from what was an intolerable situation, while for others it is a joyous entering into the next stage of development. Some people grew up in large families, others in small families, and some were only children. Some people grew up with illness and financial difficulties, while others grew up with good health and financial prosperity. All these are factors that will affect one's reactions. What is important for you to know is how you and your spouse were both affected by your individual life history. Different people will be affected in *different* ways by similar experiences.

A rational thinker will devote much time and effort to gathering knowledge and information about those subjects that will make the most impact on his life. Similarly, anyone who is married will gain greatly by attaining as much understanding as possible about the way his or her spouse thinks and reacts.

A short while after my daughter was married, my son-in-law told me that when he was engaged he heard the following from a few people:

"Here are two rules to remember after you get married. First, many women are afraid of bugs. So if your wife sees a bug and is afraid of it, don't laugh. Be a hero. Rescue her. Always go to the bug and step on it. Second, when your wife mops the floor, never step on the floor until it dries.

"The question that is asked in yeshivah circles is: What do you do if there is a bug on a wet floor when your wife has just finished mopping it?"

I remember that when I heard this for the first time, I appreciated the beauty of the question. This question expresses the concept: Don't just do or not do something that will affect your spouse. Think first about the proper course of action.

The humor in the question is that no one can answer this question for another person. The proper and correct thing to do is to ask the one and only individual who can decide and that is one's own wife. You can't act according to the vote of the majority or even that of authority. Everyone is different and unique. The only person's opinion to rely on in similar matters is the one to whom you are married.

Computer programs can give you a valuable lesson in how to view the reactions of your spouse. Computer software programs work on the following principle: The buttons you push or click on elicit reactions. Knowing what buttons to push is the key to making the best use of any program. Each human being is unique and is similar to a unique program. Knowing what we say and how to say it, and what to do and don't do are the keys to bringing out the best in the individual to whom you are married. When you speak and act in ways that the receiver subjectively perceives as being positive and refrain from what he or she considers to be negative, you have found the keys to peace, harmony, love, and joy.

Someone who doesn't understand the reactions of his or her spouse is likely to repeat the same mistakes over and over again. If you kept pushing a button in a wall that was near a light switch, and instead of turning on the light it just gave you a mild shock, how many times would it take until your brain said to you, "If you want to turn the light on don't press this button; this button will shock you; use the light switch"? Most people would catch on quite quickly. Only someone who was incapable of rational thinking or had an extremely faulty memory would keep pressing that same wrong button over and over again.

Be wise in your marriage. Learn from previous reactions. If you see that something you say or do needlessly gets your spouse angry, irritated, or upset, stop doing it. Of course, it can be difficult to change your pattern, but it's worth it.

I was married over a year and there were many things about my spouse that I couldn't understand. At times I said things that I considered to be positive, yet the reaction it brought out was negative. There were also times that I said or did something without thinking anything of it and, surprisingly, saw that it elicited a positive reaction.

I remember a time that I came home in a slightly irritable mood and spoke in a manner that reflected my state. For the next two hours my spouse was silent. I understood this to be an angry silence and therefore my own anger kept increasing even though neither of us said a word. Later on I realized that my own irritability gave a message to my spouse that I wanted space, and what I interpreted as anger was meant to be an act of allowing me to unwind in a quiet atmosphere.

Another example is that I would ask my spouse, "How was your day?" I meant this to be the opening of a friendly discussion of the day's events. I found out that this was taken as an attack, with the implicit message of, "I think that you wasted a good part of your day so I am checking up on you."

Sometimes I made a joke and we both laughed, and other times I made what seemed to me to be a similar joke and I received in return an icy, "I didn't find that funny."

I spoke to someone who has a deep understanding of people and this is what I was told, "There are many rules about human nature that are given over both in the written word and orally. But each person is a product of unique genes, a unique family, and a unique environment from childhood to the present. You probably will never understand another person with total clarity, but listen and observe carefully. You will hear from your spouse, often indirectly and subtly, what you need to refrain from and what you need to increase.

"Even after you feel you know a lot about your spouse, realize that every person has inconsistent reactions. Depending on our emotional state at a given moment, some things that are usually positive will be considered negative, and vice versa. Don't let this throw you. View it as an adventure in solving the mystery of marriage. With a sincere desire to give your spouse pleasure and to avoid causing pain, you will become an expert, even if you never attain perfection."

After this conversation, I found the entire process of understanding my spouse much more enjoyable. I felt more confident. My spouse appreciated the fact that I wanted to understand and to improve and this made everything much easier.

I was very diligent in my Torah studies when I was single. I was friendly with other students in the yeshivah whose whole interest was learning, but not with those who would talk about other topics. I wanted to marry someone who would appreciate me as I was and who wouldn't make demands on me to talk about non-Torah topics.

I was under the impression that the person I decided to marry would appreciate my Torah learning to such an extent that she wouldn't make any demands on me except for when she needed practical help when she wasn't feeling well.

When I was engaged, a number of people told me that I would have to become a little more worldly and interested in other topics. I argued at first that I was certain my kallah wouldn't want this. I was told, "She might speak in elevated ways now, but after you are married, she will want you to talk more." This was repeated to me by people I respected and I accepted it.

During the week of sheva berachos when I went out of my way to talk to my kallah about so-called worldly things, she said to me, "I feel that you are purposely trying to talk about this to make me feel good. I feel best when I see that you are learning Torah. Just keep learning. My dream is to be married to a super masmid, who doesn't do anything else but study Torah. If I ever change my mind, I'll be sure to let you know."

We've been married ten years and she still hasn't let me know about any change in her attitude. I appreciate her more than words can express and my feeling is that she feels the same.

❖ ❖ ❖

When I was single I heard that when you get married your wife will always want to cook your favorite dishes for you. I used to eat Shabbos meals at the homes of many people. Whenever I especially enjoyed eating something, I called up the family after Shabbos and asked for the recipe of that dish.

After I became engaged, I handed my kallah a thick notebook of recipes that I told her I would like her to use after we were married. The look on her face told me quite clearly that she was less than enthusiastic about the entire idea. She politely handed it back to me and said, "I don't think that I need that right now."

After we were married for a couple of months, however, on her own she asked me if I still had the notebook. I was thrilled.

A Torah scholar who lectures in a large yeshivah related that the saddest marriage story he ever heard was from a Rebbe of his. He heard it twenty-five years ago and it has remained with him as a lesson on how saichel (common sense) is needed to apply the ideas one hears.

His Rebbe was the prominent mashgiach of a major yeshivah, known for his extreme piety. The wife of one of his students called him up and complained bitterly about her husband. She had many complaints, but the central one was that her husband wasn't warm enough towards her. She felt lonely and miserable. The fellow wasn't mean or cruel in any way, but was sort of in his own world and tended to ignore her.

The mashgiach spoke to the young man the next day and told him to be more expressive towards his wife. On a practical level he advised him to be more openly affectionate. The fellow dutifully followed his teacher's suggestion, but told his wife, "I'm doing this because the mashgiach told me to." Needless to say, the mashgiach received another call with a further complaint.

The sad part of the story is that the husband meant well and was willing to do what his Rabbi told him to. Lacking an understanding of how his wife would react, he ruined what could have been the beginning of improvement in his marriage.

I once heard from a teacher of mine, "If your are on the telephone when your husband comes home, tell the person you are talking to, 'I have to go now. My husband just came home.' This way you will be showing your husband that you respect him."

This made sense to me and I made it a habit. It took me over two years to find out that my husband hated this. He finally said to me, "It's fine with me if you continue talking to your family and friends on the telephone when I come home. I hate it when you tell someone that you have to get off the phone just because I've entered the house. To me it feels that you are making me seem like a highly controlling person and I dislike that. If you personally want to end your conversation please just say, 'I have to go now.' But don't say the reason is because your husband just came home."

This made me realize that even though I should take the rules I hear as general principles, I always need to see how to apply them specifically, based on the unique reactions of both of us.

I have been married two months now and without false modesty I have to state that I am a great cook. I enjoy cooking elaborate dishes, my husband enjoys eating them, and I appreciate it when I get positive feedback.

After a number of weeks of constant high quality meals, I served some leftovers that I thought were still edible. My husband, who is usually very hungry at suppertime, took a couple of bites and stopped eating. The face he made when chewing told me that there was something wrong with this meal.

"What's the matter?" I asked. "Is there a problem with the way the food tastes?"

"No," he said. "Your food is as good as always. It's just that I'm not hungry right now."

"Are you certain that there is nothing wrong with the food?" I asked.

"There's absolutely nothing wrong," he said very

unconvincingly. "I just don't feel like eating right now." I didn't believe him, but I wasn't certain, so I took a bite of the food myself. As soon as I tasted it, I spit it out laughing. It tasted rotten. I could see that he must have read or heard that a husband shouldn't criticize his wife's cooking. Since I had confidence in my own proficiency as a cook, I wanted honest and accurate feedback in order to prevent mishaps in the future. I appreciate my husband's trying to spare my feelings, but he needn't have worried. I know that he cares about me and I don't consider it an attack when he states his honest reactions.

Someone once approached me and said, "I don't understand the laws of *lashon hara*. It's not that I have questions about specific details of the laws. Rather, I can't understand why people react the way they do. Why should anyone be bothered about things that others say about them? As long as someone doesn't physically harm you, you are safe. I know from the importance of the laws of *lashon hara* that I am missing something. But I can't understand. I've spoken to many people and I am just as confused and puzzled as when I started trying to understand many years ago."

After interviewing this person, I saw that even though he was mathematically brilliant, in the area of emotional intelligence he was what could be considered learning disabled. He had an amazingly high I.Q. but when it came to emotions and the subjective reactions of other humans, he was almost like someone who was retarded. Nothing made sense to him. Upon further questioning it came out that as a child he had always had difficulties making friends. He couldn't understand his wife and children and would argue with them, demanding a consistently rational and logical reaction.

I explained to him that the world of emotions is a valid world and that it is a world in which most of the people on this planet live. His problem was that he wanted to understand how the emotions of other people worked, using his own brand of logic.

He personally was never offended or hurt by what anyone said to him. It didn't make rational sense to allow words to hurt him. He also couldn't understand why other people had better reactions when something was worded one way and worse reactions when something was worded differently. "It all means the same, so why do people react differently towards different versions?" he kept asking.

I told him to temporarily give up trying to "understand" why people react the way they do, because his way of doing it was not working. Rather, he should view himself as a being from another galaxy who has just come to visit planet earth. He might never totally understand earthlings, but at least he would need to learn how to get along well with them. Just as most people use electricity without understanding exactly how it works, so too we can learn which buttons human beings perceive as positive, eliciting positive reactions, and which turn people off. He told me that he never thought about doing it that way. While it was still difficult for him to gain total proficiency, he found that by giving up trying to understand why people react the way they do and objectively observing their reactions, he was able to improve greatly.

SEE THINGS FROM YOUR SPOUSE'S POINT OF VIEW: TO DO CHESED, TO PREVENT DISTRESS AND PAIN, AND TO AVOID QUARRELS

We always see everything from our point of view. It's a natural tendency to perceive our own point of view as the actual reality of a situation. The only problem is that every other person in the world will see things differently, with varying levels of discrepancy. To understand the dynamics of any marriage situation it is necessary to enter the mind of both parties. A husband only knows his own mind firsthand and the same goes for the wife. Each needs to understand the other from the other's perspective. It is easy to project and develop a theory as to why the other person is acting the way he or she is, but this can easily be way off the mark.

Lack of seeing things from another person's point of view increases the quantity and intensity of quarrels. It increases anger and resentment. This is especially problematic when someone has a tendency to view the other person's point of view in a very negative way and then considers his or her thoughts on the matter to be the actual reality.

When you master the ability to see things from the other person's point of view, you will be more compassionate and understanding. You will do more *chesed*. You will save yourself and the other person from experiencing distress and pain. You will avoid many quarrels. It is important to keep in mind: With my spouse's life history, what does this mean to him/her? With my life history what does this mean to me? Meet your spouse at his or her frame of reference and address the primary concerns of your husband/wife.

When there is strife in a marriage, both sides inevitably suffer. Each partner experiences his or her own suffering. Both need to be aware that they both have suffered. Arguing, "You didn't suffer as much as I did," is usually not conducive to peace. When both the husband and wife acknowledge that they both have suffered, it helps the cause of peace. Statements that are one-sided and fail to reflect the pain on both sides are not helpful. When both the husband and wife perceive and acknowledge the other's pain, they are both more likely to be motivated to make positive changes that will be beneficial to both.

This is how Rabbi Eliyahu Eliezer Dessler, a master at understanding people, put it: "Develop the habit of seeing other people as they see themselves. All anger, all hatred, all quarrels arise because a person views the situation from his own perspective, and fails to see himself from the viewpoint of the other person. For example, if a poor person asks someone who is wealthy for a large donation, the wealthy person might view the request as insolence and become angry. The poor person feels insulted and perplexed. He thinks to himself, 'The Almighty has given him so much, why doesn't he share what he has with me?' They separate from each other with a quarrel and mutual bad feelings. If each would try to understand the position of the other, however, even though they still might not agree, the majority of conflicts and complications that arise in interpersonal relationships could be avoided.

"Seeing things from the other person's point of view will have a profound effect on your personality, since all the traits that deal with how we relate to others are dependent upon this concept. You will find it easier to master this when you realize how beneficial it is for your happiness and success in life to have many people love and care about you. When you master the ability to view others as they see themselves, you will gain the love of everyone.

"In your dealings with other people, do not relate to them only with cold logic. Rather take their emotions and individual personalities into consideration" (Rabbi Eliyahu Eliezer Dessler; *Michtav MeEliyahu,* vol. 4, pp. 243-5).

The Vilna Gaon emphasized the importance of seeing things from another person's point of view when you communicate with someone who is different from you: "When talking to someone who thinks very differently than you, especially when the person is being irrational, enter the other person's world and answer him according to his line of reasoning. It is important to remember not to reply according to your own logic, but in a way consistent with his distorted way of thinking in order to ensure that your communication will be accepted" (*Beur HaGra* to *Mishlei* 26:5).

People might demonstrate similar patterns of behavior and yet these patterns can arise from different motives. By understanding the "Why?" of your spouse from his or her view, you have a better chance of coping better with his or her patterns. For example, some people who are controlling do so in order to be protective and caring. Some do so because they are certain that they are almost always right and they know that their opinions are superior to others. And there are even some people who will openly tell you that they like to take charge and be in control because of the powerful feelings that result. If you feel that your spouse is controlling, your understanding of the motive might give you a sense of direction as to what approach might be helpful.

To influence your spouse, see the situation from his or her point of view. Why should he or she want to do or stop doing something? If your spouse does something that doesn't seem to make sense to you, try seeing the situation from his or her point of view. Ask yourself, "From his/her point of view why is he/she doing this?"

When two people disagree strongly about a matter, they both have a better chance of being given a hearing by the other when the other feels understood from his or her point of view. That is one reason why an objective third party can often get two people to listen calmly to each other. Since the third party is not emotionally involved in the issues under contention, the third party can be sympathetic to both views. When someone sincerely understands you and how you are feeling, even if that person does not take a stand as to who is right and who is wrong or what should actually be done, you tend to feel more relaxed and at ease. The goal is for both parties in a disagreement to do the same as a third party would. Understand your spouse's position and feelings even though you have an entirely different position. By being respectful to the other person, you build up the chances of the other person being respectful to you. But ultimately we should be respectful even if the other person is not equally respectful to us. This is a difficult feat. But it is the right thing to do and the most strategically wise thing to do.

If your spouse keeps denying what he or she said or did, look at the situation from his or her point of view. Perhaps something you say or do contributes to your spouse's fear of being open and honest. Could it be that your spouse is afraid of your being critical or condemning? What could you say or do or avoid saying or doing that would enable your spouse to feel safer? There is a minority of people who engage in what is called "gaslighting." That is, purposely denying things they've said or done to get their spouse off balance. The majority of people who deny their words or actions do so as a result of their own fears and insecurities. They hate to be criticized or condemned. They therefore deny they said or did something that would cause you to look down at them or to be critical of them. While you still would want your spouse to be honest with you, knowing that the denial comes from fear is likely to make it easier for you to deal with it.

There are certain patterns that are more challenging than others. For example, if you are rigid, aloof, and emotionally distant, it is difficult for a warm person to relate to you. If you are critical, argumentative, and always finding fault, it is difficult for a sensitive person to deal with you. If you lose your temper frequently, someone who likes peace and harmony will have a challenging time. If you are deeply emotional and constantly need reassurance, it is difficult for someone who is less emotional to understand you and meet your needs. By realizing the challenges your spouse is faced with when dealing with you, you will be more accepting of your spouse's reactions.

When you practice seeing things from your spouse's point of view, it will become almost automatic. Exactly how long this will take depends on how much you already see other people's point of view in general, and your spouse's in particular. In the beginning this can take a concerted effort, but after a while it will be part of your spontaneous thinking process.

> *S*ome women have told me that they wish their husbands would read a few books on marriage, but I have an opposite problem. My husband reads everything he can on the subject, but he makes one error and it is a major one. He tries to follow what's written in each book as if the rules and suggestions were absolute Torah from Heaven.
>
> His following of the rules is similar to the type of strike where the employees go by the rule books. There they purposely follow every single bylaw in a way that slows everything down and spitefully causes inefficiency. My

husband means well. It's just that he is inflexible and understands everything in too literal a manner.

When I complained to him that I didn't like something, he would say, "But it says in the book I read that women appreciate this."

One day he came home with an expensive necklace that to me seemed ugly. "Why did you buy this?" I asked him.

"I attended a lecture on how to treat a wife," he told me. "The speaker said that at times your wife might want something strongly, but will feel uncomfortable about asking directly for it." I asked him, "Like what?" and he said, "Like an expensive necklace. So right after the class, I ran to a jewelry shop and bought this necklace for you."

"I don't have a problem with asking you for what I want," I told him. "We have different tastes, so please ask me what I want before you go to buy a gift for me."

"You are wrong," he said. "You are supposed to appreciate the necklace I bought you."

I frequently feel exasperated. He doesn't notice who I am and doesn't try to find out what I like and what I don't like. I wish he would understand that in a marriage the tastes and feelings of your spouse are what counts. He's close-minded and argues that the experts know better than I do. This may be true about people in general, but I am the biggest expert when it comes to knowing what I like and what I don't like. I wish that I could convince my husband to accept this.

I began to take computer lessons given by a friend of mine. She was very patient and her fees were less than most companies that taught the basics of word processing.

When I came home from my first lesson, I was excited. I saw a whole new world opening up before me. I shared my enthusiasm with my husband, but his response was cool, and even a bit distant.

"Is there anything bothering you?" I asked.

"No," he replied. "It's all right." But his tone of voice gave a message loudly and clearly that something was bothering him.

"Please tell me what's bothering you," I said with concern.

"Nothing's bothering me," my husband said, not sounding very convincing.

"Please tell me," I pleaded. "It's healthier to discuss any issues that are bothering you than burying them and letting them fester."

"I would have preferred to just let it pass," he said. "But since you insist, I have to admit that I did feel offended. I am an expert in computers. I felt hurt that you didn't ask me to teach you. I have much more experience with computers than the person you chose as a teacher."

"I know that," I replied. "But that's exactly why I asked her. You are so brilliant and knowledgeable that I get confused with all the information about computers you tend to tell me. I just need someone who can teach a total beginner the basics. At times, I need points to be repeated over and over again. I hope that you understand how much I respect you. I didn't want to take your time."

I felt a sigh of relief when I saw that my husband accepted my explanation.

*A*husband and wife were going for marriage coun- *seling to resolve major personality differences between the two of them. They had already signed*

up at the Jerusalem Rabbinate for a divorce. They came from diverse cultures, their native languages were different, they had different interests in life and didn't feel that their marriage had a chance.

As a last minute try, they decided to go for counseling to see if there was a possibility to save their marriage. The Rabbi they spoke to found that although at first glance they did not look as if they had much in common, deep down they loved and respected each other and were still hoping that some changes could be made that would enable them to remain married.

The husband kept looking at his watch the entire meeting. The wife noticed this and became irritated. In an accusatory tone of voice she said to him, "You aren't interested in this."

"I'm very interested," he replied. "I feel that we are making progress here and I am beginning to have hope that we can make it together."

"What makes you feel that he isn't interested?" the counselor asked the wife. "To me the way he keeps responding in this room shows that he is strongly interested in doing what he can to stay married."

"Because he keeps looking at his watch," she replied. "And he is not very verbal about his responses."

The husband responded, "I always like to know the time. It's a long-standing habit of mine. I am not in a rush and this meeting is my highest priority in the world right now. I am willing to stay as long as it takes."

The counselor pointed out that the husband kept nodding his head and this was his nonverbal way of communicating his agreement. He was used to communicating with other professionals who also would nod their heads to express agreement, and he hadn't realized that this wasn't totally obvious. The wife was much more emotional and verbal and, to her, agreement needed to be expressed verbally and explicitly. The husband was *taught that he should explicitly express his agreement and learn to acknowledge verbally if a point made sense to him. The wife, on the other hand, needed to learn to interpret his head motions to increase her ability to read him accurately.*

Once they learned how to give and receive messages in a way that would be understood by both, they were on their way to reaching agreement about a number of the issues that previously had been a source of contention. Many of their arguments had been fueled by their lack of ability to acknowledge agreement and now this was no longer an issue.

❖ ❖ ❖

My husband has a habit that gets on my nerves. Wherever we go, he finds potential dangers and points them out to people. He protests if anyone tries to cross the street against a red light. He tells people to stick in their arms when a car is moving, even though no one else thinks there is danger. He tells people to stop smoking, and reprimands anyone who does anything he considers dangerous. At times I am embarrassed when he does this to complete strangers.

I have told my husband to stop, but he replies, "I'm not allowed to. It's a big mitzvah to save lives and we are forbidden to pass up an opportunity when we can protect and save anyone from harm."

I told him he's exaggerating dangers. But he says, "You can never tell. Dangers are everywhere."

After ten years of this, I recalled an incident that I had forgotten. On our very first date, he picked up a messy banana peel that was on the sidewalk and carried it until we found a trash can. I remember how impressed I was. He also told the taxi driver to drive carefully and he made certain to take me up to the door of my house even though I said he didn't have to. I was highly impressed with his general care and concern and figured that he would always be kind to me.

While some people might consider this practice more than a bit strange, I try to see what he does from his point of view. As he always says, "If I save just one life during my entire lifetime, all my efforts will have been worth it." Understanding his perspective makes this pattern more acceptable.

LISTEN TO UNDERSTAND

When you listen to your spouse speak, you will constantly gain more insights into who your spouse is. Very often we listen to people speak about themselves and our response can be viewed as critical. "I wouldn't react like that." Or, "You don't have to get upset about this." Or, "Why should this bother you? It doesn't bother a lot of other people." Learn to listen objectively. Without judgment, take in the information you hear.

To understand other people, you need to understand them from the way they describe themselves. You need to understand what they say about themselves, and what they really think about themselves even if they don't say so explicitly. Be careful about adding your own interpretations, because this is likely to distort your seeing others as they really are or as they think they are. If you do develop any theories about the other person, be careful to observe the data comprehensively and objectively.

When you listen to understand, you will find out a lot of useful information about your spouse that will enable you to avoid doing and saying things that will cause him or her pain, and you will gain many new opportunities to do acts of kindness. Listen with empathy. When your spouse has complaints, it's easy to argue or counterattack. Don't. Understand what your spouse is saying and what is bothering him or her. For example, if your spouse says, "This doesn't bother me, but ...," it usually means that it bothers him or her. Therefore if your spouse says this to you, take it as a message: "This bothers me to some extent, take my feelings into consideration."

People can be married for many years, but if they haven't listened to understand there will be an immense amount of potentially beneficial information that they have missed.

From now on be resolved to listen to understand. Whether your spouse is talking to you or to someone else in your presence, listen carefully to understand what is important to him or her.

It is helpful if you can recognize your spouse's language pattern. Is your spouse predominantly visual, auditory, or kinesthetic. We each are all three, but usually one of these systems provides a key to understanding what we are experiencing. Visual means that a person thinks in mental pictures. Such a person will often speak faster than average. A person who does so will use visual language, such as, "I see what you are saying." "I need to get a clearer picture of that." "I can't see myself being able to do that." "Do you see what I'm saying." By using visual language, you will gain better rapport with such a person. Auditory means that a person thinks in terms of hearing words and sounds. A person who does this will use auditory language, such as, "I hear what you are saying." "That doesn't sound right to me." "Do you hear what I'm saying?" Kinesthetic means that a person thinks in terms of feelings. Such a person will often speak more slowly than average, and will speak in terms of feelings, "That does/doesn't feel right to me." "I want you to get in touch with this idea." "Does that feel right to you." By using the language pattern of your spouse, he or she will understand you better. He or she will either hear what you have to say, or your response will look right to him or her, or he or she will get a good feeling about your reaction.

For some people, breaking through the pattern of compulsive eating is a major issue in their life. Many people who deal with weight issues find that self-esteem and weight problems are tied in with each other. If your spouse has an issue with eating, food, and weight, be sensitive to his or her individual needs and feelings. Someone who has never had to deal with this challenge needs to be open to hearing how their spouse views these matters. Knowing about the struggles, victories, setbacks and resilient moments in your spouse's life will help you understand him or her better. The same applies to such issues as learning difficulties, health problems, and addictions.

When your spouse talks about his or her childhood or family of origin, you will be able to glean precious nuggets of understanding. Based on positive or painful childhood experiences a person will view what happens in his or her own unique way. Someone who felt very deprived during childhood will grow up feeling differently about things than someone who grew up feeling that he or she always had whatever was needed. Those who experienced much fear in childhood will have different sensitivities than someone who felt very comfortable and secure. Those with a happy childhood will have different emotional experiences than someone with an unhappy childhood. Those who had a difficult time in school will need their spouse's compassion and sensitivity to understand what he or she went through, as well as encouragement in the present.

If your spouse shares with you any difficulties he or she had with a parent, be careful to use this information compassionately. There are people who sometimes use this information insensitively or as an attack. "You are only reacting to me this way because of the way your father treated you and I'm not your father." This usually just causes pain.

If your spouse takes a long time in getting his or her message across, try to summarize what you consider the key points. You might say a sentence or two as a summary, and then ask, "Is this the main point that you mean?" At other times it might be worthwhile to ask, "Could you please clarify for me the main point you want me to hear?"

What are a number of the key words that your spouse frequently uses that can be used by you to generate greater rapport? For the next few weeks, listen carefully. Keep a list of words that you would consider his or her favorite positive words. Some examples of words that show a pattern are:

[1] The right thing, practical, balanced, down-to-earth, effective, efficient, good use of time, saving money, getting things done, being careful.

[2] *Yiras shamayim, middos tovos, ahavas Hashem, olam habah, ratzon Hashem, avodas Hashem, eved Hashem, mesiras nefesh.*

[3] Understanding, caring, compassion, kindness, gentle, feelings, warm, considerate, friendly.

[4] Brilliant, analytical, depth, insight, creative, comprehensive picture, innovative, ingenious.

[5] Bottom line, profit, gain, benefit, time-effective, long-term planning, strategic thinking.

[6] Reframes, states, anchors, patterns, role models, outcome thinking, mental data base.

When you listen to understand, avoid needless arguments. Your goal isn't to prove that you are better than your spouse, or that you spouse is making many mistakes. When you listen to understand, don't talk about yourself as soon as the opportunity arises. Rather, be patient. Imagine that you would be writing an objective report after the conversation. As you listen carefully, you will pick up on points that you've probably heard many times before, but now you will understand with more compassion and sensitivity.

I am used to taking people's statements at face value. If someone tells me he likes something, I assume he does. If someone tells me he is feeling well, I assume that he is really well. In the family in which I grew up, if someone did not like something, he explicitly said so. If someone wasn't feeling well, he or she would say, "I feel ill today."

When I got married, I assumed that what my spouse said to me was an expression of actual feelings and reactions. But quite often I would get a feeling that even though what was said to me was, "Everything's all right," everything was not all right. Even though what was said to me was, "I feel okay," the inner feelings were not okay.

One day my spouse said to me in anger, "You are so insensitive. You don't take my feelings into consideration."

"But I always ask you how you feel," I protested.

"Yes, you do," I was told. "But you don't understand my answers."

"You keep telling me that you feel all right and okay," I said. "What is there to understand?"

"You don't understand nuances," my spouse said. "I don't feel comfortable to complain. My mother always understood that I had different ways of saying, "all right," and "okay." There is the way I say something when I really do feel all right and the way I say something when I don't feel well, but it's difficult for me to say so straight out."

From then on, I listened carefully to the way the "all rights" were said. After a while, the tone of voice of a "not all right" was the same to me as if these were the actual words spoken.

I t takes me a while to get in touch with my feelings. When I begin to talk about my reactions, I don't know exactly what I am going to say. As I express myself in words, my feelings become clearer.

When I was single, I was concerned that I never would find anyone who would have the patience to listen to my groping for the right words. My previous experiences with trying to express myself were that if anyone was impatient with me, I would become tongue-tied and unable to speak.

My husband realized when I met him that he would need to be patient with me. He had a sister he was close to with a similar personality and he had practice with this pattern. I felt his commitment to understand me and this made the whole process of understanding myself so much easier and smoother.

I am so grateful to him for his patience that I go out of my way to do things for him that otherwise I probably would have found too difficult to do.

❖ ❖ ❖

*M*y spouse took a course on how to do counseling. I was very supportive of the idea at first because it is a great act of chesed to help other people who are suffering and in distress.

But what my spouse learned began to cause us problems at home. My spouse is naturally intuitive and sensitive. When someone describes a painful situation, my spouse feels the pain. At the course, however, my spouse was told that this isn't a healthy way to react since it can become overwhelming quite quickly.

My spouse was told to respond to people who related their stories with, "Tell me more about that," "I see that this caused you pain," "Have you wondered why this upset you?" and "In what ways does this remind you of your childhood?"

I didn't think that this would be helpful to most people. But the worst part in our home was that my spouse started talking this way to me and the children. My spouse began to sound like a parody on therapy. Where was the spontaneous and real person that I had been married to until then?

I kept complaining that canned responses sound unreal and robot-like, but my spouse argued that these new responses are what was being taught in the course.

I couldn't convince my spouse that the spontaneous, intuitive responses that came naturally were so much better, but after my spouse started dealing with real-life clients the reality of what I had been saying fully registered.

The first client my spouse saw refused to come back for a second session. The feedback was, "The counselor sounded programmed to just sound like a counselor. When I tell my problems to someone, I want a real human being who actually understands me, not someone who is like a parrot."

ASK THE RIGHT QUESTIONS

When you listen to your spouse to gain greater understanding of who he or she is, asking the right questions will increase your understanding. The wrong questions will be looked upon as challenges, debates, and attacks. The right questions are clarification questions. You ask them in a gentle tone of voice. You are asking to understand why exactly something bothers him or her. You are asking why he or she is interested in something.

If you find that your questions are becoming distressful to your spouse, don't ask them right now. Questions can be asked in a way that makes them seem like prying.

Your questions should serve a dual purpose. They should further your understanding of your spouse and they should indicate sensitivity to the issue on your part. For this reason a long list of questions that you can ask might be misleading. If you find that your spouse becomes annoyed at you for the type of questions you do ask, wait for an opportunity to listen to how someone else asks questions your spouse appreciates.

A general question to ask is, "What does this mean to you?" This basic question can also be asked in a variety of ways. For instance, "When you became irritated with me, what exactly bothered you?" Or, "Why did you feel so good when you heard that news?" Be careful to ask these questions in a tone of voice that expresses your sincere wish to understand. If asked in other ways, they could be understand as confrontations and attacks.

Questions that you can keep asking are, "How do you view the situation?" and, "How do you feel about this?" Another question that can supply much insight into present reactions is, "What does this remind you of?" Also, observe changes in facial expression and muscle tension and ask, "Would you like to share what you are thinking about?" Some highly important questions to ask are, "What can I say or do to enable you to feel respected and loved?" "What do you need to feel appreciated?" "What shows you that you are important to me?"

If your spouse is cooperative some of the time and not at other times, ask yourself, "What is different about this request?" If you can ask your spouse, terrific. You might get a clear picture. You might hear that certain ways of making a request create cooperation, and other ways prevent it. It could be the words you said. It could be your tone of voice. When you know what does work well and what doesn't, you can speak in the future in ways that will bring out the best in your spouse.

If your spouse replies, "I don't know," perhaps you can work it out together. It might be that the way you make your requests make the difference, or it might be a difference in your spouse's emotional state. In a rested, calm state, your spouse will be more open to meet your requests, needs, and wishes.

Make a list of the family rules that were spoken about in the home in which you grew up. Ask your spouse to make a similar list of rules. In what way are those rules compatible? In what ways do they conflict?

Part of understanding your spouse is to know what questions not to ask him or her. By observing facial expressions and body language, you will pick up the knowledge of what not to ask in the future. Even if your spouse is often open to answer your questions, there are times when your spouse would prefer privacy and you should respect that. Don't ask unnecessary questions when you see that your spouse would prefer not to talk about something.

I *have a very controlling nature. When I wish for some-*
thing to be a certain way, I make certain that is the
way it will be. My intense determination has enabled
me to accomplish a lot. Without acting mean or becom-
ing angry, others are intimidated by my strong demeanor
and usually back down.

When I was married, I was certain that my spouse
would be devoted to meet my wishes. My need for con-
trol was manifested in many areas of our lives. This
began with my insisting that the wedding be exactly the
way I wanted it to be.

After our first anniversary, I looked back at how my
spouse acquiesced to my wishes and felt that I had a
great marriage.

"Now that we are married an entire year, how would
you rate the quality of our marriage?" I asked my spouse.
This was one of the first times I had explicitly asked my
spouse for feedback.

"I'm glad you asked," was the unhappy response. "I
probably wouldn't have had the courage to tell you what
I really feel. But now that you expressed your willingness
to hear what I have to say, I want to tell you that I had
never imagined that marriage would be so painful. Your
controlling manner has caused me to give in to you. But
I resent you immensely. I was thinking to myself that I
don't know how long I can last with things being the way
they are. Either you become less controlling or you will
lose me entirely."

This hit me like a ton of bricks. I never realized that
my desire to control was leading me on a road to lose
what I had. After a number of long discussions it
became clear to me that only by giving up my demand
to control and becoming more sensitive to my spouse's
preferences, wants, and needs, would our marriage
work for both of us. I saw that by giving up the demand
for total control I would gain so much more than if I
tried to make everything be just my way.

PERSONALITY DIFFERENCES MAKE A MAJOR DIFFERENCE

Each person on this planet has a different personality than anyone else. Nevertheless, some people are more similar than others. The more similar two people are, the easier it usually is for them to understand each other. Regardless of how similar any two people are, they will be different in many ways. Regardless of how different any two people are, they will be similar in many ways. The task of marriage is to understand your spouse's personality in order to interact in the best possible ways, and to benefit from the differences in your personalities. When you understand your spouse's personality, there are many things that you might have considered as faults and problems and now you will view them just as differences that create challenges for growth.

Personalities vary between those which are highly complex and those which are relatively simpler, less complicated ones. What makes a personality complex? When someone has many diverse and contradictory parts; when someone has an intense emotional nature with wide mood swings; when one has a deep and creative intelligence together with a secretive nature.

When two people work in harmony, personality differences can help both of them to utilize their individual strengths as a team. When there isn't harmony, differences cause clashes and quarrels. The challenge of personality differences is to create a peaceful relationship even when it takes much effort to do so. After you get married, whether theoretically it is better to have married someone similar or different is academic. What is important is to get along harmoniously with the person you did marry. Some especially challenging personality differences are:

- When one partner is very cold and the other is very warm.
- When one partner loves action, risks, and excitement, and the other wants routine, the familiar, and is highly conventional.
- When one partner is very rule-and-regulation oriented and the other cherishes freedom.

- When one partner loves talking about feelings and the other cherishes logic and reason and considers talking about emotions a total waste of time.
- When one partner has a strong need for togetherness and the other has a strong need for privacy and to be alone.
- When one partner is highly organized and the other thrives on chaos.
- When one partner loves having many guests and company over to visit, and the other loves peace and quiet and feels uncomfortable in the presence of even small crowds.
- When one partner lives by the clock and always wants to do things on schedule, and the other is always late and the exact time for anything is not important.

Husband and wife will need to work out their personality differences in ways that work for both of them. In some instances, this can go relatively smoothly. In other instances, this can be very difficult. It can take much effort. What is of vital importance is that each one respects the other, and that both want to work things out in a way that is in their mutual best interests. There is growth to be found when two people are similar and growth when they are different. True growth is elevating oneself in the situation in which one finds oneself.

Some people relate to specific personality systems and others don't. Some people feel that they have gained greater understanding of themselves and others by knowing a system, while others feel that systems are confusing, misleading, and potentially harmful. If your spouse relates to a personality system and you don't, by gaining an understanding of that system you will gain a greater understanding of your spouse. The very fact that your spouse relates to that system and you don't illustrates that you have differences in your personality. By viewing marriage as an opportunity to grow, those differences become exactly what you both need to challenge you and help you develop different aspects of your character.

If you relate to a personality system that you feel describes you, and your spouse disregards it, be patient. The fact that you feel a personality, temperament, or type describes you means that your spouse would gain better understanding of you by knowing that system. Wait for an opportune time to explain yourself. It could be that your choice of language is a key factor in whether what you say will or will not be accepted. I have seen many instances when a spouse totally discounted a description, but later understood it differently and was more open to it. Try to understand what is bothering your spouse about the system. It's possible that some of the critique might be valid. All systems are generalizations and are never an exact description of any particular person. Nevertheless, knowing generalities can be helpful in understanding a specific person better as long as individual uniqueness is taken into consideration.

Be careful. When we have a theory about how someone's personality operates we tend to view that person in ways that will be consistent with that theory. We are likely to miss many ways in which this person is different from what he or she should be according to that theory. This might cause us to overlook virtues, strengths, and positive qualities of the person with whom we are dealing. We might miss a potential solution because it does not fit into the way we perceive this person. We might not focus on how we can motivate and influence. We might not focus on how we can help this individual develop aspects of his or her character and personality that he or she has not yet developed.

The Torah ideal is to constantly develop our character. Personality differences can give us many challenges in this area. Focus on the benefits of both the similarities and differences.

I am a night person, while my spouse is a morning person. I am very tired in the morning, and as the day progresses my energy increases. My spouse, on the other hand, has a lot of energy right away in the morning, but gets tired as the day goes on.

As soon as my spouse wakes up, I hear a cheerful, "Good morning! Good morning!! It's time to wake up and have a super great day."

"Spare me," I say to myself. "Cut it out and keep your good cheer to yourself." It takes me a couple of hours to really wake up.

My spouse often tells me that I have been rude in the morning. I definitely don't mean to be rude or unfriend-ly. But I need a quiet environment for a while until I feel really awake.

I didn't realize how hurt my spouse felt about this until one day I was told, "I feel rejected when you ignore me in the morning. I know otherwise, but I feel unloved and not respected by the way you react towards me in the morning."

I explained at length that in the home in which I grew up, we all avoided each other in the morning. We were a caring family, but it took us all a couple of hours until we were friendly and outgoing. My spouse was understanding after I explained my emotional tenden-cies, and no longer took my lack of enthusiasm in the morning as being personal. I accepted upon myself to speak in a friendlier manner as soon as I woke up. Not having my spouse trying to get me to be more cheerful than I actually felt, enabled me to increase my energy level faster.

I hate personality systems and my spouse loves them. My spouse would constantly say, "You hold this position because you are such a personality type. But I hold this other position because I am this other personality type." I felt that this precluded dealing with the actual merits of each position.

There was almost never a discussion about our relatives, neighbors, business associates, and anyone else we encountered without one or another personality system being mentioned. We were both careful not to speak lashon hara. On the contrary, my spouse's love for personality systems was a constant source of judging other people favorably. "Don't blame 'X' for what he just did to us, it is because he is 'Y' personality, and that's why he acted that way." Or, "She said that because she is a 'Z' personality, so she is not at fault."

I couldn't take it anymore. "To me categorizing people belittles them," I said.

My spouse disagreed. "Understanding someone's personality is respectful of them. It gives you greater awareness and understanding and makes you more sensitive to the individual needs of people. By speaking someone's 'language' you get along better and have greater rapport. Knowing someone's personality will prevent mistakes."

My spouse challenged me, "What exactly bothers you about any of these systems?"

I mentioned a few factors:

No one is exactly any personality, we are all mixtures.

By thinking in terms of generalities, you overlook individual differences.

You limit people by categorizing them.

Stereotype thinking prevents ahavas Yisrael, and unity. Looking at people as types creates distance.

My spouse conceded that there are dangers in any system. "However," said my spouse, "there are major benefits in understanding the factors that are dealt with in each system. These patterns are helpful if individual differences and uniquenesses are acknowledged. True, every person is different, but by knowing someone's likes and dislikes you avoid causing pain and become more of an expert at helping people."

This made sense to me. My spouse agreed to limit the use of terminology that got on my nerves, and I agreed to gain a greater understanding of these systems. By our understanding of each other's positions, we saw that we agreed on the basic core issues and it was only misconceptions on both our parts that got in the way. My spouse pledged never to put me down by saying, "You aren't correct. You only think that way because you are an 'X.'" And I agreed to ask my spouse questions to gain more knowledge of what specifically was meant by the terms in the system. If it were necessary for us to know what a certain person's personality was like, for a practical and constructive purpose, we would use the terminology of the system. We both agreed to be highly cautious not to allow this to lead into lashon hara. Rather, we would use this for chesed, for judging favorably, and for finding ways to have a positive influence on the lives of others.

We both agreed that we could and should develop aspects of ourselves that were not yet developed. A total Torah personality is one who utilizes all of his and her attributes in the most appropriate way.

I have two opposite parts. Part of me is bold and willing to take emotional risks. The other part of me is highly cautious and finds it difficult to approach people or ask for things that most others would be able to do without a second thought.

My wife has difficulties with both these parts. She is very grounded and balanced. She has no fear of speaking up, of negotiating, and of requesting refunds in standard situations, but she doesn't like to take bold risks like I do. On the other hand, she can't understand why I find it difficult to confront others in standard situations. "What will they do to you and what loss will you have?" she asks me. Of course, she is right. But I still have these two parts.

I don't find my two parts in conflict. Each one has its time and place. My "bold risk part" has enabled me to accomplish much. I'm not one for major financial risks, so my risk-taking is more in the area of not fearing failure.

"You really must overcome your fears of approaching people when it is appropriate to do so," my wife told me one day. "Learn from the times you are able to do so spontaneously."

That was a valid point. I also saw that my wife herself could serve as my role model. I made a list of situations she handled remarkably well that I didn't. Then I asked her what her inner thoughts were when she confronted those people or negotiated.

She told me a few ideas that I have begun to integrate. One, you always have a right to speak up for your valid rights.

Two, the only power anyone else has over you is the power you give them. Don't empower others at your own expense. Realize that you have the power that anyone else has. Just allow yourself to feel it.

Three, if you find it difficult to confront someone, imagine him or her as a young infant, or see him or her as he or she will be in 120 years from now.

Four, imagine a powerful role model and see yourself talking and acting the way that person would.

When my wife saw that I wanted to learn from her, she began viewing herself as my coach and that made it easier for her to accept my weaker part at the same time that she was strengthening it.

I am much more emotional than my husband. I tend to get easily excited about things, both when good things happen and when something goes wrong. I speak rather quickly when I am excited, and I become enthusiastic about many things. I am very expressive with my emotions and the look on my face will broadcast the emotional state I am in at any given moment.

My husband, on the other hand, has a mathematical mind. He speaks more slowly and deliberately than I do. He generally hides his true feelings and his face usually isn't very expressive. Even when he is very happy about something, he speaks calmly. He doesn't have as many emotional ups and downs as I do.

We both care for each other very much, and appreciate our differences in temperament and personality. But I have a problem trying to convince my husband about the validity of my position when we disagree with each other.

The more excited and enthusiastic I am, the more wary and cautious my husband becomes. This used to make me speak in an even more excited and enthusiastic manner, and my husband would react by becoming even more cautious.

I finally realized that the only way I could convince my husband of the validity of my position would be to speak to him via his own style of communicating. I had to contain my enthusiasm. I had to try to speak more deliberately, as my husband does. I cited proofs that my position was valid. I don't always get my point across this way, but I am much more successful than I used to be.

I have a compulsive personality and my spouse has a histrionic one. I love lists and I am totally dedicated to using all my time and effort at succeeding at what I do.

I tend to be a perfectionist and am willing to repeat doing things until they are done to my satisfaction. Even then I feel that I could do better, but I accept that there is a limit.

My wife tends to be histrionic. She is excitable and dramatic. She overreacts when things go wrong, and shouts with excitement when she hears good news. Her emotionalism is a bit too much for me. And she constantly complains that I am too cold and rigid. She often tells me that I need to be more spontaneous and relaxed. I, on the other hand, tell her that she needs to take things in a more balanced manner.

We realized that what attracted us to each other was exactly our differences. I liked my wife's emotional expressiveness, and she liked my emotional stability. But after the marriage, these differences created frequent challenges. We each wished that the other would be more similar to ourselves. When my wife sounded too excited and enthusiastic about something and tried to convince me of its merits, I became increasingly skeptical as her emotional intensity increased. When I had to convince her about something, I tried to point out the logic and the facts and did this in a calm and rational tone of voice. But since I didn't sound enthusiastic, she wasn't convinced.

After many conversations about our personalities, we came to the conclusion that to make things work best for both of us, we would both need to make changes. I knew that I would need to become more emotionally expressive. My wife saw that she would need to decrease the drama when she spoke. This was not an easy task for either of us, and we both still need frequent reminders about our commitment. This, however, is much better than both of us insisting that we are who we are and that the other will just have to grin and bear it.

*W*hen my husband and I need to make a decision, I find myself feeling tense and frustrated. We were both in our thirties when we got married and were used to making our own decisions by ourselves. Now that we were married, we needed to come to common conclusions.

My husband tends to push off decisions until the last minute. He was fond of quoting a sign he once saw in a business office, "If it weren't for the last minute, nothing would ever get done here." Even with our marriage, I wasn't 100 percent certain that the wedding was going to be held until I was marching to the chuppah. Before that my husband would go in circles weighing each option. He himself is calm about weighing options as long as possible. Making the decision causes him anxiety, while thinking about possibilities is enjoyable for him.

I am just the opposite. I feel much more comfortable after a decision is made. I like to come to a final conclusion as early as possible. Then I can work out the details and solve the problems that arise. I would prefer coming to a decision that isn't perfect as long as the decision is already made.

The reason decision making is so difficult for us is that my husband and I can both see many possibilities in everything we discuss. Each possibility has its pros and cons. Even after seeming to come to a decision, my husband will usually say, "Wait a minute. I just thought of a few more possibilities."

One example that comes to mind is the decision we needed to make about where we should be for Pesach. Should we stay at home in our small city? Should we go to New York where we have many friends? Perhaps we should go to my parents or to my husband's parents? Maybe it should be fifty-fifty? Then there is the option of traveling to Yerushalayim for Pesach and staying in a hotel to be near the site of the Beis HaMikdash. Where will our children feel best? Maybe we should go to Australia, England, or Switzerland where we have relatives we haven't seen in a long time. If we stay home, however, we would be able to invite a number of people who were unfamiliar with making a proper seder.

We were discussing this for a few weeks and the more we discussed it, the further away we were from making a final decision. I was getting more and more nervous. If we would be staying home, I would need to hire help to assist me in cleaning our house and preparing the food. My husband kept telling me not to worry. We would certainly be reaching a decision in a day or two. But would we? I was skeptical. I was afraid we would decide at the very last minute, and then only by default. If it would be too late to make travel plans, we would end up staying home, and I would really need more time.

I analyzed the situation. I saw that my husband would accept any decision about which I felt strongly, but I wanted us to decide together. I didn't want to make the decision on my own. I felt that if I were the one who decided, my husband would blame me if anything went wrong. I told my fears to my husband and he assured me that he wouldn't blame me if anything went wrong. Even though he said this, I knew that he might convey his displeasure nonverbally. However, when I focused on what would enable us to have the greatest amount of shalom bayis, I realized that we both would be best off if I made a quicker decision. So I did.

Making this decision taught me a few principles I now follow when we need to decide on something together. I now write down the pros and cons of each possibility. If either my husband or I feel strongly about an option and the other doesn't feel so strongly about it, we agree to do what the one who feels strongly about suggests. I also see that when one path is much better for me than the other because the other path will be highly distressing, I tell this to my husband and he is open to spare me that stress. He might kvetch a little about this, but he has given me permission to ignore the kvetching. If we both don't mind too much which option we take, we arbitrarily choose one option so I don't have to experience the frustration of indecision.

❖ ❖ ❖

My husband had been Mr. Cool in his yeshivah. He learned well and had good middos. When anyone would talk about him, they would say, "He's very cool."

I always liked this quality in people. It's the diametric opposite of members of my family who were emotionally effusive. I would be uncomfortable when my friends visited if anyone in my family would be embarrassingly open.

When I first met my husband, everything about him was an expression of his being a bit aloof. He wasn't arrogant or conceited, just cool. He was careful not to speak lashon hara, but when there wasn't a question of lashon hara, he was on the slightly cynical side. His touch of aloofness and cynicism, yet at the same time his kindness and consideration, were very attractive to me.

A few months into the marriage, however, I began to miss some of the emotionalism that permeated my family. I told my husband a number of times that I wished he would be more emotionally expressive. I still liked his basic personality and was happy with my marriage, but I wished he was more emotional.

One day I bumped into the teacher who made my shiduch and expressed my concerns to her. She smiled a kind smile, and said to me, "I expected you to come to me one day to discuss this. If you recall, I mentioned to you that while I feel the two of you will be a good match, *you will need to accept that you will be missing some of the emotional warmth of your family. I know that for you, being in that environment all the time was too much, but it's normal to miss it, and the further you are away from it, the more you might build up in your mind how wonderful it was, even though you found it difficult. The personality of your husband is definitely better for you than someone more emotional. I feel certain that in your case, with time and the birth of children, you will be able to elicit more of your husband's emotions. Meanwhile, try to accept him and value his positive qualities."*

I like to be on time. When I attend a meeting, I am frequently the first one there. I come early to weddings and other celebrations. If I need to catch a plane, I leave for the airport way in advance of the time the flight is scheduled. I leave extra time in case the ride to the airport takes longer than expected. My spouse, however, comes from a home with a large family and they are usually late for things. My father-in-law's motto was, "Nothing will happen if you come late. Whenever you get there, it's all right."

When I first got married, my spouse's attitude about being on time almost drove me crazy, and I'm certain she would say the same about my opposite approach. But as I waited and waited for her when we went places together, I felt like climbing the walls.

The more I tried to speed things up, the longer they took. My spouse hates to be pressured and rushed. Coming late was normal in her home, and my arriving early was viewed with humor.

I saw that I needed to take a more lenient attitude towards being on time. If it was crucial for me to be on

time, I would leave earlier, by myself. I got used to uti-
lizing my waiting time efficiently and now whether we
are early or late it doesn't affect our shalom bayis.

ROLE REVERSAL

There is an approach that is very helpful for two people to use when they become involved in a quarrel or misunderstanding. This is known as role reversal. The husband and wife each play the role of the other and act out the problematic scene. For example, if the wife feels that the husband is very controlling, the wife will play the role of the controlling husband and the husband will act out the role of the wife. When the husband hears how his orders and commands feel to him when they are said in the tone of voice that he often uses, he will gain greater understanding of why his wife finds them oppressive. Or a husband might wish that his wife would greet him in a much more friendly way when he comes into the house. The husband and wife can act out a homecoming with the husband greeting his wife the way she usually does. Then the husband might act out the way that he wishes his wife would greet him when he comes home.

Role reversal won't be for everyone. But for those who are open to try it, it can serve as a real eye-opener. Both husband and wife can gain a much greater understanding of why their spouse reacts the way he or she does. If you don't try role reversal as an exercise, be open to opportunities when you spontaneously experience a role reversal. This can motivate you to change a problematic pattern.

W*hen my spouse does something that gets me angry, I find it difficult to let go unless I am explicitly asked for forgiveness.*
"If I just move on, I'm letting my spouse get away with things. That's not fair and I'm not willing to do it," I told my Rabbi.

"So what do you do instead?" he asked me.

"I hold onto the anger and insist that my spouse apologize," I replied.

"Do you usually get an apology?" he asked.

"Sometimes yes, and sometimes no. I frequently get excuses and rationalizations why an apology is not necessary."

"And if you don't get an apology, you hold onto your resentment. Wouldn't it be better for you spiritually, emotionally, and health-wise to let it go?" my Rabbi gently challenged me.

"But my spouse would get away with it then," I defended my position.

"Yes. You've said that. And you are right. No one wants to help others to hurt them," he acknowledged. "But when you hold onto your resentment, you're the only one who suffers this way. By letting go, you free yourself from needless emotional suffering and from the physical ailments that resentment breeds."

"That makes sense intellectually," I replied. "But if only my spouse would acknowledge that I have been wronged, it would be easier for me to forgive and let it go."

"Do you think your spouse purposely tries to wrong you?" he asked.

"No. But it's obvious that some things that my spouse says and does cause me suffering. My spouse should realize this."

"Let's look at the entire situation from your spouse's perspective. Make believe that you and your spouse have made a role reversal. Let's imagine what you would think and how you would feel if you were in your spouse's position and had your spouse's personality."

I found this exercise difficult to do. But when I did view things from my spouse's perspective, the entire situation looked different. I still would have liked an apology, but now I found it easier to let go of my resentment.

Why hurt myself just because from my spouse's point of view an apology is not forthcoming?

I am intensely phobic of dogs. I was chased by wild dogs a few times when I was a child and the fear has remained with me into adulthood.

When I am irritated with my spouse, I tend to speak like a marine drill sergeant. One day my spouse and I were taking a pleasant walk together. A dog on a leash jumped at us and barked furiously. My spouse isn't afraid of dogs, but I reacted with terror.

My spouse then told me something that I will never forget. "When you bark at me, I feel the same as you just did now when that dog barked at you. You show your emotional distress more demonstratively, but I dislike your barking as much as you disliked the way that dog barked at us."

I don't know the root cause, but I have a tendency to always be late. I become involved in conversations and discussions wherever I am and this frequently causes me to be behind schedule. When I am in a rush, someone will often ask me to do him a favor, and then I'll be late for my original appointment. For the first six years of our marriage, I would often do this when my wife and I were leaving someplace together. If we went to a wedding or bar mitzvah and made up to meet at a certain time, I would never be there on time. The same happened on trips and vacations. My wife constantly complained to me about this habit of mine, but history kept repeating itself. My wife would be irritated, although I didn't want to cause her distress. Somehow this pattern continued.

One day the tables were turned. We were at the bris of a nephew, and my wife, feeling extremely hot and tired, left before I did without telling me. I ran all around looking for her. I went up and down a large flight of stairs. I asked everyone I knew if they saw her. Eventually I assumed she had gone home alone.

As I took the bus home, I was fuming. "How could she keep me waiting like that? How could she be so insensitive? How could she leave without me?"

By the time I entered our house, I was in a rage. I stormed through the front door, and slammed it shut. "Why didn't you tell me you were leaving?" I shouted furiously.

My wife stopped me in my tracks. "First of all, I didn't do it on purpose." Secondly, we are married six years and this is the first time you needed to look for me when you couldn't find me. Do you know how many times you disappeared and I couldn't find you? How do you think I feel when that happens?"

She got her point across and I made a strong resolution not to keep her waiting for me without telling her where I was.

Whenever I am uncomfortable with what someone else says to me, I tend to retreat and withdraw. I hate confrontations, and I avoid arguments even if I end up losing out because of this. I did this with my parents. I did this with my friends. And now that I am married, I tend to do this with my spouse.

"It's better to withdraw than to get into a shouting match," I rationalized.

But my spouse didn't agree. "I don't mind if you disagree with me," my spouse said, "but I find it unbearable when you just withdraw and remain silent."

My spouse's discomfort with my withdrawing didn't make me feel more comfortable with speaking up and discussing issues that I preferred to avoid.

"Did anyone ever withdraw from you when you felt a strong need to discuss something?" my spouse asked me. "Please try to remember times when this happened to you so you will understand how I feel."

"Did you ever feel so overwhelmed because of what someone else said to you that you found it difficult to speak up?" I challenged my spouse without answering the question that I was asked.

"Let's both try to answer each other's questions," my spouse suggested.

We did. I remembered three incidents when I felt a strong need to discuss issues with people who refused to enter a dialogue. I recalled how frustrated I felt. And when I shared my incidents, my spouse, who is usually not at a loss for words, remembered an incident from elementary school. A teacher made an unfair accusation. My spouse as a child was blamed for a serious matter which never actually happened. The feeling of being overwhelmed prevented the formulation of a coherent defense. These memories made us both more understanding of what the other was experiencing.

MAKE IT EASIER FOR YOUR SPOUSE TO UNDERSTAND YOU

Would you like your spouse to understand you better? Most married people would. Make it easier for him or her to understand you. Explain your reactions in a way that will enable your spouse to understand you.

Don't explain yourself in anger. If someone does, the only message that the other person hears is usually, "I am angry at you." Human beings are usually not open to learn when they are presented with information delivered in anger.

Don't expect your spouse to understand you without your clearly expressing your likes and dislikes. Telling him or her, "You should know on your own," is futile. If he or she did know, you would have no need to say this. If he or she doesn't know, saying, "You should know," isn't very enlightening. It is more likely to cause friction than to lead to understanding. If your spouse didn't understand you the way you were hoping that he or she would, you have to make a choice. You can choose to be angry that you weren't understood, and by staying angry or by refusing to explain yourself, you are helping yourself not to be understood. Or, you can make the preferred choice of explaining why you reacted the way you did.

It isn't helpful to say, "You don't understand." Instead say, "It's important for me that you understand."

Both you and your spouse will gain a lot by your explaining yourself and your patterns. It is very helpful if you could tell your spouse how to handle you when you are in a difficult state. This takes away the guesswork and you both gain. Think of specific pieces of information about yourself that would make it easier for your spouse to interact with you. For example, you might say, "If I am in this or that unresourceful state, give me some quiet time and then I will get back to myself." Or, "If I act unreasonably, say this or that to me and I will be able to think more clearly." If at the time of this reading you don't know what to tell your spouse, observe yourself and your reactions carefully. Share the knowledge you have about handling yourself as if you are a manual for the management of a computer program.

A useful pattern to express your thoughts and feelings is:

"When you ..., I feel ..., because I think it means ..." For example:

- "When you don't look at me when I talk, I feel hurt, because I think it means you don't care what I say because I am not important to you."
- "When you forget what I asked you to do, I feel angry, because I think it means you want me to do what you should really be doing."
- "When you raise your voice when speaking to me, I feel frightened, because I think it means you are attacking me and might even hit me."

Some people are very open and easily express who they are and what is important to them. They talk about their goals, aspirations, and dreams. They are happy to share their memories of childhood and growing up. They know their likes and dislikes and enjoy telling others about them. They are aware of their emotional reactions and like discussing them with their spouse.

Yet other people tend to be secretive. They like privacy and it is important for them that their borders should be respected. They view personal questions as prying, and are irritated if others ask them about matters that they would like to be kept secret. The curiosity of others is a source of annoyance to them. If both parties have this pattern, they can enjoy each other's company and each gives the other a large amount of personal space. They will not have as close a relationship as when two people are both open, but they can have what will be for them a very happy and successful marriage.

It becomes a problem when one party has a strong desire to understand and be understood and the other party has a strong desire in the other direction. The goal should be to find a workable compromise in which both parties feel that their needs are taken into consideration. Each couple will need to work this out in a way that is acceptable to both of them.

Some people have unstated concerns. They would probably gain much by discussing these concerns with their spouse. If you have hesitated to bring up an important matter, think about how to word what you say in a way that will resolve the issue. Some people find that they can express themselves better in writing than with the spoken word. They are able to write or type their thoughts on paper and this gives a clearer picture of their message. When you write you are in a much quieter state. You can think about what you want to express, you can edit, and you can rewrite.

My husband and I are very different from each other. I always wanted to have a close relationship and thought that we would be able to discuss everything. What I liked about my husband when I first met him was that he was careful with what he said. I observed that he thought about what he said before he said it in order to be sensitive to my feelings. This is one of the main reasons why I decided to marry him.

Now he tends to say what is on his mind without thinking about how I will react. This is difficult for me, but I am strongly motivated to work things out. The habit he has developed that causes me the most pain is this. He keeps saying to me, "You don't understand me."

I tell him, "I would like to understand you."

"You're only saying that," he replies, "but you don't really mean it."

"I really do," I say.

"No you don't," he repeats. "You can't understand me and you're not interested in doing so."

When he denies my reality like this, I do become irritated. Then he says, "Your irritation is proof that that you don't want to understand me."

I was told to be patient with him. Deep down he has a strong need to be understood. Unfortunately, he is going about this in the wrong way. But for my part I need to show him that I am willing to listen to him trying to describe himself, his thoughts, and his feelings, and I am willing to spend as much time on this as it takes for him to feel understood. I hope that he will be more open to discussing the issue with me and stop telling me that I don't understand him.

I would love for my spouse to understand me better. I have a complex inner world with many feelings. I myself don't always know what I am feeling until I express myself in words. But my spouse is very practical and considers the whole idea of understanding oneself a waste of time and energy.

"What do you mean you need to be understood," I would be told. "Don't waste time on nonsense. Take action and accomplish more."

I appreciate my spouse's integrity, practicality, and accomplishments. It is disappointing for me not to be as understood as I would have wished, but it is impossible for human beings to get everything they would want in life. Every once in a while I find people with similar personalities to mine who understand me, and I have decided to be happy with that. Instead of making myself miserable about what I don't have, I am enjoying the benefits of what I do have.

The two previous passages demonstrate how important it is to be able to examine one's situation, place the cards on the table, and arrive at an individual solution that works.

I liked the idea of asking my wife, "What would you want from me?"

I used to ask this form of question to my parents, teachers, and friends, and with good results. I couldn't always meet all of their requests, but knowing in what direction they would want me to go made my life a lot easier.

I expected my wife to tell me what she wanted of me when I politely asked her this question. But I was taken by surprise when she said, "If I have to tell you, what good is it?"

"But that's the only way I can know what you want," I protested.

"You should know on your own," she responded.

"But I don't," I pleaded.

"If you can't do things spontaneously, you're only acting and it isn't real, so it's not worth telling you."

"But we'll both lose out this way," I yelled.

"I for sure don't want you to talk to me like that," my wife said.

"But what should I do?" I asked.

"It's awful to be stuck with someone who lacks intuition," she said as she began to cry.

I then spoke from the bottom of my heart. "I love you and want to make you happy. I wish that I would know on my own what I should say and do. But, unfortunately, the reality is that I don't. Please be my coach. After a number of lessons, I will know on my own. But I need you to help me right now."

My depth of sincerity came through and my wife apologized for giving me such a rough time. She explained that she needed to be certain of my sincerity and now she heard it in my voice. This was a turning point in our lives.

Chapter Six

QUARRELS:
Go from lose-lose to win-win

∽ *Disagree without quarreling*

∽ *Seek win-win solutions*

∽ *Start off with agreement frame:*
"Who is to blame?" The question
that will lead you in the wrong direction

∽ *Take the initiative to stop*

∽ *There is tremendous power in silence*

∽ *It's amazing what "pattern interrupt" can accomplish*

∽ *Quarrels over irrelevant or trivial issues*
are one of the worst ways to spend your time

∽ *Develop the inner strength and courage to give in*

∽ *Consult a Torah scholar, when appropriate, to clarify*
the right thing to do and to resolve quarrels

DISAGREE WITHOUT QUARELLING

t is normal for people to disagree. We all have our own ways of looking at things. We all have our own needs and preferences. We all have our own tastes. But it is not inevitable that these disagreements in viewpoints, opinions, needs, preferences, and tastes must create a quarrel. They can become topics of discussion and even debate. And this can be done peacefully. What is the difference between a quarrel and a discussion? When you discuss an issue with someone, both parties speak with respect to the other. Both listen to what the other has to say, and each one has a chance to express his or her own thoughts and opinions in a relatively calm manner. A quarrel is when voices are raised and tempers flare. Many things that are said are inflammatory and unnecessary. Insults are thrown at one another, and feelings are hurt. In a quarrel both parties lose out.

People will have different feelings about what exactly makes a quarrel into a quarrel. Some people who have intense natures and speak with much emotion might enjoy a lively give and take, while other people who usually speak in a calmer manner might consider that to be a quarrel. If either spouse in a marriage considers something to be a quarrel, then there is a quarrel.

At times you will need to agree to disagree. Some people find this fairly easy to accept. But there are husbands and wives who feel much discomfort if they have different opinions on important issues even though there isn't a practical everyday difference. Since each person is unique, differences in thought are to be expected. *Shalom bayis* doesn't necessarily mean that two people think exactly alike. Rather, that they have a harmonious relationship even though they might think differently.

At times, both a husband and wife will want to express their opinions first. Each is impatient to say what he or she feels a need to say. This can cause frustration and can transform a discussion into a quarrel. If you find that you are being constantly interrupted, you can say, "I listened to you, so please give me five uninterrupted minutes." If you haven't listened to the other person yet, either do so for five minutes, or say, "Please listen to me for five minutes and then I'll listen to you without interruptions."

Be resolved to express your thoughts and opinions without quarreling. There are many issues in a marriage about which you might have a stalemate. You have a choice to keep arguing about them over and over again, or deciding to leave your differences unsolved but to enjoy other aspects of each other. When you see that there will not be a settlement of an argument, state your position. State it as clearly as you can. Then stop. Since it won't be accepted there is no difference whether you say it once or many times.

This is similar to an incident that was reported on the BBC World Service. A customer in a cafe said to a waiter, "Please give me a cup of coffee without cream." The waiter came back without the coffee, and asked, "We're out of cream today. Would you like your coffee without milk?" Some people tend to argue without listening to what the other person is saying. About such people it has been said, "The difference between a monologue and a dialogue is that in a monologue only one person is talking to himself and in a dialogue two people are talking to themselves." Before arguing, listen to the other person's position. At times, you will see that you have less to argue about. Even when you do feel a need to disagree, you will be able to address the actual points that were raised.

When you argue about a specific issue, keep the discussion to the issue at hand. By bringing up arguments and resentments about other issues, nothing will be resolved, except that hurt and angry feelings will be increased. Don't say anything that would be a putdown of your spouse. For example, "If you would have any sense, you would realize that I am right and you are wrong."

People have subjective tastes. Some mistakenly view them as absolute realities. In issues of taste, instead of saying, "You have awful taste," you can say, "I prefer something different."

When two people disagree, if both parties repeat the essence of what the other said to show that they understand the other one's position, it usually helps to keep the situation under control. In issues of opinion, instead of saying, "You are all wrong," Or, "You don't know what you are talking about," you can say, "I hear what you are saying. Let me express another way of looking at the matter." It can also be helpful to say something like, "I can see why you feel that way. Let me explain how I feel about it." The more respect you personally show to the other speaker, the more likely it is that the other person will listen to you also with respect.

We were married for five months and were shocked about how much of the time we argued. When we first met, we seemed to agree on the important issues of life. During the engagement, all discussions about plans for the wedding went smoothly. We were both certain that we would have an ideal marriage.

But after the excitement of the wedding and the sheva berachos was over, we found ourselves quarreling over scores of trivial matters. Buying food for Shabbos, cleaning the house, inviting guests, or going places were all grist for the mill of our frequent verbal battles. If there were at least two ways of doing something, we would find ourselves arguing over the best way to do it.

Then we visited an uncle and aunt of mine in another city and stayed for three days. I had been at their home before, but now I noticed things I had never noticed before. They were very different from one another in personality and in background. They often had different opinions on things, but there was consistently a harmonious atmosphere in their home.

They openly discussed differences of opinion with each other, and I was able to see them talking calmly and respectfully about their plans and about things that needed to get taken care of. They both would listen patiently to what the other one had to say on a matter. Then they would either take turns as to whose preference they would follow this time, or they would find a third alternative on which they both could agree.

When I was single, I saw and heard them discussing issues peacefully, but it didn't register that this was quite an accomplishment when you are interacting with someone who is so different from you. My own parents were much more similar and their life situation didn't call for so much negotiating. Each one had his or her domain and things just worked out. Now, however, I saw a model that was necessary for my marriage.

My spouse and I each perceived our disagreements as an attack on each other's judgment and taste. We would each try to get the other to agree that we were right. I pointed out this pattern to my spouse, and suggested that we both watch my uncle and aunt's pattern of behavior carefully to learn from it how we could talk about our differences in opinions and tastes.

I saw that this was beginning to work, because we had an immediate argument on whether to test this out.

"I don't think it's proper for us to discuss the way they communicate," my spouse said to me.

"Why not?" I asked.

"It's an invasion of their privacy."

"I'm not suggesting we eavesdrop," I clarified. "Only that we listen to how they speak to each other during the meals we have with them. They see us sitting right in front of them at their table and they don't seem to mind that we are listening to what they are saying. I'm 100 percent certain that if I ask my aunt and uncle if we can learn from them, they would both be thrilled to help us out. But I don't feel a need to mention it to them."

My spouse agreed with me. I was proud of myself for the way I handled that discussion. Previously, I would have gotten angry and said, "You don't care about our marriage. You want to keep on fighting and arguing, don't you?" This never went over too well, and I desperately wanted to change things. I am grateful for the hashgachah pratis of having role models for three whole days.

My wife and I would fight like cats and dogs over both major and minor issues. As soon as one of us said something the other didn't like, the battle began.

We were quite well off financially, and this was part of our problem. We had enough money to buy many of the things we wanted, but we argued over the details. We had differences of opinion about which organizations should receive donations. We argued over how many guests to have for Shabbos. The list went on and on.

But we received a loud wake-up call one day. My wife and I were in the middle of one of our daily round of arguments. The telephone rang and on the other end was someone who had a complaint about a business deal we had made. If I had been in a positive frame of mind, I *could have handled it smoothly. But the argument with my wife had aroused my anger. I told the person who called me, "You are an idiot if you feel you could win a lawsuit if you sue me. See if I care. I guarantee you that I'll definitely come out on top."*

My challenge was effective, but not in the direction that I wanted. The fellow raised his voice and said belligerently, "We'll see who the real idiot is. I'll see you in court." I had to hire an expensive lawyer and the case dragged on for over two years. I didn't lose as much as the other fellow thought I would, but my expenses were high, and I did lose a substantial amount.

Even though the lawsuit was stressful, it brought my wife and me closer. We now had a common enemy and we stood together. We both saw the harm of our angry arguments and were careful to speak respectfully to each other even when we disagreed.

I might seem to others to have things under control when the stress is high, and I must agree that I do. But it is all because of my sensitive husband. Whenever I feel totally overwhelmed and ready to give up, my husband will give me a reassuring smile and say just the words that I need to hear.

"You've been through this before," he would say to me, "and you've managed exceptionally well. I know that you can handle it again."

His total belief in me has enabled me to believe in myself. I would thank him profusely for all his help, and he would say to me, "You're the one who manages so well. I only say a few words of appreciation." His so-called few words of appreciation are the work of an artist. He always knows exactly what to say to make me feel good. When I feel discouraged, he is so thoroughly confident in my abilities to handle things that it is almost impossible for me not to believe in myself.

If you would ask what exactly he says to me, I would be hesitant to answer you. The answer might seem too simple. He doesn't give long speeches. He doesn't preach or give me unwanted advice. But what he does do is point out how I've done so many things well in the past. He points out how much I mean to him. He points out how he appreciates all that I've done for him. When I ask him, "Such as?" he just smiles and says, "If I would start giving specific details, I would be taking away from the totality of all that I owe you."

"Come on," I would protest. "You are so confident and competent. You don't really need me."

"I only seem like that on the outside," he would say with all sincerity. "But I know that I would not be able to do all that I'm doing without you. Your essence is precious to me. It's not just this thing about you or that thing. It's you in your entirety."

When he says things like this to me, I'm touched on a deep level. I find it hard to believe that I mean so much to him. But I see that he is sincere in what he is saying. I do believe in him. I do think he's the greatest. But I don't think this way just in order to make him feel good. I think this way because it is the truth. And I guess that is how he feels about me.

It wasn't always like this, however. In the beginning of our marriage we argued and fought quite regularly. It took us a long time to get used to each other's habits and idiosyncrasies.

There was a turning point in our marriage. And for this I am thankful to my husband. We were in the midst of another one of our typical arguments. We both were feeling bad about what the other had said. Then all of a sudden my husband said in a very emphatic voice, "That's enough of this already."

I was taken aback by the way he said this. And then he went on, "I've been thinking lately about our marriage. We are causing each other so much pain and for no reason. We both love and care about each other. Let's agree to discuss any disagreements we ever have in a mutually respectful way."

I was thrilled to hear this. Of course I agreed with him. We were both committed to overcome any negative feelings that we had. We were committed to treat each other the way the Torah requires. And since we were both dedicated to improving the situation, we did. My marriage is now so wonderful that it seems like the rough part was from a different lifetime.

As I think in retrospect about the early part of our marriage, I recall the thoughts that went through my mind. I remember that although my marriage was a constant struggle, my spirit was unbroken because I knew that there was promise of renewal. I felt at the core of my soul that Hashem had a purpose for me. Oh, how I wished at the time I knew what that purpose was. I had many unanswered questions, but the big one for me was, "For what purpose did I suffer so much in my marriage? What can I do with the knowledge that my experiences gave me."

Now I know at least partly why I suffered. We started out with a rough marriage and we transformed it into one of spiritual beauty. I am able to give encouragement to young women whom I meet who seem to be suffering in their marriage. I realize that everyone's situation is different. But I believe that many other couples are like us. Once they learn how to disagree with mutual respect, they can begin to bring out the best in each other. When you do this, you don't need to work on your marriage. Your appreciation for each other makes you both feel good about one another and about yourself.

SEEK WIN-WIN SOLUTIONS

We all have needs, wants, and wishes. It is normal that our needs, wants, and wishes will sometimes clash with those of the person to whom we are married. Just as a couple can disagree peacefully, so too can they work out win-win solutions. These are solutions that you work out together in a way that both your needs are met and therefore you are both basically satisfied with the results.

When either a husband or wife tries to insure that only he or she will "win," this is not going to really be win-lose, but lose-lose. Unless both a husband and wife feel that the other wants him or her to have his or her needs met, there are likely to be hurt feelings and neither will be happy. Be willing to make sacrifices. We all know that you have to give up something in order to get something.

The question for you to keep in mind is: "How can I have my needs met while at the same time my spouse also has his/her needs met?" Definitely this takes more work than just one party being satisfied, but all the efforts exerted in finding such solutions are a wise investment. In some situations a win-win solution might mean that this time one of the parties gets his or her way and the next time a similar disagreement comes up, the other gets his or her way. For many couples learning to say, "I'll make you a win-win deal," is one of the best tools they can acquire. Instead of quarreling about things, they can negotiate an agreement that both would find acceptable.

Take, for example, the following: Some people love analyzing everything that is said. Others hate it. If both husband and wife have the same pattern all can go well. If one wants to analyze and the other one doesn't, they have a few options:

- They don't analyze. The one who would really like to learns to accept this.
- They analyze. The one who doesn't enjoy this, does so for the benefit of the other partner.
- They analyze more than one wants and less than the other would wish. They can both feel good that part of their

wishes are met and that they are meeting some of the other person's needs.

If you feel that your spouse is trying to solve a situation in a way that will be win-lose, you might find it helpful to explicitly say, "Let's try to find a way that will be win-win. Let's see how we can work this out in a way that both our needs are met."

Be careful not to attack your spouse. In most situations it isn't necessary to say outright, "That's not fair. You're trying to make me lose out. You are only considering your needs and not mine." This form of statement is usually not conducive to making your spouse more open to meeting your needs. And when you try to just get your way, you are pushing your spouse into a position of just trying to get his or her way. By just stating that you want it to be good for both, you are presenting this request in the way most conducive to creating goodwill.

"Who won this time?" This was the theme of our arguments. Winning, rather than loving, was a key element in our marriage. Whenever my spouse and I disagreed, the issue of who was the winner and who the loser was uppermost in our minds.

When we had minor arguments, winning and losing was almost like a sports competition. But when we argued over major issues, the battle to win was more like an all-out war. At times this was even over seemingly trivial issues, but the underlying themes were major to us.

We saw that we weren't able to resolve our differences on our own. We both found it difficult to speak to a third party about our quarrels. But after an especially ugly quarrel, we came to the conclusion that the pain we were suffering was so bad that we just had to do something about it.

The person we consulted asked us to describe a few of our arguments to see what they looked and sounded like. It was clear that regardless of the content of our arguments, the main goal for both of us was to come out the winner. This was especially difficult to determine because we didn't have a referee or a judge, and we both were highly biased.

We received a homework assignment. After each argument that week we should both write down who we think won. We should keep a journal of the topics argued about and our criteria for determining the winner.

Before we reported that week's win and lose record, we were asked, "Looking back at this week, how do you feel about your arguments and quarrels?"

We both answered that we feel awful about them. Even the winner is left with a bad taste in the mouth. And the loser feels even worse.

"So, in essence, you both lose out by trying to win, don't you?" we were asked. And it was obvious that our pattern was painful for both of us.

"This coming week, look at yourself as two people who are friends on the same team," it was suggested to us. "Act as if it were important to both of you that you should both end up winners and neither of you a loser."

We had been aware of the idea of win-win, but our automatic reactions were, "I need to win, and you need to lose." Spending a week on making certain we both felt like winners was a wonderful experience. We were both rooting for each other and came up with a few creative solutions that we hadn't thought of before.

I love to have guests for Shabbos. The more people, the better. I consider this chesed a high priority. It is also very difficult for me to refuse someone who asks me if he can come to our house, and many guests ask if they can bring along a friend or two who need a place to eat. My wife also likes to do chesed, but she has a stronger *need for privacy. Moreover, she is the one who does most of the work when we have guests.*

When someone calls me up to ask if he or she can come to our house for Shabbos, my tendency is to say, "Of course, you can come for Shabbos. We are happy to have you as our guest. Let me check with my wife to make certain that it's okay with her."

My wife complained that this wasn't fair to her. When she feels too tired for company, she wants to be able to refuse, but she knows that I will feel disappointed. Her biggest objection to what I say is, "You make me sound like the mean one. The person sees that you are happy to have him over, but I am the one who refuses. Right from the start you should give a cooler response until you consult with me."

I argue that this will make the person feel unwelcome. Then even if we let him be our guest, he might feel bad that we were hesitant at first.

I asked someone for a suggestion as to how to handle this. I was told, "Definitely, you should sound enthusiastic about having the person be your guest. But you can say, "We would love to have you as a guest. Let me first check out the present plans for this Shabbos to see if this week will be okay." This way in case my wife is not up to having company, it doesn't sound as if I am blaming her. The reason for not having the person over sounds impersonal. This approach was acceptable to us both.

My wife and I had frequent quarrels over a number of issues that were important to both of us. We spoke to some people for advice about what we could do to improve our relationship. Some of the ideas we heard lasted for a short time, but after a

week or two we would once again repeat our old problematic patterns.

The technique that finally helped us make a lasting change was our writing a contract of agreement. We each wrote five rules that we would follow. Since we would both gain a lot if the other one kept to the rules that he or she had agreed upon, we were highly motivated to follow our own rules.

The rules that I had written for myself were:

- I agree to greet you enthusiastically every time I walk into the house.
- I agree to talk without raising my voice. If I ever do raise my voice, you just need to say, "Please speak in a quieter tone." I agree to accept this without arguing that I am speaking in a quiet tone.
- I agree to discuss your thoughts regarding any plans I make that will affect you; and I will not make plans unilaterally.
- I agree to stop using the expression, "There's no defense like a good offense," since I know that it bothers you.
- I agree not to speak to you with sarcasm.
- I agree to study with you at least three times a week.

It took a lot of effort on my part to keep to these rules consistently. But since I saw that my wife was also making the effort to keep to the other set of rules, I kept reviewing my list with a strong sense of commitment.

My husband is a man of peace. This is a wonderful quality and I greatly appreciate it. But there is one aspect of my husband's attitude of "peace at all costs" that distresses me. One of his favorite mottoes is, "It is permissible to distort the truth for the sake of peace." He takes this to such an extreme that I can never believe him.

If he thinks that something will get me even a tiny bit upset or irritated, he will distort the truth. When I ask him how much he paid for something, he will frequently tell me a lower price so I won't argue that he could have obtained it for less. If he forgot to buy something for the house, he will tell me that the store is out of the item. If he didn't get around to calling one of the children's teachers, he will tell me he called but the line was busy. If he didn't ask for a raise because he feels uncomfortable when confronting the boss, he will make up an excuse why it's not the right time to do it. If he gave me the wrong information about something, he won't correct it even when he realizes that what he said was wrong, because he is afraid I will criticize him.

I've repeatedly told him that I would prefer that he tell me the truth. He tells me, "Of course I will," but he doesn't. I don't know about all the times I didn't find out that he did not tell me the truth, but the amount of times that I have found this out leads me to believe that he has done this very often. This gives me a strong feeling of lack of trust in what he says. I know that my husband is basically an honest person when it comes to financial matters, but not when it comes to preventing a potential quarrel.

I finally told him, "I will make you a deal. I am resolved to refrain from giving you a hard time when you tell me the truth and you can test me out. If, in the future, you aren't satisfied with how I react to your honesty, please tell me that you would prefer a different response." I kept my word and my husband has been much more open and straight.

A few weeks after my marriage my husband forgot to buy something for me that he said he would.

"I want you to ask for my forgiveness," I demanded.

"What for?" my husband asked in a puzzled tone of voice.

"Because you showed you don't care about me," I said with a tear in my eye.

"No, I didn't," he replied. "I do care about you very much. I just forgot to go to the store."

"To me that's a sign of a lack of caring," I said. "So apologize."

"I won't apologize when you speak that way to me. You have hurt me more than I have hurt you. When I thought about getting married, someone told me the well-known story of Rabbi Shlomo Zalman Auerbach, the Rosh Yeshivah of Kol Torah and a world-renowned halachic authority. At his wife's funeral a member of the Chevra Kaddisha told him to ask forgiveness of his departed wife as is the standard custom.

"Rabbi Auerbach refused. 'I never said or did anything to give her pain so I have no need to ask for forgiveness.'

"My dream is to emulate him. I feel devastated that you think I need to ask for your forgiveness. I don't think I should be blamed for forgetting that which is beyond my control."

"Okay," I said. "I accept what you are saying. I take back my request. But in the future if you agree to buy something for me please write it down in a place that will enable you to remember to take care of it."

My husband was grateful and agreed. I didn't tell him that my initial reaction was to say, "Well this just proves that you aren't on the level of such a talmid chacham and tzaddik." But I immediately caught myself. It's in both of our best interests that my husband continue his goal to emulate Rav Auerbach. It would be stupid of me to destroy his dream.

There are some arguments that at first glance might seem to be unsolvable. Either one party or the other must give in for things to work out, but neither side wishes to budge. Frequently, there are solutions available. But the way you look at the situation must be changed. The following story told by a world-famous negotiator illustrates this:

There is an old story about a father who died and left a will about how his estate should be divided up. He had seventeen camels and wrote that they should be given to his three sons. When he wrote the will, he didn't know exactly how many camels he would have at the time the will would be read. So he wrote the amount in percentages, not in the number of camels each one would receive.

"My oldest son should receive half the camels I leave over," he had written. "My middle son should receive a third of the camels. And my youngest son should receive a ninth."

When they tried to divide up their father's inheritance, they had a problem. They had to share the seventeen camels, but they couldn't be divided by two or three or nine. They argued and argued, but couldn't reach an agreed upon decision. Finally they went to a wise aunt of theirs and asked for her opinion. She asked them for some time to think about the problem.

"Come back in two days and I hope to be able to think of a solution," she told them. "I don't want my brother's children to quarrel. I know that your father would have wanted you to settle this peacefully." When they returned in two days, she told them she had a plan. "I will give you one of my camels and now you have eighteen to divide up. The oldest will take half of the camels, so he gets nine. The middle son will take a third, so he gets six. The youngest will take a ninth, so he gets two. Nine, six, and two add up to seventeen. Now I will take back the camel that was originally mine."

By looking at the problem from a different angle than you did at first, you might be able to come up with a mutually acceptable solution yourselves, as this aunt did. If you can't do it yourselves, perhaps you can consult someone with whom you both feel comfortable.

START OFF WITH AGREEMENT FRAME: "WHO IS TO BLAME?" THE QUESTION THAT WILL LEAD YOU IN THE WRONG DIRECTION

Would you like to hear one piece of advice that will save you from many quarrels throughout your life? If you don't want to avoid quarrels, don't listen to this suggestion: "Don't blame." Following the advice of these two words can transform a marriage from an arena of many heated battles and quarrels to a marriage of peace and harmony.

In a courtroom, there is often a major difference in clarifying whose fault it was. But in a marriage, it is often irrelevant. Moreover, when the husband thinks it's the wife's fault, and the wife thinks it's the husband's fault, battling over the issue will usually result in a more negatively entrenched position, rather than in a positive agreement.

In the vast majority of situations it makes absolutely no difference who was at fault. Why destroy one's *shalom bayis* over an irrelevant issue? People who make it a high priority to pin the blame on their spouse cause much ill-will. The more you try to pin the blame on your spouse, the greater the likelihood that your spouse will try to pin the blame on you. People who blame will say, "It was your fault." The other spouse will respond, "You are blaming me? You are the one to blame." This just increases the intensity of the quarrel.

Rabbi Chaim Shmulevitz used to say on the verse, "You shall not act similar to Korach and his company" (*Bamidbar* 17:5): "Besides the literal meaning of the verse, that this is a prohibition against maintaining disputes (*Sanhedrin* 110a; *Mishnah Berurah* 156:4), the Torah is telling us another lesson. The verse can be understood, 'There won't be like Korach and his company.' That is, Korach and his company were 100 percent wrong, and Moshe was 100 percent right. In other situations, each side will be partly right and partly wrong."

In many situations when a husband and wife argue about who was to blame, they both can take part of the credit. They can always argue about who has a larger percentage and who has a smaller percentage, but usually they each will feel that the other bears the main burden of fault. They will start off thinking this way and that's the way they will feel at the end of the argument.

It can be difficult to accept responsibility when you feel that your spouse was also to blame, but refuses to take his or her share of responsibility. Going out of your way to take the blame in order to have a harmonious home is an act of courage and is spiritually elevating.

The classic work *Orchos Tzaddikim* (ch. 21) wrote: "If two people quarreled and afterwards made peace, neither should later say to the other: 'The reason I behaved as I did is because you did this and this to me.' Even if the person saying this does not intend to resume the quarrel, such a remark is apt to rekindle the dispute, since the other person will probably retort, 'No, it was your fault.'" This pattern is especially important in a marriage. Even if you think that your spouse was at fault, forget it. Live in the present and enjoy your marriage rather than fighting about who started a quarrel that is already over.

Often, a partner who is afraid to face his or her patterns of speech or behavior will deny that he or she has any issues. If you want your spouse to accept the fact that you both have an issue that needs a solution, make it as easy as possible for him or her to discuss this. Say explicitly that you are not interested in focusing on blame. What do you want is positive changes in words and deeds, and be willing to do your share to make it easier for your spouse. Some people feel such an important need to blame their spouse for what is wrong that they insist on using an approach this is almost guaranteed to create resistance. Focus on the solution. This statement is so important that it needs to be repeated again and again.

Think of all the married couples who lived during the last 2,000 years. Just try to imagine all the hours husbands and wives spent blaming each other. Don't let your spouse and yourself be counted among them.

If you grew up in a house with a lot of blaming, it is possible that your first impulse will be to blame. If this is true for you, know that with a concerted effort, you can stop this pattern. It's amazing to realize that if no one is blamed, things usually don't get worse. By respectfully and pleasantly pointing out what needs to be done in the future you will get your point across. For example, if a glass was put at the edge of the table and fell down, you needn't make an issue of blaming your spouse for being careless.

Master the ability to speak:

- Assertively
- Without blaming
- With respect
- With compassion

When you have to speak about a matter over which you are upset, irritated, resentful, or angry, use these four guidelines. Don't speak aggressively but don't just be passive either. Rather, speak up assertively. Don't blame. And speak with respect and compassion.

I have spent years trying to prove to myself and my spouse that all the difficulties we have been having in our marriage are my spouse's fault. Since my spouse has thought that any arguments, disagreements, and problems that arise are all my fault, I constantly had to maintain my innocence and my spouse's guilt.

We were like two lawyers arguing a major case in front of a court. Neither budged a fraction of an inch regardless of how strong a case the other one made. We were both biased and nothing the other said made a drop of a difference. I knew it was all my spouse's fault and felt that my spouse really knew this, but was just too stubborn to admit it. The trouble was that my spouse felt the exact same way, but with the identities of the right and wrong parties exchanged.

We would explain our positions as clearly as we could. Since we didn't get anywhere, we would repeat our views over and over again. After a while this became frustrating and we would raise our voices and shout our mutual blame. This never got us anywhere either, but when you are angrily screaming at your spouse, you don't stop to think, "Is this getting me anyplace?"

One day at a large supermarket I heard a couple arguing about whose fault it was that they hadn't brought along enough money to pay for all that they wanted to buy. The wife said to her husband, "It's all your fault. Why didn't you bring more money?" And the husband said to his wife, "It's all your fault. Why didn't you tell me at home how much you wanted to buy?" They were getting louder and louder, angrier and angrier. Everyone in the store was staring at them, but they were oblivious to it. The only thing that counted was to get the other one to see who was to blame.

The saleslady was getting impatient, and politely said, "There is a long line. Could you please stand aside until you finish your discussion?" Her request went unheeded and the angry couple kept up the debate in front of a large crowd. Finally, a stranger with a loud voice who was standing in a different line, called out to them, "Both of you cut it out. It was all my fault." Everyone laughed. The arguing couple stopped for a moment and did move aside.

I felt a powerful hashgachah pratis message was given to me just then. My spouse and I would never argue like that in public, but at home we do. I saw clearly that in this couple's situation it didn't make a drop of a difference whose fault it was. They would have to find a practical solution to their difficulty regardless of who was to blame. They both were right. Each could have done differently. The husband should have brought along more money, and the wife should have told the husband how much she planned to buy. It's likely that neither of them knew in advance exactly how much they would buy and how much money was needed.

From then on whenever I noticed that my spouse and I were each trying to blame the other, I immediately saw a mental picture of that couple arguing in front of the crowd in the supermarket. This image caused me to stop trying to argue about who was at fault. "Let's handle this situation right now even if I am at fault," I would say.

Looking back I can see that this would have saved me a lot of pain and frustration if I would have had the wisdom and courage to say this instead of responding, "No, it's not my fault. It's all your fault." After acknowledging that it could be my fault, and at times even saying that it is my fault, it has become a relatively easy action. It's only an illusion that it's difficult. I see that I lose absolutely nothing by claiming it's my fault. My spouse, of course, finds this easier to accept than when I try to pass the blame. And I feel an inner good feeling of having greater shalom bayis. Giving up the battle of deciding whose fault it is enables us both to think of more practical solutions to the issue at hand.

*E*very time I voiced a complaint to my husband, he would say, "Before I was married this wasn't a problem for me. So it's all your fault that I am now acting the way I am."

If I told my husband that I would like him to be more cheerful, he would say, "Everybody always told me that I was a happy person. So it's your fault I'm not cheerful now."

When I complained about his anger, he would say, "I never became angry before I was married, so it's all your fault that I lose my temper. You can ask my family or my roommates and you will hear from them that I didn't used to get angry."

If I told him that he was being self-centered and not thinking enough about my needs, he would say, "Everybody always told me that I was a great guy. People always knew that they could ask me to do favors for them. It's only because of you that I seem self-centered."

I was puzzled and curious: What did my husband feel he would gain by blaming me for all his faults?

He might have talked himself into believing that none of his faults were truly his own. I was to blame for everything and before we were married he was a paragon of virtue. I would have been much more impressed with his character if he would have taken responsibility for correcting his faults instead of blaming me for them. I was skeptical about his claim that all of his faults began only after he was married to me.

I finally reached the conclusion that now seems obvious: I would gain nothing by trying to blame him for his faults, since he consistently threw them back to me. I told him, "I accept that the way I talk and act has caused you to act the way you do. Nevertheless, let us make a team effort to both improve."

Once I stopped trying to convince him that his faults are not my fault, he was much more open to change the problematic patterns.

"Did you take care of what I asked you to do?" the husband or wife asks the other.

"You never asked me to do it," replies the other one.

"Yes, I did. You must not have been paying attention."

"You only think you told me. It was an imaginary conversation."

"You are just being defensive. I did tell you and you know it."
"Are you calling me a liar."

This dialogue is a fairly common one. Who is usually right? I don't know and invariably it doesn't make a bit of a difference. I usually tell people who are quite certain that they mentioned something while the other one claims it wasn't mentioned to them, "Assume that you told him/her, but he/she doesn't recall it. Everyone has an imperfect memory. Very few people consistently get 100 percent correct on every single test they take in every single subject. We all forget. It could be that your spouse was distracted. And it could also be that you didn't speak loudly enough when you said your message. Repeat your message as if it is the first time you are stating it and let it go at that."

Those who follow this advice don't get caught up in an endless give and take that just frustrates everyone involved.

*M*y wife and I used to spend a lot of time arguing about who was to blame when anything went wrong. Then one day my wife said, "Let's blame this one on the yetzer hara."

I agreed. "Yes, let's blame the yetzer hara instead of each other. That makes sense. Let's focus our anger and hate on the yetzer hara and reserve our love for each other."

Since then, if either of us wants to place the blame for something on the other, the response usually is, "It was the yetzer hara's fault, of course."

TAKE THE INITIATIVE TO STOP

Quarrels are easy to start but difficult to stop. Once you get into a heated quarrel, you want to get the last word. The only problem is that your debating partner feels the exact same way. Each one wants the other one to hear his or her point and if possible to agree that he or she is right. The problem with a quarrel is that when emotions are flaring, neither is open to hear what the other has to say. Neither feels like giving the other the satisfaction of thinking, "He/she concedes that I am right and recognizes that I have won." Therefore it is difficult to stop.

It takes courage to stop an argument. Some people might fear that their spouse will consider their stopping right now as a sign that they now know they have made a mistake. It takes strength to say to oneself, "Even though I don't feel that I have won this argument, I see that I probably won't get my spouse to see my point right now. So I will stop." Knowing that stopping a quarrel is an act of inner strength makes it easier to do so.

Even in the nastiest of quarrels, have the courage to say, "I apologize. Let's stop quarreling." If you find this difficult to say, practice over and over again. This is so useful that it is worth repeating to yourself even thousands of times until it becomes second nature.

Some of the things you might say to stop a quarrel are:
- "Let me think this over."
- "I see that we both feel strongly about our positions. Right now neither of us is convincing the other. Let us agree to disagree."
- "Let us discuss this at a different time when we are both calmer."
- "This is getting out of hand. Let's call a truce."

A Torah scholar once told me, "In my house I always have the final word. When my wife says, 'Take out the garbage,' I say, 'Of course, I will.'"

While he said this to me as a joke, the lesson is valuable. If you want the final word, the way to be sure to get it is to say things that your spouse will enjoy. This is especially true when you are involved in an argument. If you want the last word each time you quarrel, try this, "I love you, and I'm sorry that I spoke to you the way I did."

THERE IS TREMENDOUS POWER IN SILENCE

There are many different forms of silence. There is an active silence and there is a passive silence. There is a silence that comes from being intimidated, and there is a silence that comes from an inner strength. There is a silence that is meant to be passive-aggressively giving a message, "I am angry right now. And even though you would like me to talk, I refuse. I want my silence to cause you some of the suffering you've caused me." And there is the silence that says, "I would like the situation to cool down right now. I will remain silent so we can both become calmer."

The silence that is an expression of inner power is when you have the option to say something that would be an attack or a counterattack and yet, out of a sincere desire to restore peace, you remain silent. This silence is only positive if you feel that speaking right now would make the situation worse. If your spouse would like to discuss the issues that you argued about in order to work it out, and you refuse to do so, this silence is a fault, not a virtue. It is in reference to the positive forms of silence that the Vilna Gaon cites the *Midrash* that for every single second that a person keeps his mouth closed, he merits a special eternal light that is beyond the comprehension of even celestial beings (*Iggeres HaGra*).

I've been married over fifteen years and I have a problem with anger which I'm trying to conquer. Until now I have failed over and over again in trying to control my temper. Sometimes I get upset and have a complaint against my husband. When I tell him my complaints in an angry voice, he just listens quietly with a blank face. He refuses to show any recognition that he hears what I'm saying. Now if I were on a proper spiritual level, I'd convince myself that he just refuses to get involved in a quarrel because that's what the Torah asks of us, and that someone who can keep his mouth closed during a quarrel is a great person.

However, when I see my husband's blank face it goads me on to reiterate what I said. Unfortunately, I start getting heated up and resent the fact that my partner does not even acknowledge that I spoke to him. I then say a bit more. Even then he refuses to comment. Then I get really upset.

I felt certain that the Rabbi I consulted about this would answer me, "You're a mature adult who wants to work on her middos. You recognize the greatness of your husband. Why don't you control yourself?" Of course, I know this is true, but when I see that after all these years I'm not coping, I feel a different strategy on the part of my husband is necessary.

I humbly suggest that keeping one's mouth closed is the appropriate approach for a stranger or an enemy. But I feel it would be much more productive if my husband would reply to an angry outburst somewhat like this, "I can't say I agree with you, but I'm sorry you're upset. I really don't mean to hurt you. I'm sorry, I can't discuss the matter with you when you're angry and talk like this. But when you calm down, whether in a few hours or tomorrow, I'll be happy to talk to you about it and see if we can come to a mutual understanding."

I asked a Rabbi, "Wouldn't that be more beneficial than just making a blank face and pretending you didn't hear your wife speak?" To my pleasant surprise, the Rabbi agreed wholeheartedly with me. "Since I haven't heard your husband's side, I can't comment at all on the content of your argument. But certainly the type of response you would wish for is the appropriate one in such situations."

IT'S AMAZING WHAT "PATTERN INTERRUPT" CAN ACCOMPLISH

When you find yourself in an argument with your spouse, it is often wise to use the technique known as "pattern interrupt" to stop the quarrel. What is "pattern interrupt"? It is the ability to say something that will enable your spouse to focus on something else besides the argument. At times you might say something that is totally irrelevant to the issue at hand. By doing so smoothly and naturally you will gently stop a quarrel and restore harmony.

It is usually quite easy to interrupt someone's pattern. You just start talking about something else. This happens often in conversations. People change the topic all the time. When this is done smoothly, it often goes unnoticed. So if you find yourself in the midst of a quarrel with your spouse about a matter that doesn't call for a decision, start talking about a different topic.

One form of pattern interrupt is to say, "I don't know why but this reminds me of …" (Right now think of a few neutral topics that quarrels will remind you of.) Then you can talk about any other topic in the world.

You might point to something and say, "What is that?" You might take a deep breath, and ask, "Is that smell dangerous?" (Quarrels are, you know.)

If you want to become proficient at the skill of "pattern interrupt," keep on practicing even when you are not in the middle of a quarrel. Then you will find it easier to do it if you need to apply this technique in the middle of a quarrel.

You can interrupt a pattern by saying words of Torah on the weekly portion. You can interrupt a pattern by relating a funny joke or story. You can interrupt a pattern by asking questions. You can ask, "Why do you feel so strongly about this issue?" Or, "How long have you felt this way?" Or, "What is the exact time right now?" After being told, you might say, "It's getting late. I have to take care of something right now."

A particularly powerful pattern interrupt is to smile and throw a kiss. Another pattern is to take some food or drink and slowly make a *berachah* over it. Then comment on the food, or even on the miracle of the digestive system.

Listen carefully to how people use "pattern interrupt" on you. Almost everyone will do it when you want to talk about one subject and he or she has a strong need to talk about something else. By observing these patterns in others, you will eventually master this worthwhile skill. "Pattern interrupt" is also the tool to use when you want to prevent someone from speaking *lashon hara*.

QUARRELS OVER IRRELEVANT OR TRIVIAL ISSUES ARE ONE OF THE WORST WAYS TO SPEND YOUR TIME

We are all on this planet for a limited amount of time. Each moment we make a choice about how we will utilize our time. Some choices will be wise. These are the choices that are spiritually elevating. These are the choices that give us a higher quality emotional life, the ones that enable us to live in harmony with others and give us more joy. Other choices are spiritually debilitating. These are the choices that decrease the spiritual and emotional quality of our lives.

One of the worst ways to spend one's life is to waste time quarreling and arguing. This causes pain while you are quarreling, and it has distressful aftereffects. If someone is arguing over a major ideal, it can at times be justified or at least understood, but when a married couple argues over trivial and irrelevant issues, it is much worse than wasting precious time. It is taking time that was given to build and accomplish and misusing it to destroy and ruin.

How much time would you really like to designate in the future for needless quarrels over trivial matters? Almost everyone will answer: none. No one wants to plan ahead to cause themselves and their spouse pain. So if you're not interested in planning to have a needless quarrel, don't allow yourself to get caught in one unintentionally. Both before you begin or as you suddenly find yourself in one, ask yourself, "What is the difference?" If there's no real difference, don't waste time on trying to accomplish nothing.

At times an argument over a topic that seems irrelevant or minor might have a more serious underlying issue. The issue might be that one or both feel a lack of respect, love, appreciation or gratitude. One or the other might be experiencing a lot of frustration, resentment, or stress. When this is the case, the underlying issue must be dealt with and resolved. There are many times in a marriage when either the husband or wife is angry at the other for doing and saying something and yet the other party is totally unaware of this. The person who is irritated might feel that the issue is too minor to mention, but feels very angry, or the person who is angry might not be totally aware of how much this actually means to him or her. When there is a lot of pent-up resentment and rage a small spark can cause a major blowup. Getting in touch with the core issues that cause the quarrels can enable you to work them through, sometimes by yourself and sometimes with your spouse and this will prevent future quarrels.

*M*y husband and I were in a taxi going to the wedding of a relative. The taxi driver told us the meter was broken and asked for a price that was higher than it should have been. My husband began to argue with the driver. The driver answered that it was a fair price and if we didn't like it, we could get out. It was raining and we were late for the wedding so his offer wasn't realistic for us.

My husband began lecturing the taxi driver on the value of honesty and the harm of deception. I felt embarrassed and motioned to my husband to stop, but he kept on delivering his sermon. I whispered to my husband to stop, but he kept on going. I was feeling very uncomfortable and I repeated my request in a louder tone of voice. My husband's anger at the driver then carried over to me. In an incensed voice, he said, "First of all, as my wife, you should be supportive of my position. Second, I am trying to teach this person some lessons that will help him both in this world and the next. It's selfish of you to try to prevent him from gaining spiritually just because you feel a bit uncomfortable. Thirdly, if you were on the right level, you would feel happy that the driver has an opportunity to be straightened out. Fourthly, you are an emotional baby for feeling bad in such situations."

"And you are emotionally evil for making me feel so bad with your insensitivity," I said in self-defense.

I stayed in emotional pain the entire wedding. I even left early and let my husband come home by himself.

The lesson I learned from this is that in the future it is better for me to feel slightly uncomfortable in situations than to provoke a quarrel that disturbs our shalom bayis. This minor discomfort is suffering for a mitzvah and is elevating.

I have to add that my husband apologized the next day, but the memory of this incident has saved us from many quarrels.

My wife and I battled over every conceivable question that one can imagine. Not only did we quarrel about issues that needed to be decided right away, but we would argue over issues of five, ten, even thirty years in the future.

I remember one especially bitter struggle over where we would live after I would retire. We argued, called each other names, said spiteful things — and I wasn't going to reach the age of retirement for another thirty-five years!

We both loved each other and knew that we had mutual care and concern, but we fought like kindergarten children over a favorite toy.

My wife became seriously ill at a relatively young age. I did all I could to help her recover. I found the best doctors. We tried every treatment but to no avail. She died before her fortieth birthday.

I am broken and guilt-ridden about my quarreling with her. Almost all of the issues we fought over were so minor that I'm embarrassed to tell anyone else about them, and to my everlasting sorrow many of the things we argued about, such as what kind of weddings we should make for our children, will take place when she is no longer with us.

DEVELOP THE INNER STRENGTH AND COURAGE TO GIVE IN

I was standing near a Rabbi who was happily married for over forty years when he was asked by a member of his congregation, "What do you consider to be the secret of a long and happy marriage?"

"Give in!" was his concise but powerful advice.

In a healthy marriage, neither party will always give in. Rather, each will take the other's needs into consideration. Both will be giving in at times. Yet in an ideal situation neither considers this as a loss. It's as if you have to choose at a wedding between two dishes for the main course. You know that you like both, but you have to choose just one. This isn't giving in. It is choosing one thing you like over the other thing you like. In an ideal marriage both the husband and wife want the other one to be happy. Therefore without keeping score they both give in at times, and this giving in is an act of love and caring.

On the way to Har HaMenuchos Cemetery in Jerusalem for the yahrtzeit of my grandmother, a cousin of mine related the story of another couple who celebrated their fiftieth wedding anniversary in the presence of their children and grandchildren. The wife, mother, and grandmother, said, "I would like to share with you how devoted I was to zaidi. For the last fifty years I've eaten the bottom of the chicken even though I prefer the top. I wanted my husband to have the top of the chicken which he prefers. I've been happy to do it since he is such a wonderful person."

"What!!" exclaimed the zaidi. "I've always preferred the bottom part of the chicken. I only ate the top because I thought that you preferred the bottom."

Someone commented on this, "Isn't it a shame that they both lost out those fifty years."

"They both gained immensely," one of my sons said. "Each one was expressing care and concern that the other should eat the part they liked best. For fifty years they've been giving, even though it meant a sacrifice to themselves. That is an essential part of why they had a happy marriage for all those years."

In the beginning of our marriage my wife and I would both try to be so good to each other that it caused us quarrels. One example stands out strongly. It was cold outside and my wife walked me to the bus. I told her, "Go back into the house. It's cold outside."

"No. I don't want you to wait by yourself. I'll wait until the bus comes," she insisted.

"Don't do that," I said, raising my voice. "It's too cold."

"Don't tell me not to wait," she said, becoming irritated. "I want to wait with you."

I spoke to my Rabbi about this. He smiled, and said, "If you're going to have problems, this is the way to have them."

"What should I do?" I asked him.

"Give in to your wife, and express your appreciation for how wonderful she is."

CONSULT A TORAH SCHOLAR, WHEN APPRO-PRIATE, TO CLARIFY THE RIGHT THING TO DO AND TO RESOLVE QUARRELS

Just as people ask a Torah halachic authority for rulings on whether food is kosher or not, whether something is permissible or forbidden on Shabbos, and all other areas of Torah law, so too should a couple consult a halachic authority if they get into a dispute about any matters dealing with Torah law. This way they won't need to argue over the matter, for they will have a clear ruling about the proper Torah way to act in a given situation.

My wife is very honest, too honest in fact. I keep telling her that while honesty is a trait in which we need to excel, we still need the sensitivity to know when not to say things because they can cause pain. We also need to protect ourselves from people who might try to take advantage of us financially.

My wife in turn tells me that I am not honest enough. She complains that I will praise people in exaggerated ways. I will say I like things that I really don't so as not to hurt someone's feelings. I will tell people who want to borrow money that I don't have any, even though I do. I say this because I don't feel they are reliable about returning the money on time.

We got into heated discussions about this topic with both of us feeling that the other is wrong. We eventually agreed to speak to a halachic authority for a clarification of Torah guidelines on when we must be totally honest and when it is preferable to distort the truth for the sake of peace, so as not to hurt someone's feelings and to pro-tect our money and property. This resolved our disagree-ments on this subject. We both felt that we should have consulted the posek earlier for it would have helped us avoid a number of arguments.

❖ ❖ ❖

A few months after our wedding, I observed my spouse reading private mail that was sent to me. It was a letter from a former classmate describing various difficulties that this person was experiencing and asking for my advice, or at least encouragement.

"Why are you reading my mail?" I asked.

"Because now that we are married your letters are my letters," was the innocent reply.

"I still want and need privacy. Besides, when someone writes to me, they want me to keep what is written confidential."

"It's not breaking confidentiality to share things with your spouse," I was told.

"Yes, it is," I disagreed.

"No, it's not," my spouse argued back.

After a ten-minute argument, we agreed to consult a halachic authority. Of course, the posek said that mail is private and also that confidentiality relating to information about other people should be kept secret. From then on we both followed this ruling.

Chapter Seven

INCREASING SELF-ESTEEM
FOR A HAPPIER MARRIAGE

⚯ *The need for self-esteem*
  (and problems caused by lack of)

⚯ *The Torah attitude towards your intrinsic value*

⚯ *Avoid saying and doing things that decrease your*
  spouse's self-esteem

⚯ *Help your spouse increase feelings of self-esteem*

THE NEED FOR SELF-ESTEEM
(AND PROBLEMS CAUSED BY LACK OF)

*Y*ou are valuable. Since the way you view yourself creates you, knowing this gives you the inner strength, confidence, and the type of feelings you need:

- To live life at its fullest
- To accomplish in this world
- To make wise choices
- To cope with the challenges that life provides
- To be the kind of person who will create a fulfilling and happy marriage

A limiting self-image will limit what you think you are capable of doing. It will limit the kinds of choices you make. It is will limit the entire quality of your life and what you will accomplish. Learning to unlimit yourself opens up many doors that would otherwise have remained closed. You might not even have known that those doors exist.

Be resolved to accept the birthright that Hashem gave you from the moment you were born: The birthright of being created in His image, the birthright of being His child, and the birthright of viewing the entire universe as having been created for you. When you view yourself in this light, others might still say and do things that express their failure to see you from this perspective, but inwardly you will always know: "My Creator has given me infinite value. No human being can take this away from me. Not even myself."

A person who has ideal high self-esteem, a realistic positive self-image with appropriate humility, will realize that he or she has basic intrinsic worth and value that is independent of the opinions of any subjective mortal. It will also be independent of any shortcomings, limitations, or handicaps. Humility is the awareness that all that we have — whether possessions or personal qualities, strengths, attributes, and natural talents and skills — are gifts from our Creator. Therefore our ideal person takes pleasure in those gifts, but does not feel arrogant or conceited because of them. If our ideal person has any handicap or natural limitation, he or she realizes that this is part of his or her personal life challenge in this world. This handicap or limitation in no way has any bearing on the individual's intrinsic value.

A person with ideal self-esteem will live a joyous life. Such a person will be free from worry or concern about how he or she is perceived by other people. Such a person will never be intimidated emotionally by any other person. He or she will be respectfully assertive whenever appropriate. He or she will appreciate valid criticism if it will help him or her grow. He or she will easily be able to ignore insults or put-downs, and will have no need to speak against any other person or put them down in order to bolster his or her own ego or self-image. Since he or she feels so good about himself or herself, he or she will want to help others also feel good about themselves.

This ideal picture is a goal for which to strive. When it comes to self-esteem it is not that we either have it or don't have it. Rather, it is a matter of degrees along a continuum. We all have some degree of self-esteem, and since self-esteem is subjective and based upon how we are feeling about ourselves at the moment, for many people it can go up and down depending on the situation and circumstances. What is quite standard is that when a person feels emotionally in a very good state and things are flowing smoothly in life, a person's self-esteem is high. On the other hand, when a person feels emotionally down and things are not going so well with studies, with financial matters, with relationships with people who are important to him or her, it is easy for one's self-esteem level to drop. We will see in the next section that internalizing the Torah view of your value will give your self-image such a strong foundation that external factors will not take away from your self-esteem.

A person with high levels of self-esteem combined with appropriate humility will have the basis for a happy marriage. He or she will not take things personally and therefore will be spared from much anger and many quarrels. Even if problems arise, these will be issues that need to be dealt with, but these issues will not be viewed as challenges to one's intrinsic value or worth.

Sometimes people with high self-esteem might even be shy or self-conscious around certain people, but for them this is a learned emotional reaction rather than a statement about their feelings of self-worth. When they are by themselves, they feel a tremendous sense of intrinsic value, but in the presence of certain people, they have developed a conditioned reaction of not being at their best, and not being able to interact as they do when they are around people with whom they feel comfortable. These social graces can be viewed as a skill that one needs to develop. The lack of them does not reflect negatively on self-esteem. This issue will be discussed in the chapter on "State Mastery." It is easier to learn to change your state than to change a picture of self-esteem. Most people will find that their level of self-esteem will rise once they learn how to access positive states in the presence of any mortal.

Now let us take a look at some of the problems caused by feelings of low self-esteem.

[1] **Lack of joy**. "A person who has low self-esteem will usually feel needlessly unhappy. When one feels he is inferior to others, he is likely to feel miserable. Since humility is a

great virtue and arrogance a great fault, the importance of feelings of self-esteem might be overlooked. To be happy and to accomplish in life you need positive feelings about yourself, while avoiding conceit" (*Gateway to Happiness,* p. 115).

Awareness that you are a valuable person just by virtue of being alive, gives you the foundation for living a joyous life. Life is full of opportunities to have the joy of *mitzvos.* Life is full of opportunities to appreciate and be grateful for the multitude of gifts the Creator has put in your world. Take, for example, a beautiful blue sky. Knowing that it's a gift from the Creator to you will help you view it not just as an expensive great painting that belongs to someone else, but rather as something that is yours too.

[2] **Sensitivity to criticism**. A person with low self-esteem is likely to be defensive and hurt if someone criticizes him in any way. One aware of his own self-worth feels safe enough to listen to criticism and is willing to improve, while a person who feels inferior becomes irritated and upset whenever someone tries to point out his faults. As a rule, the weaker you feel, the more you try to conceal your shortcomings instead of working on improving.

In marriage someone who is highly sensitive to criticism might feel strongly depressed or dejected if his or her spouse criticizes him or her, even if this is delivered in a respectful and caring manner. Others who are oversensitive to criticism will become angry at their spouse and will blame their spouse for attacking them even though an objective observer would not consider what was said as an attack.

A person who lacks positive feelings about himself or herself is more likely to take offense by what his or her spouse says to them. For instance, a wife might say to her husband, "Drive carefully." This can be understood as a caring statement. "I care about you and want you to drive carefully." However, if a husband doesn't feel good about himself, he can misinterpret this statement as a lack of trust and confidence in his driving ability.

Similarly, a husband might ask his wife, "What time is it?" The husband really wants to know the time since his watch isn't working properly, but the wife might take this as criticism. She is in the middle of making supper and takes this to mean that her husband is critical of her for being behind schedule. People with high self-esteem are not bothered by similar statements. They know that they are competent and therefore don't read into what is said as a criticism.

Knowing that you are valuable even if you have faults and have made mistakes gives you less of a need to defend yourself in the face of criticism. Even if the criticism is true and valid, it just gives you an opportunity to improve yourself. Your value and importance is never in question whether or not you actually improve.

[3] **Over-response to flattery or disbelief of sincere praise**. One who has low self-esteem is likely to be excessively overwhelmed when others praise him. Such a person can be manipulated by insincere flattery. Others with low self-esteem feel so low about themselves that they cannot believe any praise about them could be true. In marriage, someone who feels that he or she is intrinsically inferior will not believe the spouse's positive statements about him or her.

Knowing that you are valuable and have been created by the Creator gives you the belief that it's possible you have strengths and virtues of which you are as yet unaware. When someone praises you, learn to appreciate an honest and sincere statement delivered by someone who is expressing his or her appreciation for you and what you did, or for strengths that you have. You will be more objective, and therefore will be able to analyze what is said and how it was said. If the person said it just to be polite, you can respond politely in return. If the person said it to be manipulative, it is still appropriate to be polite, but you will be able to make a wiser choice about how to respond. In marriage, appreciate praise that you feel is sincere. If you feel that your spouse is just saying positive things to make you feel good, you can give him or her credit for trying. If you feel that the praise is just to get you to do something you don't feel like doing, you still have a choice to do it or not.

[4] **Hypercritical attitude**. A person who looks at himself as inferior might feel a strong need to criticize other people. He tries to elevate himself by putting others down. The more faults he finds in others the better he feels about himself. In marriage someone who feels this way is likely to constantly criticize and find fault with his or her spouse.

A person who has high self-esteem will not have such a strong need to criticize. Some people keep on criticizing their spouse because they feel that their spouse's behavior reflects on them to a great extent. They want their spouse to be viewed as perfect by others. This will then reflect well on them. When someone knows that his or her own value and worth is independent of how anyone views his or her spouse, it will give him or her a more objective approach as to when to be tactfully and sensitively critical and when to refrain from criticism.

[5] **Tendency towards blaming**. A person who feels inferior tries to place the blame for his or her faults and shortcomings on others. He is afraid to take the responsibility for what he does and blames everyone except himself. Whenever something goes wrong in the marriage, he or she will always claim it's the other one's fault.

A truth seeker with a positive self-image will be willing to accept responsibility for what went wrong when that is justified. He or she will be free from the need to blame his or her spouse in order to clear his reputation. He or she will be secure enough not to feel that any action of the spouse reflects badly on him or her. When necessary he or she will be willing to consult an objective authority to hear an unbiased opinion. A person with low self-esteem will refuse to speak to anyone. There is a fear that his or her position might not be validated. A person with true self-esteem will be happy to find out the truth even though it might not be the way he or she originally saw things.

[6] **Tendency towards seclusiveness and shyness.** A person who looks at himself as inferior is afraid of other people and tries to avoid them as much as possible. In marriage, such a person is likely not to utilize his or her strengths and talents to the degree that is possible. He or she will be afraid to take social risks and his or her fear of other people can prevent him or her from taking action to earn money that the family needs.

A person with high self-esteem might still be a private person and prefer peace and quiet rather than being with a crowd, but whenever necessary or appropriate, he or she will be able to interact with other people.

[7] **Tendency towards boasting and status seeking.** A person who lacks intrinsically good feelings about himself or herself will have a strong need to boast and do things that will give an illusion of importance. What is boasting? It is telling others, "Look at me. I am important." Of course, you are important. And when you realize your true value, you won't need other people to view you as important in order for you to view yourself as important. Status seeking is also a sign that a person doesn't value himself sufficiently. Certain people with low self-esteem will do things to gain status, while yet others with high self-esteem will do the same things but with a far different and more elevated motivation. Some people with strong feelings of inferiority feel a need to make up stories and lie about their successes and accomplishments. The very fact that a person needs

to be untruthful to feel good about himself shows that his or her self-esteem needs a boost.

A positive self-image frees you from the need to boast. You still might enjoy sharing your successes, victories, and accomplishments with friends and family, but you do this because you are excited about it and want to share your joyous feelings. It puts people into positive states to talk about successes, so they enjoy talking about them. But with high self-esteem, the need to share accomplishments comes from a healthy place.

[8] **Complaints that others don't treat them with respect**. As a rule, a person who keeps saying, "You don't respect me," needs to increase his or her sense of intrinsic value and worth. When you have self-respect, you will want others to treat you with respect. This is a universal need, but if someone doesn't treat you properly, you realize that this is the other person's issue even more than yours.

[9] **Tendency towards negative behavior.** When people look at themselves in a negative light, they are more likely to act in a way that is consistent with their negative view of themselves. It has been said that behind all crime lies the fact that the perpetrator never learned to feel good about himself as a person. If someone looks at himself as a being who is incompetent and unsuccessful, it will have a negative effect on his actual behavior. A positive self-image will lead to more positive behavior.

[10] **Tolerance for unacceptable behavior**. In an abusive situation, someone with low self-esteem is more likely to tolerate the unacceptable behavior of his or her spouse. Feeling lowly about oneself makes one feel that one doesn't deserve better. A person who has low self-esteem might expect others to treat him or her badly and this is often a self-fulfilling prophecy. Someone with positive self-esteem

is much more likely to have the strength of character to stop others from treating him or her shabbily. And if one is in a situation where that isn't possible, and others treat one with disrespect, one realizes that the problem is with the other person, not with oneself.

My husband caused me much distress. He acted reasonable when he was calm, but not when he lost his temper. Then he would insult me by pointing out my faults in a vicious manner. My problem was that I believed his put-downs and my self-esteem was shattered.

He told me that I had bad middos, that I was selfish and self-centered. He had a great memory for my faults and would prove his points by recalling my failures. I feel that I am kindhearted, but I don't always have the energy and time to help others as much as I really should.

Throughout the day, my mind would replay his negative comments and I felt lowly and miserable. My parents had also been critical of me and believed that I was inferior and unworthy.

Then I heard a story that changed my life. During the Holocaust, a mother and her teenage daughter were on a cattle car headed for Auschwitz. The mother told her daughter, "Always remember: They can take everything away from you but they can't take away what you yourself put into your mind."

That's right. I am the boss of my own mind. My husband, or anyone else, might say negative things to me. But I have the choice of accepting them or rejecting them. As I heard how the girl had survived by choosing thoughts conducive to survival and not giving in to exhaustion, hunger, or physical pain, I too decided that I would survive.

When my husband called me names, the thought that went through my mind was, "You sound like a Nazi." I was afraid to say this to him, but that's what he reminded me of. Now that I accepted upon myself that I would control my thoughts, I chose to have compassion for him instead of contempt and hatred. It was certainly an exaggeration to consider him an enemy of our people and I was going to think more objectively.

I made up my mind that I wouldn't tolerate his putting me down when he lost his temper. I decided to wait at least a month to give him an ultimatum. During the month I would repeat strengthening messages to myself. I would acknowledge my intrinsic value and worth. I would repeat to myself that what he said to me was incorrect and that he was blind to my strengths and positive qualities. At the same time, I would treat my husband with proper respect regardless of how he would treat me.

After the month I felt much better about myself. I then said to my husband, not with anger but with iron strength and determination. "I am giving you a choice. You either stop the insults or I'm going to the Rabbinate for a divorce. I don't know exactly why you feel a need to put me down, but whatever your reason, I'm demanding that you stop. If you feel you can't stop, let's get divorced right away. If you need help or therapy, I'm willing to wait. But I refuse to be spoken to like the Nazis spoke to our people in the concentration camps."

The way I said this was powerful. I didn't know I had it in me. But my month of mental preparation had built up my confidence.

"I'm not a Nazi," my erstwhile bully of a husband stammered.

"Of course not," I said, "so stop talking like one."

My husband who had caused me so much pain was shaken. He saw that I would no longer tolerate an intolerable situation. He would have to make a choice. Either he would begin to treat me with the respect which the Torah demands for every person, all the more so one's wife, or else I was determined to get a divorce.

"I don't want to get divorced," he said to me the next day. "I want to make our marriage work and I agree to go with you to a counselor. I will do whatever it takes for me to talk consistently like a Jew should. Being called a Nazi was the worst thing anyone ever said to me, but looking back I can understand why you felt that way. I hope that I never cause you to think that way again."

I could see that for the first time, he really was sorry. Time will tell if he makes a lasting change or not. But regardless of what he says to me, I know it's his problem, not mine. Now that I view myself more positively, I won't tolerate anyone trying to pour poison words into my mind.

How does a potentially good marriage become a disaster? I know. You can ask me, if you wish.

I kept nitpicking. I wanted my spouse to be exactly the way I wished. I would constantly correct the way my spouse said things. Whatever my spouse did, I would focus on what still could have been done better. I kept asking my spouse to stop doing things that were even slightly not to my liking.

When we got married, my spouse was good-natured and loved me, but I felt that I could never be satisfied unless my spouse fit the exact picture of what I wanted. My constant criticism wore away at the love that was there from the beginning until what was left was smoldering resentment and feelings of animosity.

I also kept challenging my spouse's motives when he did things for me. "Why did you do that?" I kept asking.

If my spouse said, "I did this because I felt you would

appreciate it," I would say, "And why do you want me to appreciate things?"

"Because I want you to be happy," my spouse replied.

"Why do you want me to be happy?" I challenged.

"So you will feel good," I was told.

"What's the difference to you if I feel good or not?" I asked.

"I feel good when you feel good," my spouse told me.

"So you admit that you are only trying to make me feel good because of your own selfish reasons," I gloated.

Why did I do this? When I tried to analyze the factors that ruined my marriage, I realized that I was profoundly insecure. My own lack of self-esteem led to my finding fault with my spouse so I could feel superior. I wanted to be reassured that my spouse loved me unconditionally. But unfortunately I did this in a way that demolished that love.

I teach in a High School. My main focus is on character development. I will be the first to admit that I personally have much to improve, but I find that teaching Torah ideals has had a positive impact on me.

One difficulty I face is that when I lose my temper, become impatient, or refuse to do an act of kindness, my spouse says to me, "You have so many faults. How can you have the chutzpah to teach those lofty ideas?"

I have thought a lot about this. There were times I even thought of quitting. Maybe I should not be the one who teaches these lessons even though I love to do so.

One day I asked my spouse, "Please tell me the truth. Do you think that I should stop teaching?"

"Of course not," my spouse admitted. "I respect the work you do."

"But you have often challenged my inconsistencies," I continued.

"Yes, I have," my spouse said. "But it's usually because I am feeling inferior myself at those moments. I really should never do it again, and I apologize. If I do say anything similar in the future, please don't take it seriously."

I just wished that my spouse would have told me this before. It would have saved me a lot of distress. But at least now that I understood my spouse's true feelings, I felt encouraged to continue teaching.

M*y marriage of about five years was a total disaster for me. If I could have imagined the worst, what I would have come up with would not have measured up to how much I was actually suffering.*

My husband seemed like a nice fellow to others but to me he was a tyrant. He would yell and shout at me for mistakes and oversights. He would attack my intelligence and tell me that I was stupid and brain damaged. He would criticize me for not being religious enough. He would tell me that I didn't know how to cook, clean, or sew.

This constant attack on everything I did and said tore down my self-esteem. I was insecure as a teenager and now as an adult I had profound feelings of inferiority because of the way my husband treated me.

I was desperate for help. It was only years later that I realized I wasn't as bad as my husband portrayed me. Even if I constantly made mistakes, my heart was in the right place. I wanted to be a Torah observant, G-d-fearing wife. I wanted to make my husband happy, and I wanted his approval. But my good intentions were consistently trampled upon. At the time, I believed my husband's point of view. I feel now that my own feelings of inferiority goaded my husband on. My own lowly view of myself fueled his anger and contempt.

I heard about an older woman who gave helpful suggestions on how to be a good wife and how to improve one's marriage. She didn't have much time, so I had to summarize the tragic history of my marriage.

"My husband and I laugh a lot," she told me, assuming that this would be helpful for me. "You should laugh together with your husband." I saw that she was in a rush and so I politely thanked her for her time, and meekly left her home.

I was resolved to laugh together with my husband, but any aspirations I had to do so were quickly ruined by the reality of our relationship.

Years later when I developed a healthy self-image, I realized that she didn't understand the depth of my suffering and anguish. She didn't know what it was like to be constantly criticized for everything you do. It was impossible to be as flawless and perfect as my husband demanded.

Oh, how I longed for understanding. Even if someone wouldn't be able to help me in a practical way, at least I wished to be able to share my life story with someone. I was ashamed to tell my parents how bad things were. I felt I was to blame for our unhappy marriage, but deep down I knew I was a victim. My husband was wrong for treating me so brutally. He didn't hit me, but his words were on a par with being physically punched.

I am grateful to G-d that I have met understanding people who have given me strength, bitachon, and self-esteem. My inner strength enabled me to finally give my husband an ultimatum. I would no longer be a verbal punching bag. The verbal attacks would either stop, or I was going to get divorced. When I myself finally came to believe that I did not deserve to be belittled, my husband finally started working on his behavior. It was a long process. My husband chose to stop criticizing me, and he even apologized for the pain he had caused. In retrospect I can see clearly that the turning point came when I really awoke to the fact that no matter what my faults and weaknesses were, I was a child of Hashem and deserved to be treated decently.

I hope that the person who gave me the advice to laugh, presently realizes that one can't laugh together with someone who treats one with cruelty and is totally blind to the Torah concept of the inestimable value of each human being. What I needed most was a realization that my self-worth was Divinely given and that nothing my husband said to me in his frequent anger tantrums was a reflection on my intrinsic value. Once I felt this, my own sense of worth had a major impact on how he spoke to me.

THE TORAH ATTITUDE TOWARDS YOUR INTRINSIC VALUE

The Torah perspective on who you are is that each and every human being has unlimited intrinsic worth. This means that you have immense value that is not conditional on your intelligence, your knowledge, your wealth, your popularity, your looks, your health, your weight, your emotions, or on any other factor. It is easier for someone to feel positive about himself or herself when others also see him or her in a positive light. The reality is that your value is your birthright and that can never be taken away.

You are created in the Creator's image. You are a child of the Creator, Who is our Father and King and is the Creator and Sustainer of the entire universe. You are obligated to say, "The world was created for me." Imagine how wonderful you would feel about yourself if you actually internalized the reality that everything on this planet and in all the billions of galaxies was created for you.

The entire idea of self-esteem from a non-Torah perspective is arbitrary. Where is the universal inter-galactic secular law about how you should view yourself? Since those who feel good about their basic essence live better quality lives than those who don't, it makes sense to view oneself as a worthy and valuable individual independent of anyone else's opinion of you. There are definitely skills and talents you might have or be missing, there are attributes and qualities that are valuable to have that you might have or not have, but this has nothing to do with your value as a human being. Your emotional states will have a great effect on how you feel, or better yet, your emotional states are the essence of how you feel, but this has to do with feelings, not value. While it is preferable to be joyous rather than to feel miserable, depressed, and discouraged, even if you feel simply terrible, your value as a person is not affected, only your feelings are. So it makes sense for a person to view himself or herself as being a ten on the arbitrary self-worth scale, with ten being the highest.

Someone who is confident and assertive has a skill that is worthwhile emulating. But this is a skill, not a measure of your value. Even if someone is very self-conscious, and becomes intimidated easily by other people, his or her value as a person is not in question. Confidence and assertiveness are skills that you and everyone else can learn either by training yourself, or by getting training from someone else. One can learn how to walk, talk, act, think, and feel confidently, but your internalized level of self-esteem is up to you. If you consider yourself as being valuable and important, you have self-esteem. If you choose not to view yourself this way, it is your choice.

Definitely, our life history affects the way we view ourselves. Definitely, the messages we heard from our parents, siblings, teachers, and friends have affected the way we view ourselves. But this is arbitrary. From the Torah perspective you have infinite value and worth independent of how any mortal treats you now, or has treated you in the past. Anyone who has not treated you with the utmost respect has violated a basic Torah principle of how fellow human beings should be treated. This is their problem, and while this can be stressful, you have the ability to still view yourself as a tremendously worthwhile being created in the image of our Creator.

When you realize and internalize that you are created in our Creator's image and that you are one of His children, you will have such a strong inner sense of self-respect that others will just have to have some degree of respect towards you.

I grew up in East Baltimore. My father was a major Torah scholar and a person who had compassion and respect for every human being he met. On Shabbos we needed to walk two miles through a rough neighborhood to get to my father's synagogue. I have a lasting memory of total strangers from a totally different culture and way of life approaching my father and asking him for his prayers and blessings. Where others were afraid to walk, my father radiated self-respect combined with compassionate kindness, and this was felt by those who saw him walk by.

Another basic Torah principle is that we are souls with bodies, rather than bodies with souls. When you view your essence as an immortal soul, you realize that any imperfections on the financial, physical, intellectual, or emotional level are your challenges while living in this world. They do not detract from you on the soul level, which is who you actually are.

All the problems caused by a person perceiving himself or herself as lacking self-esteem will vanish when one has internalized the Torah view of who we are. People differ greatly as to how they personally integrate this concept. Some people are able to do this faster than others. Some people need to hear it from many sources, repeated over and over again for quite a while, until an abstract idea becomes their inner reality. Because of the broad ramifications and tremendous difference the Torah view of self-image will make, it should be a high priority for us to integrate it.

Every time you touch a *mezuzah* you can have a self-esteem boost. The *mezuzah* contains the *Shema Yisrael* which states the Oneness of our Creator. This Oneness means that you are part of the creation of the Creator and so is every person who exists. You and the person you are married to are created in the image of the Creator and are His children. This one-second reminder will consistently strengthen your awareness of your eternal and infinite value.

AVOID SAYING AND DOING THINGS THAT DECREASE YOUR SPOUSE'S SELF-ESTEEM

One of the worst crimes anyone can commit is to rob someone of his or her self-esteem. The highest level of charity is to help someone earn a living himself. When you do this, you give a person a positive feeling about himself and you enable him to be independent of the charity of others in the future. Destroying or harming someone's feelings of self-esteem is the opposite. You hurt a person in the present and the damage you have done gets carried on in the future.

Even though ideally and theoretically we can develop such a strong positive feeling about our own intrinsic worth that someone else's negativity won't belittle us, in reality most people have not reached that level. Therefore we need to make it a high priority to bolster the self-esteem of others and refrain from doing or saying things that will have a negative effect on another person's self-view.

Husbands and wives have a tremendous influence on the self-esteem of their spouse. A wife whose husband is constantly critical, constantly putting her down, constantly belittling her competency and intelligence, will suffer tremendously. She is then likely to question her own value as a person. Similarly, a husband whose wife constantly criticizes him and puts him down will usually be greatly affected. Usually, woman are more vulnerable to the opinions of their husband than men are to the opinions of their wives, but it can be devastating to most men to be belittled by their wives.

If a husband or wife feels a strong need to put the other one down, the specific topic that is being complained about is not the real issue. The real issue is that one party has a goal to make the other one feel inferior and incompetent. This is in direct contradiction to our obligation to love and respect other people, all the more so our spouse. Take, for example, these destructive sentences: "You never do anything right." "You are an awful person." "Even when you do something good, you do it for the wrong reasons." "You are totally rotten." If someone makes his or her spouse feel that he or she is stupid, incompetent, and unworthy of respect, that person is harming both partners.

If you have been saying things that have lowered your spouse's feelings of self-esteem, be resolved to completely refrain from doing so again. It can take much effort to repair and heal a broken self-image, but if you go out of your way to totally upgrade the way you speak to your spouse, hopefully you will be successful.

I find my spouse very critical. I am frequently asked, "Why did you do it that way?" and, "What's the reason you said that?"

I would explain myself at length and justify why I spoke or acted the way I did. When I did this, however, my spouse would say, "You don't need to defend yourself."

Of course I did. My spouse spoke to me in a condemnatory tone of voice. This tone of voice, regardless of the content, gave me a very uncomfortable feeling, and to add insult to injury, to be told that I didn't need to defend myself was yet another put-down.

These encounters had a negative effect on my self-esteem. I tried to tell my spouse that being challenged all the time, was highly distressing, but I was told, "I'm just asking you why you do and say things. Why do you take offense?"

"Are you trying to tell me that I am deficient and an awful person," I asked my spouse.

"Definitely not," my spouse replied. "I am just trying to understand why you do things."

"But I feel judged and condemned," I said.

"It is you who choose to feel that way," my spouse challenged.

It hit me that my spouse didn't realize the strong effect

the tone of voice and this pattern of question-asking had on me. I explained that if the tone of voice was gentler and would sound more like neutral information gathering, I wouldn't feel attacked. We tried out a few different tones of voice and I saw that if my spouse used the tone of voice we agreed on, I would feel comfortable giving factual answers and wouldn't feel a need to be defensive.

I am an expert at seeing the faults of others. In the beginning of my marriage I used to take it as my obligation to point out all of my wife's mistakes, errors, and shortcomings. I looked at this as the biggest positive service I could do for her. Now that she would see what she needed to correct, she could improve herself. I naively thought that she would appreciate this.

When we were first married, my wife had a very cheerful personality. I had heard from many people how she was one of the kindest people you will ever meet. She had a heart of gold and was compassionate and good-natured. But after being married a few months, I saw that the person I was married to was unhappy most of the time. She lacked energy and rarely smiled.

I was critical of my wife for not being more joyous and grateful for all the good things in her life. I was afraid that maybe she had something like chronic fatigue syndrome. I insisted that she go to a doctor, but all the tests showed that nothing was wrong with her physically.

I took her to a Rabbi hoping that he would lecture her and tell her to be happier with what she has. Instead, after getting a comprehensive picture of the state of our marriage, the Rabbi told me that I needed to change my pattern. My constant criticisms were devastating. It is exactly because my wife is such a sensitive and kind person that she is unable to handle my way of trying to improve her. The Rabbi told me, "You also wouldn't like someone constantly criticizing you for your faults the way you do to her. Nobody would. Your task, especially during the first year of marriage is to give your wife reasons to be happy, not to make her miserable. For the rest of this first year praise her at least five times a day."

"But that's quite a lot," I protested.

"But it's fewer than the amount of times you are now criticizing her," he told me. "Besides praising her, stop with your criticisms. They are destroying your wife's confidence and healthy energy. Ultimately you and your future family will suffer greatly if you keep this up. You need to make a special effort now to improve the situation. Your intentions might have been positive, but the reality is that what you have been saying is highly problematic and dangerous. I believe in your ability to change this pattern and create a wonderful marriage. I know that you can enhance your wife's feelings about herself and you. Let's meet in two weeks for a progress report."

I was resolved to refrain from saying anything that would lower my wife's self-esteem. I made it my highest priority to keep expressing appreciation and gratitude. I focused on everything about my wife that was positive and kept giving only positive feedback. Now that I was looking for the good, that is what I noticed. I observed that after two days my wife was smiling more. By the end of the two weeks my progress report was so positive that I was intensely committed to keeping up my new pattern.

HELP YOUR SPOUSE INCREASE FEELINGS OF SELF-ESTEEM

One of the biggest acts of kindness that you can do for someone is to raise his or her level of self-esteem. When you make someone feel valued, competent, respected, and loved, you enhance his or her self-esteem. Not only do they feel good in the present, but the positive effects will be manifest in many areas. This is important when interacting with everyone, and it is especially important in your relationship with your husband or wife. Make it a high priority to say and do things that will enhance your spouse's self-esteem. When your spouse thinks of an idea, comment on the fact that you appreciate the idea, "That was smart." "That was a clever thought." "I'm proud of you for that."

If you feel that your spouse's self-esteem needs boosting, clarify your spouse's strengths, virtues, and inner resources. Then keep pointing them out in a way that your spouse will appreciate. Whenever your spouse feels low, say something empowering. Remind your spouse about his or her accomplishments and successes. Some people appreciate when this is given clearly and overtly, while others prefer that it be given to them in subtle ways. Some people appreciate continual positive feedback. There are those who have a strong need for this, while others would consider this irritating, and only need small doses of feedback every once in a while. Your approach in giving positive feedback to your spouse should be based on his or her needs, not on your automatic tendency. It is much better, however, to err on the side of giving more positive feedback rather than less.

Just telling someone in a general way, "You deserve to see yourself in a positive light," is often not as effective as pointing out specific strengths. Nevertheless, if you can sincerely say, "It's not this or that positive quality that makes you so wonderful, your entire being is fantastic," it is highly likely to have a powerful positive effect on your spouse's self-image.

> *I*n the beginning of our marriage, my wife would almost always agree with me when I expressed my thoughts and opinions. I wanted to have lively discussions rather than just hear an agreement. I liked it when someone challenged my point of view. Then I could clarify exceptions, conditions, and modifications.

My wife was intelligent and I knew she had a mind of her own, so why wasn't she expressing herself? I spoke to my older brother about this.

"I'm glad we can discuss this," he said. "I find that even with me you tend to state your ideas in an authoritative manner. You sound so certain of your opinion that nothing I say will make a difference."

"But I am open to hear the truth from everyone," I said.

"Perhaps," he said. " But you give the feeling that what I say won't make a difference. You will just staunchly uphold your position. If you intimidate me, you certainly do so when you talk to your wife."

I asked for his suggestions, and this is what he told me, "First of all, speak in a lighter tone of voice. And add the words, 'It seems to me,' and, 'At present I think.' Secondly, whenever your wife has a thought or opinion, explicitly acknowledge your agreement. Even when you disagree, if you find the idea interesting or creative, acknowledge it. Thirdly, keep asking her, 'What do you think about what I said?' or, 'How did that make you feel?' or, 'What questions come to your mind about this?'"

This made sense to me. I wrote this down and made certain to apply it in our next conversation. After using these approaches for a few weeks, I saw that my wife felt more confident and began speaking up more. We began having enjoyable discussions and my wife's entire self-image became stronger.

*O*ur marriage was clearly falling apart. I was frustrated about my entire life and my marriage was only one disappointing element in a totally futile picture of what life should not be like. I hated my job. I wasn't davening properly. I had no time for learning Torah. When I came home in the evening, I would lash out at my wife for all sorts of reasons, none of them truly important.

I realized that it was only a matter of time before my wife would no longer tolerate the way I treated her. I could argue that it wasn't my fault. I grew up in a chaotic home. My parents sort of cared about me, but I was a complicated child and they had no idea about what I really needed to set me straight. They would punish me for my negative behavior, when what I really needed was unconditional love and understanding. When I grew up, the term "child abuse" wasn't used as often as it is today. They weren't cruel or sadistic, so no one would have called me an abused child. I now realize how frustrated they were with me, and right now I am frustrated with myself.

Whether or not I was totally to blame for the situation, I still had to figure out what I was going to do with the rest of my life. My most pressing problem was how to keep my marriage together. My wife had repeatedly suggested that we speak to a marriage counselor, but I was too proud to ask anyone for help. If I felt that someone could tell me something new, maybe I would have agreed to go for counseling, but I realized that I knew what had to be done. It was just a question of whether I would have the motivation to put into practice what I already knew.

I asked my wife if we could go to a quiet spot where we wouldn't be interrupted for a few hours because I wanted to talk over our entire situation. I was afraid that she would tell me it's too late, that she's already reached a decision about the dissolution of our marriage. But she replied, "I'm very happy that you want to discuss things. I've tried to discuss our marriage for a while now. And you kept brushing me off. I feel that it's never too late to improve things."

Her response was exactly what I needed to hear. I did not expect an excessively optimistic response from her. But I saw that she was clearly open to giving our dying marriage a new chance for life.

For the first time since we were married, I shared my deep feelings of inferiority. I told her that I felt I had ruined my entire life and I wouldn't blame her if she gave up on me.

"I'll never give up on you. I've always believed in you even when you didn't believe in yourself. I'm not a miracle worker and if you don't want to try to improve yourself, I'm afraid that there is nothing that I can do. But your willingness to discuss your life and our marriage so openly is a sign that you are sincere. I'll stand by you and together we will begin our life anew."

That was twenty years ago. Since then we have celebrated that day with more joy than we celebrate our wedding anniversary. I have made it a habit to tell my story to at least one person each year. I want others to learn from my experience. If you truly want to make a major change in your life, you can. My wife and I have worked together as a team. Her belief in me is the most precious gift Hashem ever gave me. I am profoundly grateful.

Chapter Eight

Living in the Present

- *Your present choices create your future*

- *Learn from the past to be wiser in the present*

- *Keep asking yourself, "What can I do now?"*

- *Forgive and let go (don't hold onto resentment)*

- *Don't needlessly bring up the past*

- *Reinforce positive attempts and improvement*

YOUR PRESENT CHOICES
CREATE YOUR FUTURE

*T*he rest of your life begins this very moment. And this is true for your marriage also. Regardless of what you have ever said or done in the past, you can presently make new and better choices in every area of your life. Whatever you say or do now is going to be part of the foundation of your future.

Definitely everything that we have done in the past and everything that has already happened to us has an effect on who and what we are. But when tomorrow is today, whatever you say and do today will ultimately become part of the past, creating the person you are now, and in the future.

One of the most inspiring and motivating thoughts for many people is that we can begin again right this moment. You might have made mistakes and errors until now. But from now on you can be totally resolved to act in new and better ways. Just having insight about why you are the way you are isn't sufficient. We need new actions to bring about new results. This moment you can create a new reality for yourself. Regardless of what happened in the past, the past is not the future. When you realize your previously unrecognized abilities to make positive changes, you are a new person.

Reading this book and integrating the ideas presented here is a choice that will affect the rest of your marriage. You can think about ways that you can enhance your marriage and begin to apply them. Even if you have not always spoken to your spouse or acted in the optimal way in the past, from now on you can choose to elevate the way you talk and act.

You have been laying the groundwork for this moment your entire life. As you are reading this, you have in your brain your entire life history, all your knowledge, both the knowledge of the things that you consciously remember and those that are subconscious. You can read this now because you once learned how to read. You need to start learning the alphabet one letter at a time. You needed to build up your vocabulary. What is true about this very moment of your reading is also true of each moment in your marriage. Your entire life history, all of your knowledge, will play a part in what you will say and do in each encounter with your spouse. At each moment it will be true that "You have been laying the groundwork for this moment your entire life." Now, whatever you read in this book is part of the groundwork for your future interactions.

When you make a choice in the present to act a certain way, that pattern gets added to your mental library. Every time you repeat a positive behavior the neural pathways in your brain that lead to that behavior become stronger and the likelihood increases that you will continue to act this way. This principle can work for us or against us. When you choose positive ways of talking and positive actions, the principle will be working in your favor.

Before they actually consider getting married, many people visualize the type of person they wish to marry. They have their "shopping lists." After you are married, however, your goal is to cope well with the actual situation. Many people add much frustration to their lives by wishing things were different. But wisdom dictates: Make the best of what you have. Live in the present in your marriage.

Our lives are a continually changing process. We are never the exact same in any given day. Rabbi Chaim of Volozhin wrote that we never pray the same *Shemoneh Esrei* twice. The words are the same each of the three times a day that we repeat this prayer, but you are always different. Your life situation keeps changing. Your needs change. Your spiritual level goes up and down. Your emotions will be different either slightly or drastically, depending on what is happening in your life. This applies both to you and to the person to whom you are married. You are never exactly the same as you were the day before. For this reason, what you and your spouse need from each other will keep changing. Live in the present. Focus on making the best choices for what is needed right now.

LEARN FROM THE PAST TO BE WISER IN THE PRESENT

Every experience you have ever had in the past can serve as your teacher. The wise person is someone who learns from each person (*Pirkei Avos* 4:1). We can learn from the strengths and good qualities of each person, and we can learn what to avoid from his or her mistakes. We can learn from ourselves and from our past experiences.

Wisdom dictates that we live in the present, learn from the past, and prepare for the future. Positive memories of the past can sustain us in times of difficulty. Talking about the past can illuminate the present. If someone had a painful past, being able to express painful feelings can be cathartic and healing if there is a compassionate listener. Visualizing the past in new ways can free us from its painful effects. But after all is said and done, we live only in the present. And whatever we do and whatever happens to us can be used as a source of wisdom for the future.

Whenever you make a mistake in interacting with your spouse, and you find that you become excessively upset, realize that you are now wiser than you were before. The same is true with everything you've ever said or done that created pain or quarrels. Having had those experiences and having added them to your mental library increases your wisdom as to what to avoid from now on. Every time you acted wisely in the past, you now have that as a valuable resource for the future.

The way my mind works is that as soon as anything happens in the present, I immediately project it to the future. In school, when I received a good mark on a test, I would imagine how my life would be if I would keep this up for years to come. When I didn't do so well on a test, I would visualize my entire future being one big failure.

On the first meeting I had with my spouse, we got along wonderfully. I right away visualized us getting married and raising a family together. I even saw us at our first grandchild's wedding.

During our wedding and sheva berachos, we were both exceedingly happy, and I would see us sustaining this happiness our entire lives; but when we had our first bitter argument, I immediately saw a life of total disaster. I could see us fighting again and again throughout our lives. This put me into a state of panic.

My spouse saw how panicky I became, and was puzzled. "True this was a bad argument and we both felt awful about it, but why did it have such a strong effect on you?"

"Because I am afraid that this means we will continue to argue this way all the time and that would be terrible," I said.

My spouse asked me, "Just because we argued this way once doesn't mean we will always do so. I assume that from time to time our disagreements might get out of hand, but we both love each other so much that we will always work things out in a way that is acceptable to both you and me. We will both learn from our mistakes to be more careful in the future."

I explained how my thought patterns worked and we

both understood why I felt so bad. From then on it became easier for me to live more in the present. I increased my realization that we end up learning from each situation that we experience, and therefore we improve our ability to handle similar situations better.

KEEP ASKING YOURSELF, "WHAT CAN I DO NOW?"

The tool that will help you live in the present is to keep asking yourself, "What can I do now?" There are two very important words in this question. One is the word "I" and the other is the word "now." At times you might be able to say, "What can we do now?" You can ask this if you and your spouse are able to discuss an emotionally laden issue peacefully. But as a general rule keep the main focus on what you personally can do now. When you act with sincere love and respect, there is a strong probability that your spouse will also make a positive change.

This question has many variations:

- "What can I do now to enhance my marriage?"
- "What can I do now to make up for what I have already done?"
- "What can I do now to stop this argument?"
- "What can I do now that will create a joyous and loving environment in our home?"
- "What can I do now to prevent repeating a problematic pattern in the future?"

"What can I do now?" is the opposite of telling your spouse, "You should have ..." When someone makes a "You should have" statement, there is blaming. It is blaming one's spouse for the past. At times, this is appropriate. By pointing out a mistake or error, you might prevent it. But in marriage, this form of statement is often just the beginning of a long drawn out quarrel that leads nowhere. Or it creates resentment. So weigh the situation carefully before making statements that point the blame. Often it is worthwhile using the plural "we" when you talk about past mistakes. "We could have done this differently. And hopefully in the future we will."

Instead of asking, "Why didn't you ...?" which implies blaming, it is preferable to say, "I would greatly appreciate it if you would please ..."

If you need to repeat yourself, live in the present. Ask the tenth time with the same patience as the first time. This skill takes time to develop. But marriage and child-raising give you many opportunities for practice.

FORGIVE AND LET GO
(DON'T HOLD ONTO RESENTMENT)

Living in the present means that you forgive and let go. When you hold onto resentment for past wrongs, you are carrying along the weight of the past into the present. This makes a heavy burden. The present can be difficult enough on its own for us to handle. When someone adds it to the resentments of the past, it can become unbearable. That is why many people who hold onto past resentments suffer from psychosomatic illnesses. The past resentment drains our strength and we don't have the energy we need for the present. Keep your mind off past resentments. Would you keep listening over and over again to a tape that you found unpleasant? If your mind spontaneously keeps going back to the past, tell yourself, "Next," and focus on something else.

If someone we have never met before starts speaking to us, we invariably speak politely and respectfully. Since we don't have any negative history with this person, it is relatively easy to speak with respect. But when we feel resentful toward someone for not meeting our requests and needs, and all the more so if we are resentful of things this person said and did that caused us distress, we are likely to become angry easily.

The Vilna Gaon expressed this in his commentary to *Mishlei*

(10:12): "When someone feels an inner hostility towards another person, even a minor offense can arouse feelings of animosity. Even though what has actually occurred right now could be trivial, the previous negative feelings create quarrels. However, when someone feels love for another person, he is able to forgive whatever the other person does."

Forgiving and letting go doesn't mean that you are denying that this person has done something wrong, but it does mean that you are releasing the emotional attachment you have towards that wrong.

When we talk about a painful incident of the past, whether it was emotionally painful or physically painful, right now in the present our muscles tighten up. This tightness can easily be measured with biofeedback technology which measures the tightening and loosening of our muscles. When our muscles are tighter, they give off more electricity. When our muscles are relaxed, they give off less electricity. Even slight changes are detected by EMG (electromyograph) machines. When someone thinks about the distress that someone caused him, one's muscles tighten and energy is wasted. If, however, you have totally and sincerely forgiven that person, when you mention that person's name you will feel calm and relaxed. I personally have witnessed this experience with someone who totally forgave another person. This is an important principle to master for a happy marriage. Forgive your spouse for what went wrong, and begin to create a harmonious marriage in the present.

People differ greatly in how easy or difficult it is for them to let go of the past. Some people perceive the past as behind them and spontaneously keep their focus on the present and the future. Others perceive the past as happening right now. They feel the pain and anguish of the past as if it were occurring right now. When others tell them to live in the present, they often don't realize how difficult it is for these people to let go of the past. Nevertheless, this is the task they need to master. They need to reflect on the thought, "I will let go of the past and totally forgive." Some people find that by repeating this while breathing slowly and deeply it eventually becomes their reality. It can be very difficult to let go of past resentments. And that's why there is so much spiritual growth in letting go of them.

When I looked at the state of my marriage, I felt depressed. My husband and I have had so many unpleasant interactions that when I thought about the future of our marriage, I saw a dark cloud. I felt a great deal of resentment towards my husband for all the nasty things that he has said to me. I often hate the way he acts towards the children. He has a temper and acts mean if the children misbehave when he is in one of his foul moods. He is very controlling and demands respect although he doesn't always treat me with respect.

One day he was especially cruel towards the children, and I decided that I'd had it. I wasn't going to put up with the way he acted any more. I called a few people for support and they told me that if I were smart I would get out of the marriage now instead of ruining the rest of my life — but I was afraid. My husband had told me a number of times that if I would try to get a divorce, he would hire the best lawyer he could find and he would claim that I was unfit to raise the children. Every time he told this to me, I hated him for it.

Now that I had spoken to a number of people and heard their reactions to the way my children and I were being treated, my resentful feelings increased. I began speaking to my husband in anger and this got him angrier than ever before. I was resolved to get out of the marriage, but after going to the court, I got cold feet. I was even more frightened about getting divorced than I was about staying in the marriage.

I kept thinking the matter over and was in extreme pain about the entire situation. When I actually thought about divorce I saw that there were many positive things *about my husband that I did respect. He was always polite and respectful to other people. The problem was that he lost his temper too frequently in our home.*

I spoke to someone who told me to weigh the entire situation as objectively as possible. First of all, if I would keep up the resentment about the past, I would end up speaking to my husband in ways that made the situation worse. The only hope for the marriage to work was for me to forgive my husband for the past and let go of the resentment. Then I would need to tell him in a firm but kind voice that I could no longer tolerate his past behavior in the future. If he would agree to go for counseling and treat me with respect and be kinder to the children, I would be happy to continue the marriage. If not, the marriage was over. The choice was his.

I don't know yet how the future will turn out. But I realized that only by letting go of the past resentment was there any hope for a marriage based on mutual respect.

DON'T NEEDLESSLY BRING UP THE PAST

"It is forbidden to remind a person of his past misdeeds or the misdeeds of his family, for this will cause him distress" (*Choshen Mishpat* 228:4).

When someone's spouse has said or done things in the past that caused pain or distress, it is easy to keep talking about it. At times this is necessary in order to work out the issues. The person who suffered doesn't feel that he or she can just let this go without discussing it. For some people this need is very strong. The problem is that the person who said or did something wrong, often dislikes to talk about it. Talking about his or her mistakes and errors are painful, but if the hurt party has a need to discuss the issue, that is the price the perpetrator has to pay. Hopefully the realization of his or her own distress now will make him or her more motivated to refrain from causing pain in the future.

After the subject has been spoken about, however, and you already have forgiven your spouse, don't needlessly bring up the issue. If you are still in deep pain, it is understandable that you have a practical need to keep on discussing the matter. This can be a strong emotional need, but some people like to bring up past hurts even though they don't really need to do so in order to let go of strong pain. They might want to keep on retaliating. "You hurt me without provocation, so I'm going to keep making you suffer for it. I won't let you forget what you've done." If the person sincerely regrets his or her wrong, it is wrong on your part to keep making him or her suffer.

For most people it isn't easy to refrain from needlessly mentioning past offenses. As stated in the classic mussar work *Mesillas Yesharim* (ch. 11): "It is very difficult to overcome feelings of animosity and revenge when one is wronged. People find revenge sweeter than honey. It takes great strength of character to overcome the natural desire for revenge and not to hate the other person, but to forget the entire matter and remove it from one's heart as if it had never occurred. Such a level is easy only for angels who do not have normal human emotions, but not for ordinary mortals. Nevertheless, it is the decree of the King. The Torah states this obligation explicitly: 'Do not hate your brother in your heart.' 'Do not take revenge and do not bear a grudge.'

"When someone has refused to help you or has harmed you in the past, it is considered revenge to fail to do him a favor. It is considered bearing a grudge to remind him of that incident when you are engaged in doing him a favor. The evil inclination works on getting a person angry in order that he should get back at the other person, if not in a major way, at least in a minor way. The evil inclination tries to tell you, 'If you want to give something to him even though he refused to help you when you were in need, at least don't give it to him with a friendly smile. Don't help him too much. Even if you help him, don't do it in such a way that he will derive the maximum satisfaction. Don't be too close a friend with him; it's enough that you forgave him and don't consider him your enemy. Even if you do still want to be his friend, don't show him as much love as previously.' These are the ways in which the evil inclination tries to entice people.

"Therefore the Torah states a principle that includes everything. 'Love your neighbor as yourself.' As yourself — without any difference or variation. Literally, as yourself."

These thoughts from Rabbi Moshe Chaim Luzzatto are especially important for a marriage. If a couple has already made up after an argument or one of the two has asked forgiveness for a wrong, bringing it up in the present creates needless arguments. Since it is so difficult not to bring it up, appreciate the strength of character you are gaining by exercising your spiritual muscles.

Any time you feel like saying something that would be a product of feelings of animosity and you remain silent, you are fulfilling the Torah commandment of not taking revenge or bearing a grudge. This creates a great light in your soul. This is tremendous growth.

Stay in the present. It's easy to lapse into discussing past history, but that won't solve the present situation. Blaming each other for past mistakes and painful statements and actions will prevent you both from handling the present with wisdom. In a marriage, promoting change in the present should take precedence over clarifying the realities of the past. Finding out about the past is the work of lawyers in a court. It is the work of historians. And in certain instances it can be the work of skillful therapists to help a person gain greater insight. In a marriage, whether it will be helpful or counterproductive depends on the personalities and reactions of both the husband and wife. If you find it beneficial to discuss the past with your spouse, do so. If you find it counterproductive, stay in the present.

An issue in marriage can occur when one party feels a strong need to discuss what went wrong in the past in order to let go of feelings of resentment, and the other party has a strong need to avoid talking about his or her wrongs in the past. It is too painful for him or her. I recommend that both do speak about it if possible. While listening and discussing can be painful to the one who doesn't want to talk about it, it is only through this vehicle that the other one will be able to move on.

If you feel a strong need to talk about something from the past and your spouse keeps on insisting that it's wrong to talk about past wrongs, you can point out, "To me this is not a matter of the past. I am living with these memories in the present. To me it's just as if it happened recently. My goal is to be able to let go of it totally so we can have a loving relationship, but right now I have a strong need to talk about it."

When you do talk about the past with your spouse, don't talk in an attacking manner. This will usually cause your spouse to be defensive. Be respectfully assertive and non-blaming. You want to explain yourself and your feelings. Speak so you will be understood. Let your tone of voice and choice of words be conducive to a peaceful discussion. This way you both gain.

REINFORCE POSITIVE ATTEMPTS AND IMPROVEMENT

"Reinforce improvement." This is a valuable piece of advice. When your spouse does something that he or she might not keep up spontaneously, reinforce it. Express your appreciation in a way that your spouse will appreciate. Some people like direct statements. For example, "When you greeted me in a friendly fashion at the door, it made me feel wonderful. Thank you so much." Other people might see this as condescending or controlling. For them a more subtle reinforcement is necessary. It could be a slight smile, or some action that your spouse would like.

"Reinforce positive attempts at improvement." If your husband or wife is trying to improve in some area, reinforce the positive attempt even if it is not yet exactly the way you wish it would be. Small changes can lead to large changes. The trend has been reversed. That is the main thing. So even though things are not perfect yet, going in the right direction is what counts. As long as they're on the right path, express your appreciation for the fact that he or she is trying. For most people this keeps them motivated to continue doing more in the same direction. Some people are afraid that if they reinforce a positive attempt, the person won't keep trying to be better. Perhaps. But the vast majority of people appreciate your appreciation of their efforts. Unless you know for certain otherwise, assume that your spouse would like his or her positive efforts acknowledged.

Live in the present. If you didn't like something that your spouse said previously and now he or she says something that is what you want him or her to say, accept the present statement. It's counterproductive for you to act like a lawyer doing a cross-examination. What will you gain by trying to point out a contradiction? It is normal for people to change their opinions and feelings. Some people readily acknowledge, "Yes, I have changed my position." But many just change their position without being open to acknowledge that they have changed their minds. If the present position is a position that you would want your spouse to have, accept it.

"It's impossible for things to get better," I would say.

My spouse would act better, and I would say, "It won't last."

Now I understand that it would have been wiser for me to have given my spouse encouragement whenever things got better, but I was full of resentment. Moreover, I really believed that it was impossible for things to get better. Therefore, I viewed anything positive that my spouse said or did as either just a temporary try that wouldn't last, or else as just a fake, a superficial ploy to win me back. I considered it insincere and not real.

My spouse, however, believed that things could get better, and also knew with total clarity that the efforts at improvement were totally sincere. I didn't want to go for counseling. Since I felt it was impossible for things to get better, I was certain that counseling would be a waste of time, money, and energy, but my spouse kept insisting that we try anyway. An objective outsider might be able to see things that we both missed and make some helpful suggestions.

During the first session, the counselor listened carefully and objectively to both of our versions of what the reality of our marriage actually was. I said, "I'll tell you my side. But it won't make any difference. It's impossible for things to get better."

"Excuse me," he said. "I can see that the situation is serious and that change might be difficult. But right at the beginning let's differentiate between 'impossible' and 'difficult.'

"What does 'impossible' actually mean?" he asked us.

"That it can't possibly happen," I replied.

"Do you believe you can choose what you are going to say?"

"Yes," I replied.

"Do you believe you can choose what actions to take?"

"Yes, of course," I said.

"Changing patterns is often difficult and it can take time," he assured me, "but it is possible. I've seen many situations in which the participants both felt it was impossible for things to get better, but either the husband or wife started speaking and acting differently and this changed the entire nature of the relationship.

"I guarantee you one thing. If you keep repeating that it's impossible for things to get better, your belief will insure that there won't be a lasting improvement.

"I can never guarantee anyone that things will get better. For some people they don't, regardless of how many different professionals they speak to. They have incompatible goals, lifestyles, and personalities. They have so much built up resentment that they find it too hard to let go of it.

They continue to get into nasty quarrels. However, I've seen enough so-called 'impossible' situations improve to make me a strong believer in possibilities. At times, even if only one person is committed to improving the way he or she speaks and acts, a marriage can get better, even much better. When both husband and wife are willing to do whatever it takes, and will consistently work on improving what they say and do for as long as it takes, then they are almost guaranteed success. If one plan or approach does not work, they try something else. They keep trying until they are successful. I have seen couples go from being adversaries and even enemies to becoming close friends who enjoy each other's company. Some couples don't get this far, but they do get along peacefully and begin to feel more positive about each other.

"I see that your spouse is sincere," he told me. "I don't always feel this way, but in your situation I see it as clearly as I see my hand right in front of my eyes.

"I ask of you both just one thing," he concluded. "Please do it as a personal favor to me. It will also save you a lot of suffering and money."

I looked at my spouse with my peripheral vision and saw that my interest in hearing the "one thing" was matched.

"Whenever either of you likes something that the other one says or does, please say, 'I appreciate that.' Every day look for as many things to appreciate as you can. If you find that you say it too often, you might want to limit it to a specific number of times.

"Do you both agree to try this out?" he asked us. "We will discuss the results of this experiment next week."

Of course, we agreed. We had nothing to lose.

That week was the best week of our marriage since the week of our wedding and sheva berachos. I no longer felt that improvement was impossible. I became a true believer in the power of positive reinforcement.

❖ ❖ ❖

I travel a lot and am constantly busy when I travel. I am exhausted at the end of the day, and my energy is totally depleted. I know that I don't call my wife often enough. When I do call, this is what I usually hear, "How come you didn't call before? I've been waiting for you to call. You're very insensitive and uncaring."

Knowing that I will be yelled at when I call caused me to keep procrastinating. I passed up many opportunities to call my wife. If I had only a few minutes before a meeting, I wanted to be in a positive emotional state to be able to do my best. The criticism I heard on the phone was so unpleasant to my ears that it caused me to avoid calling. Didn't my wife realize how counterproductive her approach was?

Then, one day, I was totally unprepared for what my wife said when I called.

"How wonderful to hear your voice," she said. "Your call means so much to me. Thank you so much for calling. Your voice is music to my ears."

Wow!!! I never expected to hear such a beautiful greeting. I don't know if someone told her to do this, whether she read about it, or whether she thought of it on her own. Regardless of how it happened, I appreciated it immensely. I began calling more often, and each time I received a warm and loving response. We both feel great about our telephone calls. And when I come home, the effects carry over to our in-person conversations.

Chapter Nine

REFRAMING:
Builder or destroyer of marriages

∞ *Master the art of reframing and live a joyous life*

∞ *Putting things into perspective: Your view of a situation creates or eliminates problems, intensifies or diminishes them*

∞ *Internalize Torah reframes*

∞ *Marriage: Constant opportunities to reframe*

∞ *Focus on how you benefit from your marriage (rather than focusing on what is wrong or missing). At the same time work on improvement and solutions*

∞ *Unrealistic expectations create unnecessary problems*

∞ *Expecting challenges make them easier to handle*

MASTER THE ART OF REFRAMING
AND LIVE A JOYOUS LIFE

ou, like everyone else, would like to live a joyous life. One of the most important skills to master to be able to live joyously is the art of reframing. What is reframing? The way that you personally view or perceive a given situation is the way that this situation will affect you emotionally. When you view a situation in a positive light, you will have a positive emotional reaction towards it. When you view a situation in a negative light, you will have a negative emotional reaction towards it. Reframing means perceiving a situation or event differently than you did originally or differently than it is usually viewed. A person who masters the art of reframing will be the master of the emotional quality of his or her life. While you do not always have control over external factors, you always have the ability to reframe. Moreover, it is impossible not to reframe. Any way that you view a situation or event is a reframe from every other possible way of viewing it.

As we have written in *Begin Again Now* (pp. 282-3): "Anger, irritation, frustration, misery, being upset and many other painful or counterproductive emotions are all products of reframing. Each situation and occurrence that creates a negative reaction within you does so because of the way you reframed it. When you reframe the situation in a more positive way, your inner reactions will change for the better.

"People who experience much joy, happiness, and bliss in their lives do so because of the way they reframe life events. People who have mastered serenity and inner peace do so because of the way they reframe life events. People who enjoy being kind and compassionate are able to find pleasure in giving and helping because of the way they reframe their relationships with other people and because of what it means to them to be giving and kind. Interview people who are joyous, serene, and kind. Find out their attitudes and reframes, and start the process of internalizing those or similar reframes.

"People who are cynical, miserable, pessimistic, bitter, caustic, scornful, gloomy or self-pitying can only stay this way because of the unfortunate way they reframe the exciting adventures, challenges, and opportunities of the world.

"There is no event so positive that a creative negative reframer can't mess up. At the same time a person with a creative sense of humor can find humor by reframing the same things that frustrate others. Reframe is what anyone with a poetic view of the world does constantly.

"When a reframe is real to you, your feelings towards the event or occurrence will be consistent with that reframe."

This is an important point. Just repeating a positive way of looking at something will not necessarily have an effect on your emotional reaction. It is only if you actually change the way you perceive something that the new way of looking at it will transform negative feelings to positive ones. People differ greatly as to how easy or difficult it is for them to change perceptions. Some people are able to do this quite quickly. When they are upset over something that happened, they find positive ways to look at what occurred and immediately they feel better. Others need to spend much more time and effort in order to change their feelings about things.

I once overheard two people speaking on a cold day. "It's quite windy," one said to the other in a complaining tone of voice. "It's very invigorating. It makes you feel totally alive," commented the other. It was the same cold wind for both. But each perceived it differently. Hopefully, the reframe of the second person will be accepted by the first person.

You can't get away from reframing. Whether you like the concept or not, you will always be reframing. Every time anyone relates an incident or a story they are relating it from a certain point of view. For example, "We had a wonderful time." You can only have a wonderful time because of the way you reframed what happened. Instead of saying, "It was a rough day," one might prefer, "I had a challenging day, but I gained a lot and now I need to recharge my energy."

My friend, Rabbi Kalman Packouz says, "The worst disability one can have in life is a negative attitude." A negative reframer will make his or her life miserable and will be challenging to others. Since reframes tend to be contagious, a negative reframer will spread distress and misery. The highest priority of a negative reframer needs to be to master positive reframing.

Your skill at positive reframing will affect your marriage greatly. First of all, your general emotional state will be based on the quality of your reframes. Moreover, the way you view everything that your spouse says or does is ultimately the way that you reframe them. Couples who quarrel frequently, who often get angry at each other, who experience much stress and tension in their lives, have these experiences because of the way that they consistently reframe things.

Marriage will give you a tremendously large number of opportunities to reframe. Everything that is not exactly the way you wish it to be will elicit a reaction. And what that reaction will be will depend on how you reframe it. You have already been influenced by the way other people in your environment have reframed things. The way your parents, siblings, friends, and other people you have met view things will have an influence on the way you presently view things. However, even if you have previously viewed something in the past in a way that caused frustration, irritation, or anger, now you can change your reframes and find ways to gain or benefit from a situation.

When you view a situation as a learning experience, you will react more positively to it. When you view a difficult situation as an opportunity to build up your character, you will react more positively to it. When you view a difficult situation as your training ground to master perspectives that will enable you to be emotionally independent of external circumstances, you will react more positively to it.

Questions to keep in mind are, "What is beneficial about this situation?" "How can I gain from what happened?" "How can I grow from this?" or, "Why is this so trivial that it's not worth wasting precious moments of life on it?" Even before you have answers, you will be thinking in a much better direction than you would have if you weren't asking these questions.

If you have to do something unpleasant, you have a few choices of how to reframe this. [A] You can view the matter as awful and experience much distress. [B] You can think of a positive reframe. For example, you are making a sacrifice to do an act of *chesed*, and then feel good that you are helping someone. [C] You can use the time to mentally focus on thoughts you find enjoyable or pleasant. This will enable you to reframe the experience in a more positive manner. [D] You can think about how joyful or relieved you will be when the unpleasant task is finished.

Every time you need to wait for your spouse, whether this will be frustrating or not will depend on how you reframe it. When you utilize waiting time wisely, you will find positive reframes for that waiting. Waiting can be reframed as an act of *chesed*. While in the past you might have become upset with your spouse for making you wait, yet now you are waiting patiently, you are bringing the *Shechinah* into your lives and therefore your waiting has not been in vain. Rather it has been an elevating experience.

If your spouse suggests a place to go or something to do and you would find it boring, you can view your going to that place or doing that thing as an act of kindness for your spouse. This reframe will transform what was potentially boring into something that you will now do with joy to give pleasure to your spouse. This pattern of reframe will enhance your marriage greatly.

Each situation can be seen from many perspectives. A helpful exercise is to practice listing five different ways to view a given situation.

When a husband and wife are motivated to become experts at positive reframing, they can have much enjoyment mastering this skill together. They can keep asking each other, "What positive reframes for this can you think of?" If you are interested in mastering reframing and your spouse isn't, you will need to reframe this. This will give you an even greater opportunity to develop the art of reframing since you will need to do this alone, which is more difficult. If this is your situation, hopefully you will be able to master the art of reframing to such an extent that you will have a positive influence on the way your spouse reframes things also.

Using the word reframing in your house is great if both you and your spouse like the word. If your spouse doesn't like it, it can get on his or her nerves. So then think about reframing yourself. But don't explicitly use this word. For some people if you explicitly say, "I see a positive reframe for this situation," it will make them more open to hearing the reframe. Other, however, will accept a reframe if it is presented in a more subtle manner. They might resent your telling them, "Just reframe it."

It is highly important to remember that if something doesn't bother you and yet it bothers your spouse, start off by being compassionate or empathizing with your spouse's distress or pain. Immediately reacting with a reframe can be highly insensitive to what he or she is experiencing. In many instances only after you understand what your spouse is experiencing, and after you express your care and concern about the matter, will a reframe be helpful.

Telling someone else farfetched, irrational, corny, or plain stupid attempts at reframing is counterproductive. If you don't feel that a reframe you thought of will be helpful, it would be wiser not to say it, unless you have a great sense of humor and your spouse will laugh at the humor of your reframe.

If you personally are suffering from something and your spouse tells you, "Just reframe it," you might want to say, "That's a good idea. But I'm not yet ready to do so. Right now, I need you to understand me and validate my feelings. Then I might be open to reframing."

Learning about reframing transformed my life and my marriage. When I was growing up, I used to get upset very easily. When things weren't as I liked, I would get angry. I gave my parents many a rough time because of my being upset and irritated over so many trivial issues, but to me at the time, nothing was trivial. Everything that was not to my liking was a major issue. I would hide this from my friends, but at home I was quite often miserable.

When I was first married, I followed my familiar pattern. Little things upset me much more than the average person, but I noticed that the things that upset me didn't upset my spouse, and my spouse wasn't even upset that I was upset.

"Why is it that things that bother me don't bother you?" I asked one day, when I saw how calm my spouse was when a pipe burst and our apartment was flooded.

My spouse smiled and said, "I'm so glad that you finally asked me. I was waiting for an appropriate time to teach you about reframing. Now that you asked me, I feel comfortable telling you. When I was younger many things used to bother me. Then I heard a class on the concept of reframing. I realized that all of these trivial things that bothered me only bothered me because of the way I looked at them. I made a resolution to become a master at reframing. I wasn't always successful. But I kept learning from every positive reframer I met. Even people who were bothered by many things, had other things that didn't bother them. I kept asking people for the way that they viewed things. Because I needed to work so hard on reframing positively, I have become more of an expert than people who do so more naturally."

My spouse became my reframe teacher. We now have great times in situations that in the past would have been a source of distress.

PUTTING THINGS INTO PERSPECTIVE: YOUR VIEW OF A SITUATION CREATES OR ELIMINATES PROBLEMS, INTENSIFIES OR DIMINISHES THEM

There are certainly things that others would consider to be problems that you personally don't, and there are things that others would not consider to be a problem but you do. Your perspective of a situation is what makes something into a problem and your perspective will either make it easier or more difficult to find a solution.

For instance, if you mopped the floor of your kitchen and your spouse steps on the wet floor, for some people this would become an issue of lack of consideration. Others, however, view the footprints as a reminder that they are married and have a house. They still are likely to tell their spouse to be more careful, but they will do so gently and with a pleasant tone of voice. This footprint is their opportunity to elevate their character and to bring the *Shechinah* into their home. This to them will be a higher priority than having a floor without footprints.

When a couple argues, that same argument can be seen as a normal disagreement between two people, or it can even be viewed as a quarrel or fight, or it might be seen as a discussion that got a little out of hand. For some people it can be seen as a stimulating interaction. Different people will have different descriptions of the same situation. It depends on various factors, especially what you are used to from the past and what your expectations are now. For some couples what happened now was a great improvement over what used to be, while for other couples the same situation shows that things are getting worse and that improvement is desperately needed.

There are definitely serious situations that we would all consider as problems. Well not all, for those who say, "There aren't any problems, there are only challenges or opportunities," will not consider anything a problem. But yet, even for those who do consider many events as problems, the seriousness of the problem will depend on how you view it. Your perspective of a situation will often be the deciding factor whether something will be considered a problem and a source of a quarrel, or whether it won't be. Your perspective will be the key factor on how seriously you view many problems.

There was a teacher who wanted to teach his students to see situations comprehensively. He wanted them to be able to see the parts and the whole. He showed them the following experiment. He brought a sheet of paper with a small black dot on the bottom left corner. "What do you see here?" he asked the students. Every single one answered, "I see a small black dot."

"But what about the large piece of white paper surrounding that white dot?" the teacher pointed out. One of the students who never forgot that lesson became an internationally famous negotiator. "Always look at the whole picture" enabled him to see things that others missed. No human being can see the entire whole. Only the Creator can. But realizing that there is always a bigger picture will enable us to see things that otherwise we wouldn't have noticed.

This has powerful ramifications for problems in marriage. In the majority of situations when there are quarrels and disagreements, there are still many things each party appreciates about the other. Both husband and wife have gained tremendously from being married to each other. Yes, there are some black dots. But a comprehensive view will enable you to see the large white paper.

When someone has a minor pain in a finger or a toe, even though it will heal in a day or two, we focus on it while it hurts. Our brain automatically puts this uppermost in our minds. True, all our vital organs are working well. There is no threat to our life and we will be back to normal pretty soon, but it is easier for us to focus on this than to keep focusing on everything that is working well. Even though what is wrong is only a fraction of one percent compared to what is going right, it takes a major effort to see the big picture.

The same applies in marriage. When we are upset about something our spouse has said or done, that easily becomes our focus rather than all the positive things that our spouse has done for us. Compared to what can go wrong in this world, most of the things that create problems for people in marriage are trivialities. They are like the tiny dot on the white page. You can still benefit from the white page in numerous ways even though you would prefer that the dot wouldn't be there. You don't need to ignore the dot. You can think of a way to whiten it. But remember, you still have the white page.

Some people suffer a lot because of what their spouse didn't do: I am hurt because …

- You forgot my birthday
- You didn't remember our anniversary
- You didn't buy me a present
- You bought me a present but you didn't buy me what I wanted
- You didn't feel my pain
- You weren't happy for my successes
- You weren't interested in what I have to say
- You didn't notice that I cleaned the house
- You didn't notice that I lost weight
- You were bored when I said a *dvar Torah*

Your level of distress about these issues will depend on how you reframe them. If you reframe them as major problems, you will experience much more pain than if you reframe them as challenges from which to grow.

Don't assume that your spouse is purposely doing things to bother or irritate you. ("He/she is doing this *davka* because I don't like it.") In the vast majority of situations, your spouse is doing this because of his/her own reasons. If someone considers inadvertent behavior a direct act of spite, it will increase the intensity of the pain and anger. Realizing that your spouse was acting for his or her own perceived benefit and needs and not out of spite will make it easier for you to find solutions.

There are couples who stay married basically for the welfare of the children. Husbands and wives who do this as a sacrifice for their children have a choice of doing so with reluctance or with the positive feelings that they are elevating themselves by sparing their children from suffering.

When someone is tired and stressed out, what at other times can seem minor might now appear to him or her to be major and monumental. Our unresourceful emotional state increases our level of distress. Realizing that our intense reaction is more a product of our internal state than a reflection of the actual situation is a reframe that will prevent a false reframe from escalating the problem.

A person's perceptions become their reality. So the real issue in many situations isn't, "What is the objective reality of this situation?" Rather it is, "Given that the husband has this perception and the wife has this perception, what can be done now to improve the situation?" Two people who are very sensitive can love and care about each other very much but might be hurt rather easily by what the other says or does, or by what the other fails to say or do. Always keep your eyes on the larger picture. Challenge the way you view a problematic situation if you feel that there is a better way of looking at it. View setbacks as valuable learning experiences rather than failures.

Labels tend to prevent us from allowing those whom we label the chance to change. This in turn makes it harder for them to change. If you label someone as narcissistic, that is what you are likely to see whenever this person says or does something. If you label someone as a pathological liar, you are likely only to focus on his lies. Of course, if someone has a history of lying, it would be a mistake to think that all of a sudden he is going to be a totally different person. Labeling someone as a difficult person, however, often makes it much harder to improve the situation. Changing someone's pattern is often very difficult, but believing that someone's essence is a certain negative way makes it even more difficult. If you view the person as someone who will help you grow, you have a much better chance of finding compassionate or creative ways of interacting with that person and influencing him or her to make positive changes.

Having a new perspective on an old situation changes the emotional state that you associated with it. Imagine that you have had a rough time this last year. And then one day someone comes to your door and says, "We were looking for someone whose life has been rough this past year in a certain way. Yours has been exactly the picture we have been looking for. You are now being given a ten million dollar inheritance from the trust fund of someone who lived a similar life. He wrote in his will that he wanted to help someone in a way that he would have wanted someone to help him." Your perspective about that past year would be immediately changed, wouldn't it?

If your spouse has been emotionally hurt, it is always because of the way he or she perceived the situation. The first step is understanding and empathy before offering a reframe. A word of caution: If your spouse does not feel that you are really feeling empathy, just mouthing empathetic words will not be that effective. The person on the receiving end of this, however, would be best off acknowledging the effort of his or her spouse anyway.

*M*y husband uses the concept of reframe in a way that gets on my nerves without being helpful. Whenever I feel irritated, upset, or annoyed by anything, he immediately says to me, "It's not a problem. Just reframe." I want and need empathy and understanding. After I am understood, I am open to see if I can look at the situation in a different way. But I am not ready to do this until my position is sincerely understood. Even after I am understood, I need to hear a specific reframe that seems real to me. But just being told, "Reframe," is *not just unhelpful, I consider it a lack of respect for my feelings.*

Before you offer a reframe to your spouse, or anyone else, get a clear picture how your spouse presently sees the entire situation. What are all the issues that are bothering him or her? Reframing is not some magic trick that will automatically work. Rather, if you understand how this person is seeing the situation now and you are able to present another view that meets all the concerns of the other person, then your reframe has a chance of being accepted.

If you are upset over something, you might want to ask yourself, "In the entire scheme of my life, how large a role does this play?" Some people find it helpful to ask themselves, "From the perspective of eternity and the size of the universe, how important is what happened just now?" If you are faced with a practical problem, do what you can to correct it, but view it with a sense of perspective. This isn't playing a trick with your mind. Just the opposite. The *yetzer hara* is playing a trick with your mind when you allow something trivial that was said or done to cause a fight or argument. You can have the *Shechinah* in your home. Don't drive it out with a stupid fight over pettiness. Look at the challenge before you as your spiritual nourishment that will eternally enrich your soul.

> *I went to the Western Wall daily for forty days to pray that Hashem should heal my marriage. We were married close to ten years and had five small children. The first year of marriage had been tolerable, but with the financial and physical stress of taking care of a family of our size, our marriage was highly stressful. My spouse and I lacked sleep, and this created irritability and tension which led to many avoidable quarrels.*
>
> *During the forty days that I went to the kosel, I met a number of people a few times. When I saw someone praying with great fervor, I asked them to pray for me as well. I didn't tell anyone exactly what I was praying for.*

I just said that I need a healing and left it at that.

Some of the people I asked to pray for me, spontaneously told me what they were praying for. There were a few single people who prayed to find a marriage partner. There were those who prayed to be healed from a serious illness with which they were recently diagnosed, and there were those who prayed for their ill parents or children. Someone prayed for a relative who was imprisoned, and another prayed because a business venture turned into a financial disaster. And there were those who were married many years and prayed to be blessed with children.

I saw that my situation was objectively much better than that of many others who came to the kosel to pray. After the thirtieth day, besides asking for my marriage to get better, I gave thanks to Hashem for the positive aspects of my life and my spouse. After a week of this, I noticed a positive change. In general, I was more cheerful at home and both my spouse and children were in better emotional states. My prayers made positive changes in me, and I found myself feeling grateful for things I hadn't felt grateful about before.

My spouse seems so different now that I am married than before our marriage. I thought that this was unusual and it was a major cause of distress for me.

Then I came across an article written by Rabbi Simchah Cohen in a journal, "Above the Sun." There he wrote: "Studies of married couples reveal that in the majority of cases they do not view their spouse in quite the same light as they did prior to marriage. In one study, 75 percent of all participants indicated that, had they known their partners as well before as they do after marriage, they would never have married them!"

This was not a study of Torah observant people who only met each other a limited amount of times before becoming engaged, but of couples who had dated for a long time before deciding to get married.

Rabbi Cohen commented: "The obvious conclusion is that despite the long time spent getting to know each other, often years, many couples did not really know each other well enough to assure compatibility in marriage. Why doesn't dating provide the individual with a true and objective impression of his prospective mate?

"One of the reasons may be," Rabbi Cohen wrote, "that prior to marriage the young couple are unfamiliar with the nature and demands of marital and family life.

"Married life is not a utopian existence where love blooms and friendship is all that counts. Factors which barely come into play in friendship suddenly loom very large in a marriage relationship, and the awakening of reality that takes place is often very painful, indeed."

To me, reading this removed a lot of pain. Wow! Seventy-five percent felt they wouldn't have married the other person. And what about the other 25 percent? How many might have married the other person anyway, and still were faced with patterns and qualities that bothered them?

If this then is the norm rather than the exception, it means that my situation was much more common than I had imagined. It's as if a being from another galaxy reads one utopian novel about planet earth and then is shocked by the reality.

After reading this, I made a decision to continue trying to improve my own level of joy rather than focusing on my spouse's lack of total perfection.

I felt much resentment towards my wife and had a long list of grievances. She was a good person and worked hard for the welfare of our family, but the way she spoke to me often elicited my anger. When it came to preparing food for me, she tried to get by with the barest minimum of effort. She would often forget to give me messages. In general, she was more critical than supportive.

One day when I was in the middle of stewing about a specific complaint I had against her, I came across a picture of a large group of Jewish families who had just arrived at Auschwitz. The caption read that the members of the family would soon be separated forever. Some would live and some would die that same day. The cruel Nazis would make a selection among the people and some would never again see their loved ones.

It hit me that my resentment and anger were separating our family. "How could I walk in the footsteps of those evil monsters?" I said to myself. And how could I complain about the amount of food I had, when what I had was super abundance compared to what those in the concentration camps had. I saw the picture of the cattle cars in which those relatives of mine were forced to travel for days, without even the barest necessities of life.

Right then and there, I was resolved that I would gain a greater perspective of the reality of how fortunate I truly was. I was totally committed to appreciate my wife for all the positive things she did.

*M*y wife is a difficult person to get along with. She certainly doesn't view herself this way. Her friends think she is reasonable and easy to get along with, but I know the truth. She is difficult. Now, she will say the same about me. And it could be that she's right.

My wife is constantly critical of me. She complains about my personality, about my time management, about the way I handle the children. I used to find her constant complaints intolerable.

Then there are my complaints about her. I don't like her handling of the children, her ineffective time management, and her lack of skills as a housewife. I found the entire situation painful and didn't know how I would be able to cope in the years to come. We have a large family and divorce was out of the question.

Then one day someone told me the story of a great Chassidic Rebbe that changed my perspective on the state of my marriage. This Rebbe was married to someone who was considered by some as having a major personality disorder. His wife would mock him and heap scorn upon his head. The day he became the Rebbe of his followers, he came home quite late at night. He had forgotten the key to his house, and knocked on the front door.

His wife called out to him, "Do you think you are so great? You can't even remember to take your key. How can you be a leader of others?"

Regardless of how his wife treated him, he was always respectful and kind towards her.

Compared to the way this great person's wife treated him, my wife was an angel. It was still difficult for me, but since then I have viewed my own situation in a more positive light.

My spouse loves to set verbal traps. My reaction to this is at the exact opposite end of the scale. I can't stand them.

"This person and I are very similar, aren't we?" I was asked. I saw many similarities, and replied, "Yes, you are."

"No, we're not." I was told. "We are very different." I got the feeling that if I were to say they were different, it would have been pointed out to me that they were similar.

"Do you think we need to take precautions against such and such a danger?" I was asked. If I said, "Yes," I am told, "You don't have enough bitachon." If I say, "No," I am told I am failing to fulfill the mitzvah of guarding our health.

"Should we walk or take a taxi?" If I say we should take a taxi, I am challenged, "Walking is both healthier and cheaper." If I say we should walk, I am told, "Taking a taxi is faster. Time is more precious than money."

It took me some time to recognize this pattern which always left me feeling a bit stupid and put-down. Then I heard about two patterns when it comes to reactions towards ideas: matchers and mismatchers. I am a matcher. I tend to see similarities and prefer agreeing with what someone else says. My spouse is a mismatcher. My spouse tends to see differences and distinctions. My spouse prefers to debate rather than to automatically agree. I realized that my spouse wasn't purposely trying to put me down. This just happens to be the way my spouse thinks.

I began developing my ability to see a more comprehensive picture, and to be able to see both a matching and a mismatching side to questions and issues. Whenever I thought that a question was being asked that I used to consider a verbal trap, I would reply, "I see two possibilities. Each side has its merits and shortcomings. Let's analyze this together." I found that my new pattern worked well and I actually enjoyed seeing distinctions that I would have previously missed.

*M*y husband is usually a wonderful person, but he has a major problem with anger.

The latest example occurred when he was shouting on the telephone at someone with whom he does business. I feel his anger drives the Shechinah from our house and creates a toxic atmosphere. So I told him, "Lower your voice." This is something he does not want to hear.

As soon as my husband finished the telephone call, he started yelling loudly at me. He blames me for getting him angry and he curses.

He repeats the same thing over and over again to me, with his voice getting louder and louder.

Then he starts throwing things at me. He doesn't really want to harm me, but it's frightening. At times it looks as if he wants to physically harm me. At times he even shakes me.

After a few minutes, he starts paying attention to his heart. He says, "You are going to give me a heart attack." Instead of blaming his own anger, he blames me.

Then he lies down on the sofa and almost starts crying.

The next day he apologizes. He is sincerely sorry for the way he acted the day before. He will walk around the whole next day feeling badly. He is full of self-reproach and guilt.

I never know in advance when these rages will occur. It's usually after something outside of the house upsets him.

I feel trapped between my anger and my fear of being attacked in an uncontrolled over-reactive manner on the one hand, and my concern about what can happen to him. My husband needs to work through his reactions to whatever it is he doesn't want to hear.

Fortunately, my husband agreed to work on his anger with his Rabbi. He realized that this was a pattern he *learned from his father, and that it will take a lot of effort to change the pattern.*

He was told that he needs to make an intense commitment to do whatever it takes to change his pattern. He was given a breathing exercise as an emergency start. By breathing slowly and deeply, his stress level decreases. He can then think more clearly.

A key element in his changing was to learn to view my saying things such as, "Calm down," as my effort to help him rather than as an attack on his dignity.

While my husband was told that he needs to take full responsibility for his own reactions, I need to speak to him in a calmer voice. When I'm upset or afraid, my tone of voice goes up and this increases his anger. It was suggested that I look into his eyes and say to him in a soft voice, "I love you. Please calm down." I argued that when he is in a rage, I find it too difficult to say this, but I was told to look at him in his rages as at an erupting volcano and that the magic formula to calm the volcano is, "I love you. Please calm down."

Since I see that my husband is motivated to work on his anger, I'll visualize myself doing this and hopefully together we can overcome this destructive pattern.

Utilize the stories of great people to serve as a positive reframe and as positive role models to elevate your behavior. Don't misuse them as weapons of blame and condemnation if your spouse is not acting like the heroes of the stories you read and hear. This would be a negative reframe of those stories.

I had been having headaches daily for a week. My husband said to me, "Perhaps you should see a doctor for your headaches'?"

"You are an awful husband for saying that. What do you mean 'your headache.' Rabbi Aryeh Levine would

say, 'Our foot hurts us,' when he went with his wife to a doctor to treat his wife's foot. Why can't you say, 'for our headache'?"

My husband became angry at me, "I was just trying to be helpful. If you don't like the way I say things, maybe I shouldn't offer to help you in the future."

Even before my husband shot back his hurt reply, as soon as the words were out of my mouth, I realized I had said the wrong thing. He was trying to be helpful. My headache prevented me from thinking clearly. In my pain I wanted to be nurtured. I'm not even certain that Rabbi Aryeh Levine always talked in this way. Perhaps it took him years to develop this. Regardless, I am much better off appreciating the positive aspects of what my husband said, rather than getting angry at him for not being perfect.

INTERNALIZE TORAH REFRAMES

The Torah way of looking at things that occur in your life will enable you to live a joyous life. This will be a life free from much of the frustration, stress, and anger that many people on the planet experience. When you realize that all that happens to you in your life is for your benefit and ultimate good, you will have positive emotional reactions to what happens. To attain this level, it isn't sufficient just to observe *mitzvos*. Rather, what is needed is integration of Torah perspectives, making them your own personal world-view of life's events and situations. This is a lifetime process. Be patient and persistent when working on making Torah concepts your spontaneous way of perceiving things.

The way you reframe the entire concept of marriage is a key element in whether or not you will have a happy marriage. Those who view marriage basically as a vehicle for getting what they want are likely to experience much disappointment that inevitably leads to anger and quarrels. Integrate the Torah perspective or reframe, and view marriage as an opportunity for growth. You constantly grow in your character traits. You have constant opportunities to do acts of kindness for your spouse, family and guests who visit you. These patterns of reframing will give you a happy marriage and a joyous life.

In *Anger: The Inner Teacher* (see pp. 141-80) we have elaborated on reframing in general and have provided a list of Torah reframes that will have a major impact on the lives of all who internalize them. Here we will mention them concisely.

[1] "All that the Almighty causes to happen is for the good" (*Berachos* 60b). The *Shulchan Aruch* tells us that it is good to get into the habit of repeating this frequently (*Orach Chaim* 230:5), as did Rabbi Akiva. When you reframe all that happens as being for the good, you will consistently have positive emotional reactions.

[2] "The reward is according to the pain (*Pirkei Avos,* ch. 5, last Mishnah). When you realize that the difficulties you might be having in treating your spouse with the love and respect the Torah requires, will ultimately cause you to get an eternal great reward, you will find the task much easier.

[3] "All life situations are opportunities for you to improve your *middos,* character traits."

[4] "Every challenge that occurs in your life is meant to be a Divinely ordained test to enable you to elevate yourself" (*Mesillas Yesharim,* ch. 1).

[5] "This is a *kapparah,* an atonement." Every time we suffer, it is an atonement for the wrongs we have done (*Midrash Rabbah, Bereishis* 65:4; *Chochmah U'Mussar,* vol. 1, p. 347).

[6] "Love your neighbor as yourself" (*Vayikra* 19:18). Every act of kindness you do for your spouse is the fulfillment of the *mitzvah* and can be a source of joy.

[7] "Judge other people favorably" (*Vayikra* 19:15). Keep judging your spouse's actions as being inclined to be meritorious. This reframe will save you much frustration, resentment, and anger throughout your marriage.

[8] "This is an opportunity to emulate the Almighty." Being kind to someone who didn't act perfectly towards you is the fulfillment of the elevated concept of emulating our Creator. Marriage will give you many opportunities for this.

[9] "This too shall pass." Many of the issues that cause problems in marriage are so minor and trivial that if you let them pass, they will do so very quickly. When you let the trivial matters go, you can spend much more time benefiting from what is positive in your marriage.

The Torah prohibition against speaking *lashon hara* is based on the concept of reframing. When you speak against someone it is because of the way that you are perceiving that person. Listening to *lashon hara* has been compared to a computer virus. It distorts your mental programming. If you have heard *lashon hara* about your spouse and have accepted it, this will change your perspective. You now view something as negative whereas before you might have either disregarded it or viewed it positively. If this has happened to you, view it as an opportunity to fulfill the Torah's commandments to have love for other people and to judge them favorably.

My husband is a worrier. He worries about finances, about illness, about the weather, about crime, and about almost anything else that a person can worry about. I was not a worrier myself, but his constant worrying made me nervous.

I kept telling my husband to stop worrying, but, of course, that didn't stop him from worrying. I told him to have more bitachon, and he said I was just adding guilt to his distress of worrying. I told him to read a book on worry, but he said that when he was worried, nothing he read helped him.

I heard a Rabbi say that helping a worrier out of his worry is a major act of chesed. Just listening to a worrier expressing his worries lightens his burden. This made me

*realize that instead of viewing my husband's worrying as
a disturbance and a problem, I should view it as an
opportunity to do the mitzvah of chesed.*

*I no longer try to argue my spouse out of his worries,
which I saw doesn't work. Rather, I ask him questions
about his worries to understand them better. Since I
myself tend not to worry, I'm not the best person to solve
his worries, but we both see that my sincere efforts to be
helpful, together with his opportunity to express himself,
alleviate his anxiety.*

I *was home waiting for my spouse to call. I had to have
certain information to know how to plan the rest of
the day. Based on what I would hear, I would need to
either make certain appointments and cancel others, or
to continue with my original plans. I was waiting impatiently for the call, but it didn't happen.*

*My feelings of stress about not knowing what to do led
to feelings of anger. "Why didn't my spouse call? Am I not
important enough to make this a high priority? If it were the
other way around, I certainly would have called by now."*

*As my anger began to grow, the word "reframe" came
to me. "How can I reframe this in a positive way?" I
asked myself.*

*Instead of allowing anger to build up while I was wait-
ing, I utilized this situation to fulfill the mitzvah of judging my spouse favorably. Maybe circumstances that I was
not aware of prevented my spouse from calling. In place
of building up resentment, I kept repeating to myself,
"Judge favorably! Judge favorably!"*

*I remembered that I needed to make a call and I
picked up the telephone. But there was no dial tone. At
first I thought that maybe the telephone wires to our*

house were down. I then checked the telephone receiv-
er in another room and saw that it was off the hook. No
wonder the telephone hadn't rung! My resentment
totally disappeared and a few minutes later the tele-
phone rang. My spouse was on the line and told me, "I
frantically kept trying to call you. But the line was con-
stantly busy."

I saw from this that I am still very far from mastering
the ability to judge favorably. There was a major differ-
ence in my feelings when I realized the phone was off
the hook. If I had internalized a favorable judgment
beforehand, I would have felt the same before and after
I realized that our telephone was unavailable.

MARRIAGE: CONSTANT OPPORTUNITIES TO REFRAME

Your marriage will give you constant opportunities to reframe. Each encounter with your spouse will automatically be reframed in one way or another. When you enjoy and appreciate what your spouse says and does, it means that you are reframing those things positively. When you are annoyed or distressed by what your spouse says or does, it means that you are reframing those things negatively. Isn't it normal to view many things as negative? Of course it is. But everything that occurs that is not to your liking is an opportunity from which to grow. This reframe will greatly enhance your life and your marriage.

Since marriage gives you many opportunities to do acts of *chesed*, much of what you do will be spiritually elevating when you view it in this perspective.

When you need to make a sacrifice in your marriage for the benefit of your spouse, it is easier to do so when you feel that your spouse also makes sacrifices for you. However, a unilateral sacrifice might be seen as more elevating and as a higher act of greatness.

The more challenging one's marriage, the more important it is to learn to become a master at reframing. If your spouse speaks to you in a tone of voice that you don't initially like, you can reframe it as, "It is awful to be in a situation where I am spoken to like this." And it can also be reframed, "I am going to use this as a training ground to learn how to become more proficient at influencing and motivating. I will keep trying until I find a way to motivate my spouse to speak more pleasantly. This is also an opportunity for me to become more persistent."

The greater the differences between your spouse and yourself in personality and in patterns of thinking, the more opportunities you will have to become a master reframer.

Every time you become irritated, frustrated, or angry in your marriage, you are spontaneously reframing in a way that elicits these responses. Since you would prefer to experience more joy, humor, serenity, love, and spiritual elevation, you have the challenge of what you can think, say, or do to experience more of this and less of the distressing feelings.

Reframing does not mean that you will just have to grin and bear what you don't like and mumble to yourself, "It could be worse." While it is true that "It could be worse" is a valuable reframe, it is not always going to be the best one to use. Reframing might mean at times that someone will view an abusive situation as a vehicle for building up inner strengths that one didn't realize one had, strengths that may lead to resolving do do everything one can within a Torah framework to leave an intolerable situation. In many problematic situations, when the other party realizes that the marriage is over if he or she doesn't act differently, he or she will now reframe the situation as one in which he or she has a choice of improving or losing out in a major way. This reframe is frequently a strong motivator. For the majority of marriages, however, the situation is not this extreme, and that takes us to the next section.

FOCUS ON HOW YOU BENEFIT FROM YOUR MARRIAGE (RATHER THAN FOCUSING ON WHAT IS WRONG OR MISSING); AT THE SAME TIME WORK ON IMPROVEMENT AND SOLUTIONS

When you focus on how you benefit from your marriage, you will be reframing much differently than had you been focusing on what is wrong or missing in your marriage. By keeping your main focus on how you gain from being married in general, and from being married to your particular spouse, you will experience more happiness and satisfaction.

Focusing on how you benefit does not mean that you need to passively accept everything that is not to your liking. The general rule is: Change what can be changed and accept what cannot be changed. Following this logical and rational formula, you will minimize suffering and be open to experience more positive emotions.

Keep asking yourself, "What are all the ways that I gain from being married to my spouse?"

My husband isn't as interesting and exciting as I would like him to be. He is always polite and respectful, but I find his dependability a bit boring. I always know what to expect. This had created a certain sense of dissatisfaction in my married life.

One day when I had nothing special to do, the thoughts of dissatisfaction were uppermost in my mind. I suddenly remembered hearing, "Often the qualities that will bother you about your spouse are the exact same qualities that attracted you to him in the first place."

"That's true for me," I said to myself. I come from an exciting family. Too exciting. My father was a risk taker. Our financial situation fluctuated between extreme highs and lows. My father would borrow large sums of money. Sometimes his ventures would work out, and money was

flowing in our home. We would live the lifestyle of the wealthy. We would buy fancy furniture and take expensive vacations.

But at times the risks were disastrous. The business ventures failed. We had large debts and had to cut down to the barest minimum of existence.

The general emotional atmosphere of the house would also go up and down. When we were wealthy, my parents were cheerful and enthusiastic. They frequently invited a lot of company and we had a party-like atmosphere. But when the financial situation was rough, there was a depressive atmosphere in the house.

I made up my mind that I wanted to marry someone reliable and dependable, someone who would work hard, but who wouldn't take many risks. My husband fits the picture I had in mind, but now I'd like some more excitement in our lives.

Based on some advice I heard, I did two things. One, I kept my major focus on how much I gain from my husband's reliability and steadiness. Two, I asked him if he could surprise me every once in a while. He agreed. He bought me music tapes as gifts for no reason other than that he cares about me. We went on short trips to obscure places. Once in a while we go to restaurants. From time to time we would go for Shabbos to various relatives in different cities. Now I feel I have the best of both worlds.

UNREALISTIC EXPECTATIONS CREATE UNNECESSARY PROBLEMS

When I think of unrealistic expectations, I think of the request of one of my grandsons when he was a few months past his third birthday. He asked his mother to take him to the same barber he went to for his first haircut on his third birthday.

"Why do you want that same barber?" my daughter asked him.

"Because the last time I went to him he gave me *payos*. This time I want him to give me a beard."

Hearing this expectation from a three-year-old is cute. Unfortunately, unrealistic expectations when it comes to marriage can be very painful and the source of much strife and unhappiness. The way you imagined your marriage to be created your reframe of what you would consider normal and what you could expect your marriage to be like. If this picture is based on an illusion, then you could be experiencing a very normal situation and still be very unhappy because real life does not fit your picture.

An excessive amount of reverence and idolizing can easily lead to disillusionment and disappointment. When a new *chasan* or *kallah* believes every last word that is said to praise his or her *basherte*, he or she could be taken in by exaggerations. Enjoy them when they are said, but take them with a grain of salt. At engagement parties and *sheva berachos* people often speak with superlatives that would be fitting for the greatest people of previous generations. Yes, each *chasan* and *kallah* will have many real virtues, but if you expect him or her to be super humans, your blown-up balloon could blow up in your face. Real human beings have limitations and faults. Real human beings make mistakes. Don't expect anyone to be without flaws.

Both men and women often say things during the dating process that they might believe about themselves but which are inaccurate. Also, every person has a different definition regarding the exact meaning of things. (For example, wanting a large family, what is large? Wants to study Torah, how long, how diligently?) Some even say things that they know aren't totally truthful, because they wish to get married. Others omit and hide information that later creates problems during marriage. People make promises that they will improve and are sincere about their promises, but they don't take into consideration how difficult change actually is. Expect things to be different than you thought they would be and you will find it easier to appreciate the positive aspects of your marriage.

What were your dreams about marriage? Some people imagine that they will:

- Be completely understood and totally accepted
- Always be appreciated as being special
- Feel whole and complete
- Never be lonely
- Feel happy all the time
- Have all their needs, wishes, and dreams met and fulfilled

If any aspect of one's dreams are met, wonderful. But don't expect all of them to be met all of the time. Focus on growing from the reality of your actual situation.

Fantasies tend to be more exciting than reality. There are people who are never happy in their present reality. They keep hoping for a fantasized future. But present reality is what actually exists. Therefore, unless a person's main pleasure in life is his or her fantasy world, the way to live a joyous life is to find joy in your present reality, and this will be yours when you live a life of constant growth.

"The human condition is imperfection. Only G-d is perfect. Human beings are not."

Hearing this seemingly obvious wisdom in a talk that a Rabbi gave one Shabbos was the beginning of making my marriage a much more joyous one.

Previously my goal was just to make my miserable marriage into a more tolerable one. I worked on reframing, but the way I was going about it helped me just a little bit.

I asked around for some suggestions about what I could do to improve my marriage, and many of the things I did helped a little. But regardless of what I did, I was basically dissatisfied. I was a perfectionist. I wanted my spouse to be perfect and I wanted my marriage to be perfect. When I saw that neither my spouse nor my marriage was perfect, I felt so discouraged that I couldn't appreciate what was going right in my marriage.

What a relief to accept the fact that the human condition is imperfection. I was surprised that this self-evident concept had such a powerful effect on me. This reframe went deep into my mind and I immediately felt a change in my state. I reflected on the ramifications of no longer demanding that my marriage and my spouse needed to be perfect in order for me to be grateful.

I wish that I had fully realized right from the start of my marriage that I couldn't expect perfection, but that too would be an aspect of perfection. I am now grateful that I heard and integrated this concept when I actually did.

*B*efore I was married, I heard stories about great people and how they would treat their wives. The acts of kindness and sacrifice that they performed were inspiring. I was highly motivated by what I heard. That is, I was motivated to influence my husband to treat me like those Gedolim and Tzaddikim treated their wives.

There was only one major flaw. My husband had heard stories about great women who could be called super women. They never tired. Nothing was ever too hard for them. They did it all themselves and never needed to bother their husbands to help out. They earned money to help support the family. They took care of the children's needs almost single-handedly. They had guests. They ran around doing chesed. The house was always in perfect shape. They had time to study Torah and read Tehillim regularly. Somehow I think that his picture was a composite. A composite of the positive qualities of five wonderful people is a bit difficult for any one individual to emulate.

One day we had an immense blowup. I can't remember now if I started it or my husband did, but one of us challenged the other, "Why aren't you like the great people I've read and heard about?" "I have the same question for you," the other responded. And then came the explosion. We each had a lot of pent-up rage and fury and now it all came out. To say that we weren't emulating great people is an understatement.

"Wait a minute," my husband said. "Let's call a truce. This isn't getting us anywhere. We've both been comparing each other to a model of such perfection that instead of appreciating each other, all we've been thinking about is how far the other one is from the highest levels of perfection. This prevents us from focusing on what we ourselves can do to improve. Look how similar we are. We both think alike, just that we are seeing things from the opposite side."

I totally agreed with my husband. We both resolved to use stories about great people for our own inspiration and not to downplay the efforts of the other for not being everything a great person could be. Since then our marriage has improved greatly.

EXPECTING PROBLEMS MAKE THEM EASIER TO HANDLE

Someone who expects problems can mentally prepare for them and this makes them easier to handle. Someone who is consistently taken off balance when difficulties arise is reframing those difficulties in ways that make them hard to cope with. When you expect problems, you reframe them in a much lighter manner.

The ultimate in this is Rabbi Akiva who calmly recited *Shema Yisrael* when he was being tortured to death. His students were amazed at his incredible serenity. They asked him how he could possibly stay this calm and peaceful. He replied, "My entire life I was waiting for this moment." Rabbi Akiva mentally prepared himself to have such a love for Hashem that he was able to experience serenity instead of extreme pain.

Mentally preparing for problems is the opposite of worrying about problems. A person who worries about problems thinks about what might go wrong and feels anxiety in the present for what might go wrong in the future; but when you mentally prepare for a difficulty, you visualize yourself coping well with whatever occurs. Then, if a challenge actually arises, it won't catch you off guard. You are prepared for whatever will be.

When people are first engaged, they often see the other person as being "exactly like they are." In the majority of instances, as time goes on, you will find many differences. Being prepared for them makes them easier to handle.

Think about any recurring problematic patterns in your marriage. Mentally visualize yourself handling them well. Spend time with your eyes closed and see yourself speaking and acting in ways that are spiritually elevating and emotionally fulfilling.

My husband and I are both very different from one another in many ways. We come from different countries, and have different personalities. He is more rational, logical, and legalistic, and I am more emotional and fun-loving. We both considered our match a product of hashgachah pratis. After we got to know each other better, we both felt at first that our marriage would not have been our choice on our own. But we acknowledged, albeit reluctantly, G–d's superior ultimate wisdom.

The thing that was most difficult for me was that my moods kept leaning towards the depressive side. I became pregnant shortly after we were married. While I was grateful to be a mother, the physical discomfort and the emotional downs gave us both a rough time.

We argued a lot. My husband would build up cases for his position that might have been great for a lawyer in court, but were difficult for me to listen to. I wanted shorter statements that would be expressions of his love for me. Instead, I received lengthy painful lectures.

The moment of greatest pain came when I attended the wedding of a close friend of mine. The newly married couple were so happy with each other. The chasan announced loudly that this was the greatest day of his life and that he felt extremely lucky to be married to such a wonderful person. Why couldn't my husband say that about me? I was happy for my friend, but this added to my distress. Why wasn't I as happy as my newly-wed friend?

Then a number of positive changes occurred. I felt that my husband was being less critical towards me. If he had a complaint, he kept it concise. No more long lectures. My husband felt I was acting more positively towards him. We were building a positive loop, but I especially attribute one factor to having made a pivotal difference.

My friend, whom I had viewed as having the most ideal marriage, and who was a key source of my envy and dissatisfaction, confided in me that there were adjustment difficulties. She was at the beginning of a pregnancy and her moods kept changing. She didn't always feel well. Her husband said that he had a difficult time coping with his wife's mood swings. This isn't what he had expected when he got married. Seeing how similar our situations were gave me a feeling that our experiences were more common than I had thought. Realizing that challenges in marriage are what I should expect has made it much easier for me.

Chapter Ten

STATES:
The Factors that Determine the
Quality of Your Life and Marriage

- ☜ State mastery

- ☜ Express your points in a way that puts
  your spouse in a positive state

- ☜ Help your spouse access resourceful states

- ☜ Increase the positive anchors for yourself
  and your spouse

- ☜ Transform the state of frustration
  into the state of enjoyment

- ☜ Remember your finest moments
  and relive those states

- ☜ Mentally prepare yourself;
  don't get caught off balance

STATE MASTERY

*T*he quality of your life is based on the quality of your emotional and mental states. The word "states" is one of the most important words in marriage. A happy marriage is when both the husband and wife consistently put each other in good states by word and deed. A problematic marriage is when two people each put the other in distressful and unresourceful states. Mastery over one's state enables people to create joy for themselves even though their partner does not live up to their expectations.

When you are in your best frame of mind, you will think more clearly, be more creative, be more pleasant, and be more motivated to take care of things. Whatever you do will represent your best effort. You will pray and study with positive feelings and concentration. In general, you will feel good.

In your worst frame of mind, everything will be the opposite. States tend to go up and down. The interaction between any two people will depend greatly on both their states at the time of the interaction. When people are under stress, they are usually able to control what they say and do around strangers, but they might vent their frustration on their spouses.

Individual states can be considered either resourceful or unresourceful. Being able to go from unresourceful states to resourceful states is so important to your total well-being that it makes sense to consider this a high priority. Resourceful states are: joy-

ful and happy, loving, confident, balanced, calm, serene, courageous, empowered, concentrating, creative, centered, humorous, exciting, and spiritually elevated. Unresourceful states are
characterized by: sadness, frustration, anger, rage, hate, anxiety,
boredom, confusion, feeling overwhelmed or stuck, anguish,
despondence, dejection, loneliness, depression, emptiness,
chaos, detachment, and discouragement. The unresourceful
states are not the states you wish for yourself or for anyone you
sincerely care about.

Picture a life filled with these resourceful states. Compare that
with a life filled with unresourceful states. Imagine that you have
to make a choice. You can choose to consistently have food you
like, listen to music you enjoy, be in an aesthetically beautiful
environment, and be around people with whom you are excited
to be. Your other choice is to consistently have food you dislike,
listen to music that distresses you, be in an ugly environment,
and be around people who infuriate and insult you. That is the
difference between someone who consistently experiences life
with the best states and someone who consistently experiences
painful and distressing states. That is the difference between
learning how to master your states while simultaneously enabling
your spouse to be in his or her best states, or having both of you
keep saying and doing things that bring on stressful states.

Your emotional and mental states keep changing, either subtly or dramatically, throughout the day. At times you will notice
these changes, at other times you won't. For instance, when a
good storyteller tells you a fascinating story, your states will
change according to the narrative. Anyone watching your face
will be able to observe the changes in your state by the way your
facial expression and muscles keep changing. When your state
changes, your breathing rate changes, the pupils of your eyes get
larger or smaller, and your skin tone changes. When you become
aware of the state you are in, you will notice major differences
at various times of the day.

Whatever state you are in at the present moment will affect
the way you interact with people, especially your spouse. It is

quite easy to maintain a positive state when interacting with someone for a relatively short time, but when you are married you will need to interact over a long period of time, through a wide range of emotional states, some of which are resourceful while others are extremely unresourceful.

Many experiences have an effect on your states, including the sleep you've had, the food you've eaten, and your health. Doing exercise and taking brisk walks change your states. When you hear or read good news it puts you in quite a different state than when you hear or read bad news. The thoughts you focus on have a tremendous effect on your state of mind. Biofeedback technology works so that as soon as you think about a relaxing scene, your muscles relax. Think about an unpleasant scene and your muscles immediately tense up. When you act out even an imaginary joyous scene, the level of your hormones, known as endorphins, immediately increases and this gives you a natural good feeling.

States are contagious. This is why gaining greater mastery over your mental and emotional states is so important for marriage. When you are in a certain state, you tend to put other people in similar states. Think about some people who automatically make you feel good when you are around them, who enable you to access positive and resourceful states. These are the people whose presence you enjoy and with whom you want to spend more time.

State mastery means that you have mastered the skill of choosing the states in which you will be. People who use the word "mood" instead of "state" often feel stuck in the moods in which they are. The word "state" implies that the state you are in is temporary. And it is. Have you ever been in a negative state, and then received a telephone call from someone to whom you enjoy talking. Your state immediately changes. Or, how, after hearing one of your favorite songs, you can immediately change from feeling discouraged to feeling much more empowered.

People often make the mistake of focusing too much on the states in which they don't want to be, instead of focusing on those in which they do want to be. If you feel an emotional low, you might think to yourself, "I want to get out of this state." Many people think this way. But this will make you more stuck in the state in which you already find yourself. This is like fighting gravity every time you wish to take a step. Take a five-minute walk and with every step tell yourself, "I need to overcome the entire force of gravity right now and take another step. I need to overcome my tiredness. I need to overcome inertia. I need to make an effort to take my foot away from where it is and lift it up, then move it forward." See how this slows you down and makes walking much more difficult. Instead, focus on where you want to go. Similarly with states, keep your focus on the state that you do want, not on the one you don't want. Instead of saying, "I don't want to feel sad right now," it's preferable to say, "I want to access a joyous and enthusiastic state."

There are many ways to change your states from unresourceful to resourceful. Some of these ways are healthy, others are not. Addictions (e.g., smoking, drinking, gambling, and drugs) are negative ways that people use to enter more enjoyable states. People who engage in these dangerous practices do so because they haven't mastered more positive ways to access the states they wish for.

As you read about ways to change states, try to recall times when you have done this spontaneously. Imagine what your life would be like if you could access the greatest states at will, and thus effect a major transformation of your entire life, becoming joyous, confident, serene, concentrating, enthusiastic — any time you wish.

Here are more of the basic ways in which you can access the states you wish:

[1] **Change your present physiology or posture to the way it is when you are in the desired state.** For example, we have the principle stated by Rabbi Moshe Chaim Luzzatto in *Mesillas Yesharim* (chs. 7 and 23):

It is true that external behavior that expresses enthusiasm

is the result of an inner feeling of enthusiasm. But it is also true that if you behave externally as if you were enthusiastic, this will create an inner feeling of enthusiasm. For example, if someone is doing a good deed and does so with great speed and external signs of enthusiasm, little by little his outward behavior will influence his inner feelings. On the other hand, if someone's external behavior and posture is that of someone who is lazy or depressed, his inner feelings will soon be consistent with that behavior and posture. This is a fact to which experience will testify.

There is an easy exercise I suggest to people who are open to it. Look at yourself in a mirror and smile and wave to yourself. Those who are not afraid that this is too silly will immediately feel an emotional lift.

Whenever you are in a desirable state, name it and notice your posture and facial expression. When you again want to access that state, change your posture and facial expression accordingly and your brain will automatically put you into that state. Some people find this easier to do than others. Even if it takes you a while to learn to do this, the investment in time and effort is well worth it.

[2] **Remember a time in the past when you were in the specific state in which you now wish to be.** As you recall that memory, you will once again access that state. Remember the details of how you looked, how you spoke, and how you felt. The more you recall, the more likely that you will experience those states now.

You can observe this phenomenon easier in others than in yourself. Watch people talking about past events. Those events that were pleasurable and exciting will elicit aspects of those states now, while those events that were painful and sad will elicit a corresponding state now. This is why people who consistently talk about joyous memories live a happier life than those who constantly talk about situations in which they were in painful and unresourceful states.

Your brain is an entire library of various states. Every state you've ever experienced is stored away. Just as having a file name for a file on a computer enables you to access that file, so too, by giving names to your favorite states, you can access them now. Keep giving names to the states that you would like to experience again. For example, if you had an especially elevating feeling while praying in a certain place on a certain day, give it a unique name. You might have a *"Neilah* at the *Kosel"* state, a *"Purim* at the *Rosh Yeshivah's* house" state, a "speaking before a large crowd in Tzefas" state, and a "walking to the *chuppah"* state.

[3] **Imagine being in a certain state in the future.** This too will enable you to access a state in the present that is consistent with that future state. If you would like to access a more confident state, imagine that at some time in the future you feel totally confident. Then allow this confidence to permeate your entire being. Or you can imagine being in a vacation resort where you are totally relaxed and this will enable you to become more relaxed right now.

[4] **Think of people who exemplify specific states that you want for yourself.** When you want to access these, imagine for a few moments that you are someone who has total mastery of that state. Right now you might want to think of five specific people whom you would like to emulate. You only need to observe people for a few moments to access their state. Then you can stand or sit, talk, walk, and look the way they did when you saw them in that state, and the state is yours.

[5] **Ask yourself questions that enable you to access states.** For example, "When have I felt courage before?" As you recall a specific instance of courage, you are likely to feel

more courage now. Or, "How do I know that I am joyous when I feel joy?" Or, "When I am totally relaxed what do I tell myself, what do I visualize, and how do I feel?"

[6] **Your tone of voice will change your state.** When you speak joyously and energetically, you will feel that way. When you speak gently, slowly, and in a relaxed tone of voice, you will feel that way. And conversely, when you speak in an angry, hysterical, or overwhelmed tone of voice, you will feel that way.

[7] **The concept of "anchors" is valuable for state mastery.** This is crucial for a happy marriage and for this reason we have devoted an entire section to it later in this chapter.

EXPRESS YOUR POINTS IN A WAY THAT PUTS YOUR SPOUSE IN A POSITIVE STATE

When you want to get a point across to your spouse, one of the most important rules to remember is, "Express it in a way that puts your spouse in a positive state." This seems obvious, but husbands and wives often speak in a way that puts their spouse in a very unresourceful state. If you're going to make a point or ask for something in a way that puts your spouse in a negative state, what is the use of speaking just then? Unless it's an issue of life and death, wait until you can speak in a manner that enables your spouse to access a positive state.

Couples who are able to discuss issues calmly are fortunate. Before resolving disputed issues, it is crucial for a husband and wife to be calm and relaxed, or at least to be centered and balanced. What each one will say in this state will be much more beneficial and productive than if they are both angry. Even if your spouse is in an unresourceful state, you still have the ability to remain calm. This is easier for some, more difficult for others, but either way you grow.

If you want someone to understand you and be motivated to either start doing something or stop doing something, it won't make sense for you to add, "I'm going to say what I have to say, but ignore me and don't listen to what I am telling you." Essentially this is what you are doing if you deliver your messages or make your requests in a tone of voice that makes your spouse feel irritated, anxious, resentful, angry, or puts him or her in any other unresourceful state.

If you want to speak and your spouse just keeps talking, you have a choice of asking him or her in a way that will give you permission to speak, or asking in a way that creates negative feelings. For example, you might speak in a soft voice, and put up your hand as if to say, "I would like to speak now." Compare this approach with speaking in an angry voice and saying, "You never let me speak. You selfishly hog the conversation." Imagine yourself on the receiving end of these two approaches. The first way will feel comfortable; the second will access a distressed state.

If one partner is very neat and the other very sloppy, this can lend to insistent nagging and complaining. The person who tends to be sloppy might give up trying, knowing he or she will never be able to meet the standards set by his or her spouse. The neat partner needs to find ways to point things out to the sloppy partner in a pleasant way. This might take a lot of effort since the neat one is justifiably irritated by the sloppiness of the other. But what is more important, neatness or *shalom bayis?* Which is worse, sloppiness or speaking in ways that unnecessarily violate the Torah prohibition against *ona'as devarim?* Even if such a couple never reaches a situation where the neat one is satisfied with the sloppy one, they can still communicate about their situation in a harmonious way, making improvement more likely.

*M*y husband often misconstrues my concern for his welfare and safety as my not believing in him. When he is tired, I don't want him to drive. I believe he is a good driver, but he is human, and without enough sleep he might fall asleep at the wheel.

When I tell my husband to take his coat, he sometimes responds angrily, "You are treating me like a little boy. I don't need anyone to tell me to wear a coat."

When I suggest that he be careful about taking a financial risk, he tells me that he knows more about business than I do. "You should trust my judgment," he says in an insulted voice.

I used to be so hurt when he said things like this that I either remained quiet, or I would argue with him and we would get into nasty quarrels.

I gave the matter a lot of thought and came to the realization that I needed to speak in a way that expresses my concern without sounding like I am lecturing him or treating him like a baby.

I began to preface my comments with, "You are the most important person in the world to me, and I care about your health and welfare. Please realize that my concern comes from feelings of love and caring. Even if you think I am wrong, perhaps you can humor me and help me become calmer." This introduction put my husband in a good state and made a major difference in the way he accepted my comments.

My spouse tends to avoid discussing topics that are anxiety provoking. One ploy my spouse uses is to make fun of the topic, which makes me defensive. As a result, we just don't discuss certain matters, whether they relate to Torah observance, finances, or disciplining the children.

When I recognized this pattern, I tried to be assertive and insisted we stay with a topic and discuss it. We needed to overcome our anxiety and tendency to avoid confrontations, but as soon as I saw that my spouse was hurt by what I said, I backed down. I noticed that my tone of voice began to take on a pleading quality. I felt weak and we got sidetracked.

Thinking about the best approach to take, I decided to speak in a tone of voice that expressed respect and compassion while at the same time I would remain calmly firm and persistent. The next time my spouse tried to use corny humor to divert us from a stressful topic, I said in a gentle tone of voice, "The issue we need to talk about is important to both of us. I realize that it's unpleasant. Let's be mutually respectful and make the discussion as pleasant as we can."

I was resolved to repeat this basic message as often as necessary. My spouse realized that I was serious about what I said. Eventually, we've both found that discussing the issues is better than avoiding them, and we are able to work out acceptable solutions.

❖ ❖ ❖

My husband is very health conscious. He eats brown rice, whole-wheat bread, and he exercises regularly. He wants me to do the same, but I don't enjoy it.

When I was expecting our first child, his agenda to reform my eating habits and to get me to exercise regularly picked up in intensity. He gave me daily lectures on the importance of exercising and he painted bleak pictures of the damage caused by the wrong foods and other unhealthy habits. I couldn't stand these lectures and was not at all motivated to follow through on his recommendations.

My husband's elderly uncle heard him telling me to imagine a forty-year-old person in a wheelchair, prematurely old and feeble, as if this picture could motivate me *to change my lifestyle and eating habits to prevent this from happening.*

My husband's uncle said to him, "It's obvious that your approach isn't working, so save your words. Your wife agrees in principle that what you are asking her to do is in her best interests, but it would be better for her and for your future child if you could talk in ways that would put her in a positive state."

The uncle suggested that my husband ask me, "What can I do to motivate you to exercise?" and, "What is it about exercise that prevents you from doing it?"

Hearing these questions, I thought the matter over and realized I found exercising totally boring. I lacked the self-discipline to do things that I didn't like to do. Our uncle knew I appreciated my husband's sense of humor. "Instead of lecturing your wife, make her laugh," he told my husband.

My husband then asked me, "If I can make you laugh when you ride the exercise bike, will you do it?"

I agreed, but regardless of whether or not I will actually follow through, my husband consented to stop lecturing me. Deep down I feel that when the lectures stop, my motivation to exercise and to eat healthier food will increase.

HELP YOUR SPOUSE ACCESS RESOURCEFUL STATES

Two people who care about each other and consistently express appreciation, gratitude, praise, encouragement, and validation can frequently put each other in positive states. Wise communicators will speak to each other in ways that elicit positive states even when difficulties arise. However, couples who quarrel and say painful things to each other will both experience stressful states. Insults and put-downs tend to put someone into a negative state and for this reason the Torah forbids *ona'as devarim.*

When you speak the language of states, you get a heightened awareness of how you are feeling and how your spouse is feeling. You become more aware of what you say and do that is helpful, beneficial, and enjoyable, and what you say and do that is the opposite. Speaking the language of states means that you might ask, "What state are you in now and what state would you like to be in?" When you give feedback, you might comment, "When you say that, I tend to go into an unresourceful state. May I make a suggestion of how you can say that in a way that will help us both be in a better state?"

*E*ver since I was a little girl, I loved looking at wedding pictures. I must have looked through my parents' wedding album hundreds of times. I would see the smiling faces of my mother and father and could not wait to be able to see my own smiling pictures in my very own wedding album.

When I got older, I still loved to see wedding pictures. When I visited friends who were recently married, I always asked to look at their wedding pictures and my heart soared as I saw the expressions of joy in the pictures.

When I became engaged, I was thrilled that my chasan responded favorably to my request for more than the standard number of pictures at our wedding. I wanted one photographer for the men and one for the women so as not to miss anything.

During our sheva berachos, I couldn't wait to see the pictures. Someone I told this to asked me why pictures were so important to me.

"When I see a joyous picture, I personally experience joy in my entire nervous system," I said. "I feel this even with the joy of others. With my own wedding pictures, the joy I'll feel will be even more intense, since it will remind me of how happy I was at the wedding. It will be a thrill to experience my wedding over and over again."

Imagine how disappointed I felt when the photographer called up to tell us, "I am embarrassed to tell you that your pictures were ruined. This hasn't happened to me before. It was a freak accident and I sincerely apologize. Is there any way I can compensate you?"

I mumbled bravely, "I'm sure it wasn't your fault," and then burst into uncontrollable tears.

As I hung up the phone, I felt devastated. My dream of a lifetime was destroyed along with those pictures.

My chasan saw and heard my hysteria and thought that there must have been a death or horrible accident in the family.

"What happened? What happened?" he asked with great concern.

"Our wedding pictures were ruined," I gasped.

My husband looked relieved that no one was hurt, but seeing how broken I was, he was careful not to tell me, "It's all for the best," or, "This too shall pass." Bless his heart for that.

What he did say to me, I have replayed in my mind thousands of times.

"I love you profoundly. You are the most wonderful person in the whole universe. I feel that Hashem has given me the greatest gift possible. I pledge to you that I will give you so much joy that if you ever want to see a smiling face, you will only have to look in a mirror."

Despite my agony, I just had to smile. Ten years later, I don't have wedding pictures, but I do have that smile in the mirror to remind me of my husband's exquisite sensitivity.

M y wife had a difficult time becoming pregnant. We waited a few years and then started a special treatment. We were told that she needed *complete physical rest and total mental relaxation. Stress of any kind could prevent the treatment from succeeding.*

I wanted children more than anything else in the world. I was very nervous and expressed my anxiety by constantly repeating that she needed to relax. I yelled at her if she tried to lift anything heavy and I repeated the word "relax" to her at least a hundred times a day.

My wife finally became very angry. "I need you to help me relax," she yelled, "not to make me more nervous. Stop it already!"

A week later, my wife went for a test to see if the treatment was successful. It wasn't. I was profoundly disappointed. Unfortunately, I let out my feelings at my wife's expense.

"It's your fault the results were negative," I told her. "I'm certain that your yelling at me last week caused the problem."

My wife burst into tears. "Last week when I needed to have total relaxation, you made me more nervous than I already was, and now you are blaming me. That's cruel."

Her words hit home. My approach was counterproductive. Understanding and empathy would have helped her relax. My admonitions to relax were bound to get her into a worse state, and how could I honestly say it was her fault? Even the doctors didn't know the exact reason why the treatment was unsuccessful. I learned from this experience and now I am much more careful how I speak to my wife when I am under stress.

Timing determines whether a specific communication is appropriate. If you are uncertain whether to make a request, ask your spouse, "Is now a good time, or should I wait?" By giving your spouse space, you allow him or her to access a better state.

*A*s soon as I came home, my wife would bombard me with what went wrong that day. Yes, I was open to hear what she had to say, but I needed fifteen minutes of peace and quiet first in order to unwind.

When I said, "I can't listen now," she perceived this as rejection and was hurt. I didn't mean to push her off, but I felt overwhelmed. I needed quiet time to relax, and then I could listen. When I told her, she responded, "But I wait with great anticipation for you to come home, and it is painful when you don't seem happy to see me after an entire day of being away."

I read somewhere, "When your husband or wife walks in the door, give him or her time to relax before you speak about serious matters. Not everyone needs quiet time, but many people do. By being patient you both gain."

I showed this to my wife and she agreed. I told her that I understand that she needs and deserves a friendly greeting as soon as I come home. When I know that I will first have about fifteen minutes to myself, I have the energy to greet her in a friendly manner, but without this, I feel that I need to protect myself and I shut down.

When I kiss the mezuzah on the doorpost as I come into the house, I increase my energy, knowing that the oneness of Hashem encompasses everything. This reminds me that the word "echad" in the Torah can also allude to the oneness of a married couple. I then have the energy to give my wife an enthusiastic greeting.

After I rest for a quarter of an hour, I am there to help her or listen to what she wishes to share with me.

❖ ❖ ❖

*W*hen my wife doesn't get enough sleep, she tends to be irritable and cranky and she snaps at me and at the children. As soon as *she calms down, however, she asks me to express my positive feelings for her. I remember the first time this happened after we were married. She had always been good-natured when we met on dates and while we were engaged, and everyone my family asked about her agreed that she was one of the most cheerful and pleasant people you could meet. So it came as a shock for me to see her so irritable.*

The truth is that when I am yelled at, I don't feel very positive. I'm certain that other people feel the same way when someone yells at them. I decided to force myself to express positive feelings anyway. I realized that after my wife loses her temper, she needs my reassurance that I still love her. She is wonderful when she is calm, so I focus on how she is when she is in a regular state. The effort it takes me is well worth it. The more intense my positive expressions at such times, the more secure my wife feels and this decreases her irritability. Since we have repeated this pattern many times, I understand her crankiness as a message saying that she is tired and in a vulnerable state and needs my reassurance. Now that I've begun to view her irritability in this way, I am able to feel good that I can meet her emotional needs.

INCREASE THE POSITIVE ANCHORS FOR YOURSELF AND YOUR SPOUSE

The term "anchor" refers to any sound, word, picture, image, motion, or touch that causes a reaction. If the reaction is pleasant or positive, the anchor is positive. If the reaction causes distress, irritation, fear, tension, or is negative in any way, the anchor is negative. It is an act of *chesed* to make positive anchors for your spouse, in keeping with the prohibition against *ona'as devarim*.

Some anchors are made spontaneously. For example, if someone is afraid of dogs, then when he hears the rattle of a leash, he immediately becomes tense because the rattle of leashes is associated with a fearful feeling. However, someone who loves dogs might feel good upon hearing that same rattle of the leash. For one person the noise is a negative anchor and for the other it is a positive anchor.

When you smile sincerely, most people automatically smile back because your smile is a positive anchor. When you hear a song that was played at a joyous occasion, your mind will automatically take you back to that joyous occasion and you will have a pleasant reaction. Anchors can enable you to access more than just a pleasant feeling; they can help you access any state of mind you wish by consciously associating them with certain words, hand movements, body posture, songs, or images. That is, when you are in a state of joy, confidence, peacefulness, or any other positive state, you can create an anchor. Use a hand motion, a word, or make a sound that you will now associate with a specific positive state. When you wish to access that state again, just use the anchor. People who easily change states will find this easier than those who have more rigid personalities, but everyone does this automatically and unconsciously. By doing this intentionally you will have greater control over your states.

The next time you feel especially empowered, make a hand movement you can now associate with that feeling. That special hand movement will serve as a positive anchor for you. The next time you are in a very calm and peaceful environment and feel totally relaxed, make an anchor that you can associate with that place. Use that anchor in the future when you want to access a calmer state.

The principle is simple. In practice, however, you might need to make many positive associations for it to work for you. That is, if every time you feel totally confident you make a unique sound and hand movement, that sound and hand movement will enable you to feel confident. Yet, doing it just once might not be intense enough for you. Therefore you might have to feel this total confidence a number of times before your anchor spontaneously accesses this state of mind.

Every one of us has many positive and negative anchors. Each partner comes into the marriage with many anchors. Using the term "anchors" is a useful shorthand way to say, "What you just said or did made me feel good and I appreciate it." Or, "I find what you said or did distressing. Please refrain from it."

Using the language of "anchors," the reason why a habit of our spouse bothers us is because it is a negative anchor. For example, if a husband's smoking habit bothers his wife, the smell of cigarettes on his sweater is a negative anchor. If the husband could associate cigarettes with vomit, dead mice, rotting food, and other repulsive smells and tastes, or with serious illness, he would find cigarette smoking so repulsive that he would give it up. Although cigarettes used to be a positive anchor for him, they will now have negative associations.

If a husband or wife greets the other very cheerfully, the cheerful greeting is a positive anchor. A colorful note with a positive message is a positive anchor. A hand motion that is associated with praise is a positive anchor. Husbands and wives can even make up their own personal positive anchors that will make each other feel good.

As a general rule regarding anchors in marriage: When you find that something is a positive anchor for your spouse, increase the use of that anchor. When you find something is a negative anchor, stop saying or doing it.

*T*he dining-room chairs we had bought second-hand had lasted for many years, but now they had completed their mission on this planet.

I told my wife that any set of new chairs she liked was all right with me. If she wanted them, so did I.

But to my surprise, when the new chairs arrived, I did not like them. The colors had an unpleasant association for me. "Are you certain that you like these chairs?" I asked my wife.

She intuitively saw that I wasn't totally pleased and very rightly said, "You had a choice to come along and state your opinion. You chose not to."

My children all liked the new chairs, so I was the only one who wasn't pleased.

"Okay," I said to myself, "I will now create a new, positive association with the colors and design of the chairs."

"Every time I see these chairs, I will experience great joy," I said, as I visualized my favorite Purim experiences. I repeated this a number of times until my subconscious automatically made a positive association every time I saw them.

Since then, the chairs have been a constant source of good feelings, as I associate them with festive Shabbos and Yom Tov meals. They also serve as a reminder that I have the ability to create new associations to elicit positive feelings even if I start out with the opposite.

Whenever I said something that caused my wife pain, she would become angry at me and tell me that I am selfish and cruel. I thought that this was a total exaggeration. I feel I am basically a kind person with an excitable nature that is hard to control. I am working on my frustration and anger, but it isn't easy for me to totally control what I say when I am in those states.

"If you would be more helpful when I say the wrong things, I would find it easier to improve," I told my wife.

"There you go blaming me for your anger and your ona'as devarim," my wife responded.

"I'm not blaming you," I said with exasperation. "I acknowledge that I am responsible for my emotional states and for what I say even when I am upset, but if you would not attack me for it, I would find it easier to calm down."

"I don't attack you," my wife said. "You're just too sensitive."

"That wasn't helpful," I responded, having learned that this is one of the best ways to respond to verbal attacks.

Then one day I met someone who taught me the concept of "anchors." "The benefit of using the word 'anchor,'" I was told, *"is that it's a neutral term. If you don't like the way something is said to you, you can just say, 'To me that's a distressful anchor.' This way you are not putting yourself down nor are you making any accusations against the speaker."*

I immediately saw how this could be helpful for my wife and me. Now that we've been using the language of "anchors," we have found it easier to ask each other to increase positive anchors and decrease negative ones.

TRANSFORM THE STATE OF FRUSTRATION INTO THE STATE OF ENJOYMENT

In marriage, as well as in other areas of our lives, we experience many potentially frustrating moments. And the more frustrating something is, the longer it seems to last. Mastering the skill of transforming the state of frustration into a positive state will enable you to decrease the amount of time you feel frustrated. Since frustration can lead to irritation and anger, decreasing the frustration we feel is healthy for one's marriage.

How can you transform frustration into enjoyment? One way is to find a positive reframe for what you are doing. For example, suppose you need to wait for your spouse who is taking a longer time than you thought he or she would. You are becoming impatient and frustrated. If you can think of a valid reframe that will enable you to regard waiting peacefully as your way of increasing *shalom bayis* and bringing the *Shechinah* into your home, then instead of feeling frustrated, you will feel spiritually elevated. You can utilize the waiting time to review some important ideas that you would not have previously thought of reviewing. You can use this time to gain greater state mastery, and you will feel grateful for this opportunity to grow.

When engaged in routine tasks that many people find boring or frustrating, you can do them with a light and playful attitude that will make them more interesting. You might sing and dance every once in a while, or formulate a mental fantasy that will create an enjoyable setting for these tasks and chores.

I am shy, and I might seem a bit conservative to most people, but I have been blessed with a great imagination, and I fly through time and space in my mind. I relive the Exodus from Egypt, actually seeing myself leaving with the rest of Klal Yisrael. I can stand at the footsteps of Mount Sinai at the giving of the Torah. I can watch the Temple burning, and I can visualize how the Third Temple will look.

This makes helping out with seemingly mundane tasks quite exciting and dramatic. When I do things for Shabbos, I see a vision of the universe being created and now I am preparing for the great big celebration of this wonderful moment. When I prepare for Pesach, I experience what it was like to be a slave to Pharaoh in Egypt. I feel the pain of the sticks on my back for moving too slowly. Then I feel tremendous relief as I come back to present reality.

When I need to throw something into a garbage pail, I am a professional basketball player and I celebrate when the ball in the shape of garbage makes a basket. I hear the crowd cheering as I score two points.

If any member of the house does or says something that I don't appreciate, as soon as I am aware of my reaction, I mentally create an enjoyable scene out of what just happened. Sometimes, I imagine myself as the Chofetz Chaim, or Rav Levi Yitzchak of Berdichev, or another powerful personality whose compassion, self-mastery, and inner strength enable him to remain calm and centered.

It is not always appropriate to share these imaginative dramas with others. Some people find all this a bit bizarre and out of touch with reality. And yes, if a person does not have a strong sense of reality this would not be an appropriate choice, but anyone who lives in this world and harbors constant negativity, anger, resentment, and blaming, is not living in reality either. People like that are playing a mind game with themselves that causes misery to themselves and to an entire family.

REMEMBER YOUR FINEST MOMENTS AND RELIVE THOSE STATES

When you remember a great moment that you experienced in the past, you can once again relive some of that experience. Unfortunately, there are many people who keep reliving their worst moments, so they experience distressing feelings again and again. Make a concerted effort to remember your moments of joy, celebration, accomplishment, and inner peace. Every time your spouse does something you appreciate and are proud of, add it to your mental library so you can access it again. The more you recall those events, the easier it will be for you to recall them again.

My wife and I treated each other badly. We insulted each other and refused to do what the other one wanted.

My wife shlepped me to a Rabbi who scolded us. To sum up a long lecture, he said, "Do you consider yourselves to be Torah observant? What about the prohibition against ona'as devarim (causing pain with words)? What about the prohibition against quarreling? Don't you have a drop of love for other people? You should be ashamed of yourselves. You are driving the Almighty's presence out of your home. Keep this up and you will get divorced."

This approach worked wonders for the Rabbi's follow-ers who appreciated his thinking. Their ability to take his advice gave them a feeling of inner strength. They knew he loved them and knew he was even harder on himself. A gentler approach for them would be considered too weak to have an effect. Most women, however, wouldn't be able to handle this, and very few men would either, including me.

I was furious at my wife for dragging me to such a ver-bal beating. She felt good, though. "At least someone finally told you what you needed to hear," she gloated. But my wife ended up suffering. I felt so resentful from the Rabbi's lecture that I began treating her even worse than before.

Then I heard about a Rabbi who had an opposite approach. He wholeheartedly acknowledged that his approach was not for everyone, but for some people his approach was highly effective.

I went alone to the first meeting. If he criticized me, at least my wife didn't need to hear it. He greeted me with a warm smile and an outstretched hand.

I began by complaining about my wife. "That's not the way to start," he began. "First I want to hear about you. I'd like to get a picture of your life history. Also, what is your ideal picture of yourself in marriage?"

As I spoke, he kept acknowledging my positive quali-ties. "The very fact that you want to improve your mar-riage and are willing to speak to someone about it is an act of courage," he told me.

At the end of an hour, I felt great about myself and hopeful about my marriage. He told me to treat my wife better for a couple of days, and then to ask her if she would be willing to come along for a meeting.

My wife was more open than I was and was willing to speak to anyone who could help us. When we spoke to the Rabbi, he put us both in wonderful states.

"There was dancing and singing at your wedding, wasn't there?" he said to us. "You need more joy in your lives right now. Wouldn't it be wonderful if you could mentally replay the joy you had at your wedding? You can. Close your eyes and once again hear the music and the singing and see the dancing. The amazing thing about your brain is that you can add the music and dancing of every wedding you've ever attended and keep replaying it. This is something Rabbi Meir Shapiro, the Rosh Yeshivah of Lublin and founder of Daf Yomi, advised people to do."

While he was serious and acknowledged our faults and mistakes, he emphasized our strengths and resources. He told us that he felt we were compatible, and that he doesn't say this to everyone. Later, my wife and I both felt that he probably does, but we saw that he sincerely believed that we could have a harmonious life.

"It's not sufficient that you just tolerate each other," he said, "but that you both give each other joy. Remember the blessing of 'same'ach tesamach' you received at your wedding. Hashem was asked to give you the joy of Gan Eden. Now it's up to both of you to make certain the blessing will be fulfilled.

"I want you to make a commitment to continually create joy for each other. Then we can work out the details of how you can do this."

As we left the meeting, we knew that we would never return to our old patterns. We had a long way to go, but our destination was Gan Eden.

If my husband and I get into a fight, he is always the first one to apologize and make up. If a specific quarrel is especially hurtful, even if I had a major part in *starting it, he takes responsibility and apologizes. Then in a very gentle way he takes my wedding ring off and once again puts it on my finger. As he does this he says in a joyous and loving tone, "Harei at mekudeshes li betaba'as zu kedas Moshe V'Yisrael," as he did under the chuppah. This brings back my most joyous memories. Our marriage is once again consecrated with sanctity.*

In order to give happiness to my husband, I go out of my way to do things and go places even though it is extremely difficult for me. If I told him that I was only doing this because he wanted me to and it is stressful for me, he would forego many of these activities, so part of my sacrifice is that I'm not even telling him that I'm making a sacrifice.

Sacrificing for my husband is relatively easy since he is so wonderful to me. Let me share two things he said recently. He wasn't feeling well and I brought him tea. I mumbled under my breath, "I'm so tired." In the most compassionate voice, he said to me, "Tell me, dear, what's on your heart." My tiredness lifted.

A few days ago, he said to me, "You are a queen. I will do anything for you." How can I not reciprocate?

MENTALLY PREPARE YOURSELF; DON'T GET CAUGHT OFF BALANCE

When you are mentally prepared to deal with a challenge, you will find it easier to maintain a resourceful state. Think about the challenges you are likely to face in your marriage. Then visualize yourself being in the state of your choice in those situations. The more you practice, the deeper impression these visualizations will have on your brain.

When you walk into a room full of people, your state will change. If you don't feel comfortable with those people, you will most likely enter a less resourceful state, but you can overcome this by repeating positive messages to yourself. For example, if you repeat, "I will feel love and respect towards everyone in this room," you will adapt to this attitude. Those who are more open to the power of self-suggestions will be affected more, but everyone will be affected to some degree. The same principle applies to your marriage. When you enter a room and see your spouse, repeat positive messages to yourself, and you will be in better states.

When running a home, there are many times when you will have to stop the task you are involved in, take care of another task, and then get back to the first task. Some find this more stressful than others. It is a valuable skill to be able to stop what you are doing and take care of a few things and then get back to the thing you started with and to do this in a calm state.

I am highly impatient and tend to explode easily although I don't stay angry for a long time. My son's bar mitzvah was going to be in a few days and it was a tense time for our entire family. My wife knows that I tend to react strongly when things go wrong and she was concerned about my temper. She said something to me that was very helpful.

"After the bar mitzvah no one will remember the trivial mishaps and imperfections, but if you blow up, people will remember that for a long time."

I agreed with my wife and kept repeating her message over and over again. Even though a number of things did go wrong, this reminder helped me remain calm.

A friend of mine, who is presently a Talmud lecturer in a large yeshivah, told me that when he was studying in kollel, as preparation for Elul and

Rosh Hashanah, his Rosh Yeshivah spoke about emulating G-d's compassion and patience (erech apayim). This theme was repeated over and over during the entire month of Elul.

My friend said that he mentally prepared himself to remain calm and patient regardless of any potentially frustrating or anger-provoking incidents. His mental preparation had results.

That year Rosh Hashanah was on Thursday and Friday, so that with Shabbos we would have three straight days of Yom Tov and Shabbos. On Wednesday, Erev Rosh Hashanah, right before he was going to the yeshivah in a very uplifted spiritual state, his wife asked him to move a large closet from one room to another. Their young children needed more space in which to play during the next three days.

The job was difficult and took quite some time, much longer than he and his wife originally thought. He said that had he not been working on the quality of remaining calm and patient, he would have become frustrated and angry. Before Rosh Hashanah, he had wanted to study Torah and learn mussar, but because of the talks he had heard, he viewed moving the closet as his spiritual work to emulate the One he would be praying to on Rosh Hashanah.

Chapter Eleven

Middos — Building Yourself as You Build Your Marriage

- *Introduction to middos development*
- *Patience and acceptance — savlanus (vs. impatience and anger)*
- *Kindness and caring (vs. selfishness)*
- *Compassion (vs. apathy or cruelty)*
- *Gratitude (vs. being ungrateful)*
- *Seeing the good and focusing on it — ayin tovah (vs. focusing on the negative)*
- *Joy for the joy of others (vs. envy)*
- *Judging favorably (vs. judging negatively)*
- *Self-mastery (vs. impulsivity)*
- *Forgiving (vs. harboring resentment)*
- *Admitting the truth: saying, "I Was Wrong" (vs. denying your responsibility)*
- *Humility (vs. arrogance)*
- *Trust in Hashem — bitachon (vs. worrying about the future)*
- *Alacrity — zerizus (vs. laziness and procrastination)*

INTRODUCTION TO
MIDDOS DEVELOPMENT

Interacting with your marriage partner can provide some of your greatest moments of nobility and elevation. These are the moments that you act and react according to the way Hashem would want you to act in difficult situations. These are your moments of behaving in ways that are consistent with positive traits, when it would have been much easier to act in ways that are consistent with negative traits. Unfortunately, however, marriage can also bring out one's worst qualities. If we were all blessed with only positive traits and were free from potentially negative traits, the Vilna Gaon would not have written, "The purpose of life is to overcome negative traits." View marriage as your vehicle to constantly develop your character. This is a view that can enable you to make global changes in your marriage.

Mastery of our character traits is important for everything we do throughout our life. "All of G-d's service is dependent upon the improvement of one's character. Character traits are fundamental to the performance of the commandments and to Torah principles. Conversely, all sins stem from unimproved character traits" (*Even Sheleimah; The Vilna Gaon Views Life,* ch. 1). The area where this is really crucial is in marriage and in raising a family. Positive *middos* build a marriage. It is a pleasure to be in the company of someone who has elevated character traits. On the other hand, someone who has negative traits can destroy a marriage, or at least cause much distress. Marriage is a *middos* workshop. You will constantly learn lessons about which traits you need to develop. Focus on this and you will observe progress.

Imagine what it would be like to be around someone who is constantly impatient and angry, who is selfish and ignores you, who is negative and critical as well as arrogant, miserly, rigid, grumpy, and ungrateful. Add a little cruelty and you have the picture of someone who is incredibly difficult to get along with. Almost everyone will have occasional manifestations of some of these traits, but it is our task in this world to overcome all of these tendencies.

On the other hand, let's visualize someone who is kind and caring, compassionate and patient. Someone who feels grateful to you for all that you do, someone who is consistently cheerful and always judges you favorably and who is forgiving if you ever make a mistake or error. This person's *bitachon* enables him or her to be calm and serene. This person is generous and giving, and takes care of everything as quickly as possible. This person has self-mastery and self-discipline, acknowledges mistakes and takes responsibility for correcting them. In addition to all of these positive attributes, this person is also humble and easy to get along with. Someone with these *middos* would make a fine husband or wife. Our mission is to consistently develop these attributes.

A close friend of mine who is a brilliant Torah scholar and a wise counselor once put together a list of traits he felt important for a young man to have before marriage. A mutual friend of ours looked at the list and said, "I still wouldn't be married if I had to wait until I mastered all these wonderful qualities." The person saying this was also a Torah scholar and is happily married with a number of married children and many grandchildren. The higher one's level at the beginning of one's marriage, the better off one will be. Nevertheless, your Divinely ordained *middos* work starts at this moment, exactly where you are right now.

Developing character is a lifetime process, with no easy formula for instantaneous perfection, but making the commitment to elevate yourself has an immediate positive effect on who you are. The first step is to recognize your strengths and positive traits. Rabbeinu Yonah (*Pirkei Avos* 2:9) writes that when you strengthen one positive quality and master it, this will lead to further *middos* development since all traits are linked to one another. As Rabbi Yeruchem Levovitz, *zt"l*, wrote, "Every person has good traits that he acquired naturally. Be aware of those traits and strengthen them. When you work on excelling in those areas in which you have a natural talent, you will be able to elevate yourself in other areas as well. When working on your strong points, you will also improve in your weaker areas" (*Daas Chochmah U'Mussar*, vol. 1, p. 340).

Awareness of those times and moments when you acted positively makes it more likely that you will continue to act accordingly. Learning from great people as well as from your own best moments will make you great.

"When you consistently act a certain way to form a new habit, it will become your new nature even though previously your nature was the opposite" (Vilna Gaon; *Mishlei* 6:27). Marriage will give you many opportunities to do this.

If you were offered a Divine gift of mastering any specific trait, which would you choose? Start right at this moment to speak and act in ways to integrate this trait.

When thinking about character traits, it is important to mention this statement from Rabbi Tzadok HaKohen: "No trait is entirely bad. Every trait and tendency has a positive aspect. The criterion by which to measure whether any given trait you have is good or bad is to determine whether you are utilizing it according to the Almighty's will" (*Otzer HaMachshavah shel Rav Tzadok HaKohen*, Introduction, p. 27).

Rabbi Moshe Feinstein said, "Realize that every personality trait you have can be utilized for either good or for bad. One must be guided by the Torah for knowledge about how to utilize each trait properly" (*Bastion of Faith*, p. 22).

In the words of the classic *mussar* work on character traits, *Orchos Tzaddikim*, it says in the Introduction: "There are character traits that should be applied in many situations, and there are character traits that should be used only infrequently. One can compare this situation to that of someone who is preparing a dish that requires a large number of ingredients. For the food to have a good taste, the cook must use the proper amount of each ingredient. If the cook puts in too much of those ingredients that require a small amount, or too little of those ingredients that require a large amount, the final product will be ruined. Similarly, with personality traits. Each trait has its time and place, and each one must be used in the proper amount."

When it comes to marriage, which traits you need to work on the most depends on the unique combination of your personality and the personality of your spouse. As mentioned before, the life history of both of you and your present situation will be important factors. Your financial situation will play a role in your *middos* development, as well as your emotional needs. Your expectations will make a major difference, and this will be influenced by the personalities and character of your own parents. How you work out harmonious ways of interaction will bring out your character traits in the way no other testing ground would.

Take, for example, the trait of empathy. You might enjoy expressing your empathy for any aches and pains that your spouse has, but your spouse might consider this condescending. When you express your gratitude, your spouse may feel that you are overdoing it. You might want to take care of things quickly and view this as *zerizus,* but your spouse might consider you impulsive. You might tend to give in very easily and your spouse might respect you more if you stand up for your rights. You might feel a strong need to be assertive about your thoughts and opinions, and your spouse might consider this aggressive and attacking. You might like to give someone else his or her space, while your spouse wants you to express more concern and caring and considers you insensitive for not showing greater sympathy. What you consider humility, your spouse might consider a lack of self-esteem and inner strength. In these areas, almost every couple will find surprises.

When you were thinking about getting married, it's possible you had some picture in mind about the personality and character of the person you would marry. You might have envisioned someone who was quite similar to you. Of course, you knew you would be different, but still you thought that you would be more similar than you actually are.

The question is just how different you actually are. You might have been prepared *middos*-wise to interact with someone who was fairly similar to you, but you probably never guessed that the gap between your ideas on important issues would be so wide. These differences will give you many opportunities to develop your *middos* in ways that you never thought about before.

Then there are the surprises you discover in your own character in reference to traits in which you feel you excel. You might think of yourself as reasonable, while your spouse thinks you are irrational. You think you are kind and giving, and your spouse considers you selfish and stingy. You think you are calm and patient, your spouse considers you to be nervous and impatient. What happened? When it comes to interacting with a specific person, each spouse has different definitions and expectations about what it means to be kind, patient, humble, giving, grateful, etc.

Moreover, you might think, "I am kind, but not when I'm being asked to do something that is so unreasonable." Or, "I am patient, but not when it takes someone so long to get ready or to take care of things." Or, "I am humble, but there is a limit to what I'll take from another person."

Besides your basic personality and traits, some days you will feel wonderful and on top of the world. On other days, you might feel irritable and impatient. The person you are married to will also have emotional ups and downs. Therefore your traits will be especially challenged when you are both emotionally down, or when one of you feels up and the other feels down.

If you find yourself in a difficult situation in your marriage, ask yourself, "What character trait would enable me to handle this situation in a positive way?" Then act the way you would if you had already mastered that trait. Don't block yourself by thinking, "I haven't yet mastered this trait." Rather, by taking action, you are developing this trait right now.

Use visualizations to rerun scenes in which you weren't satisfied with the way you responded and reacted. See yourself talking and acting the way you would if you had already integrated the positive traits you need. This is especially effective before going to sleep. Give yourself suggestions that will induce dreams in which you act according to the highest Torah values. Be patient. Speak to yourself calmly and gently. Regardless of whether you see images vividly or not, by imagining yourself acting in better ways, you will find yourself doing so in practice.

Rabbi Yisrael Salanter said, "A person can live with himself for seventy years and still not know himself" (*Tenuas HaMussar*, vol. 1, p. 301). All the more so, someone who is single will not really have a clear picture of how he or she will act when faced with the challenges of interacting with the person he or she marries. You might have excellent relationships and demonstrate excellent traits with other people, but no one — not friends, parents, brothers and sisters, or classmates — will test you the way your spouse will. The good news is that we always have more *middos* to improve and the entire process is one of fulfilling the commandment to walk in the Almighty's ways.

"When working on self-improvement, in the beginning just try to go against a negative trait in one small way. Any positive change is already a beginning. When you take that first step and make even a small change for the better, you have already begun transforming your entire makeup. You are taking control of yourself and your behavior. With persistence, you will eventually have control over all your traits. Once you commence your journey, there is hope that you will go very far towards your ultimate destination" (Rabbi Yechezkel Levenstein; *Ohr Yechezkel, Middos*, p. 59).

You might find it helpful to ask yourself about a specific trait, "On a scale of one to ten, where am I now?" Then ask, "What will it take for me to improve one number on the scale?"

Whenever you see someone talking or acting in a way consistent with a positive trait, use that as a model for yourself in ways that are appropriate to your unique situation.

You craft a masterpiece when you utilize your strengths and overcome your faults and liabilities to make the most of yourself. Learn from your own best moments. Regardless of the context of those moments, you can now transfer your abilities and resources and apply them to your spouse. Ask yourself, "When things went well, what did I say or do?" Especially in challenging moments, ask yourself, "What will enable me to interact at my best with my spouse right now?"

PATIENCE AND ACCEPTANCE — *SAVLANUS* (VS. IMPATIENCE AND ANGER)

Marriage gives you many opportunities to master the attribute of patience. You will have to wait for your spouse, repeat requests, deal with your spouse forgetting to tell you things, and forgetting instructions. Even the most brilliant person will not remember to do everything that needs to be done. You will need to be patient and accepting when you see faults and shortcomings. Patience builds a marriage, just as anger destroys it.

Think of times when you were patient. Remember details of those situations. Think of people with whom you are usually patient. Now allow yourself to access that patient state when you interact with your spouse. In the future, be aware of moments of patience and visualize that state of patience becoming a part of you.

Anger is one of the biggest enemies of a happy marriage. When you lose your temper, you might say and do things that will be distressing to your spouse. Anger is harmful to your own health and it breeds anger in your spouse.

Rabbi Eliyahu Lopian said that a person is apt to delude himself into thinking that he has overcome his tendency to become angry. In reality he might manage to remain calm only because no one has provoked him. The true test of a person's propensity toward anger is judged by his behavior in the circle of his own family, which will undoubtedly provide opportunities for anger (*Lev Eliyahu*, vol. 1, p. 31; Heb. ed.).

"The Talmud (*Shabbos* 31a) relates how someone tried to get Hillel angry by continually interrupting him on Friday afternoon when he was in the middle of bathing for Shabbos. Although he asked Hillel ridiculous and irrelevant questions, Hillel, answered him patiently. The Talmud tells us that we all need to strive to reach this level of humility. That is, we are all obligated to work on ourselves to develop the total patience of Hillel, whom no one could anger" (Rabbi Yechezkel Levenstein; *Ohr Yechezkel, Middos*, p. 14). You might find it helpful to imagine being Hillel and being as patient as he was.

Every time you begin to feel impatient, say to yourself, "My Creator is sending me another opportunity to learn patience." Feel grateful for the opportunity. Gratitude is a much more enjoyable state than frustration. And the more you increase your inner sense of gratitude, the freer you will be from distressful states.

Adam's state of unconsciousness at the time of the creation of Chavah (Eve) illustrates how a husband should relate to his wife. At times, a husband should act in his home as if he were asleep and unaware of his wife's shortcomings. Even if a wife forgets or disregards her husband's wishes, the husband should not grow angry and shout. He should overlook minor faults in order to avoid domestic quarrels (*Toldos Yitzchak*, cited in *Mei'am Loez, Bereishis* 2: 21-22).

Some people who are impatient tend to say to their spouse, "I shouldn't have to tell you. You should know on your own." "If I have to tell you, it isn't worth it." "I'm tired of repeating myself." Every time you say something to your spouse that is difficult for you, you increase your level of patience. If your spouse needs encouragement or reassurance, you become a more patient person by patiently and repeatedly giving the needed encouragement.

*R*abbi Yaakov Yitzchak, the Chozeh of Lublin, once asked his wife to prepare his meal early so that he would have more time for the performance of a certain mitzvah, but the meal was ready even later than usual.

"It would be natural for me to become angry at my wife," Rabbi Yaakov Yitzchak said. "But I wished to eat early in order to gain time to do the Almighty's will. Shall I now go against His will by becoming angry?" (Niflaos HaChozeh MeLublin, p. 21).

A young man and woman knew each other for many years. They were both baalei teshuvah and their journey to a Torah path coincided. The young man was sure that he wanted to marry her and felt they were perfect for each other, but the woman was doubtful. She felt he was too impatient and that he had a quick temper.

"For me to marry you, I need you to become more patient," she told him.

The young man was determined to marry her, so he realized that he would have to learn to become more patient. He spoke to his Rabbi for about fifteen minutes on the importance of patience and how to acquire it. The fellow nodded and said, "Now I understand why it's so important for me to be patient. Now that I've learned how to be patient, could you reassure her that she no longer has to worry about my being impatient?"

The Rabbi was startled. How could the young man think that a trait which was so unnatural for him could be mastered in fifteen minutes? If the young man would have waited a day or two, at least he could claim that during this entire time he was patient and improving, but *if he felt that he was instantly transformed into becoming a patient person, it showed that he had no concept at all of what patience was. As tactfully as possible, the Rabbi told him that he would have to wait some time before there was proof that he really was becoming more patient.*

❖ ❖ ❖

At a wedding, I was sitting near a young fellow who had become a father only a few months earlier. After the meal, he left to catch a bus back home to a different city. A few minutes later, he returned in a great rush. With a sheepish grin, he told me, "I forgot my baby." He had left his baby in a stroller at the wedding hall. When his wife saw him waiting for the bus without the baby, she anxiously asked him, "Where is little Reuven?" He ran back at full speed to fetch their baby, who was sleeping peacefully in his stroller.

I asked him if his wife had reprimanded him for this oversight. "No," he replied. "I feel grateful that she reacted quite calmly under the circumstances. I appreciate her for not being judgmental. She knows that I love the baby and that I felt terrible about what happened. The incident taught me that I need to be much more careful in the future never to let this happen again."

The reaction of this fellow's wife is in stark contrast to that of some people who would build up an entire case against the spouse for such a serious action. You can hear them saying, "If you forgot the baby now, you might forget him in the future. Here in the wedding hall among people we know he was safe. What if such a thing had taken place in a dangerous area? If I wouldn't have been here, you might not have remembered the baby until the bus was on the highway. What would have happened then?"

Obviously this is not an incident to be taken lightly. While the young wife was praiseworthy in her self-control, a calm rational discussion of the incident is clearly necessary. However, imagining the worst is not productive either. Serious precautions must be taken to prevent similar problems in the future, but attacking or blaming will not solve anything. Patience and acceptance prevent problems in the first place, and even if a problem arises it can be settled more effectively using non-confrontational techniques.

KINDNESS AND CARING (VS. SELFISHNESS)

We are all born selfish. That is, as infants we were aware only of our own needs and we cried when they weren't met. With proper training and Torah values, we learned the importance of doing acts of kindness. The *middos* goal is not only to do acts of kindness, but to become a kind person, truly caring about the welfare of other people and meeting their needs. This is a fulfillment of the *mitzvah* to emulate our Creator, whose essence is kindness.

Previously we viewed kindness, a basic Torah principle, as a foundation for a strong and healthy marriage. Now let us view kindness as one of the attributes that we will integrate into our very being by consistently acting this way. As you increase your acts of kindness, you will become a more joyous person. Your quality of life will improve and those with whom you interact will benefit as well.

This is how Rabbi Yechezkel Levenstein expressed the concept of building up a love for kindness: "A person who has a love for money will constantly look for ways to obtain more money. So too, when you develop the trait of loving to do *chesed*, you will look for every possible opportunity to do *chesed*. Even though there might be other people who could do the same acts of kindness, you feel a strong desire to do them yourself.

"Be concerned about the welfare of others even when they do not ask you for help. Be motivated to do *chesed* because of an inner drive to help others. Your love of *chesed* gives you an appreciation for each opportunity to do an act of kindness" (*Ohr Yechezkel, Middos*, pp. 105, 174-5).

When you do something for someone who won't do any acts of kindness for you in return, it is considered a *chesed shel emes*. The original use of this term refers to attending a funeral and taking care of a burial. We cannot expect the deceased person whom we are attending to and respecting to do us any favors in return. However, doing something for someone who died is easier than doing something for someone who is alive but doesn't reciprocate. We don't expect someone who is dead to do anything for us and therefore we don't feel resentful. In marriage it is easy to feel resentful towards someone who doesn't act as we wish. The more difficult it is for you to act with kindness, the more your acts of kindness become an integral part of your personality.

"N ever be a sucker." This was very important to my father and he taught this lesson to me over and over again.

"If you let anyone treat you like a shmatah (a rag), they will, and it will be your own fault," he would tell me.

"In this world you need to stick up for your rights. If you allow people to take advantage of you, they will take advantage of others also. And you will be to blame."

If my mother asked my father to take care of something which he felt no obligation to do, he would say, "Do you think I'm a sucker?" Needless to say, this mindset caused much anger and resentment.

Before I got married, I was told by a Rabbi to view everything I do for my wife and family as acts of chesed that are elevating. This made sense to me and I felt it would be easy. I didn't realize how my early programming would create problems.

I remember the first time my wife asked me to do something that I felt she should do herself. "I'm not a sucker," I said irritably.

"Nobody ever thought you were," she said.

"Do it yourself then," I responded.

I was so involved with my own determination not to be misused that it took me a few moments to notice the look of bafflement on my wife's face. "I can't believe you wouldn't want to help me," my wife said. "You always love to do chesed."

The word "chesed" rang a bell. It reminded me of the talk I had heard about the importance of doing chesed for one's wife. Having a chesed consciousness and giving is inconsistent with "not being a sucker." We should definitely not allow ourselves to be taken advantage of. We need to take care of our own interests, but when you love to do acts of kindness, you are happy when such opportunities arise. Thinking about this enabled me to view the situation more objectively. My wife didn't want to take advantage of me. She works hard herself and needs help. Doing things for my wife never makes me a sucker. Just the opposite, it is one of the wisest investments I could ever make.

My wife is lazy. She constantly says, "I don't feel like doing that," and, "That's too difficult for me."

I tried as many approaches as I could to get her to do the daily tasks around the house that needed to be done, but nothing worked. I tried kindness. Then I tried super-kindness. When this didn't work, I tried nagging. I was told that there is power in being persistent, but this just annoyed my wife, and didn't motivate her to do anything she didn't feel like doing. I tried ultimatums. She just wouldn't do anything that required effort or that she did not feel like doing.

I asked her what she had done around her own house when she was growing up. She hadn't done too much before and she wasn't planning on doing much more now. She didn't mind if the entire house was a mess, if the sinks were full of dishes, the laundry wasn't done, and the floors were dirty.

I had a few people speak to her. She would listen politely to whatever anyone said to her, nodding her head in agreement. Then she would go home and do nothing. She had mastered laziness and made it into a fine art.

I was always known as a kindhearted fellow. My kindness was now put to the test. When I didn't pester her, she was a wonderful person, but when I tried to get her to take action, we quarreled. I didn't know how others would react in my situation, but I decided to increase my chesed level and take care of things myself. It keeps me busy, but we have a pleasant atmosphere in the house. To me it's worth it.

My mother was a very friendly extrovert, and she had many friends. When she was upset, however, she cried a lot and became very dramatic. Although most people enjoyed her company, I was uncomfortable with her extremes of emotion and consciously held my own emotions in check.

When I was single, my personality was not a problem because I was basically friendly.

After my marriage, my wife would frequently complain that I wasn't expressive enough. I would counter with, "That's just the way I am. I hope you can accept me anyway."

Then I spoke to someone about how I mentally con-

demn other people who appear to be selfish. As I spoke, I realized myself that there is an aspect of selfishness in my reactions towards those people. This made me aware that not being more emotionally expressive with my wife was selfish.

The person I spoke to pointed out that I naturally have a more flowing emotional nature like my mother, just that I put the brakes on it. He told me I should practice repeating, "I will allow my feelings of joy and love to flow from within." He suggested that I repeat this in front of a mirror three times a day, each time with ten repetitions. When I repeat this I should make an expansive motion with my hands.

I did this for over a month and found that I became more emotionally expressive at home. I'll always remember the day my wife said to me, "Your being so much more emotionally expressive now is the greatest act of kindness you could have done for me. It is worth more to me than the most expensive gift money can buy."

I was on my second marriage, but shortly after the wedding I realized that I was again in a similar situation. I was basically the same person I was the first time around. Having to do things I didn't really want to do and refrain from saying things I felt like saying was difficult for me. It was difficult in my first marriage and I saw that it was still difficult now.

I was asked, "What trait is the reason for your quarrels and disagreements?"

This was easy to answer. I was on the stingy side and hated to spend money unless it was necessary. I saw that I was arguing over money again every time my wife spent more than I felt she should.

"What quality would be the exact opposite of this trait?" I was asked.

"Generosity," I replied.

"That's right," I was told. "Try following the Rambam's formula for developing generosity. Keep giving over and over again. Every time you spend money on your wife, you are becoming more generous. Every time your wife spends money on herself, be happy she is buying things she wants. Regard this as an opportunity to develop a greater sense of generosity."

My present wife has a few children from her previous marriage. She had been a widow for a number of years and had learned to cut down on needless expenses. Nevertheless, she still spent more money than I would have originally wanted her to, but now that I was working on becoming a more generous person, I found pleasure in what used to cause me pain. Even though I still find spending money a challenge, I no longer quarrel over money.

COMPASSION (VS. APATHY OR CRUELTY)

Having compassion means sincerely feeling the distress, pain, and suffering of another person. This is how Rabbi Chaim Zaichyk described this attribute: "When you want to comfort and encourage someone who is brokenhearted and experiencing discouragement, do so with the completeness of your heart and with your entire soul. Your inner love for the person should be manifest in your sincere smile and in your whole way of talking. Do not just act dryly, saying the correct words but without your soul being involved. Do not just mutter platitudes and the standard formulas that people use in these situations. Your great and profound love for the person should pour out as water flowing from its source. You will be successful in alleviating the bitterness and depression of someone who suffers when you speak to him with sincere love. Fill your heart with so much love and kindness that these attributes will overflow. Have so much love that a person who is totally broken and discouraged will feel great warmth" (*Maayanei HaChaim*, vol. 3, pp. 9-10).

When someone suffers in any way, interacting with another person who is sincerely compassionate can be a profound and healing experience. Your marriage will give you many opportunities for developing this trait, and thereby becoming a greater person.

*M*y husband gets nervous very easily and tends to worry and complain. His constant whining and fearful predictions used to get on my nerves, and I would lose my temper. Sometimes I would restrain my anger, but the stress was wearing me out. My husband was a master at creating a gloomy atmosphere even in the brightest of times.

I spoke to a Rabbi about my anger. I wanted to change my husband and help him become more cheerful, but his anxiety has governed him for many years, and he isn't open to suggestions.

"Be compassionate towards your husband," the Rabbi told me, "that is your avodas Hashem in this world. When he complains or worries, he is suffering. Instead of complaining about his complaining, view it as your mitzvah to say things to your husband to help him relax. If you can't think of anything, you can always empathize with his suffering. Enter his world. See how much he suffers from his thought patterns. That is how he gets attention. Don't be angry at him for wanting attention. It's a universal human need. It's just a question of whom we want attention from and for what. When you are compassionate, you are emulating Hashem and that's the ultimate attention-getter from the One Whose attention we all need."

This idea clicked. That's exactly what I needed to hear. Ever since then, as soon as I hear my husband complaining,

I say to myself, "It's time for avodas Hashem. Let me see the situation the way my husband views it, so I can find it easier to think of the best thing to say." This has made my marriage calmer and happier.

Rabbi Yechezkel Levenstein quoted Rabbi Yitzchak Blauser: "*Bitachon*, trust in the Almighty, is a very precious attribute. The Talmud (*Sotah* 48b) tells us that if a person has enough bread to eat today, he is lacking *emunah* if he worries about what he will eat tomorrow. But this applies only to a person's working on his own attributes. When it comes to other people, be concerned about what they will eat tomorrow and for many days to come" (*Ohr Yechezkel, Middos*, p. 22).

When I am irritated or worried, my spouse usually says, "It's not that bad," or "That's nothing to worry about." At times I am told, "If you had more emunah and bitachon, this wouldn't bother you."

I don't like hearing a mussar lecture when something bothers me. I would love to have a high level of emunah and bitachon so I wouldn't worry, but when someone tells me, "Have more bitachon!" I take it as criticism. The time to increase my bitachon is when I am calm and open to ideas.

I also don't like it when my concerns are minimized. I appreciate understanding when I am in emotional pain. Don't tell me, "It's no big deal," when my nervous system is out of order.

I told my spouse that the greatest Torah scholars and tzaddikim didn't minimize their concerns and tell people off when they were worried. They gave encouragement and increased bitachon by presenting Hashem as a loving and caring Father. With profound compassion and sincere concern, they often gave practical advice and suggestions.

I said that I realize it takes time to develop these qualities, but as long as I saw that my spouse was trying, I would be satisfied.

While my spouse still has a long way to go, I am grateful that the negative statements have stopped.

A common mistake that many people make when someone complains is to assume they want practical advice. Some people do but very often people just want empathy and validation. This is often spoken about as a woman's needs, but many men need it as well.

If your spouse doesn't respond well to what you say, it is wise to ask, "When you express complaints about something, how would you like me to respond?"

Most likely the answer will be, "I just want you to empathize with me. When you validate my distress, I feel accepted and this makes me calmer."

Try responding, "I'm sorry you are in pain." This usually makes it easier for your spouse to cope with the situation. It is only when someone is in a comfortable emotional state that he or she can work on elevating the spiritual level.

As one Torah scholar said to his students, "Your wife's distress is your opportunity to emulate the compassion of our Creator."

One Friday I found a stray dog that seemed lost and I felt sorry for it. I took it into the house and gave it some food. My wife was nervous that it might have rabies, but it looked healthy to me. She insisted that we keep it outside on the porch. We had planned to stay with friends in a different neighborhood for Shabbos, but I felt that we couldn't leave the dog by itself without food. The stores were closed and we couldn't get dog food. My wife felt that we should still keep our commitment to our friends. She also was looking forward to being with them for

Shabbos. When she said, "We can let the dog be by itself," I became furious.

"You are so cruel!" I shouted. "Don't you have any compassion? I can't believe that you are such an awful person."

My wife had grown up with an angry father, and my explosion terrified her. At first she said she was going by herself to our friends and I could stay home alone with the dog. She went to the bus stop and acted as if she were really waiting for the bus, but a half hour later she came home. She had calmed down when she was outside in the fresh air. She told me she wasn't going to go away for Shabbos without me, but also didn't feel like being in the house with me after I yelled at her the way I did.

The next day I looked at the entire situation much more objectively. I was embarrassed by my behavior. Here I was claiming to be the compassionate one, and yet I caused my wife so much pain. The dog wasn't even ours, and yet I allowed it to get in the way of our shalom bayis. My wife is compassionate and my telling her she was cruel was unfair and untrue. This incident showed me I needed to work on my temper. I resolved to speak to someone about controlling what I say when I become angry.

❖ ❖ ❖

My wife and I were sitting on a park bench near a lake with our ten-month-old daughter.

Suddenly I felt compelled to throw a corn chip to one of the many pigeons nearby. My wife told me this was a big mistake, but I had already done it. Within seconds more birds landed near us. The baby began to shriek. My wife also began to scream. I, however, was laughing. To me, the scene was ridiculous. To my horror,

however, in a very short time we were completely sur-
rounded by hundreds of pigeons.

*I finally realized that we were actually in danger. I told
my wife to hold the baby tight and run away. I began to
yell and wave my arms. The birds were aggressive and
some were flying right into me. One even flew away with
the whole bag of chips.*

*All the pigeons finally left. My wife and baby were far
away trying to regain their composure.*

*This taught me to take my wife's concerns more seri-
ously. At first I scoffed at her fears, until I realized there
was an actual threat to the baby's safety, and I regretted
having teased her for being afraid. To go from laughter to
terror taught me that I needed to increase my level of
empathy and compassion.*

Below is an open letter to fathers of new babies, written by an
anonymous father:

*Not too long ago, my wife gave birth to a new baby.
It was not our first child, so I didn't expect anything out of the ordinary, except that I would
probably have to help out a bit more around the house.*

*However, the first week after the birth, we experienced
some strain in our home, which I attributed to the stress
of giving birth. Both of us were tired and somewhat irritable, but I figured this would pass after a week or so.*

*Well, I was wrong. Not only did life become more
tense, but my wife began to behave in ways I did not recognize. I thought to myself, enough is enough! I found it
increasingly difficult to deal with her irritability, which
often expressed itself in either biting criticism of me, or
sadness and depression, and even paranoia. Suddenly,
the birth was no longer joyous and was straining our
marriage at a time we needed to be close. It never
occurred to me then that I was part of the problem.*

I had heard of PPD (post-partum depression) before. However, I had thought that it was simply the "blues" a mother felt after losing the closeness of carrying a child for nine months. It never occurred to me that it could be hormonal, or that it could lead to severe depression, and even suicide.

Then I read an article on PPD. I was shocked to find out that my wife was suffering from a "sickness," with effects ranging from mild to extreme. I also began to hear stories about women who suffered from PPD in the past, before PPD was recognized as something needing professional treatment.

The information hit me like a ton of bricks. First of all, I realized that I had blamed my wife for an illness she was not responsible for, and one that she intensely wanted to overcome. Second of all, I learned how important it was for the husband to be understanding and supportive. Women who suffered from PPD were usually under a considerable amount of internal and external stress. If the husband didn't help relieve that stress, recovery from PPD would be delayed, and might even be impossible.

It did not take long for me to change my attitude toward my wife. Sure, it made my life more difficult, but thank G-d, I have watched my wife recover and resume a normal life. Now she even helps others who are suffering from the same illness.

I've written this letter to help you, a father of a new baby whose wife might suffer, even mildly, from PPD, whether you have many children or only this one. Don't suffer from ignorance and mistakes as I did. Do some research of your own to help you and your wife ease the strain on your relationship, and deal with your family responsibilities. Hopefully, you and your wife will have many enjoyable years raising a family.

GRATITUDE (VS. BEING UNGRATEFUL)

Being married gives you many opportunities to develop gratitude. Previously we mentioned how this is a foundation for the marriage; here we are focusing on developing this quality of gratitude in yourself. The essence of serving Hashem is being grateful for all He has given us. The more you build up this trait in yourself, the more open you will be to increase your *ahavas Hashem*, your love for our Creator.

A grateful life is a joyous life. For many people it's easier to be resentful of what they don't like, rather than grateful for what they do like. When you focus on increasing your level of gratitude, you find more and more to be grateful for, both to your Creator and to your spouse.

Every time you see or hear someone expressing gratitude to another person for anything, let it serve as a reminder for you to become more grateful in your marriage.

When Rabbi Simchah Zissel Ziv came home from the synagogue on Friday night, he would not immediately enter his home, but would pause by the door and gaze at the set table and good food his wife had prepared. He did this to feel grateful for all that she did for him (Tenuas HaMussar, vol. 2, p. 45).

❖ ❖ ❖

A Rabbi in a yeshivah who was married over ten years recalled two incidents that happened when he was single and often a guest in various people's homes.

One Shabbos he and a friend ate at someone's house. The hosts spoke a lot to him and his friend and he was not aware of anything special. When they left their host's home, the friend commented, "They have wonderful communication, don't they?"

"But they hardly said anything to each other," the future Rabbi remembered saying.

"They didn't communicate with words, but with their eyes," his friend pointed out. "Their eyes understood each other perfectly."

On the other hand, he recalls a Shabbos he spent at a home with the most elaborate spread he ever saw.

"The hostess served four different homemade desserts. The entire meal was what one would expect at a five-star classy hotel," he said.

"But throughout the meal the husband could only comment on one thing. About the delicious homemade challos, he said, 'I think the flour used to make these challos was a bit old.'

"I remember thinking, 'Where is his gratitude?' This has served as a reminder to me to be more grateful to my wife."

If you feel that this story applies to you, let this be a wake-up call to express appreciation and gratitude and refrain from voicing complaints.

SEEING THE GOOD AND FOCUSING ON IT — *AYIN TOVAH* (VS. FOCUSING ON THE NEGATIVE)

Every human being, including you and your spouse, has virtues and faults. Developing a "good eye" is the basic attribute that one of Rabbi Yochanan ben Zakkai's students reported as being of the utmost importance to master. Marriage gives you many opportunities to develop this quality as you see your spouse at his or her best and worst. Your spouse's faults will usually affect you more than they will anyone else. Keep applying "a good eye" so that the positive qualities and deeds of your spouse fill your consciousness to such a degree that there is hardly any room left to focus on faults.

When you look at a garden, you see beautiful flowers of different colors, the dirt around the flowers, and some wilting flowers or weeds. You might focus on litter that wasn't picked up, or again, you can see beautiful flowers of different colors. It's good to notice everything, but choose to focus on the pleasant and enjoyable. This is the only way to enjoy a garden and the only way to enjoy life, and this is the only way you can create a joyous marriage that is an echo of the Garden of Eden.

Often, when a husband or wife fails to be sensitive or to help out, the other spouse is upset or hurt and says, "I feel you don't care." The one on the receiving end will respond, "That isn't fair," because he or she cares and often does help out. The one with the complaint felt bad, so he or she made a general or global statement. Instead, have a comprehensive view of the good that your spouse does. Then you can look at any failure in the context of the entire relationship. When you voice your complaint, express it in a way that acknowledges the positive.

*M*y husband has many positive traits, but he is sloppy, a bit careless, and forgetful. Although he accomplishes a lot, has a positive influence on others, supports the family, and conducts himself so that most people see his good qualities, his faults and mistakes get on my nerves.

I attended a lecture given by a guest to our town, and heard a citation from the classic mussar work, "Tomer Devorah," that influenced me to change. The quote was taken from the first chapter, "If someone has done something you feel angry about, focus on some good quality of that person. That person might have done you favors in the past, he might have done much good for other people, or he might have certain virtues that you respect. Even though you don't appreciate the way he interacts with you, you can still respect him for the positive things in his life." The speaker added that this is especially important in a marriage.

In the beginning it was difficult for me to change my thought pattern. But when I imagined pressing the buttons on a computer to change files, this metaphor made it easier for me. While I still need to correct my husband's mistakes, I am no longer so annoyed. Each fault is an automatic reminder of his positive qualities and achievements.

❖ ❖ ❖

*T*here is a Torah scholar in Jerusalem who is always calm, and so is his wife. They frequently consult major Torah authorities whenever an issue arises about running their house and raising their children. They have a large family and a number of their children are already married. One day I asked him to comment on marriage.

I was referring to marriage in general, but he thought I meant his own marriage. "Kulan shavin l'tovah." That is, all the years of my marriage are equal in having been good. This was stated in the Torah about the years of the life of the Matriarch Sarah, and he applied it to his marriage.

As soon as he said this, he added, "Of course, there are ups and downs." I was skeptical about any really serious downs, so I asked him, "What were the downs?"

He thought for a few moments, but couldn't recall even one down. "Surely there must have been downs," he concluded, "but I just can't remember any."

The attitude of perceiving all of our years as good, was the level of Sarah Imeinu. Only one permeated with emunah and bitachon in Hashem can experience this regardless of life's many ups and downs. But inwardly we can develop Torah attitudes that enable us to see the good and perceive everything that happens as manifestations of our Creator's love for us.

JOY FOR THE JOY OF OTHERS (VS. ENVY)

"When you envy the good fortune of others, you destroy your own happiness and well-being. On the other hand, when you sincerely wish for the welfare of others, you give them heartfelt blessings. In the process of making others feel good, you yourself live a good life" (Vilna Gaon; *Mishlei* 11:25).

Feeling joy for the joy of others might at first glance seem to be a highly altruistic quality. And it is. But it is also the wisest trait to master for someone who wishes to live a good life himself. Feeling joy for the joy of your spouse will enhance the lives of both of you.

When you identify with the success and good fortune of another person, you feel joy for their joy. This is the joy that a parent has for the good fortune of a child. The more love you feel for others, the easier it is for you to feel their joy.

Envy is one of the three traits that destroys one's life. A person who is consumed with envy can't enjoy what he or she has because the focus is on experiencing pain for the good fortune of others. A person who is envious of others is likely to be unhappy with many aspects of life and this will detract from having a happy marriage. The way to free oneself from envy is to realize that Hashem gives you exactly what you need to fulfill your mission in this world. Moreover, when you master the attribute of experiencing joy for what you have, you will live a joyous life. The only reason anyone envies another person is because he or she wants to have the positive feelings and emotions that the other person has. When you master experiencing joy for what you have and for what others have, you will be free from envy.

*A*ttending weddings where the chasan and kallah appeared joyous was painful for me. Seeing other couples taking walks and talking animatedly was distressing, as was hearing other women praising their husbands. Even reading about happy marriages made me envious. I got used to my non-nurturing marriage, but when I felt envious of those with happier marriages, I felt resentful towards my husband and this resentment led to anger.

Believe me, I felt guilty about my reactions. I felt that if I had more trust in Hashem I wouldn't feel the way I did. However, knowing this didn't automatically increase that trust.

I spoke to an older woman who had a difficult marriage. A few months after her wedding her husband had a serious accident and his brain injury limited him physically. Although he was able to handle a simple job and earn a living, he wasn't very communicative.

"How do you feel at weddings and when you see happy marriages?" I asked her.

"I feel joyous for those people. Because of my husband's injuries, he isn't the same person he was at our wedding. I am devoted to taking care of him and I view this as my life's mission. The joy that I am missing in my own life, I experience vicariously through the joy of others. Whenever I see a happy couple walking together, I feel joy for their joy. When I was growing up, my mother always told me, 'Feeling joy for the joy of others is a wonderful opportunity to increase your own joy.'"

I felt inspired. I had that conversation over two years ago. It's still a struggle for me, but I am increasing my ability to feel joy instead of pain for the joy of others. I have my ups and downs, but I want to use my brain wisely, and its wiser to increase one's joy than to needlessly torture oneself.

JUDGING FAVORABLY
(VS. JUDGING NEGATIVELY)

The *mitzvah* in the Torah to judge people favorably is one of the 613 commandments and refers to a character trait you keep on developing every time you assume the positive. When a husband and wife consistently judge each other favorably, they will be saved from much of the resentment, anger, and quarrels caused by judging negatively.

The first step in judging favorably is to refrain from jumping to conclusions. Realize that you don't have a true picture of what the other person really said or did until you know all the facts. Someone could have been trying to help you, but without knowing all the facts you might assume he or she intentionally did something to cause you distress. Even if you don't like what was said or done, the motives could have been positive. Knowing that your husband or wife meant well should exonerate him or her even if things didn't turn out the way you would have wished.

"The Almighty loves those who constantly find merit for others" (Vilna Gaon; *Mishlei* 16:13). Some people are afraid that if they keep judging people favorably, they will eventually make mistakes. And they are probably right. Every human being will sometimes make mistakes of judgment. But when the question arises as to which direction is the safest to err, judging favorably is by far the best. Of course, if you or someone else is in physical or financial danger, you need to take precautions to protect yourself or that person. But usually when questions arise about whether to judge someone favorably, pride is involved. If we make a mistake in the process of finding merit in others, we will attain the Almighty's love; this outweighs by far any loss of ego.

*I*t has always been a high priority of mine to make my wife happy, even though she doesn't realize it. It is also very important to me that whenever my wife does something that will affect both of us, she consult me first.

We were a bit older than the average couple when we got married and were used to making our own decisions. We both realized that we needed to take each other's thoughts and feelings into consideration before inviting company for Shabbos, buying furniture, and making commitments to go places.

One day when I came home in the evening, there was a message from the the office of our travel agent. "Tell your wife your tickets are ready."

"What tickets?" I asked.

"I'm not her travel agent and I don't know the details. But there is a sealed envelope here with plane tickets."

I was furious. How could my wife make a reservation for a trip without discussing it with me first? I wouldn't do such a thing without talking it over with her.

As soon as my wife came in the door an hour later, I screamed, "Why did you order tickets for a vacation without first discussing it?"

"It was an emergency. Your brother called and said we should come immediately to your parents' home. Your father is in a coma and your mother is frantic. Your brother immediately reserved places for us on tomorrow morning's flight. I tried to reach you but couldn't get through. I didn't want to shock you, so I didn't leave a message."

This certainly taught me a major lesson about not jumping to conclusions.

I walked a Torah scholar to a local taxi stand on a rainy day. He asked the dispatcher to order him a taxi.

"There are three taxi drivers standing around," the dispatcher said, "ask any one of them to take you to your destination."

But none of the drivers felt like taking that trip. The roads leading to the destination were notorious for their frequent traffic jams. All three of them said, "Tell the dispatcher to order you a taxi on his telephone."

But the dispatcher refused saying, "One of these three should take you. I'm not going to call anyone else."

The Rabbi then walked down the road to stop a taxi from another company.

"Why didn't you protest?" I asked the Rabbi.

"I understand them. While I don't approve of their refusal, for me this is an opportunity to view the situation objectively without a condemnatory judgment. I'm certain that if I could have accessed a sincere love state, I could have influenced at least one of them to help me out, but I wasn't on the right level myself just then. If I wasn't, how could I blame them for not being at their best?"

I wonder if the Rabbi realized how much his reaction helped me with my marriage.

SELF-MASTERY (VS. IMPULSIVITY)

"Who is the mighty person? The one who has self-mastery over one's impulses" (*Pirkei Avos* 4:1).

There are people who can pick up great weights and accomplish physical feats. The Torah tells us how Yaakov, our forefather, picked up a heavy stone that was covering a well to help shepherds who couldn't do it themselves. There are mighty warriors whose heroism and bravery can help win a battle, but the truly mighty person is the one who has self-mastery. This means that day in and day out this person has impulses, but is not automatically governed by them. Rather, the mighty person thinks carefully, "Should I say this?" "Should I do this?" Even though he might feel like saying something, he controls what he says if it's not consistent with Torah principles or if it will cause problems. Even though he might feel like taking action, he won't if it's not the right thing to do. This means that he is the victor in constant battles.

Impulsivity in words and actions means that we don't stop to think about what we do. We just impulsively say what comes to our mind, or we just take action right away, and only after it's too late do we consider the full ramifications of that action. In marriage we all need to control what we say and do. This is especially important when we don't feel like it. Every action of self-mastery builds us. Many people have found that keeping a self-mastery journal enables them to increase the number of times that they accomplish self-mastery.

We find in the Torah that because his oldest son, Reuven, did something impulsively, Yaakov took away his right to being considered the firstborn. This was a great loss to Reuven. The firstborn was to be the leader. But to be a leader one must think carefully about the ramifications and consequences of actions.

When Yaakov was on his deathbed, he said to Reuven: "Unstable as water, you shall not have preeminence" (*Bereishis* 49:4).

Rabbi Yeruchem Levovitz of the Mirrer Yeshivah commented that the Torah does not usually give metaphors. The Torah's metaphor is showing us the living reality, that the trait of impulsivity is like water. Just as water flows quickly, so does the behavior of the person who acts impulsively. If you do not weigh the consequences of your behavior, you will make many harmful mistakes and will cause much damage. The Torah's metaphor of water serves as a constant reminder of the dangers of being impulsive. Whenever you see water flowing, tell yourself thoughts that will slow down your reactions (*Daas Torah: Bereishis*, p. 275).

Many people act in ways that are out of sync with their highest nature. They would prefer to act in ways that are consistent with the spiritual, eternal needs of their soul, but they allow the impulses of the moment to rule them. If you are ever aware of this in yourself, stop a moment and think, "What actions or words would be most nourishing for my soul right now?"

Realize that with every act of self-mastery you perform, you are strengthening this attribute in yourself. Allow yourself to feel joy for your accomplishment each time you express self-mastery. It can be very helpful to keep a self-mastery journal to chart your progress.

I was in the middle of eating supper and my wife asked me to lower the flame under a pot that was cooking on the stove. I went over to the stove and lowered the flame.

Apparently I didn't lower the flame enough and some of the food got burnt. My wife came over to the pot and said that lowering the flame means lowering it more than I had done.

"Do you know what my mother would say about this?" my wife commented. "'What you don't do yourself, won't get done.' That's what my mother would say. But I won't say it."

I smiled to myself. Quoting what someone would say and then saying you yourself wouldn't say it is a form of saying it. This is known as "saying it with quotes." But I did appreciate my wife's statement about not really saying it since this relieved the intensity of what was said. And I didn't say back, "And do you know what so and so says about people who are too afraid to say what they want without the use of quotes ..." I feel good that I had the self-discipline not to respond. Perhaps I should feel bad for having wanted to say it, but that just shows I'm human and this prevents me from having too much pride.

*M*y spouse would keep telling me I was clumsy whenever I dropped anything. On a Friday afternoon when preparing for Shabbos, my spouse dropped a large pot and dented it. Although I realized that

I could retaliate by saying, "See, you drop things also," I remained silent. I felt good about having the self-discipline not to say the first thing that came to my mind.

In these situations it takes self-discipline not to make an attacking statement. It requires an equal amount of self-discipline not to say, "See, I'm not like you. I won't insult you the way you insult me." In most instances this will be perceived by the person hearing it as an attack. Usually self-mastery is what is called for. After exercising the restraint not to insult in return, if your spouse does something like this again, you might feel that it is beneficial to mention it. But score-keeping is counterproductive. If you want your spouse to refrain from saying things you find offensive, point it out the next time he or she speaks that way. When you do so in the right way, there is usually no practical benefit from pointing out that you don't do the same. This often appears to be boasting and a way to be one-up. Having self-mastery can be such a reward in itself that you won't always feel a need to point out that you have it.

FORGIVING (VS. HARBORING RESENTMENT)

A wise person will forgive instead of harboring the heavy burden of resentment. It's bad enough that you've suffered already; don't needlessly add to it.

When you let go of resentment and forgive, you elevate yourself. There is an aspect of spiritual greatness and heroism to letting go and forgiving. Knowing that forgiving makes you great will make it easier to forgive. But even so, forgiving can be difficult, and it is exactly for this reason that it is a noble character trait.

When your spouse repeats mistakes and sincerely asks forgiveness, you might feel, "Why do I have to keep forgiving so many times?" However, the more times you forgive, the more you elevate yourself. However, If someone tries to take advantage of you because of your willingness to forgive, you have a right to withhold forgiveness until you feel that the person sincerely regrets causing you pain. But if the asker of forgiveness is sincere, appreciate the spiritual elevation you experience by forgiving.

"When someone feels love for another person, he is able to forgive whatever the other person does" (Vilna Gaon; *Mishlei* 10:12). Part of the art of being able to forgive others is to increase your love for other people. By increasing your love for your spouse, you will find it easier to forgive.

We don't always want to let go of our resentment, but resentment is as dangerous as an acid that wears away at the person who holds onto it. Attachment to resentment can give someone an illusion of power. "I'm in charge and I won't forgive you." Realize the harm you cause yourself by holding onto resentment in contrast to the eternal benefits of elevating yourself by forgiving. As you forgive, feel the emotional freedom you gain and experience your emotional and spiritual elevation.

ADMITTING THE TRUTH: SAYING, "I WAS WRONG" (VS. DENYING YOUR RESPONSIBILITY)

It takes courage to say, "I was wrong." These three words can be the most difficult words that a person can say. Even people who are usually very honest might tend to deny responsibility. The ironic thing is that most people will respect you more for having the integrity and inner strength to admit that you made a mistake.

Those who tend to deny their responsibility are usually not very convincing. You might feel it is easier to deny responsibility, but you actually gain much more when you exercise your inner confidence and acknowledge that you were wrong. Every act of honesty makes you an emotionally stronger person. Admitting the truth is the training ground for emotional independence. Focus on truth and not on the potential disapproval of another mortal.

If you used to find it difficult to admit the truth, look for opportunities to say, "I was wrong," or, "I made a mistake."

I am imperfect. I make mistakes. I sometimes say things that I shouldn't. But, let's face it, it's not the biggest pleasure in the world to have your wife remind you of this.

When my wife pointed out my imperfections and mistakes, I gave all kinds of reasons why I wasn't at fault. But whom was I kidding? My rationalizations didn't carry much weight with my wife, and deep down I knew that I was wrong.

I was resolved to work on the attribute of "modeh al ha'emes," acknowledging the truth. At first this was extremely difficult. I found it unbelievably hard to say, "You are right. I made a mistake." However, I realized that this was the right thing to do.

I tried to understand myself better. Why did I find it difficult to say that I was wrong? I felt that I was lowering myself by doing so. I also felt that if I acknowledge being wrong, my wife would think that I probably was wrong in other situations as well, and therefore I was making myself more vulnerable.

I learned a lesson about how counterproductive it was to deny your mistakes, especially when it is obvious to others that you were wrong. A reporter asked a politician during a major election campaign a hypothetical question about what he would do in a certain situation. His answer implied that he supported and condoned political crime. The opposition attacked him for his statement. He kept saying that he was right in saying what he did, but then his own party members challenged him, and media commentators were almost universally against him. Since I wasn't involved, I was more objective and could see how the wisest thing would have been to admit that his response was not thought out and that he had made a mistake. Then everyone would have left him alone about this issue.

The thought that made it easier for me to admit I was wrong was the awareness that I lost absolutely nothing by *doing so. Instead of making myself vulnerable, I saw that my wife respected me when I admitted I was wrong. She realized it takes courage to do this. I actually gained in self-esteem by knowing I had the inner strength to acknowledge my mistakes. Moreover, if I tried to deny my mistakes, my wife would continue to argue that I had made a mistake. This led us into heated quarrels. When I conceded my errors, the episode was minimally unpleasant.*

As I admitted my mistakes immediately without any rationalizations, I saw that it became easier. All my fears about doing so were illusions. I felt emotionally lighter and now I actually feel pleasure when I say, "You are right. I made a mistake."

HUMILITY (VS. ARROGANCE)

"Arrogance can be the source of two opposite ways of behaving. Some people are arrogant and have such a high opinion of themselves that they consider everyone else as nothing. On the other hand, there are people whose arrogance is a source of their wanting to have power and control over others" (Vilna Gaon; *Mishlei* 8:13).

Both of these patterns described by the Vilna Gaon can cause serious problems in a marriage. Someone who is controlling will create much distress for the spouse, and so will someone who doesn't value his or her spouse.

Whereas arrogance destroys, humility, on the other hand, builds. Humility builds your life, your marriage, and yourself.

Humility is the awareness that all you are and all you have is a gift from our Creator. Humility is the awareness that there are other people in the world and their needs and preferences are important. Humility is the awareness that you aren't perfect, that, like everyone else, you make mistakes. Humility is the awareness that you are on this planet for a relatively short time to serve your Creator and do His will.

Someone with humility is pleasant to get along with, doesn't get angry at others, and isn't controlling. He takes your needs and wishes into consideration, is open to hearing other opinions, admits mistakes, is flexible, and won't demand that everything be exactly the way he or she wants it. Humility is a prerequisite for a harmonious and happy marriage, and is an attribute that you will consistently be building as you and your spouse interact with a Torah consciousness.

If my husband had written an autobiography, I have no doubt he would have called it, "The Greatest Person Who Ever Lived." However, to show he was humble, he would have been forced to give it a more modest title.

Being married to an egocentric and arrogant husband is no picnic. When I first met him, I was impressed with his supreme self-confidence. I had struggled with feelings of insecurity and a low self-esteem my entire life. I felt that if my husband had a positive self-image, he would help me raise my own. I was wrong.

Almost everything I asked my husband to do to help, he considered beneath his dignity. He felt his opinions were infallible, so he didn't even argue with what I said, but just discounted that with which he wasn't in agreement.

I would walk around thinking, "My husband is totally conceited," and I felt there was nothing I could do to improve the situation.

I became aware that we have a tendency to notice the faults of others in exactly those areas that we ourselves need to correct. I began to introspect and look for ways in which I was conceited and arrogant. As I increased my humility, my husband's level of arrogance towards me decreased. When I was more humble we didn't argue as much as we did before, and my husband felt less like speaking in what I considered an arrogant manner.

Most amazing was that as I expressed my opinions modestly, my husband was more open to listen to what I had to say. When I didn't challenge him directly, he did not feel a need to protect his dignity. By changing myself, I was able to improve the marriage for both of us.

A husband once called me up to complain: "My wife doesn't trust me."

"What does she say to indicate this?" I asked him.

"I had stayed up the entire previous night," he told me, "and I planned to drive my car on a long journey. She insisted I share the driving. Doesn't this prove that she doesn't trust me?"

"This has nothing to do with lack of trust," I told him. "She wants to make certain both of you will be safe. She is right. Lack of sleep is dangerous on a long driving trip. Even if you feel confident you can still drive safely, she is entitled to be concerned."

This reminded me of a sign I once saw on the back of a public bus: "Driver! Are you tired? Let go of your ego. Let your wife drive the car!"

❖ ❖ ❖

H usband: "I want my wife to recognize that whenever we disagree I am always right. On the practical level, as long as she realizes that what she is doing is only second best, it's all right with me if she does things the way she feels she needs to do them. I don't want to be a dictator. It's just that my way of doing things and my opinions are always correct."

Wife: "I usually don't mind doing things my husband's way. But I want him to accept that when I do things my way it is just as valid as his way. I don't claim infallibility like my husband does. But my opinions are frequently correct. I want him to accept that when I do things my way it's not second best, just a valid alternative approach."

It is obvious that these two positions produced many heated quarrels. The person this couple spoke to first tried to get the husband to see that his wife was intelligent and wasn't always wrong.

"No," he argued. "You don't understand. She might not always be totally wrong. But my opinion is always totally correct. I am willing to restate this as many times as it takes for you to see that I am right."

This position in not very flexible and the husband would benefit from a greater sense of humility. The wife was advised, "You have a choice. You can keep trying to convince him your opinions are equally valid as you've been trying to do for years without success. Or perhaps someone else might be able to convince him he should acknowledge the validity of your opinions. Maybe you will be able to find someone who will be successful at this and maybe not. It seems to me, however, that you will be best off not arguing at all. When you think you are right, know that in your heart. Give up your need to convince him you are right. You probably won't succeed. Since he does give you a lot of practical leeway, you can live a more harmonious life by just not arguing about who is more right."

The wife agreed. Let's hope that she was successful.

TRUST IN HASHEM — *BITACHON* (VS. WORRYING ABOUT THE FUTURE)

"There is nothing greater in the world that can give a person serenity and tranquility than *emunah* and *bitachon*, awareness of the Almighty and trust in Him. This awareness is the tried and true method to alleviate all of a person's emotional pain. It will calm the spirits of the brokenhearted. Having *emunah* and *bitachon* will enable you to have serenity in the face of the Almighty's decrees, and joy in appreciation of the intense ecstasy of the reward which awaits you in the afterlife. This is the best path to tranquility in the world" (Rabbi Chaim Zaichyk; *Maayanei HaChaim*, vol. 3, p. 175).

When you develop the attribute of *bitachon*, you feel calm and don't worry about the future. You know that everything that Hashem causes to happen in your life is for your ultimate good. You maintain a calm and peaceful state and your home has a peaceful atmosphere where everyone experiences this inner *bitachon*.

Therefore, view every challenge that could worry you as an opportunity to increase your level of *bitachon*. Think to yourself, "If I felt that Hashem is doing this to help me trust Him more and that this is for my eternal benefit, I would feel calm. I will now allow myself to feel some of that inner calm." As you say this, you might even breath slowly and deeply a few times and appreciate each breath.

> *I am much more timid than the average fellow. At home, my parents and older brothers took care of the practical matters. I wasn't very assertive. I found it difficult to ask strangers for directions, ask questions when I didn't understand something, make telephone calls, return things to stores, and speak to people with whom I didn't feel comfortable.*
>
> *When I thought about getting married, I was highly anxious. How would I manage to support a family? How would I be able to take care of the hundreds of things necessary to set up a house and to keep things running smoothly?*
>
> *Whenever I tried to express my anxiety, I was told, "You are intelligent. You'll certainly be able to manage*

like everyone else. Don't worry. Increase your level of bitachon and you will be okay."

But I was worried. I read more about bitachon, but it was difficult for me to actually feel this inner trust in Hashem. I had normal intellectual abilities, but my social skills were lacking. So I pushed off going out as long as I could. Even though family and friends asked me, "When are you going to get married already?" I would smile an embarrassed smile, while feeling that I wasn't ready yet.

Finally someone made a suggestion that sounded just right. I was set up with a girl who was just as shy as I was. We didn't have lively discussions, but we both felt that we understood each other. While most people intimidated me, she didn't. I viewed her as a kindred spirit in a hostile world.

We were both worried about how we would manage with daily living. But since we were so similar, we were able to encourage each other. We began to reinforce each other's courageous steps. These were things that most people would have taken for granted, but nothing was easy for us.

We never argued. Both of us were terrified of disapproval and neither could take being yelled at or insulted. If there was ever a misunderstanding, we both would apologize profusely to one another. I was just relieved that my wife wasn't blaming me, and she felt equally relieved that I wasn't blaming her. Slowly, we began to express ourselves more and more.

Every act of assertiveness showed us that we could speak up. The thing that helped us the most was the thought, "If anyone else can do something, so can you. Everyone in the world can serve as our role model. Observe people who can do things that you can't and model yourself after them."

I was told, "Don't empower anyone else. The power you view someone else as having all comes from inside you.

Because you view that person as powerful, you are intim-idated. Empower yourself. Treat everyone else with respect. But realize that you can choose to empower your-self the same way that you empower the other person." This made sense to me and enabled me to speak up.

My wife and I work together to increase our level of bitachon, our assertiveness, and our courage to handle situations we previously viewed as intimidating. We repeat verses from Tehillim that mention bitachon and this has been helpful. Outgoing, confident people still look at us as meek, but we are happy with each other and are grateful to Hashem for His kindness in bringing us together.

ALACRITY — *ZERIZUS* (VS. LAZINESS AND PROCRASTINATION)

There are so many things to take care of when you are mar-ried that you will have many opportunities to keep on develop-ing the character trait of *zerizus*, that is, taking action promptly and quickly. With each action you do with *zerizus*, you will be integrating this trait more and more.

The opposite of *zerizus* is laziness and procrastination, the root of many quarrels. In a marriage, your laziness will cause your spouse much frustration. When you neglect to take care of something your spouse considers important, it can breed anger and arguments. The person who procrastinates also suffers because he or she constantly needs to think about the things that were unpleasant to do.

The Vilna Gaon wrote, "A person is lazy because he wants serenity and quiet; comfort-seeking is the root of laziness. But realize that although the lazy way might at first appear to give comfort, in the long run, a person who is lazy will lose much because of this trait. The path of laziness will be extremely rough" (Commentary to *Mishlei* 15:19).

To master *zerizus* feel more pleasure in taking care of the things that need to be taken care of than you do when you push things off.

Each day do at least three things with *zerizus*.

"Zerizus" is my middle name. I tend to take care of things right away. I become edgy and restless if I have to wait for someone who does things slowly.

Wouldn't you know, the person I married has a dilly-dallying, lethargic disposition. I constantly need to wait for anything to get done, finding the wait excruciatingly painful. When walking together I need to walk less than half my normal speed and even this is much too fast for my spouse.

Before our seventh wedding anniversary, I asked my spouse what kind of present she would appreciate.

"The best gift you can give me is to become more patient. I know you love me, but your impatience gives me the opposite message."

"Okay, I'll do all I can to develop patience," I responded.

I began reframing every situation to enable me to be patient as an expression of love for my spouse. While I was usually highly proactive and continued to do most things quickly, I now found it easier to act patiently. Exercising patience became a far better use of my time than concentrating so hard on zerizus.

Chapter Twelve

Thinking Clearly in the
Face of Challenges

INTRODUCTION: THINKING CLEARLY

One of the most important life skills to master is being able to remain mentally and emotionally centered in order to think clearly about the best course of action. Mastering this skill will enable you to remain clear thinking in the face of criticism, insults, anger, nagging, or negativity, enabling you to bring out the best in yourself and your spouse.

All of us experience challenging moments when we face people who are critical, frustrated, angry, and even hostile. Before saying or doing anything in such situations, we need to either stay in or access a centered state. This is the state that then enables us to think clearly about the wisest thing to say or do. We need to apply these two steps when dealing with anyone who is critical, and this is especially important when these challenges arise in marriage.

Everyone with young children is faced with frustration and anger. It is of immense value to both yourself and your children to stay relatively calm and clear-thinking, and to use opportunities to develop these skills. When it comes to interacting with one's spouse, some marriages will be more challenging than others. In some marriages these challenges will be subtle, and few and far between, while in others they will be dramatic and quite frequent. All these challenges, however, are opportunities for growth. Those who are relatively free from these challenges can increase their sense of appreciation and gratitude. Those who have been chosen for these challenges need to mentally prepare for them.

Let us look at both these steps. The first involves staying centered. We have already mentioned the importance of working on mastering your states. Being centered is a state, and so is being angry, frustrated, overwhelmed, or hostile. If someone's spouse is in any one of a number of unresourceful states, there is a strong tendency for that person to also access an unresourceful state. When one person is frustrated and lets it out at his or her spouse, this often serves as an anchor for the other person to pick up those feelings. If someone's spouse is angry, even mildly so, or outright hostile or mean, it takes much effort and practice to maintain an optimum resourceful state, exactly when we need to the most.

The benefit of a resourceful, centered state is that it is conducive to clear thinking. Decide upon the wisest course of action. Is it best to remain silent or to say something? What should you say to enable you to reach the desired outcome of protecting yourself and at the same time enabling the other person to become calmer and more reasonable? Both your tone of voice and the words you say will either escalate the situation and make it worse, or have a positive effect and calm things down.

Let us imagine a five-minute unpleasant interchange when both husband and wife are angry. Let us suppose that each one says something to the other for approximately twenty seconds. That gives each one seven or eight times to fire at each other with unpleasant statements. However, at any stage in the interaction either one could have accessed a resourceful state, thought clearly about the next best move, and restored peace.

The best way to learn to stay centered in the face of a challenge is to mentally prepare yourself to do so. Think about the benefits to you and your family, the emotional and spiritual benefits, and the great losses caused to you and your family by acting at your worst in these challenging moments. These are long term gains and losses that can either benefit you for your entire life, or cause pain for many years to come.

If someone paid you a large sum of money to develop the skill of remaining calm and centered when faced with criticism, anger, and other unresourceful states, you would definitely be motivated to do so. If the amount would make you one of the wealthiest people in the world, you would read anything you could, consult experts, and practice daily until you mastered this skill. Living a joyous life with a happy marriage makes you wealthier than the richest person if that wealthy person is unhappy. Spend as much time as you personally need on mastering the ability to remain centered and to think clearly in the face of any challenge. Developing this ability will save you much suffering and heartache and it can transform challenging situations into moments of great growth and joy.

Do you ever feel that your marriage partner is purposely trying to get you off balance? Perhaps yes, and perhaps it is an incorrect assumption. Regardless of the accuracy of your assumption, the person who gets you off balance is yourself. As soon as you realize you are off balance, repeat to yourself, "centered and balanced." Talk to yourself in ways that enable you to become calmer and more at ease. Visualize a relaxing scene or a centered and balanced role model, and imagine yourself being that person.

On the screen of your mind visualize any new action or pattern of talking you would like to integrate into your regular behavior. When you practice this enough times, it will become part of you.

THINKING CLEARLY IN THE FACE OF CRITICISM

Loving criticism is the ideal to strive for. This is listed in the last chapter of *Pirkei Avos* as one of the forty-eight tools to acquire Torah. The verse in *Mishlei* (9:8) states: "Do not rebuke a scoffer, lest he hate you; rebuke a wise man, and he will love you." The Vilna Gaon comments: "A wise person is someone who continuously wants to grow in Torah. He appreciates it if you point out to him that he is doing something wrong. His goal is self-improvement, and he loves every opportunity to become a better person."

The way someone tries to correct us is a key factor in our being open to accepting criticism. Speaking with love and compassion, some people can point out ways that you can improve and you can feel grateful for their care and concern. We have a strong awareness that this person is not criticizing us out of personal motives such as power or arrogance. Knowing that this person sincerely cares about our welfare gives us positive feelings about listening to suggestions and corrections.

When someone corrects us, we usually prefer that they be concise and to the point. Some people tend to give long speeches when they want to correct us and the entire process is highly distressing. If this is a problem in your marriage, tell your spouse, "I can hear you better when you are concise."

If your spouse tactfully tries to correct you and does so in a way you appreciate, you don't need to make any special effort to stay centered and to think clearly. However, if your spouse tends to be highly critical and seems to be constantly criticizing you in a way you don't appreciate, make the effort to stay centered and think clearly. Don't immediately respond with a counterattack such as, "You have the same or worse faults." Or, "You don't like it when I criticize you, so why are you criticizing me?"

As you stay in a relatively calm state, think about the criticism you just heard. Is it valid? If it were said differently, might you be totally open to hearing it? Perhaps it could have been said in fewer words. Perhaps the tone of voice could have been more loving and compassionate. Perhaps the choice of words could have been more tactful. If so, you can respond, "Thank you for pointing that out. You have a valid point. And in the future I would prefer it if you points things out … (in a gentler tone of voice / with fewer words / more tactfully)."

If you feel the criticism is not valid, you can calmly and respectfully say, "I realize you meant well, but I would like to explain why your criticism isn't valid."

If your spouse keeps arguing that you deserve the criticism and you still feel you don't, it's wise to stop. You might say, "I'll think it over."

Realize there is a possibility that you are wrong, and the criticism was valid. As the Vilna Gaon wrote in his commentary to *Mishlei* (26:12): "A person who is 'wise in his eyes' will not make positive changes. Since he thinks he is right, he is not aware of his negative and counterproductive behavior; but if a person is aware of his improper behavior, there is always hope he will correct himself."

You might feel that the criticism is valid but you are presently working on improving yourself in so many areas that this point is lower on your priority list. Perhaps if what you are doing is bothering your spouse, you might raise the priority status of this complaint.

Then there are situations when your spouse is not criticizing your actions in areas of Torah observance, but in areas that you consider inconsequential. Even though your spouse pointed it out, it is so minor that it won't make any difference at all in either of your lives. If your spouse is open to stop making these comments since they annoy you, just point out that you would prefer not to hear these criticisms at the present. If your spouse isn't open to stopping, realize that they are essentially harmless if you don't let them bother you.

I heard a husband constantly correcting what his wife said.

The wife said, "A week ago we went to my parents' home for supper."

"It wasn't a week ago. It was nine days ago," the husband corrected.

The wife said, "I paid twenty dollars for the gift we bought."

"It wasn't twenty dollars," said the husband. "It was only $18.50."

The wife said, "I returned the call the next day."

"It was two days later," the husband corrected.

The wife said, "I asked five people to bake for the occasion."

"I heard you ask six people," the husband once again corrected.

Finally, the wife burst into tears and said, "He corrects everything I say."

"Not everything. Only your mistakes," the husband interjected.

"There he goes again," said the wife. "I feel as if I am walking on eggshells. I can't stand his constant nitpicking. Whenever I open my mouth to say anything in his presence, I am nervous because I know he is ready to pounce on me and correct me. Most of the things he corrects me about are insignificant and irrelevant.

This pattern is quite common and either spouse can be just as critical over minor discrepancies. The critical party would be wise to modify his or her criticism and let it go, especially when the exact details don't make any practical difference.

Some people argue, "If one doesn't correct minor mistakes, then major mistakes will take root. It's especially important for me that my husband/wife be accurate. Mistakes are untruths and I want only truth in my home."

The Torah priority is that peace between husband and wife takes precedence over saying the truth if that will cause needless resentment. In the Torah we find that Hashem distorted the truth to prevent a lack of *shalom bayis* between Avraham and Sarah. All the more so, it is permissible to refrain from correcting a trivial and inconsequential error to protect *shalom bayis*.

If the critical party refuses to be less critical, it is important for the person on the receiving end of the corrections to become more empowered and to learn to handle the criticism with dignity and objectivity.

If your spouse is going to keep correcting you, master a positive or humorous attitude. As you mentally prepare yourself to hear corrections, imagine a large group of people cheering for you. Add music. In your imagination, keep practicing until you are able to desensitize yourself and you will be free from pain.

One Shabbos morning before I left for shul, my wife said, "When you put hot water in the thermos on Friday, you didn't fill it to the top. If you can't do the job right, tell me and I'll do it myself."

My initial reaction was, "I did approximately three hours of work around the house this Friday. I did the shopping, washed dishes, peeled potatoes and carrots, swept the floor, set the table, and took care of a number of other tasks. Why do you focus only on what didn't get done? If you aren't satisfied with the way I do things, I agree with you, do them all yourself."

Before I said this, however, I thought about how hard my wife works all the time. This week she wasn't feeling well, and it was important for her to have hot drinks. She was right. I should have realized that the thermos wasn't full and should have boiled up more water on Friday. Even though I would have preferred for her to have worded her observation differently, it was careless of me not to have filled the thermos to the top.

Fortunately, I calmly said, "I'm sorry. I'll try to remember next week to fill the thermos to the top."

This was the end of the entire discussion. As I walked to shul, I felt grateful that I didn't deliver the counterattack that had entered my mind. This would have led to an unpleasant exchange on Shabbos. I would have walked to shul licking my wounds, and my wife would have felt bad until I came home and apologized. The pleasure I experienced for exercising my self-control was greater than the dubious pleasure of responding angrily.

❖ ❖ ❖

I used to react with intense pain and distress whenever my spouse pointed out that I made a mistake.

"All I did was point out a minor detail that needs correction," my spouse used to say. "Why does it cause you so much suffering?"

I also didn't know why. All I knew was that I couldn't stand being criticized. I spoke to someone about it, and he said, "In my experience someone who has adequate self-esteem takes criticism as feedback. It's important to evaluate the feedback to see if you agree with it or not. Either way, your value as a person is a given and nothing anyone says to you can detract from it."

It was suggested I become more aware of the exact words and associations I had when someone, especially my spouse, pointed out a mistake.

The next time my spouse said, "This wasn't done right," I paid attention to my inner voice and images.

While all that was pointed out was a trivial error, I heard my parent's voice telling me, "You are incompetent. You keep making mistakes. What's wrong with you?"

My self-image has been one of incompetence. I have always been more aware of what I couldn't do when, in reality, I have accomplished a lot and there are many things I do well. I need to focus on what I am able to do, remembering that even if someone can't do anything, our value as a child of G-d is immense.

I was told to be patient. It takes time for a positive self-image to be totally integrated. At the same time, I need to internalize that if a specific action or statement is criticized, I don't need to magnify it into a global statement about my self-worth.

It was also suggested to me to create a new inner voice saying, "I love you. You are precious to me. Therefore, I *want you to correct whatever you can, but you are valuable whether or not you make any changes." I repeated this over and over with great intensity. If the old voice started playing, I immediately worked to drown it out with this new, improved voice.*

I looked forward to testing my visualization ability to prepare for the future. I mentally saw my spouse criticizing me and saw myself handling it with ease. In real life, it was not so easy for me to make the change. But when I saw that I reacted better, I knew that I was on the right track.

❖   ❖   ❖

My playful nickname for my husband, "Mussar man," relates to the fact that on an average day he will give me three or four mini-lectures on how I can improve.

My husband's cousin was in our home for a meal and heard me say, "Thank you, mussar man," after my husband gave one of his little speeches on how I can do something differently.

We both feel very comfortable with this cousin and free to express ourselves. We are open to his feedback and he has given us some good tips on communication.

"Do you enjoy these little speeches?" he asked me.

"I don't love them, but I do love my husband," I replied. "I know he has good intentions. By calling him 'mussar man' I add a drop of humor and it makes it easier for me to swallow his medicine."

THINKING CLEARLY IN THE FACE OF ANGER

When your spouse is angry, how you react will either increase his or her anger or decrease it. We find this wisdom in a well-known verse from *Mishlei* 15:1: "A soft reply turns away anger" (*Mishlei* 15:1).

As the Vilna Gaon elaborates in his commentary: "When you communicate to others in a soft manner, this will calm someone who is already angry with you. [Note: This refers both to your tone of voice and the substance of what you say.] When the person who is angry with you has a valid complaint, admit it, and this will calm him down.

"There are some people, however, who frequently say the wrong things. Such people cause others to become angry even when the anger was not present at the outset" (*Mishlei* 15:1 and 14:30).

When interacting with someone who is angry, the most important thing to remember is: Don't say anything that would just add fuel to the fire.

Try to understand why your spouse is angry. Why does what was said or done elicit such a strong reaction? What does this mean to your spouse? When you understand why your spouse is angry, you might be able to deal with the issues that are bothering him or her. If your spouse has a valid reason for being angry with you, apologize. Sincerely express your regret at having caused him or her distress.

What if your spouse has a reason for being angry, but you feel that the present anger is much more intense than necessary or appropriate? It is usually wisest to apologize. In most instances, nothing will be gained by attacking your spouse's anger right then. After the issue is worked out, you might say, "You had a valid reason for being upset before. In the future I would appreciate it if you would word your complaints in a softer manner."

At times you might think that the anger is based on a mistaken assumption. If so, be careful how you word your clarification. Don't start off by saying something that sounds like a put-down, "You are all wrong. You are getting angry for no reason." It is preferable to say, "I don't blame you for getting angry since the way you understood what happened would be upsetting. Please allow me to clarify."

When you are calm and in a peaceful state it still might be difficult to think clearly about what to say when you are spoken to angrily. But that is still much easier than when you yourself are also angry. If your spouse speaks to you in anger, that energy can easily elicit anger on your part, but you can still maintain a centered state and think clearly. If you had a group of people encouraging you, it would be easier, so imagine a multitude of people saying, "We know you can do it. Stay calm. Speak softly." Since it's impossible to have this multitude when you need them, you must create this inner voice saying, "You can do it. Stay calm. Speak softly." By repeating this over and over again, you will have created an inner voice that will reinforce your ability to actually stay calm and speak softly when you are faced with anger.

Anger is pain, so have compassion for an angry person. When you view your spouse's anger with compassion, what you say is more likely to be helpful. The challenge is to access compassion when you are the target of someone's anger. This level can take much time and effort to master, but those who do so live elevated, joyous, and loving lives. When you actually feel compassion, your facial expression, the look in your eye, your tone of voice, and your words all give the message, "I care about you. I am sorry that you are suffering. Is there anything I can do to alleviate your pain?"

When someone is angry with you, the best thing to do at times is to allow the person to let off steam. If this person usually calms down after a couple of minutes, then just brace yourself for those moments. If you are married to someone who can go on and on for a long time when angry, and some people can maintain angry tirades for quite a while, then it becomes more important to think of what to say to calm your spouse. Before thinking of what to say, however, exercise your self-mastery and maintain a centered state.

When someone gets angry or is intimidated by someone else's anger, breathing is usually shallow and almost stops. By breathing slowly and deeply, your entire muscular system relaxes. If your spouse is receptive, you might say, "Let's both breathe slowly for a few minutes. Then we can talk reasonably about the issue."

Some of the things you might be able to say are:
- "I'm sorry that I caused you distress."
- "I was wrong. I apologize."
- "I see that you're angry. Let's work this out in a peaceful manner."
- "I want to understand your feelings about this. Please explain them to me in a gentle way, so I will find it easier to understand." (It's doubtful that someone will counter with, "No, I want to keep speaking to you in a way that you won't understand." If your spouse has a tendency towards sarcasm, and says something like, "No matter how anything is said to you, you won't understand," stay centered, but try a different approach next time.)
- "If I were you, I would be just as angry as you are."

Then there is always "pattern interrupt." You might start off with, "You have some good points there … Oh, I just remembered …" (Then remember something that is likely to change your spouse's state.)

> *I have a tendency to come home late and do other things that get my wife angry. But I am peaceful by nature and hate an angry tone of voice and facial expression. When my wife gets angry, it's usually out of proportion to what I have actually done and I have to admit that I am intimidated by her explosions. I usually handle this silently while waiting for her to calm down, but inside I feel weak that I don't insist on being spoken to with respect. At times, my wife's explosions get me angry and I scream back at her. This, of course, just gets her so angry it could last a whole day, and even a few days. When she calms down, she acknowledges that she has a problem, but still, this pattern has repeated itself for many years.*
>
> *I asked someone for advice and was told I should try to come home when I say I will, but since it is certain I will be late once in awhile, I should mentally prepare*

what to say. "Don't let your wife's anger intimidate you," I was told. "She's not going to hit you. She's just going to yell. By overcoming your fear, your mind will be able to think about what you can say."

I remember the joy and pride I felt the first time I said the right thing to calm my wife after her anger began to escalate. My wife asked me to come home early to help with the children. I agreed, but I was delayed and came home later than usual. I was hungry and was looking forward to eating, but as soon as I entered the house, I could see that my wife was angry. She was tired and started saying things that weren't relevant.

Looking her straight in the eye, I calmly said, "I want to discuss what's bothering you, but right now I'm hungry and tired. As soon as I take a bite, I will have the energy to discuss whatever you want and to help out."

It was amazing. Immediately, my wife's anger dissolved. This gave me the confidence that she would calm down if I stayed calm and said the right thing. I wish I had done this years ago, but at least I see now that I don't need to fear my wife's anger. I just need to stay calm and think of something concise that will defuse the situation.

❖ ❖ ❖

My spouse is a blamer. Whenever something goes wrong, she says, "It's all your fault this happened." The words together with the angry tone of voice are very painful.

I was blamed a lot as a child and easily became intimidated. So now I tend to overapologize. It's as if I needed to apologize for my very existence.

It was suggested I become more aware of the thoughts in my mind and note how I view my spouse and myself when blaming occurs.

I became aware that I view my spouse as a powerful giant. I have associations with times that my parents blamed me for misbehaving, or for breaking or losing things even when it wasn't my fault. I remember teachers who blamed me for things that were beyond my control.

I was told to realize that if my spouse blames me in an angry manner, it's because of bad feelings my spouse is experiencing right now. It's an expression of vulnerability and lowered self-esteem, so I can view the frustration and anger with compassion.

It was suggested to me to view myself as a powerful, mighty giant, and at the same time to view my spouse as a tiny midget who just went into a temper tantrum. I laughed at the thought, but visualized how it would work.

It was amazing. The next time I was blamed, I immediately went into an, "I giant, you midget," mode. I was then able to calmly say, "Let's take a look at this objectively and work it out." This enabled both of us to discuss the issue as two intelligent adults.

A couple once told me that whenever they see that they are getting angry at each other, one of them will say, "Mental vacation time." Then they both spend at least five minutes mentally visualizing such places as lakes, gardens, waterfalls, jungles, mountains, interesting cities around the world, uninhabited islands, and national parks.

They set an alarm to go off in five to ten minutes. When the bell rings, they are both in such a peaceful state, that the issue at hand is easier to deal with. At times, the one who previously had a grievance will say, "I feel so great right now that things don't bother me anymore."

THINKING CLEARLY IN THE
FACE OF NAGGING

Being nagged is irritating. A spouse who nags is also frustrated and that is why he or she is nagging. If you are on the receiving end of nagging, you have a number of positive alternatives and probably a greater number of negative alternatives.

Sometimes your spouse's nagging is a wake-up call for you to take action. Although you might have preferred more enjoyable ways of being reminded, if the thing you are being asked to do is something that really needs to get done, do it right away, or at least as soon as possible. When you are being nagged, you might not feel that you are in your *chesed* state. That is exactly why accessing a *chesed* state would be a wonderful growth choice. "According to the difficulty is the reward" (*Pirkei Avos* 5:26).

At times you agree that you should take care of the matter, but right now you are not yet ready. Speak to your spouse in such a respectful or loving way that he or she will be willing to wait.

You might even feel like procrastinating and are not in a state to speak at your best. If so, you should think about what you can say to your spouse so you can continue to procrastinate. We are not advocating this position, but realistically speaking, if you are going to procrastinate, you still need *shalom bayis*. We are not advocating just pushing your spouse off by saying, "Oh sure, honey. I'll take care of it soon," when you have no intention of taking care of it. You might try, "I know I should take care of it today, but I'm not in the mood. [Note to the procrastinating reader: Here, if you use the word "state," you might give your spouse food for thought about how to put you in an active state.] So I'm asking you for a favor. Please don't nag me now and I'll be so grateful that I'll take care of it faster than I would have otherwise."

You might say something such as, "I realize that what you are asking is valid, but I'm not on the right level now to meet your requests. I realize that it's self-serving of me, but perhaps you can be on the level of being more patient." Some people might appreciate your honest admission of your weakness and let you go for a while longer. If not, at least this won't escalate matters. Your spouse might say, "You can't get away with things just by claiming that you aren't on the right level." If this happens you can answer, "I'm really not open to taking care of what I should right now. We have a choice of getting into a quarrel or of waiting. I vote that we wait. I'll try to make it up to you in another way." You should try to get yourself motivated to take care of things you know you should take care of, but even before you motivate yourself to do so, always speak with respect.

When you are deciding what to say, remember your goal is to maintain a good state yourself and to enable your spouse to be in a positive state. This is true even when you feel that what you are being nagged about is not a valid request. It might be for something that is too time-consuming, too expensive, too difficult for you to do, too boring or distressing.

If you access an unresourceful state when faced with nagging, you are apt to quarrel. But by staying centered, you might say something to make your spouse laugh or feel so positive about you that he or she feels as if he or she has attained the desired goal.

M*y wife is a world-class nag. When I think about it objectively, I realize I am on the forgetful side, and also a bit lazy. However, I find the nagging highly annoying. I work on not getting angry and therefore the nagging does not lead to quarrels, only to irritation on my part.*

I keep telling my wife, "Don't nag," and she responds, "If you don't want me to nag, take care of things right away." That makes sense, but it is as unlikely for that to happen as for my wife's nagging to miraculously stop. She is practical and also frustrated. So this has been a minor lose-lose situation for both of us.

I thought about what I could do to eliminate the nagging, besides changing my personality and mastering my middos. Then I realized what we could do.

I told my wife, "We are both in agreement on the basic principles, but our patterns bother each other. Can I suggest that you remind me with humor? I can't promise that this will magically turn me into an energetic ball of fire, but at least we will have shalom bayis."

My wife agreed. We began enjoying each other's company more. And of course I did increase my speed, not as much as my wife would have wanted, but there was definitely improvement.

❖ ❖ ❖

My husband is the persistent type, highly determined to accomplish in every area of life. His determination has made him a Torah scholar. While he spends most of his time studying, he also is involved in a few business ventures and we live comfortably. He is a volunteer fund-raiser whose persistence and determination have enabled him to raise large sums.

There is a reason, however, that I find his persistence problematic. When he wants me to do things or go places he will persist in his requests, even if I'm not interested. He doesn't lose his temper, but he also doesn't give up very easily. He is considerate, and if he knows that I really can't do something, he accepts it good-naturedly. But when he feels that it's laziness or lack of motivation on my part, he will persist. I am usually the one who gives in and agrees to go along with his plans.

In the beginning, this bothered me. I come from a home where we were all easygoing types. When I ask for something, I will usually only ask two or three times, then give up. But not my husband. He is willing to repeat requests even thirty and forty times. I am used to this and accept it, realizing it is the price to pay for his wonderful accomplishments for himself and our family. Now, *whenever I think about this, I smile. It's a more than fair deal on my part. What I gain outweighs the loss of comfort I sometimes experience. As a matter of fact, my initial reaction of irritation is an immediate reminder of his positive applications of this trait.*

THINKING CLEARLY IN THE FACE OF NEGATIVITY

As the Rambam states in *Hilchos Dei'os,* human beings are influenced by their environment, including the attitudes and perspectives of the people around them. Our own emotional states in varying degrees respond to the emotional states and energy of those in our presence. When we are around people who have a balanced optimism and tend to be cheerful, we tend to feel better.

In the presence of someone who is excessively pessimistic, bitter, cynical, and consistently negative, we feel worse. Unless, of course, we share this outlook. Then we might feel good in the presence of a kindred spirit. "Here's someone who thinks as I do." Someone growing up in this environment may adopt this as his or her reality and will need to work hard to develop a more optimistic and helpful perspective on life in general and on the specific challenges that one is faced with. It can take a lot to upgrade his or her thinking.

If you are married to a person who is consistently negative, how this will affect you depends on how negative your spouse is and how positive you are. In the short-term his or her negative energy can be contagious, or at least put a damper on your positive energy in any situation when you are together. In the long-term, you might pick up your spouse's outlook on life and make it your own.

How can you positively influence a person who constantly thinks negatively? How can you change someone from being bitter and cynical into someone who is cheerful, optimistic, and consistently appreciative of the good and the positive? It isn't easy, but before you try to change someone, your first priority is to protect yourself from being brought down. Influencing the other person requires a long-term plan based on strategic thinking. You need patience and a willingness to have a positive influence one small step at a time.

Be totally resolved that every negative statement of your spouse will automatically be met with a mental defense on your part. It might be inappropriate and counterproductive to express these statements, but you can think whatever you like. Strive for the goal of responding to every unnecessary negative statement with a statement that is Torah-consistent.

We all have automatic associations. For example, suppose someone says to you, "Please tell me the first letter you think of after I say the letter A." Most likely you will think of "B."

If the person then asks you for the first number that comes to your mind after he says, "1," most likely it will be "2." We respond this way because we have made these associations repeatedly.

Similarly, we can build up an association of thoughts of gratitude and appreciation whenever we hear an unnecessary negative statement. Therefore the negativity of someone else can set up a positive response in our minds. Then not only will someone's negativity not bring you down, but it will be a catalyst to make you into a more positive person.

Be careful how you try to influence someone who is negative. If this person suffered a lot in his or her life, be compassionate and empathetic. Try to understand his or her pessimism and bitterness in the context of his or her entire life history. Perhaps life has been full of suffering; perhaps he or she grew up in a chaotic or dysfunctional environment. Then judge what is appropriate to say, and what would better be left unsaid. When compassion is required, that is our Torah obligation. A person who is suffering can't listen to a long lecture about being more positive. Only after feeling genuinely understood can this person hear about another outlook and attitude.

If a person who tends to be cynical and pessimistic views himself or herself as highly intelligent and sees you in a lesser light, he or she will usually ignore the positive things you say. They will think, "This person is naive."

Some people have found that being more negative than a negative person sometimes works to make them a little less so. For example, if the person says, "Things are falling apart around here," instead of saying, "No, it's not that bad," you might say, "They sure are. We are in the midst of a total disaster and catastrophe." Then they have a choice of either agreeing or saying, "Well, it's not that bad."

Asking questions might help this person see things more positively. You might ask, "Is anything going right in your life?" or, "Can you think of anything that is already the way you want it to be?" You might even ask, "Can you think of a plan to improve the situation?" Suppose they say, "No." Then you can say, "Perhaps you can find someone who could suggest improvements."

Some people who are cynical need to be told, "You think your thoughts are reality, but anyone who has a more comprehensive view will see that your perspective is limited." Maybe the person will concede you have a point and his or her way of thinking is just a habit that can change. Then you are making progress.

Remember that the negativity of people in your environment is your Divine test. You need to maintain your dignity and Torah perspective, regardless. Keep practicing. Imagine the negative statements that your spouse or anyone else might say to you, and immediately change your images and words to reflect a positive state. As you keep practicing, this will become a spontaneous and automatic reaction.

Chapter Thirteen

Specific Issues in Marriage

- ᔕ *Money and debts*

- ᔕ *Child rearing*

- ᔕ *Illness and health*

- ᔕ *Erev Shabbos*

- ᔕ *Growing up in different cultures*

- ᔕ *Religious differences*

- ᔕ *Marriage counseling*

- ᔕ *Back from the brink —
  saving marriages at the last moment*

MONEY AND DEBTS

oney can be a major source of marital quarrels and disputes. Recently in the United States there was a lottery with a grand prize of 292 million dollars! The chances of any specific ticket actually winning were minuscule. Nevertheless, the Associated Press reported that one wife said, "If I win, I'll have a fight with my husband. I want to invest it all, and he wants to invest it in playing every golf course in America." The odds were totally against their winning, nevertheless this woman was already visualizing the quarrel it would cause.

The Talmud (*Eruvin* 65b) states that money is one of the three ways by which we reveal our personality. Everyone will be challenged by money; the only question is the form those challenges will take. Money means different things to different people. To some it's security, to others it's buying power. To some it's a measurement of self-worth, to others it's a means of gaining respect from other people. To some it's a powerful obsession, and to others it's a necessary but distressful aspect of their lives. To some it's a way to elevate themselves spiritually, and to others it's totally materialistic.

The attitude towards money in our parents' home and our personal financial situation determine how we presently view money. The Torah attitude is that money, like everything else, is part of our life test. We need to acquire it and use it according to the principles set forth in the Torah (*Mesillas Yesharim*, ch. 1). Regardless of whether a couple is wealthy or constantly struggling to keep out of debt, money will supply them with potentially elevating tests.

In marriage, money is the cause of many quarrels. It can create anxiety and tension, and arouse much anger. But it can also be a means by which a couple becomes closer and develops their character as they handle money wisely. View money as a key element in your Divine program of constant growth.

Build up your ability to view money from both your own point of view and the point of view of your spouse. Then try to view the situation as an objective observer and think of what he or she might advise you to do. Maintain respect for each other the entire time you work on practical ways to handle your differences.

> *H*usband's version: "My wife spends way too much of the money I work hard to earn. My salary would be sufficient if she were thrifty. She isn't careful to check prices to see where to buy things at the cheapest possible price. If she worked herself, she would appreciate the value of money and wouldn't waste so much. I keep telling her to cut down on expenses, but she doesn't listen. She just keeps spending as much as she can."
>
> *Wife's version: "I try to live on the limited amount of money that my husband earns. He doesn't appreciate how hard I try to economize. If he worked harder and longer hours, he would earn more and we could live better, but he's a bit lazy and doesn't put in enough effort. There are so many things I really need to buy that we can't afford. He doesn't realize how much I sacrifice to keep us out of deep debt."*

Who is right? Perhaps both. Their challenge is to create a loving and respectful atmosphere even if they see things differently.

I like fancy things and my spouse likes to live simply. When we need to make purchases, we disagree about how much money to spend. I don't mind going into debt, but my spouse hates to owe anything.

My spouse felt that I was wrong for wanting expensive items, and I felt that my spouse was excessively limited in taste. We both brought spiritual arguments into the picture. My spouse argued that spending more money than absolutely necessary was "bal tashchis," wasting things that shouldn't be wasted. My spouse pointed out that others might be envious of us if we splurge. We would get used to living on a higher budget and then, if in the future we couldn't keep it up, we would suffer more than if we were used to living frugally. I argued that the Talmud states that we will be held accountable for pleasures in this world that we failed to make use of. I felt greater gratitude to Hashem when we had expensive things in the house. When we spent more money on things, I felt happier, and it is a mitzvah to be happy.

I would not tell my spouse the true price I paid for things, but eventually my spouse would find out that things often cost more than I claimed. I would say I bargained and got a special deal, or that the item was in the shop's window so they sold it for less money than the regular price. My spouse didn't always believe this and we would repeat the same arguments over and over again.

I claimed that a luxury and a necessity are relative. One's upbringing and personality played a major role and my spouse should accept the fact that my needs cost more. Hashem who gave me my upbringing will provide for our unique needs. My spouse argued that I wasn't really on such a high level of bitachon, and my claims that expensive things are healthier for my emotions and our shalom bayis were just rationalizations.

If we had spent time earning more money instead of

wasting time on arguing, we would have made up for the differences in price between what we both wanted.

After one heated battle, which left us both defeated, I realized that it was more important to have harmony in the house than to have more expensive items. My spouse and I agreed to discuss each purchase calmly. As soon as either of us became angry, we would stop and breath slowly for two minutes. While we still have long discussions on major items, at least they are almost always peaceful.

❖ ❖ ❖

M y husband and I grew up in homes with different attitudes towards money. In my husband's house, every penny was counted. Before they bought anything, they checked several stores and always bought from the cheaper one. If something wasn't necessary, they didn't buy it even though they could afford it. Save your money, or invest it, but don't waste it.

In my home we were more relaxed about money and didn't make a fuss about small amounts. We chose the more convenient store that was closer even if it was slightly more expensive. We hired the best doctors regardless of cost, and spent whatever was necessary for health.

I once wanted to see an expensive doctor, but my husband disapproved. He didn't explicitly stop me from going, but I felt intimidated and went to a less experienced doctor who charged less money. Later, I had medical complications I could have avoided if I had gone to the expert. Moreover, when I was recuperating, I wanted to spend money on hiring help, but my husband wanted to get as little help as possible.

I felt resentful. "What's more important, my health, or money?" I asked him. I wanted to judge my husband favorably, but I had trouble doing so.

Someone who understands human nature explained that people who have a frugal mentality don't view spending as a choice; it's as if the option to spend more money doesn't exist. I wasn't told that I have to like this attitude, but by understanding it, I won't feel as resentful. In the future, if I need to spend money, I should explain how spending money now will save us money in the future.

*I*n my family, if any of us lost anything, we were reprimanded sharply. We were told about the importance of being careful with our belongings, like Yaakov, the Patriarch, who put his life in danger to retrieve small containers. We were told that if we were careless with minor items, we would eventually be careless with more valuable things.

When I was first married, I felt awful if I lost anything. If the item belonged to me, I never told my spouse about it. "Why ask for needless trouble?" I told myself.

I still recall the first time I lost something that was valuable to my spouse. When I mentioned it, I was anxious about being censured for my carelessness. But the response I received was a relief.

"Don't worry. I know you didn't mean it. When we lose something it's a kapparah (an atonement for our wrongs). It gives me pleasure that we are both receiving atonement. Your remorse gives me an opportunity to cheer you up, which is one of my favorite acts of chesed."

To say the least, this reaction made my heart soar.

I am very emotional and intuitive while my husband is rational and grounded. I find his stability exactly what I need. The differences in personality create challenges and opportunities for growth. He is a tzaddik and I have a profound respect for him. One incident I remember is his attitude towards my losing a large sum of money. He works hard and we are not wealthy; nevertheless he calmly accepted my costly mistake. We were scheduled to take a trip overseas. I was late getting ready for our flight so we missed it and had to buy expensive new tickets for the next flight. I felt awful, but my husband comforted me, "It's only money," he said. "Your feelings are more important to me than money." He can't imagine how profoundly I appreciated this.

I grew up in a home where money was always scarce. My father worked hard but we never had enough money. I always felt bad about not being as financially well-off as most of my friends. I planned to marry someone with greater financial ambitions than my father.

When I met my husband, he told me about his adventurous plans to earn a great deal of money. His dream was to be a big baal tzedakah and give money to support Torah institutions and charitable organizations, and help the poor get married. I was impressed with his aspirations and eager to be the wife of a major tzedakah giver.

But, "Humans plan, and G-d laughs." My husband was more often in debt than rolling in money. We didn't have enough for basic necessities, let alone to carry out his lofty philanthropic projects. Unlike my father who was hard-working and satisfied with a little, my husband took major risks borrowing money and investing in schemes *that promised a lot. When things worked out, we could pay off the debts and give some money to charity, but when things didn't work out, we had to live on the barest minimum.*

I tried to convince my husband to take a reliable and steady job so we could live more securely, but he refused. "I might be able to do so for myself," he said. "But how can I do so at the expense of all the Torah institutions and charitable organizations that I will eventually be able to support?"

"But who says you will succeed?" I asked.

"Have bitachon," he replied. "Hashem will give us major financial success any day now."

I had to admit that with all our financial ups and downs, we always had a place to live and enough food to eat. This calmed me down. It was easier for me to increase my level of bitachon than to try to influence my husband to change his approach to money. I have more bitachon now and am much calmer than I used to be. By accepting what I cannot change, we have shalom bayis in our home even when we are going through financial difficulties.

CHILD REARING

Children can be a parent's greatest source of *nachas* or the greatest source of pain. In ideal situations children can bring a husband and wife closer together. Parents have a common life's goal of raising children to serve Hashem. Both father and mother love their children and work in harmony to teach and train, to inspire and encourage, to nourish and support. Even if parents disagree about specific details, they both respect the positive intentions of the other.

But children can be a source of stress, and the focal point of strife and dissension. They can be the topic of arguments and quarrels, and the victims of power struggles. If parents don't get along, children are likely to suffer.

View your children as the greatest gift your Creator has given you and the greatest responsibility as well. You have an obligation — for the spiritual and emotional welfare of your children — to treat their other parent with respect. Every time you speak to your spouse in front of your children you are teaching them lessons about marriage, about putting Torah ideals into practice, about ways of communicating, about *middos,* about who their parents are, and ultimately about themselves.

Be careful not to take out frustrations with your spouse on your children. Part of growing from your marriage is growing from raising your children. Your children will test you in many ways. They will supply you with innumerable opportunities for personal growth and for developing your *middos.* Learn from your mistakes and constantly upgrade the way you talk and act. Clarify the internal resources and attributes that will help you interact at your best with your children.

Learn from your own best moments. Remember the times you reacted to difficult situations with love, patience, compassion, and respect. Let these memories empower you whenever you feel tempted to react with frustration or anger.

Pray for Hashem's assistance to act wisely when you need to make difficult choices about a specific course of action in a given situation.

W*ife's version: "My husband is too strict with the children. He isn't realistic about his demands and wants them to be perfect angels all the time. He has no patience if they misbehave. Also, he punishes them in a way that is a bit cruel. He learns with our young son much too long for his age level and refuses to ask anyone about what a proper amount of time would be. During the Shabbos meal, if a child acts even a little wild, he is sent to his room for the rest of the meal. I think that a five-minute time out would be sufficient to get the point across. My husband feels that most other people don't really know the right way to discipline children."*

Husband's version: "My wife is too lenient with the children and lets them get away with murder. If they are not taught how to behave when they are young, they will grow up thinking that improper behavior is all right. They are able to accomplish much more than my wife thinks. I would be doing them a disservice if I let them do less than they are really capable of. I look around and don't like the way most people are raising their children. I want my children to be great, not mediocre. I know that I am right and don't want anyone to give me another opinion."

Even among the greatest people, there are many different approaches to disciplining children. Shlomo HaMelech (*Mishlei* 22:6), for example, tells us to raise each child according to his nature. Husbands and wives can easily have different ideas about what is too strict and what is too lenient. When in doubt, they should consult a recognized Torah expert on raising children. If either the husband or wife refuses to consult anyone, this indicates a fear of not finding anyone who agrees with him or her. With minor disagreements, maintain a united front regardless of whether it is slightly too strict or slightly too lenient, but if you are afraid that a major error might be made, speak to a knowledgeable Torah authority about the best thing to do in your unique situation.

This morning I was in a mad rush. I had a number of important things to take care of and didn't know if I would be able to finish them. My nine-year-old son was dawdling, so I told him I was in a hurry and he should rush.

Instead of speeding up, he slowed down. The more I rushed him, the more he stalled. Finally, I lost my temper.

"I hate you," I found myself saying. "You are a stupid idiot. You are acting like a retard."

As soon as I said this, I hated myself. I felt terrible. How could I have said something so untrue and insensitive!

After my son left for school, I called my husband to tell him what I had said. I was a bit nervous that he might reprimand me. But to my relief, he consoled me, "We all know how much you love the children and how proud you are of them. Fortunately our son knows that we both love him and he has healthy self-esteem. He's a bright child and knows you don't mean what you said. He knows that when he comes home from school, you will apologize profusely, and he probably forgot about it already."

I was grateful for the reassurance and made a resolution to do all I could to control what I say even when I am under stress.

❖ ❖ ❖

We have a son who wasn't turning out the way we wished. He didn't study much and wasn't enthusiastic about praying. His level of derech eretz was below par, and he frequently got into trouble in school.

"It's mainly your fault," I said to my spouse. My spouse's reaction was to follow my example, "You're just saying this because you don't know what to do. Besides, it's mostly your fault."

"You don't really care enough," we both shouted at each other. We both cared immensely, but we hadn't a clue how to help our son improve. Blaming each other was our way of releasing our deep feelings of frustration and inadequacy.

We went to a Rabbi who specializes in influencing children who don't listen to their parents.

"The first step you must both take," he said to me, "is to stop blaming yourselves and each other. If you continue to blame one another, you will view your son as *the cause of your unhappiness with each other and this will increase your anger.*

"When your son sees that you are making changes in how you treat each other, you will begin to see a positive change in him. Every approach and technique you implement in dealing with your son has a prerequisite — your united position. Let your love for your child, which you both have, serve as a powerful motivator to improve your own relationship."

We left his office totally committed to each other and to saving our son.

ILLNESS AND HEALTH

As the *Mesillas Yesharim* states in the first chapter, everything in our lives is a test in this world. One of the greatest tests is the test of illness. Even a minor and transient illness is a challenge. It disrupts our prior plans and affects our emotional state. All the more so, a major illness has a great impact on one's life and marriage.

Illness, either your own or that of your spouse, is part of the Divine plan to enable you to develop your character in a way that good health wouldn't. The traits that enable us to grow from an illness include: *emunah* and *bitachon* (the realization that all that occurs in our lives is from our loving Creator for our benefit), compassion, humility, patience, courage, cheerfulness, and acceptance even when life isn't going the way we wish.

A relatively common issue is when one party complains of pain and the other party questions whether the complaints are authentic or exaggerated. As a general rule, if someone complains about pain, believe him or her. If the person is not in physical distress, he or she is experiencing emotional distress, and your own growth comes from being understanding and compassionate.

I have the most beautiful memories of the one year that I was married to a wonderful man. When I was single, I had leukemia and wasn't certain if I ever would be able to get married. The doctor who treated me also treated a fine young man for the same illness. He thought that we would be suitable for each other. He suggested that we meet with the possible intention of marriage. He was frank with us that he didn't know how long either of us would live, but he felt it was worth being married for a short while rather than not being married at all.

My husband lived for an entire year and I survived him. It was the most amazing year of my life. We both knew that we didn't know how long either of us would live so we appreciated every day we were together.

I cherish the joyous memories of being married to my late husband. I am deeply grateful for the time we had together.

❖ ❖ ❖

My husband and I argued a lot. We agreed on the most vital issues, but frequently bickered about trivial matters. When we were tired, rushed, or under tension, the angry exchanges increased. This went on for over twenty years.

Then one day we received some news that shook us to the core. My husband was complaining of pain for a few weeks, but assumed it wasn't significant. I insisted he go for a medical check-up and tests. The days we had to wait for a diagnosis were stressful beyond description. Finally the doctor called us in to tell us he had a malignant tumor that had spread.

My husband and I both felt as if we were stricken by lightning. I felt numb and terrified, and was certain that my husband felt even worse.

"How long do you think I have to live?" my husband asked.

"I have to be frank with you," the doctor answered.

"Optimistically, between one year and a year and a half."

My husband reacted with great courage and bitachon. "I accept the will of Hashem. Let us use the time for spiritual elevation. "

It is now two years later. Objectively, we have had more stress than ever before, with frequent trips to doctors and hospitals. But we've felt a sense of togetherness, grateful that my husband has lived longer than the doctor's prognosis. Ever since the fateful day of the doctor's pronouncement, I have appreciated my husband's positive qualities more than ever before and respect the way he has been handling the illness.

We don't know how much longer my husband will live. But we definitely aren't going to waste any precious time on pointless quarrels.

If your spouse is doing something you feel is unhealthy, it is a *mitzvah* to try to influence him or her to guard his or her health. But people differ as to how careful they are with what they eat, how much sleep they get, and whether or not they engage in habits that are potentially dangerous to their health. While it is a *mitzvah* to help someone remain healthy and to try to prevent him or her from doing something harmful, we must realize that we are limited in the degree we can influence another adult in this area. If your spouse doesn't listen to what you have to say, seek ways to influence him or her, but don't allow your valid concerns to turn into a constant source of arguments.

My husband smokes and I detest it. I worry about his health and I find the smell of cigarettes repugnant. My husband claims he is a light smoker and knows smokers who lived long lives. I argue that it is still dangerous to his health to smoke.

I've begged my husband over and over again to quit. Unfortunately, when I see that I'm not getting anywhere,

I get angry. My husband tells me that my anger is just as unhealthy as his smoking.

After seeing that my anger wasn't having any effect except to make him angry, I decided to decrease the intensity of my protests. I told my husband I care about him too much to let him continue smoking without trying to influence him to stop, but I was resolved to voice my opinion gently. I asked him to please view my attempts as messages of love and concern. He agreed to this. He's hoping I will get tired of trying and will give up. I, however, am hoping that my messages will eventually motivate him to quit this dangerous habit. In the meantime, we don't get into fights. My more pleasant approach and his reframing have helped us have harmony in our home even though neither of us has totally gotten our way.

EREV SHABBOS

We are different when we are in a rush than when we are calm and relaxed. Being in a rush can easily cause stress and tension. But it doesn't have to. Shabbos is our weekly celebration of the creation of the universe. Everything you do to prepare for Shabbos is part of your expression of gratitude to our Creator. Allow this sense of joy to permeate your entire being and make your preparations in a positive emotional state.

Anger and quarrels about preparing for Shabbos are incongruent with its essence. It should be a high priority to perform all your actions associated with Shabbos in a state of self-mastery. Shabbos signifies peace and connecting with our Creator. Make this the reality in your home.

*B*asically, I have a calm nature which I am able to maintain even under pressure. After being married about a year, I noticed that on Friday afternoons as it was getting late, I felt tense. My interaction with my husband reflected this pressure. My husband didn't complain, but I realized the habit I was falling into.

"How does it help to speak this way?" I asked myself. I was resolved to remain calm. Previously, I assumed I needed to get nervous and panicky in order to complete everything on time. However, by remaining calm I worked with the same speed as before and I was more efficient. This creates a much more peaceful atmosphere in our home. That was six years ago. Now, with three children and a morning job, I'm much busier. But since I've developed the habit of remaining calm when preparing for Shabbos, even when I have a lot to do in a short time, the whole process is enjoyable.

*M*y spouse and I would get along just fine the entire week. The only time we'd have problems with each other would be on Friday afternoon. We would both feel the pressure of having to take care of a ton of things before Shabbos. Our young children weren't always cooperative and this added to our stress and tension. We would have more anger towards each other on Friday than on all six days of the week put together.

Then I heard a tape about how Shabbos is our weekly celebration of the creation of the universe and everything in it. If the entire planet were to be in danger of exploding and then were miraculously saved, there would be worldwide celebrations and parties. One can just imagine the joyous reaction of people all over the world. Shabbos is our weekly celebration of the greatest event that ever took place. Anything else that anyone gets excited about is minuscule in comparison. Every aspect of Shabbos and preparing for it should be greeted with joy.

I heard this tape on a Friday while I was washing the dishes and I replayed this part of the tape for my spouse.

"Let's put this celebration into action," I said.

"That would be great," my spouse agreed.

What happened that Friday afternoon was an almost miraculous transformation. We actually had fun when previously we'd had tense outbursts. Can we keep it up? Only time will tell.

GROWING UP IN DIFFERENT CULTURES

Even within the Torah world each culture has different priorities, customs, patterns, and ways of behaving. What might be taken for granted by one group could be unacceptable to another. Regarding expectations of a husband and wife, what is considered appropriate will differ with Jews from different countries, yeshivos, chassidic sects, and social and economic groups. Many husbands and wives who come from very different backgrounds are not initially aware of how profoundly these differences have affected them and their expectations about each other.

The greater the difference in their backgrounds, the greater the challenge and the greater the opportunity for growth. The Torah principles of love, respect, appreciation, gratitude, *chesed*, and judging favorably will probably be tried and tested, but by treating each other with mutual respect, differences can be overcome. The more different the couple, the more effort they need in order to develop compassion and understanding necessary for a harmonious marriage.

The more different you are, the more important it is to see the situation from your spouse's point of view as well as your own. It is usual to feel that your way is "normal" and the way of your spouse isn't, but that is because we are familiar with the patterns with which we grew up. If your spouse is very different from you, make a sincere effort to gain an understanding, and use a tone of voice and wording that make it clear you are not being judgmental.

RELIGIOUS DIFFERENCES

When both husband and wife share the same Torah values and level of observance, they already share the same goals that are the basis for a harmonious marriage. Differences, however, can be a major source of tension and strife. Every situation is unique. In Chapter 12 we spoke about remaining calm and thinking clearly. This is especially important in this area. Even if there are major differences, solutions can often be worked out if there is mutual respect and understanding. When respect and understanding are missing, even minor differences can be the source of bitter conflict.

If religious differences arise, keep your focus on outcome thinking. Clarify your goal before you speak. Be prepared to remain in a calm state and don't let statements said in frustration or anger make the problems more difficult to solve. The wisest thing to do is to consult a sensitive Torah scholar with experience in these areas.

A young man who davened in a shul in Tel Aviv consulted the Chazon Ish in Bnei Brak about an issue that troubled him. In the shul where he prayed, most of the people were not familiar with details of the laws of tefillin. They didn't put on their tefillin in the proper place and therefore failed to fulfill the mitzvah. He wanted to go up to the bimah one day and give an informal lesson on the proper manner in which to put on tefillin.

The Chazon Ish told him not to do it that way. "Your intentions are good, but a public announcement will be met with protests to leave them alone."

The Chazon Ish then told him to use the following strategy. "Approach each person individually. With respect towards the person and humility in your manner, gently suggest the proper way to put on tefillin."

A man who was married over ten years commented upon hearing this story and applying its message, "I now see how wrong I was when I corrected my wife after seeing her make halachic mistakes. I began to speak with respect and humility, instead of anger and indignation, if I saw that something needed correction. My wife expressed her appreciation about my new approach and was more open to what I had to say."

❖ ❖ ❖

M y wife was more religious than I was when we got married. We both were committed to living according to Torah, but she was more careful with details and customs. I felt that by marrying her, I would keep growing in the service of G-d and mitzvah observance.

But after we were married, it seemed to me that she became less conscious of avodas Hashem and more focused on nagging me about my failings.

As I was growing up, my mother had always nagged me in a very irritating voice, and I was certain I would marry someone different. I remember hearing a radio commercial for real estate in which, years in the future, the wife was still nagging the husband about having failed to buy property that increased in value many times over. "That's exactly the type of person I'm married to," I said to myself.

I see that Hashem tested me exactly in the area in which I needed it the most. Every time my wife returned from a halachah class, she had more topics about which to nag me. I told her that I wanted to observe all 613 commandments properly, but I didn't want to be nagged about them.

How did I respond to her nagging? Sometimes I kept quiet, just hoping she would finish quickly. At other times, I would tell her she also made mistakes and needed to improve. Yet other times, I would walk out of the room in the middle of one of her long-winded tirades.

"That's not the way to talk to me," I insisted.

"But if I don't help you improve, no one will," she responded.

"I will not listen to anything you tell me if you don't say it pleasantly," I said like a hurt little boy.

Finally, one day, she asked me the magic question. "I see that my approach isn't working. How can I speak to you so you will be open to listening?"

I told her what I needed, and we both gained spiritually and emotionally when my wife spoke to me about these topics in a way that was acceptable for me.

My husband spent too much time on his business and not enough time learning Torah. I spoke to him many times about increasing his studies, but this led to arguments, and he felt resentful towards me for badgering him.

I spoke to a Torah scholar about the proper approach to take. His advice helped me tremendously. He told me that instead of nagging my husband, I should encourage him in positive ways. I should celebrate his successes and express my respect and admiration for what he does do. I need to realize that my avodas Hashem is based on what I can do, and not on what I can't.

My husband was grateful for my new approach and found more time to study Torah.

At times, religious differences can be just a matter of style or approach and at other times they represent a wide gap between people.

*M*y wife served us and our guest a delicious soup. Right after she put down the plates, she announced, "Don't taste the soup yet."

"What's the problem?" I asked.

"I see some black spots and need to check if they are bugs," she replied. "Perhaps it's the spices I added, but it might be bugs."

"Why are you so negative?" I challenged her. "Why assume they are bugs?"

A few minutes later my wife again called out, "It's okay. You can eat the vegetable soup. It's just pepper."

When she returned to eat her soup, I observed that she was hurt.

"I don't intentionally assume the worst," she said. "But I want to make certain that the food we eat ourselves and serve others is absolutely kosher."

Of course, my wife was right. I had been the one who was negative, not her.

MARRIAGE COUNSELING

Some couples quickly develop problematic patterns which, if changed early in the marriage, could save them much pain and suffering. There are many situations when a couple will benefit from counseling of one form or another and should speak to a Rabbi or Rebbetzin, a teacher, or a professional counselor. Couples will differ as to their openness to speak to a third party and the degree to which they consider a situation serious enough to warrant consulting someone. This can range from a husband and wife who are very happy with each other but want to enhance their marriage by dealing with a relatively minor issue, to a husband and wife who get into explosive quarrels and fear they are incompatible.

Choosing the right counselor is of great importance. Both the husband and wife need to feel comfortable that the person they speak to understands them and is sensitive to their needs as individuals and as a couple.

Secondly, it is important to clarify your goals before speaking to someone. A couple will not benefit from counseling if each uses it as an opportunity to blame the other one for being at fault, rather than speaking with clear goals of what they would like to see improved.

A world-famous family therapist wrote a tongue-in-cheek article for a professional journal about how not to conduct a counseling session. Instead of calling the husband and wife "clients," he calls them "customers," and talks about how to keep the customers coming without having any idea of what to do to improve their marriage. He "suggests" that the therapist get the couple to discuss every argument they've ever had. This keeps adding more fuel to the fire. Then, after a very long time, when they've exhausted that reservoir, he has them discuss comparisons between what is going on between them and what went wrong with their parents, grandparents, and any other friendships they ever had, all to keep them coming back again. When I read this it reminded me of someone who once told me, "We've been going to marriage counseling for a year and a half and I don't feel that things have improved at all." I suggested they ask the therapist to give a time frame estimating when they should see some improvement. The therapist told them, "About ten years." This isn't the approach to take if you really want to improve a marriage.

Therapists who focus on solutions are often more effective than those whose main focus is problems. There is a big difference whether you focus all week on, "What don't I like?" and "What complaints do I have this week?" or whether you keep thinking about, "What is happening that I do like and wish to continue or increase?" and, "What can we both do to improve the way we speak and act towards each other?"

People differ greatly in many areas: religiosity, intelligence, emotional makeup, personality, family and national backgrounds, intensity, simplicity or sophistication. A counselor who is highly effective for one couple might be useless or even a disaster for another. One couple might appreciate someone who is authoritative and tells them what to do. Another couple might only want to consult someone who serves as a mediator and enables them to work out their issues in a safe environment. Some couples want to speak about the whole history of their marriage, while others just want to solve a present crisis.

Remember, when speaking to a marriage counselor you are a consumer, and if you are not getting the results you want, it is worth trying someone else.

*M*y wife was dissatisfied with the way I was acting and wanted me to change. "You need therapy," she said. My wife's nagging was so stressful, I felt that therapy was the lesser of two evils.

I spoke to someone who recommended a few possibilities. The person I decided to see had a reputation for being brilliant and deep. I was told his credentials were impeccable and I would respect him, and I did.

He told me right away that he would not make any decisions for me. But he listened to my free associating and he gave me interpretations to help me gain greater insight and clarity on my own. I spoke at length about my childhood, my parents, my relationships with my siblings and friends, my inner conflicts, my ambivalences, my defenses, my prejudices, my inner child, my personality disorders and how they had an effect on my entire life, my neurotic needs, my resistances, and a host of similar topics. I enjoyed this very much because I like talking about myself, and the therapist listened when others didn't.

My therapy was helping me in my house. Not that I had to do anything to change, but whenever my spouse complained about anything, I always responded, "That's exactly why I am in therapy. Please be patient." The fees I was paying were worth the shalom bayis I had in return.

After a year of twice weekly sessions my spouse said, "I don't know if you'll ever totally change, but at least do something practical to improve. You have three weeks to begin to act differently or else I'm going to open a file at the Rabbinate. I'd prefer you go to a therapist who will have a practical effect on you. If you don't go on your own, the Rabbinical court will put pressure on you."

As a result of this two-minute speech I made more changes than I had made in the previous year. I realized that my wife was serious about what she was saying, and that I had been stalling. Once I was really motivated I saw that it wasn't as difficult as I had thought to make some positive changes. I didn't have to change my per-sonality, I just had to be more sensitive to my wife's needs and feelings.

It is not marriage counseling that will make a difference, but your personal changes in thought, speech, and behavior. The goal of therapy is change. There are many different approaches that can be helpful. But there is a prerequisite: If things weren't going well before, you now need to do something different.

BACK FROM THE BRINK — SAVING MARRIAGES AT THE LAST MOMENT

When a husband and wife come to the conclusion that after trying to do all that they can to stay married, they will just keep on quarreling and will cause each other much misery by staying married, it is sometimes advisable to get divorced. A wise Torah authority should be consulted and counseling should be tried to see if *shalom bayis* is possible. If the counseling doesn't help and a Torah authority recommends divorce, the husband and wife should still maintain a mutually respectful way of talking to each other during the divorce proceedings.

Louis Nizer, a nationally famous lawyer, wrote in 1961:

L*itigations between husband and wives exceed in bit-terness and hatred those of any other relationships. I have represented defrauded businessmen who fight* *their deceivers for fortune and power. I have seen them pour out their venom against their opponents until they suffered heart attacks or were ulcerated. I have witnessed struggles for the protection of copyrighted property, where the pride of authorship, being dearer than life itself, consumed the creative artist. I have seen public figures libeled or accused of wrongs that could wreck their life's work, strike back at their detractors. I have observed men with spotless reputations who were indicted, suffer nervous breakdowns. I have witnessed children sue their fathers to deprive them of their businesses, or brothers engaged in fratricide contests without quarter. I have seen defendants in antitrust suits beleaguered by plaintiffs seeking treble damages or defending themselves against government actions aimed to break up their enterprise, painstakingly built over a lifetime. I have participated in inheritance contests in which relatives were at each others' throats.*

All these litigations evoke intense feelings of animosity, revenge, and retribution. Some of them may be fought ruthlessly. But none of them, even in the most aggravated form, can equal the sheer, unadulterated venom of a matrimonial contest. The participants are often ready to gouge out the eyes or the soul of the once loved, without any pity whatsoever.

The Torah ideal, however, is that even if a husband and wife feel a need to get divorced, they still are obligated to treat each other with the respect due to every human being. This can be a difficult challenge. If you feel that your spouse has major character and spiritual failings, have compassion. Spiritual ills are a worse disability than physical ones.

Even though the Torah allows for divorce, Torah scholars throughout the ages have done all they could to make peace between husbands and wives who were quarreling. As long as a couple is still married, there is a chance that one of them or even both might make changes that will enable the marriage to work.

The Sages teach us that even with a sword at his throat, a person should still not give up. He should pray that the Almighty will miraculously save him. Seriously contemplating divorce is often a wake-up call that elicits the motivation to save the marriage.

I attended a seminar given by an organization that does divorce mediation. They try to make *shalom bayis* if at all possible. But when they can't, they try to mediate peaceful divorces that are in everyone's best interests.

A number of their members told me that they have the following experience. Their policy is to have two people do the initial interview, known as an intake, and then two other people try to make *shalom bayis* or handle the mediation. They want both parties to come to both the intake and the first meeting. But once in a while only one party, either the husband or the wife, will come to the intake meeting. Then, for the first *shalom bayis* meeting, at times only the other party will show up. Whenever this happens, the following occurs. The pair doing the intake will say, "The person we dealt with is friendly, polite, and reasonable. The whole problem must stem from the other party." Then the pair handling the first meeting will say, "That's strange, because the person we spoke to is friendly, polite, and reasonable. We think it must be mainly the other person's fault."

This is quite usual. Frequently, when a couple does not get along, anyone seeing just one party or the other will be impressed by their calm and courteous manner. One party says it's all the other person's fault and the other person says it's all this person's fault. If both the husband and wife would interact with each other the way they interact with other people, the marriage could be a happy one for both of them.

One day in Israel during a major strike of government workers, the office where couples went to register for marriage was closed, but couples could register for divorce, since this was under the jurisdiction of the Rabbinical courts which were not on strike. An official who was asked about the irony of this, commented, "One can never tell. For certain couples signing up for divorce is the biggest step towards *shalom bayis.*"

I have seen numerous couples who had given up on their marriage and opened up a file at the Rabbinate. Many had contemplated divorce for a long time, but once this became a reality, they decided to give the marriage a last-minute try, and this saved their marriage.

❖ ❖ ❖

"*If you keep doing that I'm going to divorce you."
Whenever I said this, my spouse would do whatever I asked for the next few days. Seeing how effective this tool was, I used it frequently. Threatening divorce became my number one method of motivating my spouse.*

After repeating this enough times, I felt certain that my spouse knew I wasn't serious about it. To me, threatening divorce was like someone else saying, "I am displeased with the way you are acting."

But one day I came home to a note in an empty house. "You've succeeded in breaking me down with all your threats. I can't take it any more. I'm hiring a Rabbinical lawyer."

I didn't really want to get divorced. I contacted my spouse's parents and told them that I deeply regretted having used the possibility of divorce as a tool for getting my way. My spouse refused to speak to me outside of court. But I begged my in-laws to ask my spouse to give me another chance and I will never again threaten to get divorced. Reluctantly my spouse agreed. That was three years ago and I have kept my word.

A couple who frequently argued decided they weren't right for each other. They went to a Rabbi and told him that they wanted to get divorced.

The Rabbi was experienced with truly serious and fundamental problems in marriage. He saw that while this husband and wife argued frequently, they had much in common and if they adopted a proper perspective, they would have few quarrels over trivial matters and would be able to establish greater harmony.

He invited them back for another meeting. When they showed up, he told them he needed to see someone in the local hospital and invited them to come along with him so they could speak while he was driving. At the hospital, he took them to the waiting room of the burn unit and asked them to please wait for him while he spoke to someone in a different section of the hospital.

For over a half hour, they saw what real problems were. New patients were brought in screaming in pain. They saw the anguish of parents and close relatives and heard some of their horror stories.

When the Rabbi came back, they told him, "We've changed our mind. This experience has brought us closer together. We feel our new perspective will help us handle our differences."

Imagine what it would be like if the courts used this Rabbi's tactic before granting a divorce.

O ur marriage was in serious trouble. My husband's anger provoked my anger towards him and this got him even angrier at me. This destructive loop was about to destroy our marriage. I felt as if I were drowning and spoke to a number of friends and neighbors explaining that I couldn't take it anymore.

A few days before I had planned to go to the Beis Din for a divorce, my husband realized that he really did want our marriage to work. He was finally motivated to conquer his anger, and I saw that he was totally sincere.

My husband began acting towards me with kindness and respect and my feelings towards him were transformed. We had a wonderful week that gave us both hope for the future. But a few weeks later, my husband shared with me his basic concern about whether we could sustain this improvement.

"The way you are treating me now is exactly the way I wish to be treated," I told him. "Don't worry about the future. Just continue speaking to me the way you do now, and I will do the same. If we ever get off track, we'll remind each other how great it was when we were pleasant to each other."

But my husband had one lingering issue. When I had felt overwhelmed I told a number of people about how awful he acted towards me. He now felt embarrassed and ashamed. We spoke to our Rabbi about it. "Only confide in one woman from now on," the Rav told me. "The person you choose to speak to should be levelheaded, objective, and have a lot of common sense. She needs to realize that whatever you say is only part of the entire story and it is impossible to know the full picture unless both parties are present."

Our Rabbi told me to tell the people I complained to that my husband is wonderful and I greatly appreciate him. I should tell them that I now realize that I added to the problem by the way I reacted. My husband was fantastic about this. He said he understands that I felt as if I were drowning and was desperately looking for help. He saw I wanted to make amends and realized that on the practical level he wouldn't suffer from what I had done.

*M*y mother taught me a lesson that helped improve my own marriage. Whenever she wanted my father to know she was working on something that would please him, she bought a book on the topic and left it conspicuously on the table. She told us this technique was amazingly effective.

In general, I had a bad temper and needed to improve my marriage in many ways. My wife was fed up with my anger and wanted out of the marriage.

I was in debt and money was tight in our house. But I moonlighted, getting a job doing something I hate in order to earn enough money to buy my wife gifts, including her favorite candies, flowers, and a copy of "Anger: The Inner Teacher" for myself.

I started reading the book on anger and left it on our dining-room table. My wife saw that I was making an effort to eradicate my anger. We started enjoying each other, having fun, but also working on our serious issues. Our hope is to treat each other with so much unconditional love and respect that our painful memories will disappear when compared to the joy we bring each other.

❖ ❖ ❖

I had an awful marriage. My spouse and I argued about everything and found it so difficult to agree on any decision that we were contemplating the termination of our marriage.

We spoke to a compassionate elderly Rabbi who told us that the Altar cries when a couple divorces. "Do all you possibly can to save your marriage," he encouraged us. He told us we have many strengths we can call upon to make the marriage work. He advised us to speak to a person who had once been pronounced clin-ically dead. This person had a remarkable physical comeback and is today alive and well. He is one of the most joyous people you will ever meet. "Your marriage needs a spiritual comeback; perhaps you can learn something from him."

We were not able to meet this fellow in person, but we were able to see a taped interview in which he described how he had been run over by a car and pronounced dead. He described the brilliant light he saw. As he described his experience, his face radiated with selfless love and joyous energy. He and others who had similar experiences developed a transformed perspective on life. They were no longer afraid of death and felt inspired to live on a higher plane than ever before.

My spouse and I had never personally met anyone who experienced this, but I had met a Rabbi whose grandmother had experienced clinical death over fifty years ago. This grandmother was an elevated, pious woman who lived with a constant awareness of Hashem.

Thinking about how temporary our stay in this world is, and our true purpose in life, inspired us to prevent the Altar from crying. This thought itself brought a spark from the Beis HaMikdash into our home. While my spouse and I are still very different from each other and have diverse opinions on many issues, we find ourselves having a much more peaceful relationship with each other.

*O*ur marriage was clearly falling apart. I was frus-trated about my entire life and my marriage was only one disappointing element in a totally futile picture. I hated my job, I wasn't davening properly, I had no time for learning Torah, and when I came home in the evening, I would lash out at my wife for all sorts of reasons, none of them truly important.

I realized that it was only a matter of time before my wife would no longer tolerate the way I treated her. I could argue that it wasn't my fault. I grew up in a chaotic home. My parents thought they cared about me, but I was a complicated child and they had no idea what I needed to set me straight. They would punish me for my negative behavior, but what I really needed was unconditional love and understanding. They weren't cruel or sadistic, so no one would have called me an abused child. I now realize how frustrated they were with me. And right now I am frustrated with myself.

Whether or not I was totally to blame for the situation is irrelevant. I now had to figure out what I was going to do with the rest of my life. My most pressing problem was how to keep my marriage together. My wife had repeatedly suggested that we speak to a marriage counselor, but I was too proud to ask anyone for help. If I felt someone could tell me something new, maybe I would have agreed to go for counseling. But I realized that I knew what had to be done; it was just a question of whether I would have the motivation to put into practice what I already knew.

I asked my wife if we could find a quiet spot where we wouldn't be interrupted for a few hours because I wanted to discuss our entire situation. I was afraid she would tell me it's too late, she's already reached a decision about the dissolution of our marriage. But she replied, "I'm very happy you want to discuss things. I've tried to discuss our marriage for a while now, but you kept brushing me off. I feel it's never too late to improve things."

Her response was exactly what I needed to hear. I did not expect an excessively optimistic response from her. But I saw that she was clearly open to reviving our dying marriage.

For the first time since we were married, I shared my deep feelings of inferiority. I told her that I felt I had ruined my entire life and I wouldn't blame her if she gave up on me.

"I'll never give up on you. I've always believed in you, even when you didn't believe in yourself. I'm not a miracle worker and if you don't want to try to improve yourself, I'm afraid that there is nothing I can do, but your willingness to discuss your life and our marriage so openly is a sign that you are sincere. I'll stand by you and together we will begin our life anew."

That was twenty years ago. Since then we have celebrated that day with more joy than we celebrate our wedding anniversary. I have made it a habit to tell my story to at least one person each year. I want others to learn from my experience. If you truly want to make a major change in your life, you can. My wife and I have worked together as a team. Her belief in me is the most precious gift Hashem ever gave me. I am profoundly grateful.

NOTES

NOTES

NOTES

NOTES

NOTES

NOTES

NOTES

NOTES

NOTES

NOTES

This volume is part of
THE ARTSCROLL SERIES®
an ongoing project of
translations, commentaries and expositions
on Scripture, Mishnah, Talmud, Halachah,
liturgy, history, the classic Rabbinic writings,
biographies and thought.

For a brochure of current publications
visit your local Hebrew bookseller
or contact the publisher:

Mesorah Publications, ltd.
4401 Second Avenue
Brooklyn, New York 11232
(718) 921-900